Writing
the Modern
Research Paper

Writing the Modern Research Paper

ROBERT DEES
Orange Coast College

ALLYN AND BACON
Boston London Toronto Sydney Tokyo Singapore

Executive Editor: Joseph Opiela
Series Editorial Assistant: Brenda Conaway
Editorial-Production Service: Glenview Studios
Copy Editor: Susan Freese
Cover Administrator: Linda Dickinson
Manufacturing Buyer: Louise Richardson

Library of Congress Cataloging-in-Publication Data

Dees, Robert.
  Writing the modern research paper / Robert Dees.
    p. cm.
  Includes index.
  ISBN 0-205-13504-8
  1. Report writing. I. Title.
LB2369.D44   1991   91-41073
808'.02—dc20   CIP

Printed in the United States of America

10 9 8 7 6 5 4 3 2 1   97 96 95 94 93

CONTENTS

CHAPTER ELEVEN Alternative Documentation Styles: Author-Year (APA), Number-System (CBE), and *Chicago* (Footnote/Endnote) 267

CHAPTER TWELVE Preparing the Final Manuscript 305

PREFACE

Writing the Modern Research Paper provides college students in any discipline with a step-by-step guide to doing enjoyable, effective research and to writing a thorough, well-documented paper. The text explains use of traditional as well as the very latest reference materials and research technologies available in modern libraries; it also emphasizes the importance of documentation and other features of a well-written research paper.

My own years of teaching about the research paper have shown me that, in order to think critically and creatively during the research process, students need to understand the range of possibilities for conducting research and to know how to use those possibilities to their advantage. On-line databases, CD–ROMs, citation indexes, and video discs are just a few of the modern resources available to today's campus researcher. Off campus, public as well as private libraries offer additional resources on topics of local or specialized interest; onsite study can provide primary research opportunities through firsthand observation, self-designed surveys, interviews, and taped performances. *Writing the Modern Research Paper* was written to serve as a guide to these and other sources of information as well as to instill in the student researcher the kind of knowledge and self-confidence that leads to completing a research paper with which the individual can be personally satisfied.

To obtain such results, instruction should begin with the student's general understanding of the research paper and how to start a research project. Chapter 1, *Research and the Research Paper,* introduces the student writer to the meaning of research and provides an overview of the research paper. The chapter also explains the process of framing a research question, planning a research schedule, and keeping a research notebook. Referred to throughout the book, these activities provide students with easily learned, practical ways to get started and stay on track during the research and writing processes.

As any experienced researcher knows, understanding libraries and how to use them is essential to enjoying research and to getting good results. Chapter 2, *Using a Library for Research*, sets the stage by explaining libraries in general, including the two basic classification systems used. Traditional as well as modern resources for research are also discussed, including computer catalogs, CD-ROM formats, computer searches, and citation indexes.

Techniques for using such resources and familiar writing methods for selecting and narrowing a research topic are covered in Chapter 3, *Planning the Focus of Your Research*. Chapter 4, *Researching Library Sources*, discusses bibliographies and indexes and explains how to prepare a working bibliography.

Not everything one needs to know about a research topic is necessarily found in a college library. In fact, the most creative and fulfilling aspects of research often take place elsewhere, when the researcher is free to discover information somewhat more independently. Chapter 5, *Researching Beyond the Campus Library*, leads students past traditional library resources and out into their communities. In addition to encouraging research using primary and secondary materials from public or private sources, the chapter also explains how to gather information by observing onsite, conducting personal interviews, taking surveys, and utilizing such media as radio and television.

Chapter 6, *Reading and Recording Information*, discusses the importance of careful reading and notetaking—practical, time-saving skills that can ensure accurate content and source citation later. The chapter includes a discussion of how and when to use summary, paraphrase, and quotation in the research paper as well as the importance of citing sources to avoid the problem of plagiarism.

Once students have begun to assemble a quantity of research data, they are often confused about how to begin organizing it and writing the paper. Because of their importance, these activities are discussed in two separate but related chapters. Chapter 7, *Planning Your Paper*, explains how to formulate and use preliminary and final thesis statements to focus the paper's discussion as well as how to devise an appropriate outline to organize the content. Basic written patterns of development are also reviewed. Chapter 8, *Writing Your Paper*, explains a variety ways to write the introduction, body, and conclusion as well as how to revise, edit, and proofread the final draft.

Three chapters are devoted to explaining and differentiating among the most common documentation styles used for research papers. Chapters 9 and 10 demonstrate correct forms for intext citations and the Works Cited section of a research paper using the Modern Language Association (MLA) style of documentation. A sample MLA-style research paper is provided as an appendix to Chapter 10. Chapter 11 discusses alternative documentation styles for author-year, or American Psychological Association (APA), papers and for papers written according to number-system, or Council of Biology Editors (CBE), documentation.

Chapter 12, *Preparing the Final Manuscript*, addresses the many technical and stylistic matters that often confront the student writing a research paper. MLA conventions for handling abbreviations, numbers, illustrations, titles, and so forth are explained as well as what constitutes *fair use* according to current copyright law.

To assist writers using documentation styles other than MLA, Appendix A presents two additional sample research papers: the first using author-year, or APA, style; the second using number-system, or CBE, style. Appendix B provides a guide to selected subject reference sources.

One other feature of *Writing the Modern Research Paper* deserves mention: The conclusion of each chapter includes a special Working with Others section, providing suggestions to students for collaboratively reviewing their progress at each step of the research process. Such activities take the loneliness out of research by providing students with opportunities to sound out ideas and share information as they complete the research assignment. These sections are intended for groups of students to use on their own or as assigned by the instructor as part of structured classroom activities.

Acknowledgments

Many people have generously contributed their ideas and time to help bring this book to fruition. My deepest thanks go to Joe Opiela, Executive Editor at Allyn and Bacon, for his encouragement, advice, and patience throughout the process. I am also grateful to my friend Pamela Grieman, who took time away from her own writing to share in the research and provide many valuable insights as the book developed.

I also wish to thank those individuals who reviewed this book at various stages: A. J. Bradford, Northern Virginia Community College-Manassas; Kathleen Shine Cain, Merrimack College; Linda Humphrey, Citrus Community College; Rebecca Kelly, Southern College of Technology; Shirley Morahan, Northeast Missouri State University; Jack Oruch, University of Kansas; Thomas F. Shea, University of Connecticut; and Al Starr, Essex Community College.

Research and the Research Paper

Virtually every human achievement—whether making a fire, building the pyramids, or discovering a vaccine for polio—has been accomplished by someone doing research. William Shakespeare's plays grew directly out of his own historical research and creative genius; Albert Einstein might never have discovered relativity without studying the works of other mathematicians. Every film produced in Hollywood, each law passed by Congress, and all the products on our grocery shelves are the result of research. Research is observation and study. It is the collecting of information in order to make judgments and gain truth.

In this sense, you have been doing research all your life. Why does it rain? Who were my ancestors? Which college should I attend? These and other questions that you have asked are all the beginnings of research. While posing a single question is hardly all there is to doing research, the continual seeking after information, knowledge, and understanding that you have done since birth is research on a grand scale. The same process occurs when you write a research paper: You learn by asking questions, finding their answers, and making judgments for yourself.

Research Is Learning

In fact, you should regard writing a research paper as learning how to learn on your own. Your professor will not simply hand you information in the form of a lecture or notes nor will a textbook or other single source sum up all you need to know and understand about a subject. Your efforts in producing a research paper will educate you in ways of acquiring information and give you practice in drawing intelligent conclusions from what you discover. You will come to see that doing research is learning in its most fundamental form: the acquisition and interpretation of information.

Perhaps you enjoy finding out about scientific subjects, like a possible cure for AIDS or the feasibility of interstellar travel. Or you may be interested in the advantages and drawbacks of becoming a nurse, a professional athlete, or a teacher. What is happening to the earth's ozone layer? Why is teenage suicide so common? What should be done to stem the spread of drugs in our society? Has television become sleazy? Are abortion laws too lenient? Writing a research paper provides you with the opportunity to learn—really learn—about these and other subjects about which you may be curious.

What Is a Research Paper?

The research paper you write will be a documented report resulting from your firsthand acquisition, synthesis, and interpretation of information. Its content will focus upon a topic that your own intellectual curiosity brings you to study. The primary purpose of such a paper is to inform the reader about the research topic and to demonstrate the validity or reasonableness of your conclusions about it. Although it is more objective than a personal essay, keep in mind that a research paper is also an expression of your own understanding of the topic. Your personal values, insights, and experiences will shape your responses throughout the research process, eventually finding expression in what you conclude and how you write about the topic.

The Research Topic

The information you collect for a research paper relates to a research subject or, more accurately, to a particular aspect of it called the *topic*. If you were interested, for example, in researching the subject of space exploration, a possible topic might be the benefits of long-range space probes like *Explorer I* or *Galileo*. Another topic for a paper on space exploration might be the physiological effects upon humans of spending prolonged periods of time in outer space.

Once you have selected a suitable topic for research, you can begin to frame a *research question,* which will become the focus of your research and your paper's discussion. How beneficial are long-range space probes? might be one question to investigate. Should we continue sending long-range probes into space? would shift the focus to a different aspect of the same subject. A topic concerning the effects upon humans of prolonged time in space could generate a research question such as Are prolonged flights in space too dangerous for humans?

Questions like these direct the investigation of sources and focus your notetaking. They ensure that your paper raises a significant issue and provides thoughtful discussion about the topic.

Length

The amount of discussion needed to support your main point about the research topic will determine your paper's length. In general, you will probably want to select a research topic that can be adequately discussed in 10 to 12 typewritten pages (5,000–6,000 words), the assigned length for most college research papers. Depending upon your topic, the length of time you have for research, and the expectations of your instructor, your paper may be somewhat shorter or longer.

Organization

A completed research paper includes several major parts, usually arranged in this order:

Title page
Outline (optional)
Text
Notes (optional)
Works Cited/References
Appendix (optional)

The largest part of the paper, the *text* or content portion, generally consists of three major sections:

1. an *introduction,* which sets forth the paper's *thesis,* or main point
2. the *body,* which illustrates and supports the main point with paragraphs of information and discussion
3. the *conclusion,* which states a final idea or summarizes the paper's major arguments

A research paper also includes *documentation,* the citing of sources in the text of the paper, as well as their listing at the end of the paper in a section titled Works Cited or References. Figure 1.1 presents a simplified diagram of a typical research paper.

Introduction	Introduction of the topic leads to a statement of the paper's thesis.
Body	Several paragraphs that illustrate and support the thesis through discussion, analysis, and examples; acknowledgment of sources as appropriate.
Conclusion	A summary of major arguments or a final statement and example.
Works Cited or References	A list of sources acknowledged in the paper.

FIGURE 1.1 Simplified diagram of a research paper

Doing Research for Your Paper

To "re-search" a subject is literally to see it another way: You gather original information of your own or study the work of others and evaluate it from your own point of view and experience.

Finding Sources

The investigation you do for a research paper may draw upon several kinds of sources. *Primary sources* include original material from such sources as the following:

- Your own experiences
- Field observations
- Interviews
- Laboratory reports
- Diaries
- Letters
- Literary works

Or you may be involved in research that uses information written by others about your subject. These *secondary sources* are those found in most libraries and include materials like these:

- Encyclopedias
- Magazines
- Journals
- Books
- Newspapers
- Pamphlets
- Indexes
- Computer databases
- Government reports

In order to give your paper both depth and breadth in its discussion of the research topic, use both primary and secondary sources as much as possible (see Chapters 4 and 5).

Documenting Sources

Regardless of which kinds of sources you use, your paper will include *documentation,* a method of acknowledging where you found your information and giving credit for any ideas that are not your own. Depending upon the kind of paper you write and for which discipline, the documentation may appear within the text of the paper itself, in footnotes, or in endnotes. As described earlier, your paper will also include a list of all the works cited as documentation in the paper. (See Chapter 11 on documentation forms for various academic disciplines.)

Organizing Your Research

A successful research paper reflects careful planning, not only of the research activities themselves but also of the time involved to accomplish them. The due date for your paper limits the time available for research and writing, and it puts pressure on you to finish the paper by a specified date. In order to complete the research process fully and to make sure the paper is finished on time, you will need to plan a reasonable research schedule and do all you can to keep to it.

Planning a Research Schedule

A *research schedule* is a calendar of each of the steps necessary for completing a successful research paper on time. Obviously, the schedule will list the paper's due date, but you will also need to include the major research steps that are described in this text:

1. Investigating one or more potential research subjects
2. Selecting a topic and framing a research question

3. Establishing a preliminary bibliography
4. Reading and taking notes on the topic
5. Devising an outline and tentative thesis statement
6. Writing the paper
7. Listing the works cited
8. Revising and editing

In addition, you will add steps that are unique to your individual research methods and necessary for your particular topic.

Your planning for a successful research paper should begin early. In fact, you ought to start thinking about your subject, available resources, and your time for researching and writing the paper the first day you know about the assignment. Starting early like this will save time later and allow you to collect ideas and resources throughout the term.

Once you actually begin your research assignment in earnest, expect to spend at least four to five weeks of ongoing thinking, researching, and writing. Since having enough time for these activities is crucial to your paper's success, it is important to devise a schedule that leads to accomplishing these tasks and meeting the turn-in date.

Figure 1.2 presents student Ron Bonneville's research schedule for his paper about Japanese ownership of properties in the United States. The finished paper, titled Japan in America: The Meaning of Foreign Ownership of U.S. Properties, is one of the sample research papers included in Appendix A. Notice that Ron's research schedule includes the major steps given in this text, as well as several activities required by his topic and his own way of approaching it. Ron also decided to use an asterisk to mark any due dates for various steps in the research process.

Ron became interested in the subject of foreign investment in United States properties after learning that a Canadian investment group had purchased the small milling plant where he had worked the previous summer. Employees at the plant had mixed feelings about working for a foreign owner, and Ron became interested in their discussions. Though he began with the idea of writing about all foreign investment in United States businesses, Ron soon discovered the topic was too large to treat adequately in a research paper. After some library research of current books and magazines, Ron realized that the rapidly increasing investment power of Japan was being felt worldwide and becoming a major concern to Americans. He decided to make Japanese ownership in the United States the focus of his research paper.

Patterns of Research Progress

The shift in direction that Ron made is not at all unusual for someone who is approaching a research paper. His research schedule may look complete here, but it is important to remember that Ron's planning, just

```
Ron Bonneville
English 101
                    RESEARCH PAPER SCHEDULE
_____

                                            Completed

September 22      Begin thinking about research
                  subject. Start research
                  notebook.                       [   ]

October 15        Select research subject.        [   ]

November 14       Read encyclopedia, and review
                  general sources on possible
                  research topics.                [   ]

*November 17      Make topic decision. Get OK
                  from Professor Braughn.          [   ]

November 18       Start preliminary reading
                  and notetaking.                  [   ]

*November 21      Turn in preliminary
                  bibliography.                     [   ]

November 22-      Research in library.             [   ]
December 2

November 24       Visit Foreign Trade Center.
                  Make observations, take notes,
                  find sources.                    [   ]

November 28       Attend city council hearing on
                  acquisition of city golf course
                  by Japanese investment group.    [   ]

December 3-4      Analyze research notes. Make
                  up outline and preliminary
                  thesis statement.                [   ]

December 5-8      Write first draft of the paper. [   ]

*December 8       First draft due to Professor
                  Braughn for advice.              [   ]

December 8-10     Write final draft.               [   ]

December 11-12    Revise and edit final draft.     [   ]

December 14       Finish Works Cited list.         [   ]

*December 16      Final research paper due!        [   ]
```

FIGURE 1.2 Student Ron Bonneville's research paper schedule

like his original subject, actually changed several times during the assignment period. Though this guide will introduce you to the steps every research paper writer must complete, bear in mind that these steps do not necessarily occur in order or only once during the research effort. Your analysis of what you discover one day about the validity of IQ tests may lead to new discoveries the next day, then a revision of your first analysis, and so on throughout your research. The book you thought would be of no help when you began your research may suddenly become essential at some later stage.

As Ron Bonneville discovered after he shifted his research focus from foreign investment in the United States to Japanese ownership of American properties, research proceeds more in loops and zigzags than in a direct line. Keep your research efforts on track, but try not to become discouraged by this irregular pattern of progress: Looping and zigzagging is the nature of productive research.

The format for your own research schedule may vary from Ron Bonneville's, but do not overlook this important planning step in preparing to write a research paper. Your schedule will change along with your research; it will also serve as your planning guide and a source of reassurance about the timeliness of your efforts. As you move progressively further into the research process, you will also find that checking off each completed task provides satisfaction and encouragement as you work to complete the paper.

Keeping a Research Notebook

Most of the thinking for your research paper will occur during times that you have specifically set aside for research and writing. Unfortunately, however, the best ideas and sudden insights do not always occur on schedule. Many useful thoughts will spring up spontaneously, often coming only half formed at unexpected times. Seeing a neighbor who works for the city housing agency, for example, may suddenly remind you that he or she would be an excellent interview source for a paper on the homeless. While crossing campus on your way to a morning class, you might recall the magazine article you read yesterday on the cost of space exploration. At that moment, you may start to think about how your paper might use some of those statistics.

To make sure useful ideas like these are not lost, you should write them down in a research notebook. A *research notebook* is any handy-size, spiral-bound notebook that you can literally carry with you everywhere and make a habit of using throughout the research process. You will find such a notebook a useful place to record valuable information, especially the spontaneous, mental pondering that occurs both during and between your planned research activities. The research notebook is also a good place to jot down titles you want to look for later, to pose questions you need answered, or to record your progress.

A research notebook will be most useful to you if you give some thought ahead of time to a few practical considerations. Follow these suggestions as you begin to set up your research notebook:

1. Keep a particular notebook reserved especially for your research notes and writing. Mixing your research material with other kinds of writing or class assignments defeats the purpose of the research notebook, which is to record and organize all of your thinking for the research paper in one easily accessible place.

2. Use pencil or ink to record ideas and information. While you do not need to worry about neatness, write legibly and make complete entries. Nothing is more frustrating than having to retrace your steps to find omitted information or not being able to decipher a hastily written note later.

3. Record names, titles, and other bibliographic data accurately and fully to avoid errors in your final paper. Make a point of later copying all such information about sources onto 3" x 5" notecards for easier use.

4. Use as many headings or subtitles in the notebook as necessary to keep your entries organized. Headings like Notes and Ideas, Research Subjects, Topic Choices, Sources to Find, and Questions to Answer will keep your entries accessible and encourage your thinking for each section.

5. Date each entry in the research notebook. This will help you see a pattern to the research, as well as provide an occasional nudge when you have ignored something for too long.

The pages in Figure 1.3 are from student Anne Kramer's research notebook and show entries she made while preparing a paper for an American literature class. When Anne's class read Mark Twain's *Adventures of Huckleberry Finn,* her instructor assigned the novel as the subject for their research papers. It was up to each student to select a particular topic on which to write about the novel. Anne was initially fascinated by Twain's use of dialect, as well as by his positive portrayal of Jim, the black slave who escapes down the Mississippi on a raft with Huck. Later, she grew interested in how readers reacted to Twain's handling of relationships between blacks and whites in the novel. Anne eventually completed the sample research paper in Chapter 9, titled The Response of Black Readers to Mark Twain's *Adventures of Huckleberry Finn.* The entries in Figure 1.3 demonstrate how she used the research notebook to record and organize her work on the paper.

Anne Kramer
English 151   *Research Notebook*

Notes & Ideas

✓ <u>September 22:</u> *Professor Morrison described our research paper
assignment today. Ten to fifteen pages on Mark Twain's <u>Adventures of
Huckleberry Finn.</u> Start thinking of what to write about.*

✓ <u>October 11:</u> *What about Twain's use of dialect in <u>Huckleberry Finn</u>? Was
it accurate? He uses a different dialect at times to show character and
station in life—Jim's vs. Huck's. Or the Dauphine, whose phony French
dialect is as big a fraud as he is!*

✓ <u>October 20:</u> *Library research on <u>Huckleberry Finn.</u>*

✓ <u>November 13:</u> *There seems to be some controversy over Twain's depiction
of blacks in his work. Was he unconsciously prejudiced, or was he more
enlightened than others during his time? It seems like Jim in <u>Huckleberry
Finn</u> is held up for both scorn and respect. How do readers of Twain's
time vs. those of today view his representation of black people? Was he
fair, accurate?*

✓ <u>November 15:</u> *Library hours for weekends: 8-5 Sat. & Sun.*

✓ <u>November 17:</u> *There's a class on Twain at the university. Check the
bookstore to see what they are reading. Maybe attend class?*

<u>November 24:</u> *Interview with Professor Kennedy on Twain. This was a
good idea. He gave me some books and told me about other kinds of
sources to look into. Next time I'll take a tape recorder.*

<u>December 8:</u> *The paper looks good so far. I probably need more
examples. <u>Don't forget</u>—underlining for book titles, quotation marks for
short stories and essays.*

FIGURE 1.3   Student Anne Kramer's research notebook

Research Topics

1. The controversy over the ending of _HF_.
2. The use of dialects in _HF_.
3. Jim's Cairo vs. Huck's "territory" as freedom symbols.
4. Critics' views of Twain's portrayal of blacks in _HF_.
5. Huck and Tom Sawyer—a comparison?
6. The role of literary references in _HF_.

Research Questions

October 14: Why _did_ Twain postpone Jim's being freed at the end of the novel? This is the question everyone keeps asking.

October 25: How did people in Twain's day react to Huck's helping a slave escape?

November 6: What was Twain's personal attitude toward slavery and black people in general? See a biography? Encyclopedia?

November 27: How accurate is Twain's use of dialect in _HF_? Where can I find out?

December 3: How many of my own ideas go in the paper, and how much should I try to include what critics and others have said? What's the right balance?

December 7: How do I cite a video in the paper and in Works Cited? Ask Professor Morrison.

FIGURE 1.3 Continued

Sources to Find

November 5: Check library for DIALOG—computer database for available books on Twain and his works.

November 10: Find *Index to Periodicals By and About Blacks.*

November 23: Find *Mark Twain's Negroes* by Thomas L. Langley. Not in college library. Try city library or university.

November 27: Found Langley book on Twain at city library. No help.

FIGURE 1.3   Continued

As these entries show, your research notebook will contain many kinds of information, from short reminders to yourself about library hours to extended thinking about your sources. You may decide to use the notebook as a place to record all your research notes and do extensive writing for the research paper, or you may want to use it only as a place to try out ideas in very brief form.

Notice that Anne Kramer has dated each entry. She has also made a checkmark next to each task as she completed it (see p. 10). You may want to devise your own way of keeping track of what you accomplish, and you may even prefer a different format than Anne's for your notebook entries. The most important thing is to utilize a research notebook in a way that is genuinely helpful for preparing your research paper.

While there are no set requirements for what goes into a research notebook, the following kinds of entries are typically the most useful:

■ *Your research schedule.* Having your research schedule readily available will keep your efforts organized and give you direction. Make it the first item you put in your notebook.

■ *Ideas about your research topic.* Jot down spontaneous insights before you forget them. If you find yourself writing a lot, keep going. What you write could become valuable material for the final paper.

■ *Research questions.* Keep track of questions you need to answer for yourself about the paper's topic (What are my city's educational requirements for police personnel?), as well as those questions you will need to ask others (Do I hand in my research notebook with my final paper?).

■ *Sources to follow up on.* Record authors' names, source titles, libraries, data services, and other information you may need for your paper.

Since you never know when an idea or useful information may suddenly become available, make a habit of carrying the notebook with you wherever you go, not just to the library or during research times. Once you start using a research notebook regularly, you will find it an essential aid in the research and writing of your paper.

Including Your Own Ideas in the Research Paper

Unfortunately, too many beginning writers make the mistake of letting research content alone dominate their papers. Anxious to demonstrate the hours of research they have devoted to the paper or simply overwhelmed by the amount of material discovered, they end up writing a summarizing report instead of the thoughtful, creative response to research that their instructor had expected. A work that only summarizes sources instead of using them to illuminate ideas or support an argument is not a research paper.

Make sure your paper analyzes, compares, and evaluates information and sources to support your position and clarify your thoughts for the reader. As you go about writing, remember that your own ideas are not only valuable but actually are, in one sense, what the paper is about. If you are writing a paper on the subject of homeless people in the United States, for example, your reader not only wants to know about the homeless but also what the information you present adds up to. Your presentation and interpretation of the facts, your analysis and comparison of other writers' opinions, and your conclusions about all of these constitute the heart of your research content.

WORKING WITH OTHERS

Make a habit of talking over your research assignment with friends or classmates as early in the term as possible. Begin by discussing the following questions together to get a broad view of research and to be sure you understand the class assignment clearly.

- Discuss a recent film or television program you have seen that required someone to do research for its content or production. What kind of research was done? How was it done and by whom? How important to the success of the production was the research? Cite examples of how research or its results are being carried out in other areas of our society.

- Review any previous experience you have had researching information, and discuss the major steps or tasks involved. How did that kind of research differ from that involved in doing the research paper for your current assignment?

- Regardless of whether you have had previous experience doing some kind of research, what questions do you now have about research and research papers generally?

- Discuss your current research paper assignment. Do you foresee any major obstacles to your successful completion of the assignment? If so, how will you overcome these obstacles?

- Exchange ideas about potential local resources for research. What primary or secondary resources are available?

- Have you used anything like a research notebook or made up something like a research schedule in the past? Why or why not? How helpful do you feel either of these will be to your completing the current research paper assignment?

- Share any ideas you have for a research subject or topic. What interests you about these issues? How do they fit your current research paper assignment?

Each of the chapters in this book concludes with suggestions for Working with Others on a research paper assignment. Check with your instructor about any guidelines he or she may have for working together, and take advantage of any opportunities you have to share your ideas and progress. You will find that time spent discussing your research and writing with others is one of the best resources available.

Using a Library for Research

Whether writing a library-based research paper or one developed fully from your own field or laboratory studies, you will need the resources of a good library. You should use the library to discover what is already known about the research topic, what issues need to be addressed, and what sources exist for you to consider. Most campus libraries and large community libraries can provide the information you will need, first, to establish the direction of your research and later, to investigate a specific research question in depth.

This chapter will introduce you to academic and public libraries and how to use them, including newer types of library resources like computer catalogs, citation indexes, and database searches. You will need to understand such libraries and resources in order to make your research both efficient and comprehensive.

Understanding Academic and Public Libraries

It is best to begin your research at the largest library available. Access to numerous resources will ensure success in getting started and give you insight to the limitations and possibilities of the research topic. Once you have a topic and can focus on a potential research question, your goal will be to locate appropriate numbers and types of sources to investigate. Both academic and public libraries will be useful to your research for the different emphases and variety of sources they provide.

Academic Libraries

College and university libraries are created primarily to serve the study and research needs of students, faculty, and scholars. For this reason, academic libraries are your best resource for general as well as scarce or highly specialized materials. The sheer quantity of books, periodicals, microfilms, and other resources at most academic libraries makes them especially essential to competent research. (The combined libraries at Harvard University, for example, house over 11,000,000 books alone.) Since they are intended to serve research, the reference sections as well as the research support services of most academic libraries are also more extensive than those of community or private libraries.

Special Emphasis Libraries.   Most colleges and universities also maintain separate libraries for such professional areas as law, medicine, business, or technology. Such discipline libraries often contain specialized resources that you would not readily find in other libraries or at least not in such quantity. If you were researching a topic like AIDS, for example, you would most likely find a reference source such as *AIDS Bibliography for Nineteen Eighty-one to Nineteen Eighty-six* only at a college or university medical library. Similarly, you would go to a campus law library for *Index to Legal Periodicals* to locate the numerous legal journals not ordinarily found at the main college or university library. You will find that community college libraries are good resources for general research and especially for trade and vocational subjects.

The general emphasis of a college or university is often a reliable clue to its library's resources. Because of its focus on art and design, the Massachusetts College of Art, for example, has an extensive collection of slides, films, videos, and recordings in addition to a large general library. The library at Northrop University, a private California college emphasizing technology and business, houses over 65,000 books, many of them engineering and airframe-maintenance sources that would be unavailable at most other academic or public libraries.

To work in the library at a school you do not attend, you may be restricted to using materials right in the library or checking them out on a community-use basis. You may also be able to check out resources through the interlibrary loan services on your own campus. Access to the libraries of private colleges and universities may be available for a small fee. And if you do visit another school's library, do not overlook the campus bookstore as an additional place to find very recent material on your subject.

Assessing What Is Available.   You should thoroughly investigate your own campus or another academic library and its resources before starting research. Though you may feel that you can research effectively at a nearby community library, you never know what research ideas might be better developed through the facilities of a larger library. Ask your instructor or a librarian what subjects the libraries of nearby universities and colleges emphasize. Also consult the following references for information about major focuses, programs, and libraries at any college or university:

American Library Directory: 1989–90. New York: Bowker, 1989.
Barron's Profiles of American Colleges. New York: Barron's, 1988.
The Right College: 1990. New York: ARCO, 1989.

Public Libraries

If your research steers you toward topics of community, county, or state importance, you may profit by investigating the holdings of one or more public libraries in your area. Public libraries do not usually offer the extensive general holdings or scholarly reference materials found in academic libraries. Most all of them, however, carry major encyclopedias; dictionaries; subject bibliographies; indexes to magazine, journal, and newspaper articles; and other standard reference works, which can be of help when you are first starting to research.

Special Focus Materials. Local libraries also offer resource materials not available at most academic or private libraries. News that has particular local importance—say, the closing of a nearby nuclear atomic power plant or the life and career of a famous area resident—may be more thoroughly covered by the small community newspapers kept on file at the local public library.

In addition, county and city libraries are often the only resources for local or regional historical documents. Because of a particular librarian's personal interest or a patron's donation of items, local city or county libraries may have special collections of materials (such as diaries, letters, scrapbooks, or antiques) not commonly included in academic library holdings. Your local public library may also maintain small informal files of pamphlets, handbills, political advertisements, theater announcements, and other items of community interest. Check with the librarian to see what kinds of special collections may be available and useful for your research.

Locating Public Libraries. Remember that public libraries vary as much as the communities they serve. Sometimes a brief phone call can tell you whether visiting a city or county library would be worth your time. You can probably locate the nearest public libraries just by looking in the telephone book. For more comprehensive information about the location and particular collection emphases of any academic, public, or private library, consult the *American Library Directory: 1989-90* (New York: Bowker, 1989).

Do not overlook the value of using public libraries at some stage of your research. Their different emphases may provide ideas about what to research, or if you already have a topic, they may suggest a local angle for the paper to make it more representative of your individual approach. The campus library may be the best place to research the topic of teenage gangs generally; however, the local library may help you in researching a paper focusing on efforts to eliminate a widespread gang problem in your own community.

How Libraries Are Organized

You can save time and avoid a lot of frustration doing research by understanding the general arrangement of materials in a library. Although libraries are not alike in the ways they organize information, the reference, book, and periodical sections are the ones you should be most familiar with in doing your research.

The Reference Area

A library's reference area houses its encyclopedias, dictionaries, bibliographies, directories, atlases, indexes, and almanacs. Information is usually available at a reference desk from which a librarian provides assistance by answering questions or locating items that are difficult to find. The reference desk is also where you can request a librarian-assisted database search for your topic.

Since reference books are generally not allowed to circulate outside the library, plan to complete most of your working bibliography in the reference room itself. To save time and get ideas about what resources are available in the reference area, it is always wise to browse awhile in this section before settling into your research. Many libraries provide printed guides that show the general layout of the reference section and other parts of the library.

The Book Area

Also called the "stacks," this is the area containing books and the bound volumes of periodicals, including magazines and journals. Depending on the library, the stacks may range in size from many rows of shelved books to several floors of them. Some libraries have a separate "oversize" section for all books that exceed normal height or width.

Access to the stacks varies among libraries. In those with open stacks, you can go among the aisles of books yourself to find what you need. In a library with closed stacks, a staff person brings books to you after you make out a request form.

The Periodicals Room

Unbound issues of current magazines, journals, and newspapers are kept in the library's periodical room. Practice varies, but most libraries keep several back issues of a periodical on the shelf until they are ready to be bound into volumes. Some libraries provide only the current issue of a periodical, making past issues available by request.

Academic libraries seldom allow recently published, unbound periodicals to circulate, and they may not always subscribe to certain popular periodicals. In these cases, public libraries may serve your needs much better, since they subscribe more heavily to popular periodicals and frequently allow recent and unbound issues to circulate.

Other Specialized Areas

In addition to the reference, book, and periodical areas, your library may also maintain a separate microform section, a government documents desk, a media library, or a special collections library. Make a point of exploring your library and finding out which of these or other specialized areas are available.

Library Classification Systems

Libraries organize their holdings by classifying them into groups and storing items of the same group together in one place. Each item in a group is marked with a *call number*, a series of numbers and/or letters indentifying it and the group to which it belongs. The call number also accompanies the item's description in the library catalog system to indicate where it is located.

Two of the most common methods used to classify a library's holdings in this way are the Dewey Decimal (DD) and the Library of Congress (LC) subject-classification systems. Small libraries favor the DD system because it is simpler and thus fulfills their needs. The LC system is used by large libraries because it is almost infinitely expandable and has more main divisions. Most libraries use either one system or the other, though some may be in transition between the older DD system and the newer LC system. Knowing something about how both systems work can make your research more effective in any library.

The Dewey Decimal System

The Dewey Decimal classification system assigns a library book or other resource a call number according to the 10 major subject categories shown in Figure 2.1. By the DD system, a book with any call number in the 300s, for example, has a subject in the social sciences, a major category that includes group dynamics, law, government, education, and economics as subdivisions. A book with a call number beginning with 342 addresses constitutional and administrative law, while one with a call number beginning with 345 treats criminal law. Successive numbers and decimal points further classify such a book more precisely:

340	Law
345	Criminal law
345.01	Criminal courts
345.05	General criminal procedure
345.052	Criminal investigation and law enforcement
345.056	Rights of suspects
345.06	Evidence

CALL NUMBER	MAIN DIVISION
000–99	General works
100–199	Philosophy
200–299	Religion
300–399	Social sciences
400–499	Languages
500–599	Natural sciences
600–699	Technology and applied sciences
700–799	Fine arts
800–899	Literature
900–999	History and geography

FIGURE 2.1   The Dewey Decimal subject-classification system

The Library of Congress System

The most obvious difference between the Library of Congress and Dewey Decimal systems is that the LC system uses letters instead of numbers to identify subject classifications, as identified in Figure 2.2. Like the DD system, the LC system provides subcategories within each of the main divisions. In the LC system, subdivisions are made by adding a second letter and numbers. For the main division of technology (T), for example, works about motor vehicles, aeronautics, and astronautics are classified under the subdivision TL. All books classified under TL670-723 are about airplanes. The call letters TL721 indicate that a book is about commercial airplanes, while TL723 shows it is about government airplanes.

As with the Dewey Decimal system, paying attention to the subject designators of the Library of Congress system can save you valuable time during your research. If you were investigating the safety of private planes, for example, you would want to spend your time tracking down books with a TL685.1 designation—private airplanes—rather than TL685.3—

CALL LETTER	MAIN DIVISION
A	General works
B	Philosophy and religion
C	History—Auxilary sciences
D	History—Topography
E–F	American history—Topography
G	Geography—Anthropology
H	Social sciences
J	Political sciences
K	Law
L	Education
M	Music
N	Fine arts
P	Language—Literature (nonfiction)
Q	Sciences
R	Medicine
S	Agriculture
T	Technology
U	Military science
V	Naval science
Z	Bibliography and library science
P–Z	Literature (fiction)

FIGURE 2.2   The Library of Congress subject-classification system

military airplanes. Careful attention to the LC designator would also keep you from spending time trying to locate a work listed in the library catalog under "airplanes" but designated QA930—airplane aerodynamics.

Working with the Library Catalog

Without the catalog, the collection of materials in any library would be practically inaccessible. Arranged alphabetically by author, title, and subject or a combination of the three, the library catalog tells what books and other materials the library has and where they are located.

While the basic information a library catalog provides is generally standard, the kind of catalog a library uses can vary. Card catalogs, in which information about each item in the library is printed on a small card, are still predominant in most local library systems, though they are rapidly being replaced by more modern and more efficient online computer catalogs. Book catalogs, microform catalogs, and CD–ROM (Compact Disk–Read-Only Memory) catalogs have their own special uses and are generally found at academic or large public research libraries. Most libraries today use one or more of these kinds of catalogs. You will need to understand how to use each to do effective research in any library.

Using the Card Catalog

A *card catalog* consists of hundreds—or in a large library, possibly thousands—of alphabetized cards, usually filed in rows of small drawers, that list every item in the library. Separate author, title, and subject cards are stored in alphabetized order according to the first important word. The words *a, an,* and *the,* for instance, are dropped from the beginnings of titles and subjects when you want to locate a work. An author's name is reversed, putting the last name first. Thus, if you were looking for a book titled *The Life of a Forest,* you would find it in the "L" section of the card catalog under "Life of a Forest, The." If you looked the book up under its author's name, William R. Owens, you would look under "O" in the card catalog until you came to "Owens, William R." The DD or LC call number on the card would tell you where the book is shelved in the library.

The information in most library card catalogs is stored in triplicate, with every resource listed on separate subject, title, and author cards. This system allows you to find any book or other work, regardless of whether you know very much about it.

Subject Cards. Use the subject card catalog to begin compiling the preliminary bibliography or any time you need to know what books are

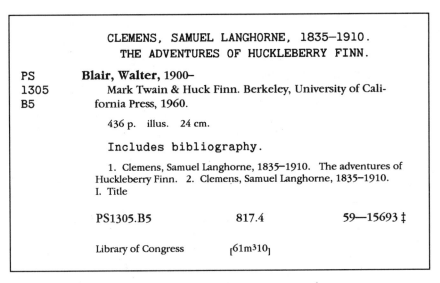

CLEMENS, SAMUEL LANGHORNE, 1835–1910.
THE ADVENTURES OF HUCKLEBERRY FINN.

PS
1305
B5

Blair, Walter, 1900–
Mark Twain & Huck Finn. Berkeley, University of California Press, 1960.

436 p.   illus.   24 cm.

Includes bibliography.

1. Clemens, Samuel Langhorne, 1835–1910. The adventures of Huckleberry Finn. 2. Clemens, Samuel Langhorne, 1835–1910. I. Title

PS1305.B5   817.4   59—15693 ‡

Library of Congress   ₍61m³10₎

FIGURE 2.3   A subject card

available on any particular subject. Begin by looking in the catalog under the subject or topic you are researching. The subject heading appears at the top of each card, with full information about each book and its location in the library (see Figure 2.3).

If you cannot locate subject cards for your research subject, you may need to look under a different subject heading. For instance, you may have looked under "Macintosh" and need instead to look under "computers." "See also" cards may direct you to other headings in the catalog. If not, you can find alternative headings by consulting the library's two-volume copy of *Library of Congress Subject Headings,* a list of subject headings and related terms used for all library card catalogs.

Author and Title Cards.   Another way to find sources for your research is to consult the author and title cards of the library catalog. If you know the author of a book or if you want to find the titles of works by a particular authority, consult the author card index. You will find a card for each book by that author filed alphabetically by title under the author's last name (see Figure 2.4).

If you know precisely which book you want, you can locate it most quickly by going right to the title card catalog. Author and title cards give the same information as subject cards. Title cards, however, also have the book's title printed at the top (see Figure 2.5).

PS   **Blair, Walter,** 1900–
1305   Mark Twain & Huck Finn. Berkeley, University of Cali-
B5   fornia Press, 1960.

                436 p.   illus.   24 cm.

                Includes bibliography.

                1. Clemens, Samuel Langhorne, 1835–1910.   The adventures of
             Huckleberry Finn.   2. Clemens, Samuel Langhorne, 1835–1910.
             I. Title

                PS1305.B5   817.4   59—15693 ‡

                Library of Congress   ₍61m³10₎

FIGURE 2.4   An author card

                           Mark Twain & Huck Finn
PS   **Blair, Walter,** 1900–
1305   Mark Twain & Huck Finn. Berkeley, University of Cali-
B5   fornia Press, 1960.

                436 p.   illus.   24 cm.

                Includes bibliography.

                1. Clemens, Samuel Langhorne, 1835–1910.   The adventures of
             Huckleberry Finn.   2. Clemens, Samuel Langhorne, 1835–1910.
             I. Title

                PS1305.B5   817.4   59—15693 ‡

                Library of Congress   ₍61m³10₎

FIGURE 2.5   A title card

Using the Online Catalog

An *online catalog* uses a computer terminal to provide a complete
listing of all the items in a library. Such a catalog provides a great deal
more than a computerized version of its predecessor, the traditional li-

brary card catalog. With an online catalog, you cannot only locate books by subject, author, and title, but many systems will also tell you which local libraries have a book if yours does not. Because they can be more easily updated, can provide more information than traditional card catalogs, and can be made available at several locations throughout the library, online catalogs have generally replaced or subordinated other catalog systems.

Locating a Subject. The tremendous amount of and number of types of information in a modern online catalog system have made research easier as well as more thorough than ever before. For example, many online systems have a browse feature that allows you to begin with a subject like birds and alphabetically scan the system's subject catalog in a matter of minutes:

Birds
Birds—Behavior
Birds—Habitats
Birds—History
Birds—Physical characteristics

As the system displays a list of subjects, you simply select the one you want to investigate. The online screen will then display a list of all the available books in the library on your selected subject.

Using an online catalog, you do not even need all the information that would be required if you were using the card catalog to locate a book. You can enter a single term—let's say "college"—and the system will display all titles, subject and author entries, and bibliographic notes in which the term "college" appears. To save time, you can also enter a title code and have the system display only titles with a particular word or combination of words in them. For example, if you know only the first word or two of a title, like *College Entrance Examinations,* you can enter any one or a combination of main words—"college," "entrance examinations," "college entrance," and so on. The online screen will display a list of all books with the words you enter in their titles.

Locating an Author. You can also enter an author's last name and get a display of all authors with that name. Selecting one author from the displayed list will produce a second display listing all available works by that particular author. Or suppose you are unsure of how to spell an author's last name—like that of Ernest Hemingway, for example. Just enter an online code, plus "HEM". The system will display the names of all authors whose names begin with HEM:

Hembree, Ron
Hemenway, Joan M.
Heming, William
Hemingway, Ernest
Hemker, H. C.
Hemlon, Marie
Hemmingway, Charles A.

Other Features.   Some online catalog systems allow you to print the information on the display screen as you view it, thereby saving you the work of copying down the information you find. One particular library's online catalog may even be accessible through the system at a neighboring library or on your own home computer through the use of a modem and payment of a small fee. Since all online catalog systems are not alike in their capabilities or operations, consult a librarian or follow available directions for using the system in your own library.

A word of caution: While online catalogs are wonderful aids to research, they are not everything you need to write a good research paper. As you use your library's computerized online catalog, remember not to rely on its systems so much that you eliminate your own creative thinking about your research. Browse the bookshelves of the library yourself. Remember that some valuable sources may even be too old to have been entered into the online system. Think of connections between sources and subjects that the system's technology may not have included. Use the online catalog all you can, but remember to approach your research subject with your own individual thinking about it, too.

Using Other Types of Library Catalogs

The most commonly used library catalogs are the card and online computer types, discussed above. Many libraries, however, also use other types of catalogs either as the main cataloging system or as a supplement. You will want to know something about each of these catalogs in order to take advantage of the assistance they can also offer the researcher.

Book Catalogs.   Available in the library reference section, a book catalog is, as the name suggests, a book listing all of the library's holdings. The pages of a book catalog may be composed of photographed and reduced copies of all the cards in the library's card catalog, or they may contain bound, computer-generated lists of each item in the library collection. Many libraries use a book catalog as a back-up to their online catalog.

Though most online catalogs have information only about local libraries, book catalogs from out-of-area libraries are additionally valuable for researching long distance. A researcher in Tampa, Florida, for example, can use the book catalog from the University of California at Los Angeles to find out what books are at UCLA, to get bibliographic information about resources there, or to obtain a book through interlibrary loan services.

Book-form card catalogs also allow you to scan whole pages of entries at once. Seeing multiple entries allows you to compare several items on the page: publication date, bibliography, number of pages, and so on. If the library allows it, book catalogs also make it possible for you to photocopy the pages themselves as a quick way to record data for several entries at once.

Microform Catalogs.   Library catalogs in microform—or COMCATS (Computer Output Microfilm Catalogs)—are copied at greatly reduced size on cards or sheets of microfilm that must be read at special machines available in the library. Because of the reduced size of its print, a single microform card, for example, can hold up to a thousand pages of regularly printed material. Microfilm, microcards, microfiche, and microprint are all varieties of microforms that differ only in their format (card or sheet) and the amount of reduction they provide.

Because of the small print and the necessity of reading them at a machine, microform catalogs are not as easy to work with as other types of catalogs. Some libraries have machines that can give you a print-out of a microform, but the practice can be time consuming and expensive. In most cases, doing your research through the library's card catalog or online computer catalog will prove more satisfying.

Compact Disk Catalogs.   Rather than working as an online catalog, the CD–ROM (Compact Disk–Read-Only Memory) provides a fixed catalog that library computer terminals read off a single imprinted disk. Similar in size and appearance to a common music compact disk, a CD–ROM disk can store well over a half million words. You read a CD–ROM catalog at a library computer terminal equipped with a monitor, keyboard, and (usually) a printer.

CD–ROM catalog information is generally the same as that given by other catalogs, although information stored on an individual disk cannot be added to or changed. The catalog is kept current by the addition of new disks as they become available. For this reason, always note the date on the CD–ROM catalog disk you are working with. If it is not current, you may need to go to the online catalog or elsewhere for more recent information.

Library Services and Resources

In order to use any library efficiently, you need to know what assistance it can provide. The services that make life easier for researchers vary with the size and purpose of a library. Naturally, larger libraries can generally give more support than smaller ones, but most libraries can offer more help than you may realize.

Librarian Assistance

Probably the most valuable assistance you can get in the library will come from a librarian. Trained in the resources of a library and the process of research, librarians are also experienced in assisting students with research papers. It is likely that your librarian has helped another student with a topic similar to yours and can tell you what resources to consult or avoid. He or she knows what is available and where to find it in the library, as well as how to access materials located elsewhere. Do not underestimate the help a librarian can give you at any stage of your research. You cannot find a better resource.

Information Service

Larger libraries often staff a telephone information service just to answer questions that can be handled with a few minutes of searching by the librarian. Most libraries will gladly answer questions over the telephone, whether you need to know what resources are available or just forgot to write down an author's name. Find out at the start of your research if your library has such an information service.

Search Assistance

A library's search service can locate books or other materials that were not on the shelf when you looked for them. Someone else may have been using a book when you were looking, it may have been at the bindery, or it may have been misshelved. If you cannot locate a book where the catalog says it should be, ask a librarian for a library search request form. You can usually get a search report on the book's status in one or two days.

Interlibrary Loan

You can obtain books and other materials that are unavailable in your own library through interlibrary loan. Your library's online catalog may tell you when a book is located at another local library, or the librarian can use a national library computer network called OCLC (Online Computer Library Center) to find where any book is available. Once a work is located, your librarian can arrange to have it sent to you at the library. Be aware that material requested through interlibrary loan may take three to ten days to arrive.

Reserve and Recall

Do not give up on library books or other items you need just because they have been checked out. The library can reserve materials for you, placing a hold on their circulation and notifying you as soon as they have been returned. At academic libraries, where books are often checked out for long periods of time, you can recall items that the original borrower has had out for over two or three weeks.

Nonprint Sources

Many libraries maintain collections of nonprint materials, including audio cassettes, phonograph records, video cassettes, and films. The forms for including such sources in your working bibliography and Works Cited list are addressed in Chapter 10.

Photocopying

Since photocopying has proven so necessary to modern research, most libraries today provide machines for that purpose. A good system of notetaking (see Chapter 6) can reduce the expense of photocopying, but such an aid can be valuable when you need to study noncirculating, lengthy, or complex materials outside the library. Read the copyright restrictions posted on most machines, and avoid plagiarism (discussed in Chapter 6) by crediting any sources from which you borrow.

Computer Facilities

Your library's online catalog and database systems will allow you to search for hundreds of sources in your own and other libraries. If you have a personal computer and a modem (a device connecting your computer to another via the telephone line), paying a small fee will enable you to link up with your library's catalogs and other databases right at home. For those who prefer to write with a library's resources at hand, most large academic libraries also have computers and word-processing programs available in the library.

Finding Sources through a Database

You can draw upon several hundred computer databases in the arts, humanities, sciences, and social sciences to produce a customized list of sources or other data for your research topic. While libraries bear the cost of making some computer databases free to their patrons, many useful commercial databases cost according to the time used. Librarians will conduct database searches for you, using their expertise to reduce the time and cost of the service. Since you will have to pay the fee charged to the library for such a search (usually $10 to $50), discuss your research goals with the librarian ahead of time to verify the need for a database search and to plan an effective, economical search strategy.

What Is a Database?

A library research database is a collection of reference information stored in a computer and available to other computers through a telephone hook-up. Libraries subscribe to commercial vendors whose systems provide access to hundreds of separate databases on a fee-for-use basis. Databases incorporate hundreds of general indexes and journal abstract sources, even the complete texts of a variety of sources:

Books	Government reports
Newspapers	Dissertations
Magazines	Grants
Journals	Conference proceedings
Reviews	

Databases exist for hundreds of subjects, ranging from agriculture and chemical compounds to the stock exchange and Chinese technology. A single large database like AGRICOLA, which covers agriculture and related subjects, contains over 2.5 million records. A national database vendor such as DIALOG, to which many libraries subscribe, can search over 300 such separate databases, offering researchers access to more than 175 million records.

Searching a Database

To initiate a library-assisted database search, your librarian will ask you to complete a search request, requiring information such as the following:

1. Describe the content and title of your research paper.
2. List key terms, subjects, or concepts for your paper topic, as well as their synonyms. Also list those terms to be excluded.

3. Explain the purpose of your search.
4. State the time period you want the database search to cover.
5. State other limitations, such as languages.

After you have returned the search form, the reference librarian will discuss your search topic with you, determine whether a search is advisable, and if so, discuss a search strategy with you.

With the librarian's assistance, you will need to identify the terminology that will direct the database search. These *descriptors* identify the characteristics by which the search program will select or reject the bibliographic entries in its databank. For example, when Anne Kramer asked for a database search for her paper on black readers' responses to Mark Twain's *Adventures of Huckleberry Finn*, she decided with the librarian to use "Mark Twain," "black," and "censorship" as the three descriptors. The computer search program recorded only those books and articles that had qualities named by the three descriptors. Eventually, Anne got a computer print-out of several possible sources on her topic, one of which is shown in Figure 2.6.

If you decide to use a database search for research sources, remember that it will take time. Allow at least five days in your research schedule to plan such a search and to get the results from the library.

```
880048       24A-03936
A BRIEF HISTORY OF THE CENSORSHIP OF THE ADVENTURES
OF HUCKLEBERRY FINN
   Rule, Henry B.
   Lamar Journal of the Humanities, 1986 12(1):9-18.
DOCUMENT TYPE:   ARTICLE
ABSTRACT:   Traces the changing efforts to censor
   Mark Twain's classic, The Adventures of Huckleberry
   Finn, initially centering on the vulgar nature of
   the Huckleberry Finn character, shifting in 1957
   to protest against the book's alleged negative
   portrayal of American blacks, and continuing
   unabated through 1985. (R. H. Fritze)
DESCRIPTORS:   Novels ; Censorship ; Twain, Mark
   -(Adventures of Huckleberry Finn) ; 1884-1985
HISTORICAL PERIOD:   1880D   1880H   1900H
   HISTORICAL PERIOD (Starting):   1884
   HISTORICAL PERIOD (Ending):   1985
```

FIGURE 2.6　An example of a database search report

Available Databases

Almost any bibliographic or other general reference information found in a library is also available from a database. The following is a representative sampling to show the variety of databases online today (with suppliers' names):

Arts & Humanities Search (Arts & Humanities Citation Index), 1980–date.
AGRICOLA (U.S. National Agricultural Library), 1970–date.
ERIC (Educational Resources Information Center) 1966–date.
Historical Abstracts, 1973–date.
Magazine Index, 1959–1970, 1973–date.
MEDLARS/MEDLINE (Medical Literature Analysis and Retrieval System), 1965–date.
MLA Bibliography (Modern Language Association), 1964–date.
National Newspaper Index, 1959–1970, 1973–date.
PAIS (Public Affairs Information Service), 1976–date.
PsychINFO (*Psychological Abstracts*), 1967–date.
SOCIAL SCISEARCH and/or SCISEARCH (*Social Science Citation Index* and *Science Citation Index* online), 1972–date.

You can contact a database vendor directly and investigate accessing a system yourself by checking the telephone directory or consulting one of these sources:

Online Database Search Directory. New York: Gale, 1987.
Directory of Online Databases. New York: Elsevier, 1989.

WORKING WITH OTHERS

Use the following suggestions to evaluate local academic and public libraries, as well as to gauge your understanding of library resources discussed in this chapter.

- Find out whether your campus library offers orientation tours or special classes for students engaged in research projects. Sign up with a classmate to go on such a tour or to take part in a library research class. If these options are not available, ask a librarian to provide a short orientation for you and a few classmates.

- Discuss your campus library with another student to review what you know of its reference, book, and periodical collections. If your college has more than one library, discuss the others also, considering their usefulness in doing your research assignment.

- What local public libraries are available to you, and what kinds of resources might they offer? Consider state, county, and city libraries in your area and how they might differ in the services and resources they provide.

- Compare your own campus library's services with those discussed in this chapter. Which campus library services may be particularly helpful in working on your research project? If you have used any special library services in the past, describe them and their usefulness.

- Discuss the advantages and disadvantages of performing a database search for research materials. Investigate the possibility of doing such a search at your own campus library. If the campus library does not provide for such searches, what other nearby academic or public libraries might offer database search services?

C H A P T E R   T H R E E

Planning the Focus of Your Research

Getting started on a research paper begins with selecting a suitable topic to investigate and write about in depth. Your goal in selecting such a topic, as well as throughout your research, is continually to refine and narrow the area of investigation in order to make the research and resulting paper significantly specific.

In general, you should start by considering a broad subject of interest to research and then move to a more particular topic within that subject. Preliminary investigation of sources should next lead you to formulate a research question that states what you want to know about the topic. Figure 3.1 illustrates the continual narrowing process of focusing your research in this way. Once you have defined a research question, use it to focus your later investigation of sources and direct notetaking toward a tentative answer, or preliminary thesis, about the topic.

Keep in mind that the actual progress of your own research efforts may not evolve as directly as suggested here. You will most likely recognize several possible subjects, topics, or research questions at the same time or in a different sequence throughout your research planning. Remember that research is an evolving process. Expect to modify an initial topic and any related research questions as your insight about the subject itself develops.

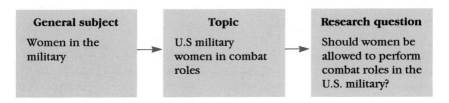

General subject	Topic	Research question
Women in the military	U.S military women in combat roles	Should women be allowed to perform combat roles in the U.S. military?

FIGURE 3.1 Focusing your research

Understanding a Subject and Topic

You will be better able to focus your research efforts if you understand the concepts of a research subject and topic at the beginning of your assignment. A research *subject* is any general area of experience, knowledge, or events that can be studied for more understanding. A *topic* is a more focused area of ideas included within a broader research subject. AIDS and acid rain, for example, are each research subjects. AIDS on the college campus and the effects of acid rain on human health are topics included within the subjects AIDS and acid rain, respectively. A subject is always more general than the topic or topics included within it. Notice how the following subjects for college research papers contain one or several more specific topics:

Subjects	*Topics*
Euthanasia	1. "Mercy killing" and AIDS victims
	2. Euthanasia in Holland
Native Americans	1. Fishing rights of Native Americans
	2. Threats to ancestral burial grounds
	3. Native languages in the classroom
Alcoholism	1. College students and drinking
	2. Pregnancy and alcohol
	3. Television beer commercials
Popular music	1. Sexual violence in popular music
	2. The social power of "rap" music

Understanding the distinction between a subject and a topic can help you to plan your research sooner and more effectively. If you begin the assignment by planning at the subject level, you can compare several potential areas of interest to research before commiting to a particular topic. On the other hand, if you begin with a topic already in mind, a sense of its relationship to a broader subject can help you to gauge your progress in focusing the research.

Finding a Research Subject and Topic

Several steps described in this chapter for discovering a research subject or topic can work equally well for finding both. Which purpose any of the steps fulfills for you will depend upon how far you have progressed in your planning or actual research. Although the steps are presented sequentially here, they may overlap or occur in different order in actual practice. The *Reader's Guide,* for example, is recommended for first dis-covering a subject; however, you will likely return to it again later for nar-rowing a subject to a particular topic or to find specific sources to investi-gate in depth. As you proceed in following the suggestions given here about a subject or topic, keep the overlapping nature of these two ele-ments in mind.

Selecting an Appropriate Research Subject

Unfortunately, many beginning writers have had the frustrating experience of wasting valuable time on subjects or topics that they decided upon too quickly. You can avoid dead-end topics, those that are unsuitable for your interest or resources, with careful planning. The best approach is to con-sider several possible subjects initially and then to move systematically to-ward a more particular topic and relevant research question.

Assigned Subjects

If your paper's subject is assigned by your instructor, he or she has already considered its suitability for research, as well as your probable level of interest and understanding. It will be your responsibility in an as-signed-subject paper to demonstrate a grasp of basic concepts through in-dependent research and thinking. With assigned subjects that are closely related to the course focus, you have the benefit of your class notes, text-book reading, and your instructor's own expertise to draw upon, though you will of course need to do your own research work, as well.

You will find that an assigned subject requires as much original thinking as one you might have chosen for yourself. Try to find an ap-proach that makes your paper different from others on the same subject. That is what Anne Kramer did when her American literature teacher designated Mark Twain's *Adventures of Huckleberry Finn* as the assigned subject for the class. Anne's research paper, The Response of Black Readers to Mark Twain's *Adventures of Huckleberry Finn,* grew out of her independent thinking and individual interest in the subject assigned.

Free-Choice Subjects

If you are like most students facing a research paper assignment, you will need to select what to write about. This means you may not have the benefit of lectures or class discussions to help you get to know and under-stand a subject, as you would if it were assigned. When responsible for finding your own research subject, you will need as much time as possible to select the right one.

For this reason, you should start thinking about an appropriate research paper subject from the day you first learn about the assignment. Use the class in which the paper is assigned or other courses you are taking as resources. As you listen to lectures, study your textbooks, or join in class discussions throughout the term, be alert to potential areas for research. The following suggestions will help you discover a research subject that interests you and is appropriate for your assignment.

Reviewing Your Interests

If there were one simple rule for selecting the right research subject, it would be this: *Work with your interests.* As you begin working with a research subject or topic, think critically about those you may be willing to spend time researching. You will recognize more potential topics in a subject you care about than in one you select because it seems impressive or easy to research. In addition to the information you gather from other sources, remember that your research paper should reflect your own insights and opinions.

You will write best on a subject you care about and already have a feeling for. Avoid any that are not part of your general field of interest or that you may be drawn to for the wrong reasons. Though a subject like uniform commercial code laws may sound impressive, you will not go very far with it unless you are genuinely interested in laws governing various kinds of commercial transactions. Similarly, microwave cooking may sound like an easy subject to write about. Unless you care enough to research and think critically about it, however, such a subject may generate only a tiring exercise for you and a dull paper for your instructor.

Recording Subject Ideas

Begin discovering the right research subject for yourself by using a research notebook (see Chapter 1) to record and later review your general interests. Title a section of the notebook Research Subjects, and use it to explore potential areas of research:

- Take time to think about your hobbies or any clubs and organizations to which you belong. Use your research notebook to discuss events that you want to know more about. What controversies need greater examination?
- Consider the subjects of magazines or particular sections of the newspaper you read regularly. What is happening that you have a strong position on? What issues need clarification or updating for an interested and even generally informed audience? Record these subjects in your research notebook.
- Think about your favorite college course, your prospective career, or even the latest book or movie you enjoyed. What subjects do these

areas of interest cover? What famous persons or events in these areas intrigue you? List these in the Subjects section of your research notebook.

■ Review the entries of possible subjects you have been keeping in your research notebook. Which subjects seem to interest you most? Which would match your interests and the requirements of your assignment best? Which do you want to learn more about?

Subdividing your interests with questions in this way will put you on the track of potential subjects. Just remember to take your time. Start with a variety of possibilities, and gradually narrow the list to the three or four most suited to your interests and the assignment. Find out more about each of these subjects to select the most promising one for extensive study and research.

Using Library Sources to Find a Research Subject

A library's reference section or book collection contains excellent sources for discovering a potential subject or topic for your paper. Use these sources to discover a research focus or to gauge the potential of possible subjects already listed in your research notebook. Before settling upon any single subject for research, be sure to consult as many such sources as possible. Preliminary investigation of standard library materials will provide important general information, as well as specific sources essential to your later research.

Encyclopedias

The articles found in encyclopedias offer excellent, authoritative discussions on nearly every subject known. Written by well-chosen experts who provide reliable facts and informed insights, encyclopedia articles are vital to effective research and writing on any issue. No matter what subject or topic you decide upon, it is wise to begin all your research with a study of relevant encyclopedia articles. You can use what you learn from them to investigate and better understand other sources.

You are probably already familiar with multivolume, comprehensive encyclopedias like *Encyclopedia Americana, Encyclopaedia Britannica,* or *Collier's Encyclopedia.* These references cover hundreds of subjects and include maps, illustrations, and highly useful bibliographies. Entries appear alphabetically by subject, and discussions vary in length from a single paragraph to a dozen or more pages. Most public or campus libraries carry one or more complete editions of such encyclopedias, as well as the yearbook supplements intended to keep them up to date.

An encyclopedia article can help you in selecting a subject and focusing on a topic at the same time. Besides offering the general information you may want, encyclopedias also cross-reference and subdivide entries. Figure 3.2 shows an excerpt from an *Encyclopaedia Britannica* article on international trade. This is an article Ron Bonneville used to begin the research for his paper's discussion of Japanese investments in the United States. The main entry includes two subsections titled "Trade among Developed Countries" and "Trade between Developed and Developing Countries." These were aspects of the subject that Ron needed to learn more about before focusing on a particular topic.

Subject heading

Topic heading

International Trade

Patterns of trade

Subtopic

TRADE AMONG DEVELOPED COUNTRIES

The greatest volume of trade occurs among the developed, capital-rich countries of the world, especially among industrial leaders such as Australia, Belgium, Canada, France, Italy, Japan, The Netherlands, Spain, Sweden, the United Kingdom, the United States, and West Germany. Generally, as a country matures economically its participation in foreign trade grows more rapidly than its gross national product.

The European Economic Community (EEC) affords an impressive instance of the gains to be derived from freer trade. A major part of the increases in real income in EEC countries is almost certainly attributable to the removal of trade barriers. The EEC's formation cannot, however, be interpreted as reflecting an unqualified dedication to the free-trade principle, since EEC countries maintain tariffs against goods from outside the Community.

Trade within the EEC

Minor topic

Subtopic

TRADE BETWEEN DEVELOPED AND DEVELOPING COUNTRIES

Difficult problems frequently arise out of trade between developed and developing countries. Many less-developed countries are tropical, frequently relying heavily for income upon the proceeds from export of one or two crops, such as coffee, cacao, or sugar. Markets for such goods are highly competitive (in the sense in which economists use the term competitive)—that is, prices are extremely sensitive to every change in demand or in supply. Prices of manufactured goods, the typical exports of developed countries, are commonly much more stable. Hence, as the price of its export commodity fluctuates, the tropical country experiences large fluctuations in its "terms of trade," the ratio of export prices to import prices, often with painful effects on the domestic economy. With respect to almost all important primary commodities, efforts have been made at price stabilization and output control. These efforts have met with varied success.

FIGURE 3.2   An entry on international trade from *Encyclopaedia Britannica*

Source: Excerpt from article "International Trade." Reprinted with permission from *Encyclopaedia Britannica*, 15th edition (c) 1990 by Encyclopaedia Britannica, Inc.

Encyclopedia entries also provide cross-references to related subjects, and they generally include a selected bibliography on the subject discussed (see Figure 3.3). Such bibliographies may assist you in further identifying subjects of interest, as well as serve later as valuable sources for research.

Cross-references
to other
sources
and topics

For later developments in the history of Japan, see the *Britannica Book of the Year* section in the BRITANNICA WORLD DATA ANNUAL.
For coverage of related topics in the *Macropædia* and *Micropædia*, see the *Propædia*. sections 934, 96/10, and 975.

BIBLIOGRAPHY

Annotated
bibliography

Physical and human geography: Two good gazetteers of Japan are *Nihon chimei jiten,* compiled by AKIRA WATANABE, 4 vol. (1954–56); and *Nihon chimei daijiten,* compiled by AKIRA WATANABE et al., 7 vol. (1967–68). The *Nippon: A Charted Survey of Japan,* an industrial digest issued annually since 1936, contains physical and economic statistical data with explanations. Representative geographical works in English include *Regional Geography of Japan,* trans. from the Japanese, 6 vol. (1957), the proceedings of a conference of the International Geographical Union; and ROBERT B. HALL, JR., *Japan: Industrial Power of Asia,* 2nd ed. (1976), which contains a brief analysis of postwar industrial development. Geomorphology is covered by AKIRA WATANABE, "Landform Divisions of Japan," *Bull. Geogr. Surv. Inst., Tokyo,* 2:81–94 (1950–51); and by TORAO YOSHIKAWA, SOHEI KAIZUKA, and YOKO OTA, *The Landforms of Japan* (1981); climatology is dealt with by EIICHIRO FUKUI (ed.), *The Climate of Japan* (1977). TAKESHI MATSUI, "General Characteristics of the Soil Geography of Japan," *Pedorojisto/Pedologist,* 12:25–36 (1968), is useful; and *Japanese Cities: A Geographical Approach* (1970), published by the ASSOCIATION OF JAPANESE GEOGRAPHERS, discusses many pertinent subjects. BUREAU OF STATISTICS, *Statistical Handbook of Japan* (annual), contains official information, and *Japan Statistical* tailed current information on various aspects of the economy may be found in publications of the Japanese government, such as the BANK OF JAPAN, *Economic Statistics of Japan* (annual); and the MINISTRY OF AGRICULTURE AND FORESTRY, *Abstract of Statistics on Agriculture, Forestry, and Fisheries* (annual). *Kodansha Encyclopedia of Japan,* 9 vol. (1983), provides a comprehensive compilation of information on Japan's history and its modern physical, social, political, and cultural environment. RYUZIRO ISIDA, *Geography of Japan* (1961, reprinted 1969), is concerned with major aspects of the physical, economic, and cultural environment. GLENN T. TREWARTHA, *Japan: A Geography* (1965), also deals with geographical aspects in detail; as does THE ASSOCIATION OF JAPANESE GEOGRAPHERS, *Geography of Japan* (1980). A detailed field survey of village life from geographical, historical, and social viewpoints is made in RICHARD K. BEARDSLEY, JOHN W. HALL, and ROBERT E. WARD, *Village Japan* (1959, reprinted 1969). Japan's cities are treated in detail in RONALD P. DORE, *City Life in Japan: A Study of a Tokyo Ward* (1958, reprinted 1965). J.D. BISIGNANI, *Japan Handbook* (1983), is a comprehensive travel guide. FREDERICA M. BUNGE (ed.), *Japan: A Country Study,* 4th ed. (1983), is a comprehensive work covering geographical, economic, social, and cultural aspects. See also *Grand Atlas of Japan* (1985), published by Heibonsha; and *The National Atlas of Japan* (1977), published by the GEOGRAPHICAL SURVEY INSTITUTE.

FIGURE 3.3 Encyclopedia cross-references and a subject bibliography for an entry on international trade from *Encyclopaedia Britannica*

Source: Excerpt from article "Japan." Reprinted with permission from *Encyclopaedia Britannica,* 15th edition (c) 1990 by Encyclopaedia Britannica, Inc.

When using encyclopedia articles, keep in mind that they are intentionally broad introductions to a subject. More frequently published sources, such as books and periodicals, usually give more detailed or current information. Use encyclopedias to acquaint yourself with fundamental facts about a subject and to understand it in broad terms. It is also wise to consult more than one encyclopedia to begin your research in order to find the most useful information or the most instructive organization of your research subject.

Current Books

Whether written for popular or academic audiences, books are excellent resources in which to discover a direction for your research. Simply browsing through a book's introduction or sampling a few chapters can tell you a lot about whether its subject will prove appropriate to your research interests and abilities. Your own textbook for a course may be a good source to begin with, or you can find the library section for a particular subject and consult several books at one sitting.

A book whose scope is broad and introductory is best for an overview of a possible research subject. (More highly focused books will prove useful when you decide about a specific topic for your research.) As you examine books to investigate possible subjects, keep in mind that your purpose is not to read the books but to get an overview of your potential focus for research.

Using the Table of Contents.   The subject a book covers is outlined by the headings found in its table of contents. You can study the contents

CONTENTS

FIGURE 3.4   A table of contents from a book

to find the major categories of interest for your subject or to see under what headings it might be discussed. If it helps, skim a particular chapter in order to learn more about the subject. (See Chapter 6 on skimming and close-reading techniques.)

Ron Bonneville used a book's table of contents (see Figure 3.4) when he began researching foreign ownership of American businesses in the United States. Using such a resource informed him of several issues about international investments in America and eventually led to his selection of Japan's role as a possible research topic.

Using the Index.   The index at the end of a book can also be useful for discovering research subjects and their specific subtopics. Figure 3.5 shows some of the entries Ron Bonneville considered when he examined the heading "Japanese investment" in the index of a book about foreign ownership of U.S. businesses.

As you skim the indicated pages for an index entry, take note of additional subjects or topics that you may want to pursue for your research. You may find it useful to compare two or more books' index entries to recognize important concepts or compare discussions of the same subject.

The *Reader's Guide*

Nearly all popular magazine articles are cataloged in one or another of several available indexes. The most well-known of such indexes is the *Reader's Guide to Periodical Literature,* which covers articles and book reviews appearing in nearly 200 popular magazines. (Other magazine indexes are discussed in Chapter 4.)

J

Japan
 American businesses in, 86–93
 automobile industry, 59–63,
   118–121, 199
 economy, 25–33, 57–77, 99,
   115–121
 educational spending, 74–77
 entertainment industry, 60–61,
   116–117
 foreign assistance, 99, 105
 government spending, 52–59
 history, 133–141, 118–119
 investment in America, 61–69,
   117, 121
 labor force, 22–31
 military status, 44–51
 nuclear energy, 187–188
 political outlook, 198,295
 role in world economy, 178–188
 women's roles, 5, 9, 55

FIGURE 3.5   Entries from a book's index

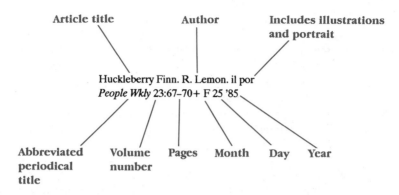

FIGURE 3.6   An entry from the *Reader's Guide to Periodical Literature*
Source: Entry from *Reader's Guide to Periodical Literature*, 1985, p. 954. Copyright (c) 1984, 1985 by The H. W. Wilson Company. Reprinted by permission of the publisher.

You can use the *Reader's Guide* to get an overview of a subject, as well as to get ideas about major topics within a subject. Figure 3.6 shows a *Reader's Guide* entry on Mark Twain that Anne Kramer used for her paper on *Huckleberry Finn*.

As this sample entry illustrates, the *Reader's Guide* has its own system of listing information. As in other periodical indexes, information about the magazine's title, date of publication, number of pages, and other useful data are abbreviated. When using the *Reader's Guide* or any periodical index, refer to the front of the volume for an explanation of the symbols and abbreviations used to describe an article entry.

NOTE: When you are recording source information on your research bibliography cards, remember that the form and data given in the *Reader's Guide* and other indexes are not the same as you will use later in the Works Cited list of your research paper.

The *Social Issues Resources Series (SIRS)*

Your library's reference section will no doubt carry several volumes of the *Social Issues Resources Series,* or *SIRS.* With over 30 different subjects titled and numbered on the spine, these large three-ring binders contain hundreds of short, up-to-date articles on dozens of interesting subjects. A Quick Reference Guide lists the subject volumes and indicates which ones contain articles on various major topics. Figure 3.7, for example, shows the *SIRS* subject volumes and a partial list of article topics included within those volumes, ranging from abortion to handicapped. In addition, a Cross-Reference Guide (see Figure 3.8) offers more specific topic listings and tells you which numbered volume contains articles about each topic.

Quick Reference Guide to SIRS Volumes	Abortion	AIDS (Disease)	Alcohol and alcoholism	Aliens, illegal	Arms race/Nuclear warfare	Baby boom generation	Behavior modification	Birth control/Contraception	Cancer/Carcinogens	Censorship	Child abuse/Child molesting	Cigarette smoking	Civil rights	Computers	Consumers	Cults	Death penalty/Capital punishment	Discrimination	Divorce	Drug abuse	Environmental protection	Euthanasia/Right to die	Future/Forecasting	Gangs	Genetics	Genocide	Greenhouse effect	Handicapped/Disabled
Aging		●			●							●	●				●	●		●	●			●				●
Alcohol		●				●		●		●								●	●					●				
Communication										●			●	●				●		●		●						●
Consumerism	●					●	●	●	●			●			●			●				●	●					
Corrections		●				●			●	●		●	●			●	●		●			●						
Crime		●			●				●		●	●	●			●	●		●		●	●	●	●	●			
Death & Dying	●	●			●			●											●		●				●			●
Defense				●								●						●		●	●	●		●				
Drugs	●	●						●	●	●	●							●			●				●			
Energy		●						●						●						●	●					●		
Ethics	●	●	●	●	●		●	●	●			●	●				●	●		●	●			●	●			●
Ethnic Groups			●							●							●	●		●				●	●	●		
Family	●		●		●		●		●			●					●	●	●									●
Food		●					●	●				●	●							●	●							
Habitat				●	●			●				●	●				●			●		●	●	●		●		
Health	●	●	●			●	●	●		●	●	●	●					●	●	●								
Human Rights		●	●				●	●	●		●	●		●	●			●		●			●			●	●	
Mental Health	●	●		●	●	●	●	●		●		●						●		●	●	●						●
Money			●	●							●	●					●	●	●		●							
Pollution			●				●			●		●						●					●		●		●	
Population	●	●		●	●	●						●					●		●	●			●		●	●	●	
Privacy	●	●		●		●	●		●	●		●	●	●		●	●	●			●			●				●
Religion	●	●		●		●		●		●		●		●		●	●			●	●		●					
School	●	●	●		●	●	●		●		●	●	●			●		●			●	●						●
Sexuality	●	●	●		●	●	●	●	●	●		●	●				●	●	●	●			●					
Sports		●									●	●					●		●		●							
Technology	●			●			●				●	●					●		●		●						●
Third World	●	●	●	●	●			●	●		●	●	●			●			●		●		●	●			
Transportation		●									●	●					●		●	●								
Women	●		●		●		●	●			●	●	●				●	●				●						
Work	●	●	●	●		●		●	●			●	●	●			●	●	●		●	●				●		●
Youth		●		●	●	●	●	●			●	●	●	●	●	●		●	●	●			●	●				●

FIGURE 3.7 A quick reference guide to *SIRS* volumes

Source: "Quick Reference Guide to *SIRS* Volumes," *SIRS Cross-Reference Guide, 1972–1989.* Reprinted by permission of the publisher, Social Issues Resources Series, Inc.

You can use *SIRS* to find a subject or to learn about a potential topic. Looking over the Quick Reference Guide, for example, may start you thinking about the relationship of aging and divorce, or you might begin to wonder about aging and civil rights as possible research interests. A brief search through the subject volume on drugs will turn up such articles as "Addicted Doctors," "The Drug Gangs," "Should Hard Drugs Be Legalized?" and "Cocaine's Children." After reading some of these articles, you can decide if one of the topics interests you enough to research further, or you can turn to a different volume to get ideas about another subject.

Air pollution, ENERGY 3, 4; HABI-
TAT 2, 3; POLLUTION 1, 2, 3,
4; TECHNOLOGY 2; THIRD
WORLD 2; TRANSPORTATION
1, 2
Air pollution, indoor, HEALTH 3;
POLLUTION 3, 4; TECHNOLO-
GY 2; THIRD WORLD 2; WORK
3
Air traffic control, SCHOOL 2;
TECHNOLOGY 2; TRANSPOR-
TATION 1, 2, 3
Aircraft, DEFENSE 1, 2, 3; ENER-
GY 4; MENTAL HEALTH 3
(Fear); POLLUTION 2, 3, 4;
TECHNOLOGY 2; THIRD
WORLD 2; TRANSPORTATION
1, 2, 3
See also Aviation
Airlines, AGING 3; COMMUNICA-
TION 2; CONSUMERISM 2;
CRIME 2; MONEY 2; TRANS-
PORTATION 1, 2, 3; WOMEN 1;
WORK 2
Alaska, ALCOHOL 4; ENERGY 4;
HABITAT 3; SCHOOL 3;
SPORTS 3
Alcohol and alcoholism, AGING 1,
2, 3; ALCOHOL 1, 2, 3, 4; COR-
RECTIONS 1; CRIME 1, 4;
DEATH & DYING 2; DRUGS 1,
2, 3, 4; ENERGY 2, 3, 4; ETH-
ICS 1; ETHNIC GROUPS 3;
FAMILY 1; FOOD 2, 3; HEALTH
1, 2, 3; MENTAL HEALTH 1, 2,
3; SCHOOL 3; SEXUALITY 1;
SPORTS 1, 3; THIRD WORLD
1; TRANSPORTATION 3;
WOMEN 1, 2; WORK 2, 3;
YOUTH 1, 2, 3
See also Fetal alcohol syndrome
Alcoholics Anonymous (AA),
ALCOHOL 1, 2, 3, 4

FIGURE 3.8   An entry from a *SIRS* cross-reference guide

Source: Entries from *SIRS Cross-Reference Guide, 1972–1989.* Reprinted by permission of the publisher, Social Issues Resources Series, Inc.

Moving from a Subject to a Research Topic

Since you cannot read or write meaningfully about everything relevant to the research subject, you will need to narrow your investigation to a more particular topic within it. Because they represent general areas of interest, subjects contain several topics suitable for research (see also Chapter 1). A broad subject like AIDS, for example, includes many potential topics:

Subject: AIDS
   Topic: The problem of AIDS on the college campus
   Topic: AIDS education in the high schools
   Topic: Employment rights for AIDS victims
   Topic: Potential cures for AIDS
   Topic: Support groups for AIDS patients
   Topic: Children with AIDS

Focusing Your Efforts

While considering several possible topics like these during the early research phase may be a good idea (in case one or more prove uninteresting or impractical), you must nevertheless also focus your efforts. A paper attempting to cover all of these topics would be shallow in content, just skimming the surface of each in order to discuss them all. Or it would arbitrarily treat two or three areas and ignore other equally important ones. To avoid a scattered, superficial research paper, you will eventually need to select a single topic to investigate at length.

Recording Potential Topics

Under a heading like Research Topics, keep an ongoing list of ideas in your research notebook. Jot down facts, questions, or potential sources as they occur to you. Mark those topics that appear most promising or that you want to discuss with your instructor. You will find that certain entries eventually dominate the list and your interest. These preliminary topics will provide a core of possibilities as you make your decision about which ones to investigate further. The list of potential research topics that Ron Bonneville kept in his notebook included the entries shown in Figure 3.9. Notice that some topics are more general than others, but all of them identify topics of inquiry for research.

Research Topics

  * 1. *SAT scores and college admissions*

    2. *Illegal aliens in the U.S.*

  * 3. *Rights of the homeless*

  * 4. *The use of force by police*

    5. *Acid rain*

  * 6. *Foreign ownership in the U.S.*

    7. *The Voyager discoveries*

    8. *College athletic programs*

    9. *Social criticism in popular music*

 *10. *Japanese vs. U.S. education*

  11. *Global peace efforts*

  12. *The war against drugs*

FIGURE 3.9 Notebook entries for research topics

Ron did preliminary reading about most of these topics, and he discussed those marked with an asterisk with his instructor and a few friends. Although he had begun with the idea that he wanted to find out about all foreign investment in the United States (#6 above), Ron eventually chose to write only about Japan's role in buying American properties. In this way, he moved from a broad research topic toward a more focused one. Having thought about the other topics in his list gave Ron useful options in case he later decided that foreign ownership was not a good choice for his paper.

Using Discovery Techniques to Focus on a Topic

A practical method of deciding what you want to research about any topic is to explore your own understanding of it. You need not follow all the methods described here; rather, use those that will help you to focus on a topic matching your interests with your resources and your assignment.

Freewriting

Freewriting allows you to discuss a subject or topic as freely as necessary to start ideas flowing to a conscious level. You begin by simply writing (with a pen or pencil or at a computer) all your thoughts on a subject as they occur to you. Do not worry about organization, punctuation, or spelling. The important goal in freewriting is to get your ideas down. Write for about 10 minutes at a time, longer if you suddenly find yourself deeply involved in a discussion on a particular topic.

Figure 3.10 shows the freewriting Ron Bonneville did in his research notebook for his paper on Japanese ownership in the United States. Notice that this exercise allowed him to identify more clearly the topic he eventually chose for his research and to discover several ideas he would later develop in the paper.

If you have trouble getting started with freewriting, try focusing with introductory phrases that will launch you directly into a discussion of your research subject. Start freewriting with introductory phrases like the following:

One unsettled question about (subject) is . . .

 (Subject) is important today because . . .

 (Subject) should (or should not) be . . .

I am interested in (subject) because . . .

Freewriting

October 14

I am freewriting about the problem—or what I think may be a problem—of foreign investors buying up all of the United States or just about. Mainly the Japanese. They buy more than anyone else, although I found out that Britain owns more U.S. land than anyone else does. Next is the Netherlands. Can you believe that? So what harm does it do? None, I guess, but what if another country buys up all the aircraft companies or all the computer chip manufacturing—then where will we get what we need in a war or even just a bad economic period? Actually the Japanese are pretty good business people. Look at all the cars they sell to Americans. Or computers—TV sets, cameras, VCRs, even sushi! Why are we selling places like Rockefeller Center and CBS? Is the Statue of Liberty next? How come we aren't buying up all of Asia? Or maybe we are. So how does it feel, America? I think we better get our act together, but then too maybe this is all good for world peace. Maybe it's a sign that America is no longer the independent giant it used to be. It seems like Japan's buying must be good for the American economy. Look at all the Japanese auto plants there are in this country now.

FIGURE 3.10 Freewriting to examine issues

After you finish freewriting, look over the results. Pick out recurring ideas or phrases that indicate a potential topic to discuss at greater length. Use such ideas or phrases as the focus of a second freewriting session. You will gradually recognize that you have a lot to say about one or two particular aspects of your subject. These particular aspects are most likely the research topics you have been seeking.

Clustering

Clustering is another useful way to discover a research topic. Begin with drawing a circle around the research subject and then connecting the circled subject with lines to any ideas that you associate with it. Circle the second idea and connect it to other associated concepts, grouping them

FIGURE 3.11   Clustering to examine issues

as you proceed. When you have run out of ideas for one line of thinking, start at the subject circle and begin again with a new connection. Ron Bonneville's clustering about Japanese and other foreign investment in the United States is illustrated in Figure 3.11.

As with freewriting, do not worry about which ideas or associations come to mind as you cluster. Get your ideas down in any order or grouping as they occur. Review and organize your thinking after recording your thoughts.

Relating a Subject to Your Interests

Your own interests should play a major role in your selection of a research topic. Once you have decided upon a research subject, relate it to your personal interests by listing them opposite each other. You can tell what they add up to by following this formula, in which X equals your paper's topic focus:

My interest + Subject = X

Anne Kramer's use of this technique in her research notebook produced several possible research topics for her paper on *Huckleberry Finn:*

1. Language + *HF* = a discussion of the way Twain uses dialects in the novel
2. Art + *HF* = an examination of the book's illustrations and what they contribute
3. Black Americans + *HF* = a look at the way Twain presents black characters or how his audience reacts to them
4. Rafting + *HF* = a study of Twain's realism about the river and Huck's raft trip

Narrowing the Focus of the Research Topic

Make any topic you select as specific as possible. Remember that nearly every topic may become increasingly focused as you learn more about it through research. Figure 3.12 demonstrates how continual narrowing of the subject environmental hazards, for example, can lead to the general topic acid rain, which in turn can be continually narrowed toward an even more specific aspect of the original subject.

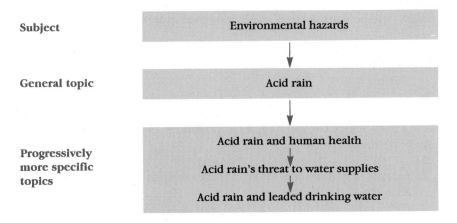

FIGURE 3.12   Narrowing a topic

A different emphasis or interest on your part, of course, will determine the direction of your narrowing and the choice of topics with which you choose to work. In the above example, the topic of acid rain's threat to water supplies could also lead to an entirely different subtopic, such as acid rain and asbestos contamination of drinking water. Regardless of whether you decide to pursue the topic of lead poisoning instead of asbestos contamination from acid rain would ultimately depend upon your interests or the availability of resources for one or the other topic.

Working with a Back-Up Topic in Mind

As you explore particular areas for your research paper, consider more than one potential topic in case your first choice later proves impractical. The unavailability of resources or a lack of time to investigate your first topic thoroughly may make another choice more feasible, or you may later learn enough about an alternate topic to make it a more appealing option. If that happens, you will find that any broad, preliminary thinking about the general subject for the first topic can provide useful background for selecting a related second topic.

For example, you might begin with a general subject like alternative automobile fuels and then progress to a narrower topic such as electric power as an alternative to gasoline. Preliminary investigation, however, may not uncover enough sources discussing recent developments in electrically powered automobiles. In this case, you could move to a back-up topic such as gasahol as an alternative to gasoline and still make use of your earlier research. Keeping a back-up topic in mind as you research will require some mental juggling and a little extra time; however, the precaution will be worthwhile should an original topic prove unuseful.

A Checklist for Topic Selection

The topic you finally select to research and write about will need to meet a number of criteria. As you narrow your general subject to one or two possible topics, check each of your most promising choices to see if it allows you to do the following:

1. Be sure the topic meets the requirements of your research assignment.
2. Focus on a topic that you want to learn more about.
3. Pick a topic for which you can meet an audience's needs and expectations.

4. Check to see that sufficient resources are available. Depending upon the materials involved, using interlibrary loan or trusting the mail may take more time than you have.

5. Avoid philosophical topics or those based on personal belief. Topics like the value of the family or why you play sports rely upon personal opinion and values rather than objective research and discussion.

6. Avoid strictly biographical topics—Abraham Lincoln as a father—that are already discussed fully in book-length studies.

7. Avoid describing processes such as how cocaine is sold on the street or why getting a suntan may be dangerous. Such information will not allow for original insight and judgment on your part.

8. Avoid topics too narrow or too recent for discussion. A paper on local airport conditions or last week's international event will not allow for adequate use of research materials.

9. Avoid standard, popular topics commonly chosen for student research papers. Unless recent developments have added new information or conditions, it may be difficult to impress your instructor with yet another paper on the death penalty or animal intelligence. Besides, all the resources on these topics will be checked out by others when you need them. Pick a topic that shows your individual abilities and interests.

10. Cease consideration of any topic that you cannot get very far with in terms of an approach or finding resources. If you seem to be meeting a dead end with a topic, ask your instructor or a librarian for help, but recognize that some topics may just not be right for you and your circumstances.

As you approach selecting a research topic, consider yourself part of the paper's audience, someone who will also benefit from its discussion. Through researching and writing, you will discover what you know or do not know about your topic. Writing will allow you to test your ideas, to analyze and to evaluate your research data to a far greater extent than before. The paper topic you select should be one you want to help others, as well as yourself, understand better.

Formulating a Research Question

Even a well-defined research topic presents too broad an area to research and write about by itself. A topic like acid rain and lead poisoning, for example, needs a more specific focus for the research to promise more than an accumulation of facts. To make your research more effective, formulate a research question about the topic. Questions like the following focus on the topics and the research required for them:

Topic

Television and race

Research questions

1. Does televison present stereotypes of racial minorities?
2. Do minority actors have equal opportunities on
   televison?
3. What does television teach us about race relations?

Topic

Fan violence and sports

Research questions

1. What should be done to curb fan violence?
2. Does the alcohol sold at games contribute to fan
   violence?

Topic

Women in magazine advertisements

Research questions

1. What image of women is conveyed by advertisements in leading national magazines?
2. Do magazine advertisements over the last 10
   years reflect any changes in the way women are
   presented?
3. How do women's groups respond to current advertisements for women and women's products?

Remember to regard any research question as a working hypothesis that your research may confirm or alter significantly. Just asking whether minority actors have equal opportunities in television, for example, implies that they may not. It will be your responsibilty to research the question objectively and to demonstrate the validity of your answer in the paper you write.

Recording Research Questions

Which questions you decide to pursue in your research will depend upon several factors, incuding your own interests, the requirements of your assignment, available resources, and the needs of an audience. As you begin the preliminary research for a topic, keep a section in your research notebook for recording ideas and potential questions about a topic. A section titled Topic Notes and Questions in Ron Bonneville's research notebook (see Figure 3.13) contained five entries for various topics he was interested in pursuing.

Ron went on to develop the last topic and research question shown here, changing both slightly as his research and further thinking led him to do so. Ron's notebook entry enabled him to identify his own central concerns and led to a research question that could answer them. The other

Topic Notes and Questions

1. Japanese vs. American education. Which is really better? There is a lot of talk about how inferior American schools are, but I don't really know why that would be.

2. Proposition 48: Is the NCAA's new rule fair to black athletes? The rule requires both a C average in high school <u>and</u> a 700 SAT score to be eligible for a college athletic scholarship. Most black athletes will lose out by such a rule, at least at first. Some say the new rule will improve student efforts to get a C average and a good SAT score.

3. Organic farming may be a good topic. People talk about how healthy organically grown foods are, but are they really better than the usual kind we buy? Why are they more expensive? Is interest in organic foods just another health fad?

4. College admissions and SAT scores. Are SAT scores and other criteria really accurate at predicting student success? Are they fair to everyone applying for admission to college?

5. Foreign ownership of American land and businesses: Japanese investors just bought Rockefeller Center in New York City. Is that good or bad? Foreign investors seem to be able to pay a lot of money for what they buy, but are we selling off our country this way? Or do we need their investment dollars to keep us going? What does foreign investment really mean for America?

FIGURE 3.13   Entries from Ron Bonneville's research notebook

notebook entries gave him useful alternative topic choices and a means of judging what seemed the most interesting and challenging issues to research.

Considering Your Audience

Part of selecting a topic and research question to investigate also involves considering your paper's audience. Naturally, the instructor who assigned the paper is your most immediate audience, though he or she is not the only one you want to think of as you consider a focus for your research.

While your instructor may be your paper's primary reader, his or her reading will have the same criteria that you would want to meet for other readers. When planning the research for your paper, you should assume that the audience is generally knowledgeable about a subject but needs additional information to understand and be convinced of your paper's main point, or thesis. This is the audience you should write for and whom you want to consider when thinking of your research paper.

When considering any topic and research question, assess your readers' needs. Ask yourself what they need to know or what you can discuss to enlighten them further about the topic. What questions do people need to have answered about organically grown foods, for example? What does an audience of chemists want to know? What questions do you need to ask and which audience's needs can your research fulfill?

Because the audience you assume is generally informed already, you will need to avoid topics and research questions that are so familiar they offer nothing new. The question of whether cigarette smoking endangers people's health is not likely to interest an already informed audience. Likewise, such an audience is unlikely to find much interest in a paper simply arguing against drug addiction: Why listen to an argument most informed people have already accepted? A good topic and research question stimulate your readers' thinking, drawing upon an assumed interest in the subject to present new perspectives.

Defining the Paper's Purpose

As you determine the focus of your research, you will also need to define your paper's *purpose,* which includes answering the research question and planning your strategy for presenting information. The kind of paper you write and the investigation you do for it will reflect the research question and the paper's purpose.

The Argumentative Paper

Research papers that aim primarily at interpreting information are *argumentative* papers. When you write an argumentative paper, the intention is to lead readers to understand and agree with your analysis of the research topic and your conclusion about the research question.

Argumentative papers are meant to persuade an audience that the writer's perceptions are correct. Such a paper states the author's argument (or thesis) and then presents the evidence to support it. Argumentative research papers also appear in the form of scholarly articles, scientific essays, legal briefs, business reports, historical studies, and government analyses. In short, writers use an argumentative approach whenever they feel their audience needs or expects comprehensive discussion and reasoned conclusions about a topic.

Because it seeks to persuade readers of her research conclusions, Anne Kramer's paper on *Adventures of Huckleberry Finn* has an argumentative purpose. After selecting the response of black readers as her topic, Anne formulated a research question that addressed her further interest in the novel: How have black readers responded to the novel's use of language and characterization? The resulting thesis statement in Anne's paper explains her answer: Language and characterization in *Adventures of Huckleberry Finn* offend black readers to the point of diminishing the novel's value as literature. After stating the thesis in her introduction, Anne went on to develop a discussion of the thesis argument and to support it with her own research and analysis of the novel (see Chapter 9).

Similarly, Ron Bonneville's paper on foreign ownership in the United States argues that Americans should view the expansive Japanese presence as a positive stage in this country's global development (see Appendix A). Ron's argument is an answer to his research question: What does the extensive amount of Japanese ownership in the United States mean for our country?

Both Anne and Ron recognized early in their investigations that their topics provided enough questions or controversy to call for further discussion and reasoned conclusions from them. While investigating your research topic, keep similarly alert to obvious—as well as implicit—questions that readers want answered.

An effective argumentative research paper should demonstrate your ability to gather information and assess it accurately. In discussing any topic, especially a controversial one, present all sides of an issue, not just those that favor your argument. You should acknowledge any facts and opinions that seem to oppose your position, offering counter-arguments or qualifying discussions as you do so. In this way, you are being fair to your audience and to your own understanding of the topic.

The Informative Paper

Informative research is primarily intended to present information for the reader's benefit. In one sense, of course, all research papers inform their audiences: They offer information to illustrate the writer's ideas and to show how the various parts of the topic relate. Informative research studies, however, minimize expression of the author's viewpoint. Topics for informative research papers are those about which readers need information more than anything else. The research questions for informative papers usually emphasize description, measurable results, or processes, as in these examples:

1. What effect has deforestation in the Amazon had upon already threatened species of wildlife?
2. What changes has the recent Persian Gulf War made to the numbers and types of volunteers enlisting in the U.S. military?
3. Do students from private schools get better SAT scores than those from public schools?
4. How are other countries coping with the growing problem of waste disposal?

You inform readers when you explain, summarize, report, chart, list, or otherwise make information itself the primary focus of your presentation. Your major role in writing an informative paper is to gather data and organize it in a more clear manner than your readers would otherwise have it. The information you gather to describe may range from entirely new data, such as a report analyzing the impact of an oil spill on local fishing grounds, to a review of the current literature in a field, as was done for the sample paper on AIDS (see Appendix A). If you foresee the need to write an informative paper, remember that it is not merely a summary of sources or a string of quotations from various authorities. Your ability to formulate and answer a significant research question is vital to an effective paper.

Knowing whether you want to write an argumentative or informative research paper will help you decide what to write about and how to shape your ideas for research. As you plan the focus of your research, keep in mind these two major kinds of purposes. You may need to check with your instructor about which kind of paper is required or may be most appropriate for your research assignment.

Working with a Preliminary Thesis

At some point in the initial stages of your investigation, you will undoubtedly begin to perceive a potential answer to the research question you have formulated about the topic. For some writers, such an answer is formed early in the research process. For others, it develops slowly or changes as the focus of the research question itself shifts in response to more information about the topic. Some writers resist forming even a potential answer to the research question until their investigation of sources has been completed.

Guided by a research question, however, most writers find it also helpful to have in mind a *preliminary thesis* as they work. The preliminary thesis is a statement in one or two sentences that summarizes your tentative response to the research question at a particular point in your investigation. Along with the research question, such a thesis statement will direct your research activities toward relevant material, helping you decide what to give close attention to in examining sources.

For example, suppose your research topic is the effectiveness of antiyouth gang programs in large cities. An appropriate research question would be: What is required for a successful antigang program? Drawing upon what you know of the topic from your beginning investigation, you might formulate a potential preliminary thesis such as this: The most effective antigang programs include community-based education and employment assistance. Key concepts such as community-based education and employment assistance can focus your reading. Defining what your paper will mean by *effective* (and its opposite, *ineffective*) can strengthen its content and add breadth to your discussion.

Remember that a preliminary thesis is not intended to be your final opinion on the topic. As you investigate the topic more thoroughly, you will most likely modify the thesis or change it entirely in response to your increased knowledge. You might begin with something like this: The average American's diet is certain suicide. Later, you may decide that this statement more suitably expresses your ideas: Americans can choose to eat better and live longer. If a preliminary thesis seems helpful at the planning stage, use it with the research question as a way of furthering the focus of your research.

WORKING WITH OTHERS

Discussing your research ideas with others will promote and clarify your own thinking. A five-minute conversation can sometimes eliminate an inappropriate subject from further consideration or make you suddenly enthusiastic over a topic you might not have thought of alone. Use the following suggestions to help you work with others in planning the focus of your research. You will find sharing your ideas and progress acts as a stimulus to your perseverance and thinking for the research paper.

- Meet with a classmate or friend to review the potential subjects listed in your research notebook. What makes each subject particularly appealing to you? Does your friend or classmate have a preference for one subject over another? Why? Discuss each subject and the kinds of resources that might be available for it. What other subjects can you suggest to each other?

- Work with another person to narrow a potential subject toward a particular topic. Try brainstorming together to come up with as many related topics for the subject as you can. What are the major concerns regarding this subject? What questions need to be answered about these concerns? What important research steps might some of these topics require?

- If you used freewriting or clustering to arrive at a topic, share the results. What pattern of ideas or interest is apparent? Does your approach seem to favor an argumentative or informative approach to the discussion? Take turns completing introductory phrases about potential topics, such as "Water conservation is important today because . . ."

- Once you have some specific topics in mind, use the topic checklist presented earlier to discuss their merits. Discuss whether each topic seems suitable for the assignment and available resources. Does any particular topic seem too philosophical or too narrow? Will it result in little more than a restatement of well-known and accepted ideas?

- After selecting a suitable topic, your next step will be to investigate specific sources and to take notes. Discuss your general plans with your collaborator, and make arrangements to review your progress together again. If you are working with a classmate, use your research schedules to plan times to meet and begin thoroughly researching sources together.

CHAPTER FOUR

Researching
Library Sources

Having determined an appropriate topic and research question, you will next need to think about locating the information on which to base your research. A large, general library, such as that found at most colleges or universities, will provide the greatest number and variety of resources for you to begin your research.

Organize your search for information by first establishing a *working bibliography*, a list of sources on the research topic. The working bibliography will serve as an ongoing, developing pool of sources to consult throughout your research. You will want to use the full range of standard library resources and reference materials to ensure that the working bibliography, and therefore your research on the topic, is as comprehensive as possible.

Preparing the
Working Bibliography

The working bibliography is a *preliminary* list of sources for your paper, one that will change as you add or delete sources uncovered throughout the research process. The list is a *bibliography* because it names and provides information about sources on a particular topic. It is a *working* bibliography because it is tentative: You use the working bibliography to record information about available sources, to determine whether there are enough and the right kind of sources for your research needs, and to locate and work with such sources as you research and write the paper. Sources included in the working bibliography—books, magazines, newspapers, journal articles, interviews, and others—lay the groundwork for the notetaking and organization of data that will come later in your research. Information for all or most of the sources in the Works Cited section of the final paper will also come from your working bibliography.

Listing Sources on Bibliography Cards

You will find it most practical to record each source for the working bibliography on a separate *bibliography card,* usually a 3" x 5" (or larger) index card, a packet of which is easily carried along anywhere you do research. Such cards offer several advantages to the researcher.

1. Cards allow for quick organization and sorting of sources.
2. You can discard or add cards as some sources prove useless or you find new ones.
3. Cards from the working bibliography will prove handy when you cite authors and titles in the paper.
4. Easily shuffled and arranged alphabetically, the cards will later provide bibliographic information for the Works Cited list.

While it is possible to keep the working bibliography in the form of a list in your research notebook or to store it on a file on computer, you will find recording each source on a separate bibliography card more practical than other means. Lists on notebook pages, for example, cannot be shuffled or easily added to as you find more resources for the working bibliography. Computerized lists are helpful, but you may find it inconvenient to copy information from your notes to a computer file to keep the bibliography up to date at the end of each day's research. Besides, you cannot take your computer to the library and everywhere else the research may lead you.

Keep a stock of blank bibliography cards with you as you hunt the library, bookstore, or other places you do research. Make a habit of jotting down titles or authors' names on separate cards every time you come across a possible resource for the paper. You will soon find a growing stack of possibilities to seek out and research.

Bibliography Card Information.   When filling out a working bibliography card for each of your sources, include the information you would need to find the source again or to include it in your paper's Works Cited section. Though you will no doubt list many sources on cards, most library sources listed will be books or periodicals.

Book Sources.   In general, record the following information for any book you list in the working bibliography (see also Figure 4.1):

813.4

Bloom, Harold, ed.
Modern Critical Interpretations of Mark Twain's
Adventures of Huckleberry Finn.
New York: Chelsea House, 1986.

— *Has an essay about Huck's speech.*

FIGURE 4.1 A bibliography card for a book (MLA style)

1. Library catalog call number
2. Author(s), editor(s), or translator
3. Title, underlined, including the subtitle
4. Place of publication
5. Publisher
6. Publication date (or latest copyright date)
7. Brief note about the book's content or usefulness

Follow the form and punctuation you will use in your paper if the form shown here is different. (Other bibliographic styles and forms are discussed in Chapters 10 and 11.)

Periodical Sources. Publications that are published at regular intervals are called *periodicals.* The information recorded on a bibliography card about an article from a periodical—such as a magazine, journal, or newspaper—will differ slightly from that for a book. It should include:

1. Author(s)
2. Title, in quotation marks, including the subtitle
3. Periodical name, underlined
4. Volume number (for professional journals but not popular magazines)[*]
5. Date of publication
6. Page number(s) the article is found on
7. Brief note about the article's content or usefulness

[*]See also Chapter 10 regarding issue and series numbers.

> *Chambers, Bradford*
> *"Scholars and Huck Finn: A New Look"*
> *Interracial Books for Children Bulletin*
>   *15.4 (1984): 12–13*
>
> *— Questions whether Twain's use of ironic dialog to attack racisim can be understood by student readers.*

FIGURE 4.2 A bibliography card for a periodical article (MLA style)

If no author is given for a periodical article, begin the entry with the article title. Do not use "Anonymous" or "Anon." in place of an author's name. If you have located the periodical through the *Reader's Guide* or another index, avoid using that source's forms and abbreviations. Either translate these into the bibliographic style of your paper as you write the data on your card, or make a new card when you later locate the periodical. Figure 4.2 shows a typical bibliography card (in MLA style) for a periodical article, but follow the format of your paper's bibliographical form if it is different.

Gauging the Topic's Feasibility

At the start of your research, the working bibliography serves as an important check against beginning to work at length on an unfruitful topic. If your preliminary search for sources turns up too many—a dozen books and 20 magazine articles on your very topic, let's say—you need to narrow the topic more or take a different approach to it (see Chapter 3). If you can find only one encyclopedia entry and a few magazine articles that discuss your research question, you may need to broaden your focus or select an alternate topic to research (see Chapter 3). In addition, check the working bibliography against the requirements of your assignment. If your instructor wants you to use particular kinds of primary sources—original material like diaries or unpublished papers—for example, and none are available, you will need to select another topic.

Expect the working bibliography to change as you delete some works and add others throughout your research. Keep in mind, however, that the working bibliography's completeness is also essential to the success of your research. The more inclusive the working bibliography, the more thoroughly you will be able to study major ideas involved with the research topic. For these reasons, you will also need to understand how libraries organize and store information, as well as how to use the resources available in them.

Using Bibliographies
to Locate Sources

A list of related books or other written works is called a *bibliography* (hence, the name for the working bibliography). While all bibliographies provide information about a source's title, author, and publication data, they also vary in their emphasis and approach. A bibliography may be *selective* and include only a few works; it may *descriptive* and provide brief annotations or reviews; it may be *evaluative* and discuss the value of the sources it lists; or it could combine any of these approaches.

The most familiar kinds of bibliographies are those commonly found at the ends of scholarly books or their chapters, at the conclusions of encyclopedia or journal articles, or at the backs of a few popular periodicals like *Smithsonian* or *Scientific American*. These bibliographies are sometimes titled References, Works Cited, or Works Consulted, and they usually list works the article authors used to prepare their own discussions of a subject. The Works Cited list that you will include at the end of your research paper is such a bibliography.

Some complete reference works, however, are bibliographies only. That is, the entire purpose of a book published *as a bibliography* is to provide a list of sources on a topic. For example, you might go to a work titled *A Bibliography of Jazz*, by Alan P. Merriam, if you wanted a list of published works about jazz. The term *bibliography* is also sometimes referred to as a union catalog or list, a checklist, sourcebook, or index. Thus, G. Thomas Tanselle's *A Checklist of Editions of Moby Dick, 1851–1976* might be a useful bibliography to consult if you were studying that novel's publishing history. Regardless of what they are termed, you will need such whole-work bibliographies, as well as shorter ones listed within other works, to locate sources for your own working bibliography and to establish a larger base of materials to investigate for your research.

Becoming Familiar with
General Bibliographies

Probably most helpful to researchers are the *general bibliographies,* reference books that tell you about the bibliographies contained in other books. Begin your research by consulting one or more of the general bib-

FIGURE 4.3 Moving from a general bibliography to an individual work

liographies described in this chapter. You can then go to the particular kind of bibliographic source, such as one of the following, to which they may refer you:

1. A bibliography of works used by an author to prepare his or her own discussion (those works listed at the end of an encyclopedia article, for example)
2. Bibliographies by or about one author (e.g., *Bibliography of the Works of Rudyard Kipling* or *Emily Dickinson: A Descriptive Bibliography*)
3. Bibliographies about one subject or subject field (e.g., *Checklist of Arizona Minerals* or *Bibliography of Mexican American History*)
4. Bibliographies describing materials relating to one country or region (e.g., *Bibliography of Africana*)

From these specific bibliographies, you will proceed to locate individual works by author and title (see Figure 4.3).

Bibliographic Index. One of the most useful general resources is the *Bibliographic Index: A Cumulative Bibliography of Bibliographies*. You can look up an author or subject in this comprehensive work to find other bibliographies that appear in books and periodicals. When Anne Kramer wanted to locate bibliographies about Mark Twain and his works, she found the entries shown in Figure 4.4 in the *Bibliographic Index*.

> **Twain, Mark, 1835–1910**
> **About**
> Sewell, David R. Mark Twain's languages; discourse, dialogue, and linguistic variety. University of Calif. Press 1987 p179–84
> **By**
> Bridgman, Richard. Traveling in Mark Twain. University of Calif. Press 1987 p ix–xi
> **By and about**
> Twain, Mark. The wit and wisdom of Mark Twain; edited by Alex Ayres. Harper & Row 1987 p263–5

FIGURE 4.4 An entry on Mark Twain from the *Bibliographic Index*
Source: Entry from *Bibliographic Index*, 1988, p. 718. Copyright (c) 1988, 1989 by The H. W. Wilson Company. Reprinted by permission of the publisher.

Sewell, David R.

Mark Twain's Languages: Discourse, Dialogue,
and Linguistic Variety.

U. of Calif. Press, 1987

179–84

FIGURE 4.5 A bibliography card for a book cited in the *Bibliographic Index*

As Figure 4.4 shows, an author entry in the *Bibliographic Index* may include bibliographies listed in works *by* an author, *about* an author, as well as *both by and about* an author. In addition to writing down all the usual information about a *Bibliographic Index* source, notice that you will also want to record where the bibliographies appear in the works cited. This information is given as the page numbers listed at the end of each entry. Anne Kramer listed the work by David R. Sewell, as well as the pages on which the bibliography of works about Mark Twain appear, on her bibliography card, as shown in Figure 4.5.

Other General Bibliographies. While the *Bibliographic Index* is probably the most available and practical general bibliography, others will also be useful to you. Theodore Besterman's *A World Bibliography of Bibliographies* (later updated by Alice Toomey) is international in scope and helpful for topics focusing on other countries or worldwide issues. It lists separately published bibliographies by subject, including those in books and periodicals.

The following list of general bibliographies includes those already discussed, as well as others that can provide valuable assistance to your research:

Besterman, Theodore. *A World Bibliography of Bibliographies.* Lausanne: Societas Bibliographica, 1963. [See also the entry for Toomey, below]
The Bibliographic Index: A Cumulative Bibliography of Bibliographies. New York: Wilson, 1938 to date.
Hilliard, James. *Where to Find What: A Handbook to Reference Service.* Rev. ed. Metuchen, NJ: Scarecrow, 1984.

McCormick, Mona. *The New York Times Guide to Reference Materi-als*. Rev. ed. New York: Times, 1986.

Sheehy, Eugene P., ed. *Guide to Reference Books*. 10th ed. Chicago: ALA, 1986.

Toomey, Alice F. *A World Bibliography of Bibliographies: 1964–1974*. 2 vols. Totowa, NJ: Rowan, 1977. [A supplement to Besterman's work of the same title, above]

Searching Trade Bibliographies for Sources

People in the book trade, mainly librarians and booksellers, use trade bibliographies to buy, sell, and catalog books. You can use trade bibli-ographies to find out what books exist on your research topic; to get au-thor, title, and publication data; and to find out if a book is still in print.

Subject Guide to Books in Print.   You will find the *Subject Guide to Books in Print* helpful in identifying current sources to include in your preliminary bibliography. Printed yearly, the *Subject Guide* can tell you which books on your research topic are in print. After writing down the information about any works listed, you can seek them out at your local library or see about borrowing them through interlibrary loan. Figure 4.6 shows how the *Subject Guide to Books in Print* lists books on the subject of college admissions.

Other Guides.   The *Subject Guide to Books in Print* is a version of another trade bibliography, *Books in Print,* which lists works in separate volumes by author, title, and subject. There is also *Paperbound Books in Print,* a good source to go to if you cannot find the hardbound edition of a book in your library and are willing to try the local bookstore instead.

For a listing and publication information about any book published in the English language, consult the *Cumulative Book Index* (*CBI*) for the year in question. If the *CBI* is not available at your library, *Publisher's Trade List Annual* lists current and past books still in print from over 1,500 publishers.

The following trade bibliographies, including those already men-tioned, are available at most libraries or bookstores:

American Book Publishing Record. New York: Bowker, 1960–date.
Books in Print. New York: Bowker, 1948–date.
Cumulative Book Index. New York: Wilson, 1898–date.
Paperbound Books in Print. New York: Bowker, 1955–date.
Publisher's Trade List Annual. New York: Bowker, 1873–date.
Subject Guide to Books in Print. New York: Bowker, 1957–date.

UNIVERSITIES AND COLLEGES–ADMISSION
Adolphus, Stephen H., ed. Equality Postponed:
Continuing Barriers to Higher Education in the
1980s. 156p. (Orig.). 1984. pap. 12.95 (ISBN 0-
87447-188-5). College Bd.
American Association of Collegiate Registrars &
Admissions Officers Staff. Certification of Students
under Veterans Law: Information for
Certifying Officials & Other Advisers of Veterans,
Their Dependents or Survivors & Service Persons.
pap. 25.50 (ISBN 0-317-20523-4, 2022849). Bks
Demand UMI.
—Retention of Records: A Guide for Retention &
Disposal of Student Records. pap. 20.00 (ISBN 0-
317-26604-7, 2024073). Bks Demand UMI.
—Survey of the Management & Utilization of Elec-
tronics Data Processing Systems in Admission,
Records, & Registration, 1969–70. pap. 34.80
(ISBN 0-317-26616-0, 2024076). Bks Demand UMI.
Applying to Colleges & Universities in the United
States 1988: A Handbook for International
Students. 3rd ed. 368p. (Orig.). 1988. pap. 12.95
(ISBN 0-87866-572-2). Petersons Guides.
*Armstrong, Robert & Armstrong Anna. Admission
Hints for Tough Colleges. (Illus.) 96p. (Orig.).
(YA) (gr. 11–12). 1985. pap. 7.95 Creative
Plantation.
Aslanian, Carol B. & Brickell, Henry M. Americans
in Transition: Life Changes as Reasons for Adult
Learning. 172p. 1980. 6.50 (ISBN 0-87447-127-3,
001273). College Bd.
Association of Muslim Scientists & Engineers. The
Educational Guide: A Handbook for Foreign
Muslim Applicants to U.S. & Canadian
Universities. rev. ed. 114p. pap. 7.00 (ISBN 0-
916581-00-4). Assn. Muslim Sci.
Bauld, Harry. On Writing the College Application
Essay: The Key to Acceptance at the College of
Your Choice. LC 86-46043. 128p. 1987. 14.45
(ISBN 0-06-055076-7, B&N Bks); pap. 6.95 (ISBN
0-06-463722-0, BH 722, B&N Bks). Har-Row.
Blaker, Charles W. The College Matchmaker. LC 80-
67604. (Illus.). 56p. (Orig.). (YA) (gr. 11–12).
1980. pap. text ed. 3.50 (ISBN 0-9604614-0-X).
Rekalb Pr.

FIGURE 4.6 An entry on college admissions from the *Subject Guide to Books in Print*

Source: Reprinted with permission of R. A. Bowker, a division of Reed Publishing (USA) Inc. from *Subject Guide to Books in Print 1990–91* (c) 1990, by Reed Publishing (USA) Inc. (p. 7463).

Using Indexes to Locate Sources

Bibliographies can tell you what books are published, but they do not list the individual items that may be included within a work. Indexes, how-ever, can help you find single works—articles, stories, poems, essays, and other written pieces—located *within* books and periodicals. There are general indexes to periodicals and books, as well as specialized indexes to particular kinds of works or subjects.

Periodical Indexes

Publications printed at regular intervals (or periods) are called *periodicals*. These include magazines, journals, and newspapers of every type and description. Because they are published more frequently than encyclopedias or books, periodicals are valuable sources of current information and opinion. Articles appearing in both popular and scholarly periodicals are indexed in a variety of sources. Use these indexes to identify possible areas to explore for research.

Popular Magazines.   In addition to journals and newspapers, periodicals also include popular magazines written for general audiences and usually available at newsstands or the local supermarket. *Newsweek, Ms., Psychology Today, Field and Stream, Penthouse, National Geographic,* and *Rolling Stone* are examples. Popular magazines like these can be useful for exploring a potential research focus and acquiring helpful background information. Because they are aimed at general audiences and vary greatly in their authority, however, articles in magazines may not be suitable for every kind of research. They are best used when you need current, nontechnical information and opinion about a subject. When in doubt about using magazines, consult with your instructor.

Magazine Indexes.   You are probably already familiar with the *Reader's Guide to Periodical Literature,* an index to more than 200 of the most popular magazines in the United States. (The *Reader's Guide* and its use are also discussed in Chapter 3.) The format for information in the *Reader's Guide* is representative of that used in most other periodical indexes. Articles are listed alphabetically by author and subject; each entry includes the author's name, article title, abbreviated name of the periodical, the date and volume number of the periodical, and the page numbers of the article. Figure 4.7 shows a typical entry from the *Reader's Guide*.

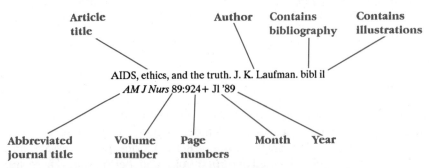

FIGURE 4.7   An excerpt from the *Reader's Guide to Periodical Literature,* September 1989.

Source: Excerpt from *Reader's Guide to Periodical Literature,* September 1989. Copyright (c) 1989 by The H. W. Wilson Company. Reprinted by permission of the publisher.

While the *Reader's Guide* is no doubt the most comprehensive of the magazine indexes, you should not overlook others that include publications it does not index. For example, *Access,* issued three times a year, includes 150 or more magazines not included among those indexed in the *Reader's Guide.* Using *Access,* you can find articles printed in such magazines as *Woman's Day, TV Guide, Penthouse,* and *Bicycling,* sources that can provide you with insight to popular taste or current information on well-known individuals.

If your research topic concerns issues related to black Americans, as was Anne Kramer's paper on black readers' responses to *Adventures of Huckleberry Finn,* you may want to consult the *Index to Periodical Articles By and About Blacks.* To find very current articles with slightly different viewpoints than those often found in many mainstream publications, you might want to consult the *Popular Periodical Index* and the *Alternative Press Index.* The first of these indexes such magazines as *MacWorld, Playboy, English Journal,* and *Columbia Journalism Review;* the second includes over 200 "alternative" publications such as *Green Peace, Feminist Studies,* and *Canadian Journal of Political and Social Theory* (see Figure 4.8).

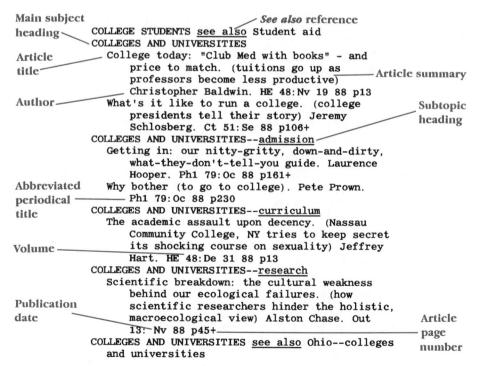

FIGURE 4.8 Entries from the *Popular Periodical Index,* July–December, 1988

Source: Entries from *Popular Periodicals Index,* July–December 1988. Reprinted by permission of the publisher, Robert M. Bottorff.

While you will obviously want to consider the *Reader's Guide* as your primary index to popular magazines, remember that you can locate useful sources in various other indexes, too. For easy reference later, the following list includes indexes already mentioned, as well as others you may wish to consult.

Access, 1975–date (includes only magazines not indexed in the *Reader's Guide*).

Alternative Press Index, 1969–date (covers politically "left" publications).

California Periodicals Index, 1978–date (indexes magazines about California cities and lifestyles).

Catholic Periodical and Literature Index, 1930–date.

Children's Magazine Guide: Subject Index to Children's Literature, 1948–date.

Consumer's Index to Product Evaluations and Information Sources, 1973–date.

Index to Jewish Periodicals, 1963–date.

Index to Periodicals By and About Blacks, 1950–date.

The Magazine Index, 1977–date (appears on microfilm and duplicates the *Reader's Guide* and *Access*).

Physical Education Index, 1978–date (indexes magazines covering nutrition, fitness, and sports).

Physical Education/Sports Index, 1973–date (includes magazines devoted to particular sports).

Popular Periodical Index, 1978–date.

Knowing Which Index to Consult. If you are unsure about which index includes a particular popular magazine, refer to a copy of the magazine itself. The table of contents page will often tell you where the magazine is indexed. If that fails, consult one of the following sources, but remember that these publications try not to duplicate each other. You may have to consult more than one before you find the particular magazine you want to know about.

Chicorel Index to Abstracting and Indexing Services. New York: Chicorel Library, 1978.

Katz, Bill, and Linda Katz. *Magazines for Libraries.* New York: Bowker, 1986.

Standard Periodical Directory. New York: Oxbridge, 1988.

Ulrich's International Periodicals Directory. New York: Bowker, 1988.

Journals. Periodicals written for scholars or audiences with special expertise in a subject are called *journals.* These periodicals report on current issues, original research, and the results of surveys and experiments.

They also often include book reviews, which are themselves useful for your research. Journals are written by informed authorities for an audience of similarly informed or interested people. The level of knowledge or experience required to read them easily varies from very accessible ones, like the film journal *Movie Maker,* to more technical ones, like *Accounts of Chemical Research.*

Journal Indexes. Numerous indexes list journal articles covering subjects in nearly every field of study and interest. Four of the most widely used in the social sciences and literature and languages are discussed here.

1. *Social Sciences Index.* Since nearly every subject has implications for social consequences, check general social science indexes on almost any topic you research. A major source to consult in this field is the *Social Sciences Index,* which lists articles in over 250 scholarly journals covering such subjects as anthropology, economics, environmental studies, history,

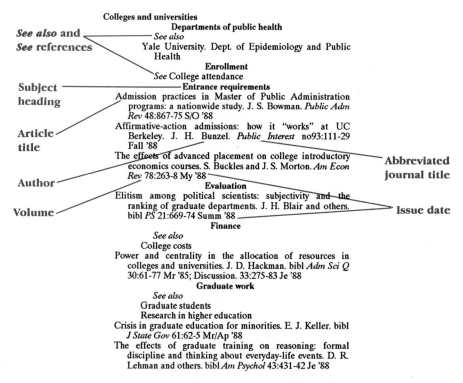

FIGURE 4.9 Entries from the *Social Sciences Citation Index,* April 1988 to March 1989

Source: Entries from *Social Sciences Index,* April 1988–March 1989. Copyright (c) 1988, 1989 by The H. W. Wilson Company. Reprinted by permission of the publisher.

law, philosophy, political science, and sociology. As Figure 4.9 suggests, a check of the *Index* may not only yield sources for research but also suggest new relationships and emphases for you to consider.

2. *Social Sciences Citation Index.* A valuable resource in the behavioral and social sciences is the *Social Sciences Citation Index (SSCI)*. This source indexes approximately 2,000 scholarly journals and is also available through online databases. Citation indexes are useful both for locating published journal articles and identifying authorities who have written on your research subject. Since it is composed of four separate indexes—Citation, Source, Permuterm Subject, and Corporate indexes—this work requires familiarity before it can be consulted efficiently.

a. The Permuterm Subject Index of *SSCI* is useful at the start of your research, when you need to become acquainted with the key terms related to your subject or need to discover who has written about it. The Permuterm Subject Index lists articles by subject headings, followed by associated terms or subheadings. As Figure 4.10 shows, looking up the subject of "college" in the Permuterm Index would yield a large number of more particular subheadings and authors whose journal articles treated them specifically. The entry "college—admissions," for example, yields one author, A. E. Roth, who has written on that exact topic. You could then use the Source Index to locate the particular article by Roth.

b. The Source Index provides publication information about each of the authors ("sources") listed in the Permuterm Subject Index and published in periodicals covered by *SSCI*. In addition, it also indicates the number of references made to each entry by other authors and

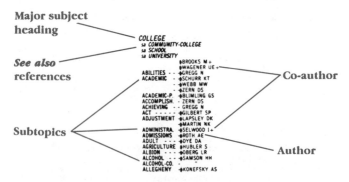

FIGURE 4.10 An excerpt from the Permuterm Subject Index of the *Social Sciences Citation Index*, 1989

Source: Excerpt from Permuterm Subject Index. Reprinted from the 1989 *Social Sciences Citation Index*[R] with the permission of the Institute for Scientific Information[R] (ISI[R]): (c) copyright 1989.

```
ROTH A
  STABILITY AND PERFECTION OF NASH EQUILIBRIA -
  VANDAMME,E ◆ BOOK REVIEW
    J ECON      51(3):308-309        90    1R  DM582
    see CEBULA RJ    WELTWIR ARC    126   393 90
ROTH AE
  CORRECTION ◆ CORRECTION
    ECONOMETRIC 58(1):275            90    1R  CV633
    ROTH AE          89 ECONOMETRICA        57  559
  VANDEVAT.JH—RANDOM-PATHS TO STABILITY IN 2-SIDED
  MATCHING ◆ NOTE
    ECONOMETRIC 58(6):1475-1480      90   12R  EL310
    UNIV PITTSBURGH,DEPT ECON, PITTSBURGH, PA 15260, USA
    CRAWFORD VP      81 ECONOMETRICA        49  437
    FELDMAN AM       73 REV ECON STUD       40  463
    GALE D           62 AM MATH MONTHLY     69    9
    KELSO AS         82 ECONOMETRICA        50 1483
    KNUTH DE         76 MARIAGES STABLES
    MONGELL S        90 IN PRESS AM EC REV
    ROTH AE          82 MATH OPER RES        7  617
    -                84 J ECON THEORY       34  383
    -                84 J POLIT ECON        92  991
    -                90 ECONOMETRIC SOC MONO
    -                90 IN PRESS AM EC REV
    -                90 IN PRESS EC THEORY    1
  ■ NEW PHYSICIANS - A NATURAL EXPERIMENT IN MARKET
  ORGANIZATION
    SCIENCE     250(4987):1524-1528 90   12R  EM931
    UNIV PITTSBURGH,ECON, PITTSBURGH, PA 15260, USA
    ANDERSON J       COMMUNICATION
    BLAIR C          88 MATH OPER RES       13  619
    CLAYDEN AD       71 BRIT J MED EDUC      5    5
    GALE D           62 AM MATH MON         69    1
    KELSO A          82 ECONOMETRICA        50    6
    LEISHMAN AG      70 LANCET               2  459
    MONGELL S        IN PRESS AM EC REV
    ROTH AE          -
    -                84 J POLIT ECON        92    6
    -                87 LABORATORY EXPT EC 6
    -                90 ECONOMETRIC SOC MONO
    SHAW DA          COMMUNICATION
ROTH B
  ■ THE MORAL ARGUMENTS AGAINST MILITARY RESEARCH
    ANN NY ACAD 577(DEC):21-33       89   12R  DB058
    STANFORD UNIV,DEPT MECH ENGN, STANFORD, CA 94305, USA
    BUSH V           68 MODERN ARMS FREE MEN
    CAMUS A          86 NEITHER VICTIMS EXEC
    EVERETT M        89 BREAKING RANKS
    GLANTZ SA        74 SCIENCE            186  706
    KING J           88 SCI PEOPLE          20   17
    MACARTHUR DM     70 DEF IND B            6    1
    MOYERS B         87 SECRET GOVT CONSTITU
```

FIGURE 4.11 An author entry from the Source Index of *SSCI*

Source: Excerpt from Source Index. Reprinted from the 1990 *Social Sciences Citation Index*R with the permission of the Institute for Scientific Information R (ISI R): (c) copyright 1990.

lists those authors and where their works appeared. Thus, once you had found A. E. Roth's name in the Subject Index under "college—admissions," you could look him up in the Source Index for full information on what he had written. The entry would also list other authors who have cited his article. Figure 4.11 shows a complete Source entry for Roth's article on college admissions

c. Next, suppose you also wanted to find out more about A. E. Roth's work. *SSCI*'s Citation Index will tell you (a) how many times and where a particular author has published during the time covered by the Index and (b) what authors have made reference to the entries indicated for that author. Note that the Citation Index does not list titles of individual publications by an author. Instead, it lists the periodical and date when an article appeared (see Figure 4.12).

You should use the Citation Index to gauge an individual author's authority on the subject (indicated by the number of publications and the frequency of citations by other authors). Also use the Citation Index to locate articles by other authors in the field, looking up the names listed there in the Source Index later.

d. The Corporate Author Index of *SSCI* has the same format as the Citation Index. Rather than citing persons, however, this index lists associations, leagues, corporations, and other groups who author publications.

```
ROTH AE
** IN PRESS AM EC REV
  ROTH AE        SCIENCE        250 1524 90
76 MATH OPER RES    1   43
  LEBRETON M   INT J GAME       19  111 90
77 ECONOMETRICA   45  657
  BLAIR DH     J ECON THEO       50  346 90
77 J MATH ECON   4  131
  BERLIANT M   J MATH ECON      19  357 90
  TAMOSIUN R   MATH SOC SC      19  205 90
  WEBER S      REG SCI URB      20   23 90
77 J MATH PSYCHOL   16  153
77 J ECON THEORY   16  481
  BLAIR DH     J ECON THEO       50  346 90
77 MATH OPER RES    2   64
  CHUN YS      ECONOMETRIC      58  951 90 N
78 J MATH PSYCHOL   17  189
  MURNIGHA JK  ACC REVIEW       65  642 90
79 AXIOMATIC MODELS BAR
  COPELAND B   OX ECON PAP      41  774 89
  FARBER HS    IND RELAT        29  361 90
  FITTS MA     MICH LAW R       88  917 90
  FURTH D      MATH OPER R      15  724 90
  HECKATHO DD  J POLIT          52 1101 90
  IOANNIDE YM  INT ECON R       31  619 90
  KENNAN J     J APPL ECON       4 S 87 89
      "        SCIENCE         249 1124 90
  LIVNE ZA     OPERAT RES       37  972 89
  SEITZING AH  AM J AGR EC      72   95 90
  SOPHER B     J LABOR EC        8   48 90
79 EC MATH SYSTEMS
  BERKOVIT E   J LAW EC OR       5  395 89
79 LECTURE NOTES EC MAT
  MOLDOVAN B   INT J GAME       19  171 90
79 LECTURE NOTES EC MAT  170
  HARRINGT JE  J RISK UNC        3  135 90
  HERRERO MJ   J ECON THEO      49  266 89
  KAMECKE U    INT J GAME       18  423 89
79 PSYCHOL REV   86  574
  COOPER R     RAND J ECON      20  568 89
  COOPER RW    AM ECON REV      80  218 90
  ELIAS N      ACC REVIEW       65  606 90
  OCHS J       Q J ECON        105  545 90
  RAPOPORT A   THEOR DECIS      28   47 90
  SHOGREN JF   ECON LETT        31  319 89
  THOMPSON L   J EXP S PSY      26  528 90
```

FIGURE 4.12 An author entry from the Citation Index of *SSCI*

Source: Excerpt from Citation Index. Reprinted from the 1990 *Social Sciences Citation Index*R with the permission of the Institute for Scientific Information®R (ISIR): (c) copyright 1990.

Figure 4.13 summarizes the relationships among the separate indexes comprising the *Social Sciences Citation Index* and typical citation indexes in other fields of study. In addition to the *SSCI*, the following reference works include source, citation, and permuterm indexes as described here:

Arts and Humanities Index, 1977–date.
CompuMath Citation Index, 1968–date.
Science Citation Index, 1961–date.

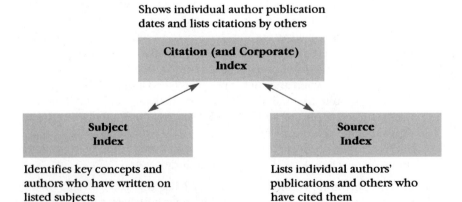

Shows individual author publication
dates and lists citations by others

**Citation (and Corporate)
Index**

**Subject
Index**

**Source
Index**

Identifies key concepts and
authors who have written on
listed subjects

Lists individual authors'
publications and others who
have cited them

FIGURE 4.13 A summary of indexes included in the *Social Sciences Citation Index*

3. *MLA Bibliography.* If you are researching a topic in languages or literature, consult the Modern Language Association's *MLA International Bibliography of Books and Articles on the Modern Languages and Literature.* This work's title is fully descriptive of its use and focus. Bound together as a single, inclusive volume and subtitled *Classified Listings with Author Index,* the *MLA Bibliography* divides articles on languages and literature into five distinct areas:

National literatures (subvolumes I and II)
Linguistics (III)
General literature (IV)
Folklore (V)

Locating an author or work in the *Classified Listings* is a step-by-step procedure.

a. Turn to the appropriate subvolume.
b. Find the section for the appropriate time period of your subject.
c. Find the alphabetical listing for the author or work you seek.

To locate items in the *MLA Bibliography* by subject, you will need to use a second separate volume, the *Subject Index,* which is organized alphabetically.

When Anne Kramer used the *MLA Bibliography,* she found sources in the *Subject Index* first and then looked them up individually in the *Classified Listings* (see Figures 4.14 and 4.15).

CLEMENS, SAMUEL (1835-1910)
See also classified section: I:7574 ff.
Used for: Twain, Mark.
   American literature. 1800-1899.
      Howells, William Dean. Relationship to CLEMENS, SAMUEL. Includes biographical information. I:7919.
   American literature. Criticism in *New York Tribune* (1870). 1800-1899.
      Hay, John. Treatment of Western American literature; especially Harte, Bret; CLEMENS, SAMUEL. I:7902.
   American literature. Fiction. 1800-1999.
      Treatment of utopia; especially CLEMENS, SAMUEL; London, John Griffith. Dissertation abstract. I:7369.
   American literature. Fiction. 1800-1899.
      Melville, Herman. Treatment of women; relationship to myth; the quest; compared to CLEMENS, SAMUEL; Hemingway, Ernest. Application of theories of Campbell, Joseph: *The Hero with a Thousand Faces*; Neumann, Erich: *Die grosse Mutter.* Dissertation abstract. I:8140.
   American literature. Fiction by Afro-American writers. 1900-1999.
      Point of view compared to CLEMENS, SAMUEL: *The Adventures of Huckleberry Finn.* I:8700.

FIGURE 4.14 An entry from the *Subject Index* of the *MLA Bibliography*

Source: Reprinted by permission of the Modern Language Association of America from *MLA International Bibliography* (Subject Index), 1984, p. G235. Copyright (c) 1985 by The Modern Language Association of America.

American literature/1800-1899

CLEMENS, SAMUEL (1835-1910)/*Novel* /*The Adventures of Tom Sawyer (1876)*

Novel/The Adventures of Huckleberry Finn (1884)

[7039]   Abderabou, Abdelrahman A. "The Human Dimensions in Multicultural Relations: A Critical Study of Twain's *Huckleberry Finn* ." *JEn* . 1986 Sept.; 14: 1-5.
[†Treatment of black-white relations.]

[7040]   Anderson, David D. "Mark Twain, Sherwood Anderson, Saul Bellow, and the
Territories of the Spirit." *Midamerica* . 1986; 8: 116-124. [†Treatment of spiritual
journey; relationship to American experience compared to Anderson, Sherwood:
Winesburg, Ohio ; Bellow, Saul: *The Adventures of Augie March* .]

[7041]   Barrow, David. "The Ending of *Huckleberry Finn* : Mark Twain's Cryptic
Lament." *CCTEP* . 1986 Sept.; 51: 78-84. [†Narrative ending.]

[7042]   Berry, Wendell. "Writer and Region." *HudR* . 1987 Spring; 40(1): 15-30.
[†Treatment of place; escape; relationship to community; the individual; society.]

[7043]   Bird, John. "'These Leather-Faced People': Huck and the Moral Art of Ly-
ing." *SAF* . 1987 Spring; 15(1): 71-80. [†Treatment of Finn, Huckleberry (character); relationship to falsehood.]

FIGURE 4.15   An entry from the *Classified Listings with Author Index* from the
MLA Bibliography

Source: Reprinted by permission of the Modern Language Association of America from *MLA
International Bibliography* (Classified Listings with Author Index), 1987, p. 175. Copyright
(c) 1985 by The Modern Language Association of America.

4. Humanities Index.   A good source for articles in religion, philosophy, literature, or any of the performing arts—such as dance, television,
opera, drama, or film—is the *Humanities Index.* It includes entries from
over 200 scholarly journals and follows *Reader's Guide* form in listing information. Figure 4.16 shows an article entry about Mark Twain taken
from the *Humanities Index.*

Notice that most of the journals cited are published quarterly rather
than monthly. Thus, for the article "Twain's Huckleberry Finn," published
in the *Explicator,* a Fall 1987 publication date is cited rather than the
month and year.

Journal Article Abstracts.   Journals and the articles they contain are
listed for nearly every field of study in a number of specialized indexes.
You can often save time by reading an *abstract,* a condensed version of an
article, in one of the many abstract references providing such article summaries. Most abstracts are identified by number and indexed according to
subject in the abstract source itself. As shown by the summary in Figure
4.17 of an article about AIDS from *Psychological Abstracts,* an abstract
gives you all the information you would need—author, title, date, volume,
page numbers—to locate the complete article. If you intend to read the
original article as well as the abstract, you should make a separate bibliography card for each.

While abstracts are useful for general or background information,
they should not serve as major sources for your research paper's discus-

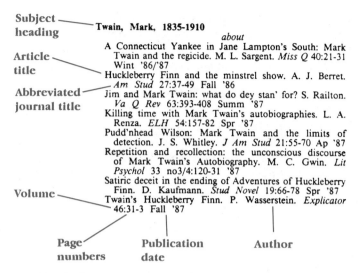

Subject heading

Article title

Abbreviated journal title

Volume

Page numbers

Publication date

Author

FIGURE 4.16 Entries on Mark Twain from the *Humanities Index*

sion. Instead, use a journal abstract to determine whether the orginal article may be useful enough to seek out and read fully. If it is, use the publication information provided by the abstract to find the article and read it in complete form.

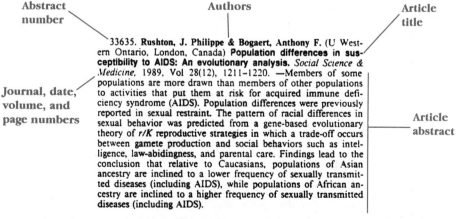

Abstract number

Authors

Article title

Journal, date, volume, and page numbers

Article abstract

FIGURE 4.17 An article abstract from *Psycological Abstracts*

Many specialized journals titled as indexes also include abstracts. Familiarity with the common indexes of your research field will acquaint you with those that do. The following list provides a small sampling of the many indexes and abstracts available at most college and public libraries:

Applied Science & Technology Index, 1913–date.
Art Index, 1929–date.
Biological & Agricultural Index, 1913–date.
Business Periodicals Index, 1958–date.
Child Development Abstracts and Bibliography, 1927–date.
Education Index, 1929–date.
Film Literature Index, 1973–date.
General Science Index, 1978–date.
Hispanic American Periodicals Index, 1974–date.
Historical Abstracts, 1914–date.
Humanities Index, 1974–date.
Index Medicus, 1960–date.
Index to Legal Periodicals, 1908–date.
Index to United States Government Periodicals, 1974–date.
Nutrition Abstracts and Reviews, 1931–date.
Pollution Abstracts, 1970–date.
Psychological Abstracts, 1927–date.
Public Affairs Information Index, 1915–date.
Social Sciences Index, 1974–date. [Previously part of *Social Sciences and Humanities Index,* 1965–74].
Women Studies Abstracts, 1972–date.

If you need to know if a particular journal is listed in an index or abstract, consult the comprehensive references given in Appendix B or one of these index sources:

Harzfield, Lois. *Periodical Indexes in the Social Sciences and Humanities: A Subject Guide.* New York: Scarecrow, 1978.
Owen, Dolores B. *Abstracts and Indexes in the Sciences and Technology: A Descriptive Guide.* 2nd ed. New York: Scarecrow, 1984.

Newspaper Indexes

Newspapers report current facts and opinions. While they do not provide the studied or scholarly insights journal or magazine articles offer, newspapers contain valuable current information about economics, social trends, politics, sporting events, crime, and fashion. Not all newspapers are indexed, but you can use those that are to find the date of an event. Once you have the date, you can locate information about the event in any nonindexed newspaper.

Subject
heading

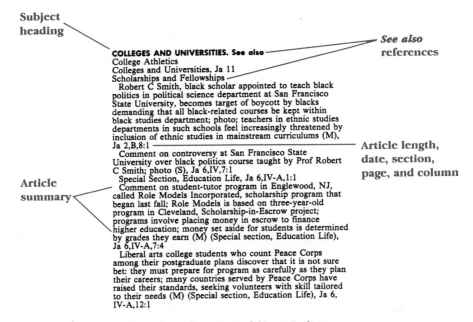

See also
references

Article length,
date, section,
page, and column

Article
summary

FIGURE 4.18 An excerpt from the *New York Times Index*

Source: Excerpt from *New York Times Index* (quarterly issue, January–March 1991), p.66.
Copyright (c) 1991 by The New York Times Company. Reprinted by permission.

New York Times Index. You will find the *New York Times Index*
(1913–date) available in book form, microfilm, or online at most libraries.
As an index to the *New York Times,* it lists news stories by subject and
provides a summary. Similar to the *Reader's Guide* in its entry format, the
Index cross-references items with "see" and "see also"; indicates whether
an article is short (S), medium (M), or long (L); and lists the date, section,
and column number for each item (see Figure 4.18).

Other Newspaper Indexes. Like the *New York Times,* other major
newspapers—such as the *Chicago Tribune, Christian Science Monitor,
Los Angeles Times, Wall Street Journal,* and *Washington Post*—are also
individually indexed. You can find and compare articles in several of these
and other newspapers at the same time by consulting the following comprehensive general indexes:

> *National Newspaper Index,* 1979–date (indexes five major news-
> papers at once: the *New York Times, Christian Science Monitor,
> Wall Street Journal, Los Angeles Times,* and *Washington Post.*
> Available online).

The Newspaper Index, 1972–date (includes articles from the *Chicago Tribune, Los Angeles Times, New Orleans Times-Picayune, Denver Post, Detroit News, Houston Post,* and *San Francisco Chronicle.* Available online.)

The Times Index, 1906–date (lists entries from five major English newspapers: the *Times, Sunday Times, Times Literary Supplement, Times Educational Supplement,* and *Times Higher Education Supplement*).

Other newspapers may be indexed locally. Use the *Gale Directory of Publications* (Detroit: Gale, 1989) to locate, by state and then by city, publishers of small and large newspapers nationwide, or check with your library for newspapers you need information about. Almost any newspaper is available by writing to the local library or arranging for a microfilm copy through interlibrary loan.

Periodical Files or Serials Lists

Magazines, journals, and newspapers available in your library are listed in a periodicals file or serials list. The list may be in book form, on microfiche, or online at a computer terminal, with each periodical title listed alphabetically. Under the title of the periodical, such lists typically provide publication information, a description of the periodical, its location in the library, and the issues included in the library's collection. Entries without call numbers are shelved alphabetically in the library's periodical section. Figure 4.19 shows an entry from a library serials lists.

```
        Title:  American Health
  Other Title:  A.H.
Dates Covered:  Vol.1, no.1 (Mar./Apr. 1982) –
    Published:  [New York, N.Y. : American Health
                Partners, c1982–]
  Description:  v. : ill.; 28 cm.
   Subject(s):  Health--periodicals
                Health--periodicals
        Notes:  Title from cover.
      Library:  BIOMED LIB    Call number: W1 AM227
  Library has:  U3N1-3, 5-9 (1984) b4-7 (1985-88)
                U8N1 (1989)
                Library has current subscription
```

FIGURE 4.19   A periodical entry from a library serials file

Indexes to Literature in Collections

Most indexes direct you to complete works addressing one major subject almost exclusively. Quite often, however, you need only a certain *part* of a work—say, a brief discussion of a minor subject, a single essay or chapter, or other selection. Fortunately, you do not have to hunt through the indexes of several different books to see if the material you want is included. Instead, you can consult subject indexes that locate material within complete works:

Biography Index. New York: Wilson, 1946–date.
Essay and General Literature Index. New York: Wilson, 1900–date.

The *Biography Index* lists information on people who have been written about in books or in the more than 2,000 popular and scholarly periodicals it cites. The *Biography Index* includes an alphabetized index, giving the date of birth, nationality, and occupation of each person listed in the volume. A second index cites individuals according to occupation. Any

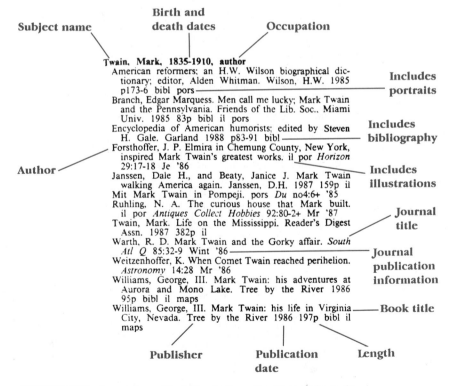

FIGURE 4.20 An entry on Mark Twain from the *Biography Index*

Source: Entry from *Biography Index,* September 1986–August 1988, p. 765. Copyright (c) 1986, 1987, 1988 by The H. W. Wilson Company. Reprinted by permission of the publisher.

biographical material by or about an individual and appearing within another work is cited, as shown in Figure 4.20.

The *Essay and General Literature Index* locates essays and parts of books for which there are no descriptive titles. Suppose, like student Anne Kramer, you wanted to find material about Mark Twain's characterization of Jim, the black runaway slave in *Huckleberry Finn*. Without checking the *Essay and General Literature Index*, Anne would never have consulted the book *Faulkner and Race*, a collection of essays about the writer William Faulkner. By checking the *Index*, however, Anne discovered the essay by S. Chakovsky, "Lucas Beauchamp and Jim: Mark Twain's Influence on William Faulkner" (see Figure 4.21).

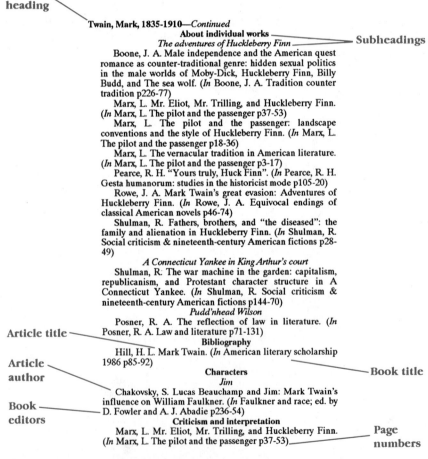

FIGURE 4.21 An excerpt from the *Essay and General Literature Index*

Source: Entries from *Essay and General Literature Index*, 1985–1989, p. 1673. Copyright (c) 1985, 1986, 1987, 1988, 1989, and 1990 by The H. W. Wilson Company. Reprinted by permission of the publisher.

Pamphlet Indexes

Libraries often maintain a collection of pamphlets and other uncataloged printed material in a *vertical file* (so named because items used to be filed standing upright rather than in a file drawer). Pamphlets, flyers, newsletters, and other printed information distributed by local government agencies, clubs, businesses, and individuals are usually filed alphabetically by subject. Used appropriately, pamphlets can add fresh perspective to your research.

1. They can provide current information.
2. They usually discuss local issues or specific minor topics not addressed by other sources.
3. The presentation of technical material is generally written for the nonspecialist.
4. Pamphlets often reflect opinions not available in other sources.

Remember that pamphlets and similar materials are sometimes written for other purposes than solely reporting information in an objective fashion. Weigh the content, authority, and objectivity of any pamphlet before relying on it too heavily in your research.

Besides investigating the vertical file of your own library, also consult the *Vertical File Index: A Subject Guide to Selected Pamphlet Material* (1935–date). Use this source to identify and order various pamphlets, brochures, and posters directly from their publishers. Figure 4.22 shows an entry from the *Verticle File Index* for a pamphlet on AIDS.

In addition, the United States government also publishes thousands of pamphlets and other small information items every year. Check your library's holdings, or consult the *Monthly Catalog of United States Government Publications* (discussed later in this chapter).

Finally, the most direct means of acquiring pamphlets and other such material is to go directly to places related to your research topic (see Chapter 5). Along with getting a firsthand perspective on your research, you may also discover pamphlet material unavailable in any other way.

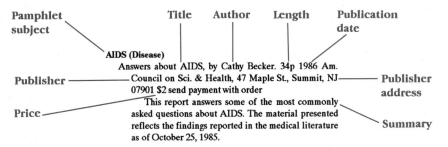

FIGURE 4.22 An entry from the *Vertical File Index*

Source: Entry from *Vertical File Index*, March 1986. Copyright (c) 1986 by The H. W. Wilson Company. Reprinted by permission of the publisher.

Indexes to U.S. Government
Publications and Documents

The documents that the United States government prints include reports, bibliographies, dictionaries, guidebooks, maps, posters, pamphlets, directories, magazines, and other resources. All government publications are sent to designated depository libraries; there are two per congressional district and several others named in each state according to a range of criteria.

Many state, county, and college libraries serve as depositories for federal publications. Most of these, however, *select* the publications they receive because of the quantity available. Consequently, you may find that your own library either has no government documents available or has only a limited selection. If you know what document you want, you can ask your library to get it for you (usually in microform) through interlibrary loan. You can also write to this address to order a free copy of any government publication:

Superintendent of Documents
Government Printing Office
Washington, DC 20402

Locating Government Documents. Government documents are not always easy to locate. In most libraries, they are not cataloged with other materials nor are they always shelved in the same areas. Indeed, you will find that the call numbers given for government publications are not those of either the Dewey Decimal or Library of Congress systems. Instead, documents are assigned what is known as a Superintendent of Documents (SuDoc) number and shelved according to the issuing agency rather than by subject. The first letter in the SuDoc number indicates the government issuing agency (J = Justice Department, L = Labor Department, and so forth). The number following the letter is assigned by the Library of Congress for cataloging purposes. Thus, a publication with a SuDoc number such as S 1.65/3:2734 is produced by the State Department and would be located with the other materials published by that agency.

This system prevents your browsing to find government materials by subject and remains complicated, even for those with experience. Until you become familiar with government indexes and documents, you would be wise to work with a librarian to locate those you need.

Commercial as well as government-published guides to federal documents abound. The most comprehensive and generally up to date is:

Monthly Catalog of United States Government Publications. Washington, DC: GPO, 1895–date (Annual. Also available online from DIALOG).

The *MC*, as the *Monthly Catalog* is known, lists the subject, author, title, and complete publishing data, including price, for all publications from United States government agencies. Published monthly, the *MC* supplies information from approximately 2,000 new government publications in each issue.

You can locate a publication by first consulting the Subject Index of the *MC* (see Figure 4.23). Then use the entry number given there to find the complete listing in another part of the *Catalog* (see Figure 4.24).

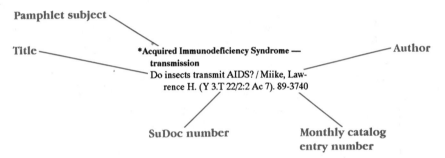

FIGURE 4.23   An entry from the subject index of the *Monthly Catalog*

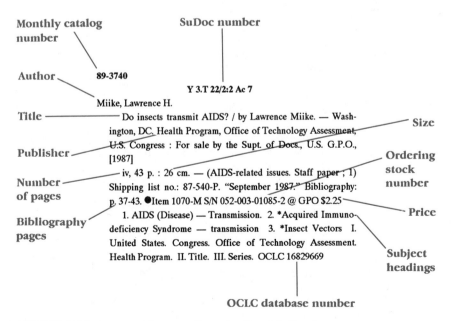

FIGURE 4.24   An pamphlet entry from the *Monthly Catalog*

You will want to remember that the *MC* is a bibliography; it therefore lists complete works, not the articles they include. You can, however, refer to the Subject Headings (Figure 4.23) given in the *MC* entry to decide whether the publication contains information that would be useful to you.

For an index to government periodicals and serial publications that does include the articles within these sources, consult the commercial guide commonly known as *PAIS:*

> *Public Affairs Information Services Bulletin.* New York: PAIS, 1915–date (Annual. Available online as PAIS).

Similar to the *Reader's Guide, PAIS* indexes about 1,500 periodicals, books, pamphlets, mimeographed materials, and state and city publications about government and legislation, economics, sociology, and political science (see Figure 4.25).

If your research requires that you examine the reports of congressional committees, testimony of witnesses in congressional hearings, communications from the president to the Senate and House, or commit-

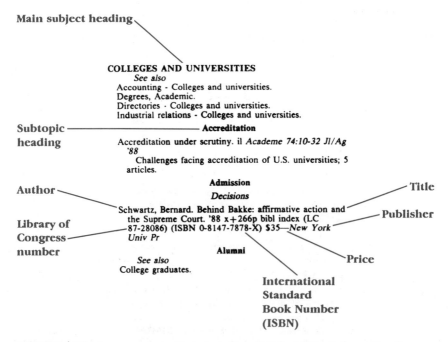

FIGURE 4.25 An excerpt on admissions from *Public Affairs Information Services Bulletin (PAIS)*

Source: Excerpt from *PAIS International in Print,* Vol. 1, No. 6. Copyright (c) 1991 by Public Affairs Information Services, Inc. Reprinted by permission.

tee-prepared background on new legislation, consult the CIS annual *Index:*

> Congressional Information Service. *Annual Index and Abstracts to Publications of the United States Congress.* Washington, DC: Congressional Information Service, 1970–date.

This useful source appears monthly, with quarterly cumulations and an annual cumulation titled *CIS/Annual.* The *Annual* itself comprises two volumes, *Subjects and Names* and *Abstracts.* You use the first volume to search out a listing for a subject or a person's name (see Figure 4.26); then use the *Abstracts* volume to get full information, including a summary of any report or activities (see Figure 4.27).

The guides to government documents listed here are only three of the hundred or more indexes and catalogs available. Every department of the government—from the Agriculture Department to the National Science Foundation to the Veterans Administration—publishes thousands of pages of information yearly. In addition to those sources discussed here, some

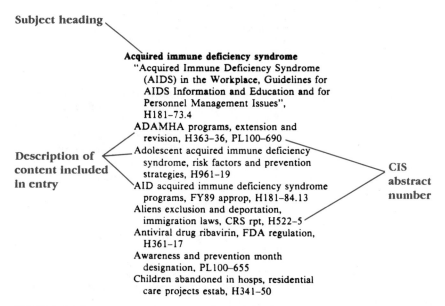

FIGURE 4.26 An excerpt from the *Subject Index* of the *CIS Annual Index and Abstracts to Congressional Publications and Public Laws*

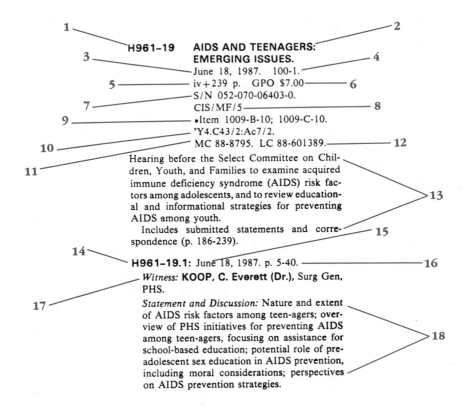

1. CIS accession number
2. Title
3. Date
4. Congress and session
5. Pages
6. GPO* price
7. GPO* stock number
8. CIS microfiche availability and unit count
9. SuDoc item number
10. SuDoc classification number
11. Monthly catalog entry number
12. Library of Congress card number
13. Abstract of the publication
14. CIS accession number for individual item
15. Date of testimony
16. Page reference
17. Names and affiliations of witnesses
18. Abstract of testimony

*Government Printing Office

FIGURE 4.27 An entry from the *CIS Index to Congressional Publications and Public Laws*

Source: Entries from *CIS/Annual 1988, Abstracts of Congressional Publications*, p. 525. Copyright (c) 1989 by Congressional Information Service (Bethesda, MD). All rights reserved. Reprinted with permission.

2,900 U.S. government publications in 83 subject areas are listed and annotated in:

> *Guide to Popular U.S. Government Publications.* Littleton, CO: Libraries Unlimited, 1986.

Reviewing Your Library Search

Before assuming that your search for available library sources is completed, take the time to review the working bibliography for balance and comprehensiveness. You will need sources reflecting a variety of viewpoints and depth of coverage. The number of books, magazines, journals, newspaper articles, or other sources you will need depends upon your topic and the research requirements of your instructor.

Thoroughly review your sources before proceeding too far with any of the activities decribed in the next chapter. That way, you can better decide how researching beyond campus and community libraries can next benefit your research most.

WORKING WITH OTHERS

Establishing a working bibliography will be easier if you share insights and experiences with a classmate along the way. Use the following suggestions to review your understanding of library resources and the working bibliography discussed in this chapter.

- Share your knowledge of the campus library's general bibliographies, indexes, and abstracts with a classmate. Briefly explain the differences between each of these types of reference sources. Does each of you know where these resources are located and how to use them?

- Exchange working bibliographies with a classmate, preferably someone researching a topic related to your own. What differences do you see in the way you are both recording information? Has either of you overlooked a source that should be included in the bibliography?

- Explain citation indexes such as the *Social Sciences Citation Index* or another that you are familiar with. How might you use such indexes in your own research? If you do not undertsand how to use a citation index, team up with a classmate and ask a campus librarian to show you how to use these useful (but complex) resources.

- Locate the abstract for a published journal article, and compare it to the original. Does the abstract accurately summarize the article's major ideas? Would it make any difference if you read an abstract rather than an original article for your research?

- Located in major cities across the nation, Government Printing Office (GPO) bookstores provide hundreds of government publications, some for free and some for sale. Check the local telphone book to see if there is a GPO bookstore near you. If there is, you will find it rewarding to visit the bookstore with a friend to find current sources for research.

- Exchange working bibliographies from time to time with a classmate to review each other's list of sources. Are there an adequate number and variety of sources? Are the sources current enough? Are the sources varied enough in the points of view they represent?

Researching Beyond the Campus Library

As you collect and study materials for the research topic, you will want to broaden your investigations by looking beyond campus and community libraries. Going out in the community to observe sites and activities related to your research topic, for example, is an exceptionally valuable way to understand it more thoroughly. Special library and museum collections can provide scarce primary and secondary sources especially relevant to local and regional subjects. You can also interview experts or people with uncommon opinions and experiences, use surveys and questionnaires to collect original data, listen to radio and television programs, or get firsthand opinions by attending lectures, addresses, and speeches on issues of community and world importance.

Getting more familiar with your research topic in any of these ways provides concrete experiences with which to illustrate and to verify your research. These approaches put you directly in touch with the people, places, events, and objects most closely relevant to your research and understanding of the topic.

Using Primary and Secondary Sources

Going beyond your campus and community libraries also provides opportunities to work with both *primary* and *secondary* materials in your research. The majority of books and magazine articles you consult in the library are secondary materials, information compiled and interpreted by someone else. Such research sources are valuable in providing information and expert insights, that would be unattainable otherwise. For most undergraduate research, secondary materials provide the foundation as well as most of the materials for studying and writing about any subject.

Primary research, on the other hand, results in your discovering your own information and opinions. When you research onsite, interview an authority, conduct a survey, or attend a lecture, your own observations and the materials you examine firsthand are primary sources. You may also do primary research in a library by studying letters, diaries, manuscripts, or literary works or by examining unpublished reports and research collected by others.

Anne Kramer used a primary source when she included a study of Mark Twain's novel *Adventures of Huckleberry Finn* in her research, as well as when she interviewed a professor who taught the novel. In a marine science course, you might do primary research charting the migration of Atlantic salmon; in a physics lab, you could do primary research measuring air samples to determine local pollution levels. As you can tell from these examples, working with primary materials means getting information directly from original sources and interpreting it on your own. (See also Chapter 1 on primary and secondary sources.)

Primary material is sometimes harder to come by and usually requires more original analysis than secondary material. Both kinds of research materials can add important dimensions to your study. When you research in the community, look for primary and secondary materials that would not be readily available at traditional campus or community libraries.

Observing Onsite

Reading as much as you can on a subject is essential to knowing it well and being able to make the most of related information. Researching onsite, however, to see and study something firsthand, engages your insight differently. By going to the places and events most directly connected with your topic, you will better understand that topic's importance in other people's lives. While books and articles can tell you about the plight of homeless people living on the streets of America, you will understand their condition far better by visiting local state or federal agencies to talk directly with people trying to assist the homeless. If you are researching the problem this country faces in disposing of its thousands of tons of trash every week, visit the local city or county dump. The experience may not be wholly pleasant, but you will understand the problem as never before.

Going onsite to explore your research topic more thoroughly will inspire other creative means to gather information for your research. Depending upon your purpose, you may need to make onsite observations to complete your research in several ways:

- *Record behavior*—For example, record social gestures of children at play; describe the actions of police officers making an arrest; test the responses of animals to human and nonhuman sounds.
- *Describe conditions*—Characterize damage from a hurricane; investigate conditions at an animal research laboratory; report on the working environment of air traffic controllers.
- *Examine primary material*—Compare organically and nonorganically grown fruits and vegetables; study a museum painting; examine an historical document; take notes at a lecture or interview.

While onsite observation may appear more interesting in some ways than library research, remember that it is not easy to do effectively. Accurate observation and reporting of data are difficult, even for a trained researcher. Thoughtful preparation before you get onsite can make the difference between a research study and a tourist visit.

To ensure the effectiveness of your onsite studies, follow these steps for any observation research you do:

1. *Plan your onsite research as early as possible.* List it in your Research Schedule, along with any arrangements you will need to make for reservations, permissions, tickets, or transportation. For any onsite visit, ask ahead of time about limitations or required authorizations. If you plan to use a camera or tape recorder at the site, find out if such equipment is allowed. In addition, be sure to schedule enough time to complete the objectives of your research visit.

2. *Make a checklist of what you want to observe.* If you will be studying patients in a hospital ward, include the frequency, conditions, and extent of the behaviors to note. If you are making a study of playground equipment at city parks, make a checklist to record the type, condition, and times of use and nonuse. If you are studying an historical document, list the features you want especially to note. Keep any checklist limited to what you can observe and record with accuracy. It is easy to get so caught up in observing as to forget the pupose of your visit. Once onsite, *use* the checklist to keep your activities focused on the research question you seek to answer. Once you get onsite, add to the checklist as needed.

3. *Take notes during and right after any onsite observation.* Use your research notebook to record factual descriptions of any artifacts or other objects you examine as part of your research study. In an appropriately labeled separate area of the notebook, write down any personal impressions and ideas for later use.

4. *Collect pamphlets, brochures, maps, and other explanatory materials about your topic or about any artifacts you observe at the site.* (Make certain that you *never* remove any artifacts themselves or other objects that are parts of an exhibit or observation site, however!) You need not bring home a whole library, but collecting available materials can prove valuable later. You might need to review the materials again or draw more extensively upon them than you had originally planned. Make bibliography cards for all such materials if you think you might use them in your paper (see Chapter 4).

The onsite investigation you do now for a research paper will prepare you for the kind of advanced field or laboratory research you may do later for other college courses or a career. It requires training for such observational research to be carried out effectively and for its results to carry any authority. Check with your instructor about your plans before proceeding too far, and exercise careful judgment when you incorporate results in your paper. Done with care and used as a supplement to your other research, any one of the activities described here can enrich the content and individualized approach of your research paper.

Researching Society and Museum Libraries

You can spend an interesting afternoon exploring your city's museum or private society libraries. These facilities may help you discover research ideas and locate primary and secondary resources that might be unavailable at academic or public libraries.

Society Libraries

Local as well as national societies exist in every part of the country, varying in size as well as purpose. Sometimes called *clubs, lodges, federations, associations,* or *leagues,* such societies are formed by people sharing interests in a particular subject. The libraries they sponsor for their own collecting and research purposes can often provide unusual or hard-to-find primary sources for your research.

Investigate the societal organizations in your local area. You will find groups interested in nearly every subject imaginable: the Civil War, gardening, the handicapped, bird watching, genealogies, literary interests, the environment, and star gazing, to name just a few examples. Almost every region has at least one local historical society, a good place to start for any topic on a local issue.

The members of such groups range from beginning enthusiasts to informed amateurs and scholars. Any members can provide assistance with your topic or may be willing to serve as the subject for an interview.

A society library may be open only to experienced researchers or perhaps just members; nonmembers may pay a small fee for public use. To locate society libraries near you, consult the telephone book or one of the sources listed later in this chapter (see "Finding Special Libraries and Museums").

Museum Libraries

Local museums are excellent sources of information and bibliographic materials on dozens of subjects, including art, history, literature, science, and popular culture. Not only can pamphlets or exhibit materials themselves prove useful primary resources for your research, but the museum's own library may also be available for limited public use.

Check ahead of time with the museum staff about research privileges and the availability of materials for your topic. If you cannot use the materials in the museum library itself, take advantage of the museum exhibits. You can add available information about them to your list of bibliographic sources. It is also likely that someone on the museum library staff may be able to give you information or direct you to other libraries and resources.

Finding Special Libraries and Museums

The telephone book's Yellow Pages are the handiest reference to societies and museums in your area. In addition to the *American Library Directory,* already cited earlier, a number of excellent guides to special libraries and museum collections found nationally are available. Entries from the *Directory of Special Libraries and Information Centers,* for example, indicate the size and type of collection a library has, if it is a government depository, and whether it offers computerized information services (see Figure 5.1). Use such sources as the *Directory of Special Libraries* to locate materials in your local area or to investigate the possibilities of acquiring them in microform or through interlibrary loan. Other guide sources to investigate include the following:

Ash, Lee. *Subject Collections: A Guide to Special Book Collections and Subject Emphases as Reported by University, College, Public, and Special Libraries and Museums in the United States and Canada.* 6th ed., rev. and enl. 2 vols. New York: Bowker, 1985.

Directory of Historical Agencies in North America. Nashville, TN: American Association for State and Local History, 1986.

Encyclopedia of Associations. Detroit: Gale, 1986.

Hudson, Kenneth, and Ann Nicholls. *Directory of World Museums and Living Displays.* New York: Grove's Dictionary, 1986.

Research Centers Directory. Detroit: Gale, 1989.

★13347★
SOLANO COUNTY LAW LIBRARY (Law)
Hall of Justice
600 Union Ave.   Phone: (707)429-6655
Fairfield, CA 94533   Yvonne Lafferty, Libn.
Staff: 1. **Subjects:** Law. **Holdings:** 15,000 books. **Subscriptions:** 16 journals and other serials. **Services:** Copying; library open to the public.

★13348★
SOLANO COUNTY LIBRARY - SPECIAL COLLECTIONS (Rare Book)
1150 Kentucky St.   Phone: (707)429-6601
Fairfield, CA 94533   Anne Marie Gold, Act. County Libn.
Founded: 1914. **Holdings:** Donovan J. McCune Collection (printing history, rare books; 1500 volumes); U.S. and state government documents depository (5000 volumes); local history (500 volumes). **Services:** Interlibrary loan; copying; collections open to the public. **Automated Operations:** Computerized cataloging, acquisitions, and circulation. **Computerized Information Services:** DIALOG Information Services; OnTyme Electronic Message Network Service (electronic mail service). Performs searches free of charge. **Networks/Consortia:** Member of North Bay Cooperative Library System (NBCLS).

★13349★
SOLAR ENERGY INSTITUTE OF NORTH AMERICA (SEINAM) - LIBRARY (Energy)
3404 Connecticut Ave., N.W.   Phone: (202)289-4411
Washington, DC 20008   Luana Moore, Pres.
Founded: 1976. **Subjects:** Economical solar energy systems, energy conservation. **Holdings:** 10,000 volumes.

★13350★
SOLAR ENERGY RESEARCH INSTITUTE - SERI TECHNICAL LIBRARY (Energy)
1617 Cole Blvd.   Phone: (303)231-1415
Golden, CO 80401   Jerome T. Maddock, Br.Chf.
Founded: 1977. **Staff:** Prof 5; Other 4. **Subjects:** Energy - solar, wind, ocean, biomass; photovoltaics; biotechnology; solid state physics. **Holdings:** 13,000 books; 3500 bound periodical volumes; 20,500 technical reports; 8000 patents; 46,000 reports on microfiche. **Subscriptions:** 600 journals and other serials; 5 newspapers. **Services:** Interlibrary loan; copying; SDI; library open to the public by appointment. **Automated Operations:** Computerized cataloging and serials. **Computerized Information Services:** DIALOG Information Services, SDC Information Services, DOE/RECON, RLIN, OCLC, BRS Information Technologies, CAS ONLINE, CIS, Pergamon InfoLine; internal database. **Networks/Consortia:** Member of FEDLINK. **Publications:** Serials Holdings List; New Acquisitions Lists, both irregular. **Remarks:** The Solar Energy Research Institute operates under contract to the U.S. Department of Energy. **Staff:** Nancy Greer, Hd., User Serv.; Joe Chervenak, Acq.; Soon Duck Kim, Cat.; Al Berger, Ref.

FIGURE 5.1   Entries from the *Directory of Special Libraries and Information Centers*

Source: Entries from *Directory of Special Libraries and Information Centers*, 12th Edition, Brigitte T. Darnay and Holly M. Leighton, editors. Copyright (c) 1989 by Gale Research Inc. Reproduced by permission of the publisher.

Finding Other Sources
of Research

Not all useful collections of books, magazines, pamphlets, business reports, tax ledgers, production schedules, flowcharts, policy statements, consumer profiles, or case histories are always stored in a place called a *library*. Your community and the surrounding area undoubtedly offer hundreds of places to investigate for research materials. Here are a few of the most common:

- Foreign consulates and embassies provide information covering the education, health care, politics, history, art, and economics of their respective countries.
- Large businesses and corporations maintain collections of data and reference materials pertinent to their operations.
- Hospitals and state and local health departments offer brochures on disease and health care, as well as maintain small libraries for staff research.
- Radio and television stations maintain transcripts of news broadcasts, documentaries, and interviews, as well as biography files and reference sources.
- Newspaper offices keep files of past issues that may not be available at a library.
- Chambers of Commerce provide visitors and interested investors with financial reports, tax schedules, transportation studies, and related business information.

In addition, police departments, social service agencies, water and power departments, zoos, museums, churches, and forestry services all keep records, as well as provide printed information on a variety of subjects to anyone interested. Your family dentist probably has a small library for his or her own practice, and many of your friends or relatives no doubt have collections of resources about a hobby or topic. Someone in your family undoubtedly has a scrapbook, a genealogy record, letters, mementos, a diary, or old news clippings that have been stored in a closet or garage for years.

In short, everyone collects information, and libraries are anywhere people store it. Think about and look into all the possible local resources for information as you begin to do your research. Remember to make out a preliminary citation card for any material you investigate in public agencies or business and private collections. Follow the appropriate form for each type, and give the necessary information (see Chapter 4).

Interviews

An *interview* can provide you with current information and personal insights that may not result from consulting other sources. In addition, information from an interview can add a dimension of human interest to a paper that might otherwise be mainly statistical or simply monotonous for other reasons. Taped interviews or those conducted on television or radio allow you to hear from experts and well-known personalities who might otherwise be unavailable to you. The most profitable interviews, however, can be the ones you conduct yourself, directing the questions to focus directly on the primary information you need for your research paper.

Determining the Purpose

Because of the time required to prepare for and conduct an interview, assess its usefulness and purpose beforehand. Do not include an interview in your research only to add a primary source to your paper's bibliography or just to avoid learning about your topic through more ordinary materials. Instead, use an interview when you need the firsthand information or insights that only a person with special experience or expertise can provide.

An interview will be useful to your research any time it fulfills one or more of the following purposes:

- Provides more current information than other sources
- Samples opinions or viewpoints not usually presented elsewhere
- Answers questions other sources have not sufficiently addressed
- Gives you examples to illustrate and support other research
- Records the responses of a recognized authority to questions specifically focused on your research topic or the research question

Selecting the Right Person

The value of interview research depends significantly upon the choice of the *interviewee*, the person to be interviewed. Remember that not everyone interested in or connected with a research topic qualifies as a good subject to interview. Your neighborhood mechanic may be an expert on the difficulties of repairing or getting parts for certain models of cars, but the local Nissan dealer knows more about consumer trends in auto buying. Your chemistry professor may have some opinions about how his Ford Bronco behaves on mountain roads, but the ideas of a professional test driver will carry a lot more weight in a paper discussing automobile safety standards.

People with knowledge about your research subject are probably easier to locate than you might think. You may already know family members or friends who would be valuable subjects. Certainly, the professors on your own college campus are knowledgeable about or directly involved with many types of research topics. City, county, and government employees—from police officers to engineers to social workers—are also informed and usually willing sources to consult. Local societies, associations, hospitals, museums, private businesses, and political organizations are just a few of the many other places you will find people to discuss your research with you. Use your local telephone directory or the Chamber of Commerce to contact businesses in your community. You can also use the *Encyclopedia of Associations* (described earlier) to locate individuals with special knowledge or experience in almost any subject.

Scheduling the Appointment

It is usually appropriate to schedule an interview a week or two ahead to allow you and the interviewee time to prepare. Contact the person by telephone or letter, identifying yourself and the purpose of the interview. Establish a few ground rules that you both agree upon concerning permissible subjects, tape recording, approval to quote, and so forth. Be sure to indicate the approximate amount of time you will need (one to one-and-a-half hours is generally long enough). Make your introduction concise and polite, something like this:

> My name is Jeanette Carson, and I'm a student at Bluffs College. I am doing a research paper on air traffic control problems in our area, and I wondered if I could have an hour of your time for an interview. I'd like to find out about conditions at the local airport and what plans there may be for changes there in the future.

Ask the interviewee what day, time, and place would be convenient, and adjust your own activity schedule accordingly.

Preparing for the Interview

Avoid using valuable interview time to ask needless or unfocused questions. Do a sufficient amount of preliminary reading and thinking about the research topic beforehand. Then plan and write out a list of questions focusing on information needed for your research. Use these questions to direct the interview, but do not follow them so strictly that you inhibit the discussion. In order to evoke the interviewee's ideas on the topic, avoid questions that promote only "yes" or "no" responses. Twelve to fifteen questions should allow enough time for you and the interviewee to get acquainted, discuss your topic, and pursue any helpful digressions in detail.

Conducting the Interview

Be on time to the interview, and come equipped with pencils or pens and a notebook (and a tape recorder if the interviewee has agreed to its use). Avoid taking notes or taping the first few questions and answers until your subject gets used to the situation.

Start the interview with a general inquiry about the person's background and interest in the interview topic. Then move on to the questions you have prepared. Maintain a polite, attentive manner while you listen and ask questions. Allow time for the interviewee to complete his or her responses. When clarification or additional information would be helpful, ask follow-up questions such as "Why do you feel the data are unreliable?" or "I don't know what a tokamak reactor is. Can you explain it to me, please?"

Interview Structures

Some researchers favor a *structured* interview that restricts responses to the interview questions and keeps the discussion closely focused. However, an *unstructured* approach, which allows the discussion to move with the interests of the interviewee, can often generate more useful material. Avoid getting bogged down in clearly irrelevant subjects, but do not worry too much if your interviewee brings up unexpected topics: Brief digressions about an exceptional incident or a personal triumph may yield rich new insights or information for your paper. If the discussion wanders too far afield, return to your prepared questions to bring things back into focus.

Quoting from the Interview

If you do not tape the interview, take careful notes throughout the session. Make a point of quoting authoritative, insightful, or fascinating comments word for word. Because they come from a live interview source, such remarks will add rich authority and interest to your final paper. At the completion of the interview, read aloud any direct quotations you have written down to check their accuracy with the interviewee.

Interview Length

Try to keep to the hour or so you had originally scheduled so the interviewee does not run out of time. That way, you will not have to schedule a second meeting in order to get all of your questions answered.

Before the interview ends, briefly read over or summarize all of your notes for the interviewee to hear and to suggest additions or changes, if

4. How do you approach the subject of racism in the novel?

Direct, open approach. Much discussion. "We try to get at Twain's message about racism and how he expresses it."

5. Do white and black students react differently to the work?

Yes— "Black students seem to resent the term because they view it as echoing the racial prejudice they alreay see in our society. White students grow into resenting the term."

FIGURE 5.2 Prepared questions and handwritten notes from a personal interview

necessary. Be sure to thank the person for the interview. Take the time later to send a follow-up note, again expressing your appreciation and indicating how helpful the interview was to your research paper.

Figure 5.2 contains an excerpt from Anne Kramer's interview with Professor Jeanne Corderman, who taught the American literature course on her campus. Anne used questions she had prepared and typed ahead of time to guide the interview. Notice that Anne recorded her own summaries and Professor Corderman's words as the interview took place.

Using Telephone or Mail Interviews

Your own time schedule, distance, or the interviewee's availability may make a telephone or mail interview more practical than meeting personally with someone. Because of the cost of telephoning and the limited discussion allowed by mail, both types of interviews require more planning than a personal conference might.

Telephone Interviews. A telephone interview is convenient, but it can also can be expensive. Another drawback is that it forfeits your opportunity to meet directly with the authority you have chosen to interview. Use your best telephone personality to encourage your source to enjoy the discussion enough to talk freely and to volunteer information. To avoid catching the interview subject at an inconvenient time, use the first telephone call to set up a time for the actual interview. Follow these suggestions for the telephone interview:

1. After introducing yourself again and reminding your source why you called, state how much time you think the interview will take and whether the call is local or long distance. This will prompt each of you to keep the discussion focused and to use the time productively.
2. Let your telephone interviewee know that you will be recording or taking notes during your discussion.
3. If you have not already done so, tell a little about yourself and your interest in the topic.
4. Briefly summarize your research and findings up to now.
5. Ask the interviewee to describe his or her background in or experience with the topic.
6. At this point, you will probably find that your interview questions enter naturally into the conversation. If not, this is a good time to begin asking them.
7. Keep track of your time on the telephone to avoid running up a huge bill or taking up too much of the person's time.
8. Thank the interviewee for talking with you, and ask if you may call again if you have questions about anything that was said.

People who take the time for an interview like to know the results. Once you have completed your paper, write or call to thank your interviewee again. If you can, explain how the information from the interview helped your research or was used in the paper itself.

Mail Interviews.   Interviews done by mail allow the interviewee to answer your questions more carefully and on his or her own time. In addition, written responses provide accurate notes for your paper and usually give you more details to work with. You can also use a mail interview to correspond with several persons at once, thus getting multiple replies to the same questions.

Of course, a drawback to mail interviews is that, like those done over the telephone, you lose the opportunity of meeting and talking directly with your source. In addition, people responding to a mail interview may not always do so quickly enough to meet a researcher's deadline. Rather than count on one particular source for an interview, contact more than a single person for a mail interview, or be prepared to go forward with your research should a response not arrive soon enough.

If you decide to use a mail interview in your research, follow these suggestions:

1. Write or call ahead to find out if the person is willing to respond to your inquiry.
2. If your source agrees to respond, prepare a list of questions to be answered in writing.
3. Keep the questions specific and their number to a minimum. Asking "What can you tell me about the recent decline in Alaska's grizzly

bear population?" is too broad: Your respondent will not know where to begin or end. Something like "How important has the recent increase in logging been to the decline of Alaska's grizzly bear population?" gives the question focus and shows you have done your research.

4. Avoid asking too many questions. You do not want to hand the interviewee a burdensome writing task, which may be refused or done poorly because of its size. Ten to twelve questions focused on the topic or research question itself will probably be enough.

5. In a cover letter sent with the questions, explain the purpose and scope of your research project, how extensive the answers should be, and when you need to have the responses returned. Include a stamped envelope with your address on it.

6. Once you have gotten the responses, promptly acknowledge their receipt with a thank-you letter to the interviewee. A brief follow-up note after the paper is finished can describe your use of the interview and, again, appreciation of your correspondent's help.

One overall suggestion should be emphasized separately: The interview source will respond more willingly if he or she sees that you are serious enough about your research to write with care. Make necessary revisions to a draft before writing and sending out a final version of any correspondence. Check a dictionary for help with spelling. Consult your college writing handbook for questions about grammar, style, or letter formats.

Documenting the Interview

For any type of interview, make a preliminary citation card ahead of time. If you make use of the interview in your paper, include it in the Works Cited list, following one of the appropriate forms outlined in Chapters 10 and 11. Shown in Figure 5.3 is a sample bibliography card for

---

Jean Cordermann.
Personal interview. Nov. 24, 1990

FIGURE 5.3 A bibliography card for a personal interview

a personal interview. Other than the identification of the type of interview conducted, information for a telephone or mail interview would be similar.

Surveys

If your research topic calls for characterizing the opinions, behavior, or conditions of people in your local area, you may want to conduct a survey. A *survey* can provide statistical data for statements like "When asked if they would flirt with a friend's date, nearly two-thirds of the 350 students surveyed answered 'yes.' " You could use a survey to learn the percentage of people in your city who are satisfied with their personal physician or to find out how many hours a week students on your campus study. Surveys are also useful when you need to identify trends or make comparisons among groups or individuals (see Figure 5.4).

Using Published Surveys

Use published surveys whenever possible. A survey of your own is best done to compare the characteristics of a local population with surveys done on a larger basis by others. For example, you may want to compare local attitudes about hunting with those identified by a national poll.

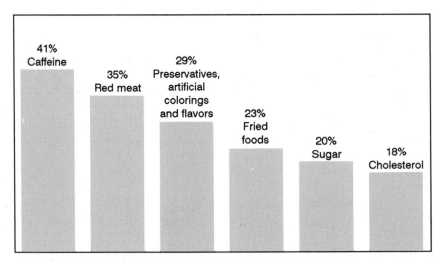

FIGURE 5.4 An illustration of survey results (showing percentage of 1,225 adults who say they are making *no* effort to reduce their intake of indicated foods and substances)

Source: Adapted by permission from *U.S News & World Report*, November 13, 1989. Basic data: The Gallup Organization.

Or you may want to compare the opinions of a certain group with the facts the rest of your research uncovers.

Before you set up your own survey, check the statistical resources in your library. It is very likely that others have already compiled the kind of information you want or can use. The following sources are only a few that provide statistical data, rankings, comparisons, and public opinion polls for nearly every subject and locality:

> *American Statistics Index.* Washington, DC: Congressional Informa-
> tion Service, 1973–date.
> *The Complete Book of American Surveys.* New York: New American
> Library, 1980.
> *The Gallup Report.* Princeton, NJ: Gallup Poll, 1965–date.
> *Statistical Reference Index.* Washington, DC: Congressional Informa-
> tion Service, 1980–date.

Conducting Your Own Survey

Once you decide to conduct a survey of your own, remember that no survey is ever entirely accurate. Those with even a fair degree of accuracy require training to design and conduct. Correctly interpreting their results is usually a job for experts. For the most part, expect to treat the results of any survey as *supplemental* to your other research. In most cases, it will be more descriptive than conclusive about, let's say, attitudes as to whether the United States should spend more money on fighting drugs through education.

Devising a Questionnaire. To get started, you will need to devise a questionnaire to poll people about the information you want to know. You will get best results from a questionnaire that is relatively short, easy to answer, and focused upon a single problem or related issues. The following suggestions will help you design a questionnaire that will be simple to administer and analyze for results.

1. *Define the questionnaire's purpose.* Begin by making a list of the specific information you want to gather. If you were researching the impact of the home video rental craze, you would make a list like this:

I want to know:

- Why people rent video movies
- How often people watch home videos
- What kinds of videos they watch
- How they feel about commercials in rental videos
- How they feel about X-rated videos
- How much they pay for video rentals

Having defined what you want to know, you are ready to write your questions.

2. *Decide upon a question-and-answer format.* Frame your questions and their answers to suit the information you seek. Several types of questions and responses are possible.

a. Open-ended questions allow respondents to answer in whatever way they choose. The variety of responses such questions allow, however, can make answers difficult to interpret and summarize. At the same time, responses to open-ended questions can also provide more details than answers to other types of questions, and they often reveal unexpected, useful information.

Examples of open-ended questions:

- Why do you think watching movies on video at home has become such a popular form of entertainment in this country?
- What do you think the government should do to prevent oil spill disasters from tanker ships in U.S. coastal waters?

Because open-ended questions require more time to answer orally or in writing, you will get better results using no more than five or six per survey.

b. Controlled-response or multiple-choice questions allow a respondent to choose from a limited number of answers.

Example of a controlled-response question:

- The government should tighten controls on tanker ships transporting oil within 10 miles of any U.S. coastline.

  _____ Agree   _____ Disagree   _____ Undecided

Be careful that your controlled-response questions include an adequate representation of answers. Had the question above allowed only "Agree" and "Disagree" responses, people who were undecided would not be able to answer truthfully or might not answer at all. Yes-or-no questions—like "Do you rent video movies more than three times a month?"—may suit one purpose or reveal some of the information you seek. Giving more choices, however, always provides data for you to make more comparisons among respondents. For example:

- How many times a month do you rent a video movie?

  _____ 1-3 times   _____ 4-7   _____ 8-12

  _____ More than 12   _____ Never

Unlike open-ended questions, controlled-response questions are convenient for respondents to answer quickly, and their results are easy to describe quantitatively.

3. *Word your questions carefully.* The way you ask a question will significantly influence the response it prompts. To prevent biasing answers, keep your language objective. Asking "Do you favor passing stronger laws to protect our valued coastal environments from careless destruction by oil tankers?" unfairly loads the question. Anyone answering "no" may be made to feel he or she does not value the environment and approves of careless destruction. Rephrase the question to be more objective: "Do you favor stronger regulation of oil tankerships operating in or near the U.S. coast?"

Also avoid asking questions that seem to implicate the respondent. People feel uneasy about admitting their shortcomings or being made to appear in a negative light just because of the way a question is worded. Asking "Do you ever cheat on examinations?" puts a respondent immediately on the defensive. Making the question more hypothetical, asking "Would you ever cheat on an examination?" will probably fulfill your research needs and get a more accurate response.

Carefully review the wording of each question in your questionnaire. Consider whether each question is free of bias and offers the respondent a chance to answer accurately. Before administering the questionnaire for research purposes, try it out on yourself and a few friends. Also ask your instructor to look it over and make suggestions. Once you are satisfied that the questionnaire will meet your needs, you are ready to administer it to a representative survey population.

Sampling a Population.   In research, *population* refers to all the members of a group. A *sample* is a representative portion of the population (see Figure 5.5). When researchers study a group of any kind, they make generalizations about it based upon sampling the population.

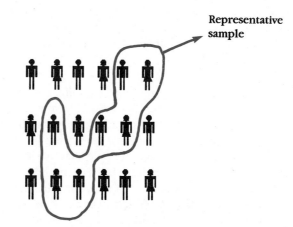

Representative
sample

Population:
Long-distance
telephone customers
in Fairview City,
May 1990 (by 100s)

FIGURE 5.5   The population and representative survey sample

Sampling is important to research because examining every individual person or item in the group is usually impractical or impossible.

Good survey results are derived from an accurate sampling of the research population. You will get the best results from sampling by following these guidelines for a survey:

1. *Define the survey population.* Who gets surveyed and who does not will obviously affect the results of your questionnaire. Begin by carefully defining the population you intend to poll.

If you intend to study the characteristics of inner-city youth gang members, how will you define the population?

- What constitutes a *gang?*
- What kind of gangs will you study?
- Which participants in gang activities are actually members?
- What age range is meant by *youth?*

These and similar kinds of questions show the need for analyzing the population and describing it accurately throughout your research.

2. *Use random sampling.* The more diverse your sample, the more accurate the results. Narrowing your sampling to one kind of group lessens its representativeness. If you want to know how many people think watching television dulls creativity, do not ask only male college students or only those who refuse to watch television at all. A good sampling would include males and females of all ages and educational levels, of varied interests and occupations, and of a range of television-viewing habits.

3. *Take an adequate sample.* Common sense may be your best guide to how large a sample you will need. Since it allows for more variety, a large sample is generally more accurate than a small one. The opinions of 15 people in a population of 1,000 has little practical value. On the other hand, a random sampling of 500 of those individuals represents a significant number for consideration. In general, large populations require proportionally larger samplings, and larger samplings carry more significance than smaller ones.

Polling the Population. Administer the questionnaire at varied times and places to the population you have identified. Choose a *polling* method that ensures getting a random sample and a good response rate. The results of a recent national telephone survey of married couples were widely challenged because people may have answered in ways to please their spouses (who may have been in the next room listening to the survey response). Another survey to find out what times people wanted college classes offered was criticized because it was done only during the day, while most people who might have preferred night classes were at work.

Almost every survey procedure has drawbacks, but you can safeguard results by consistently considering whether your method leaves out any particular group or overemphasizes the participation of another. If you survey customers at a video store to study their rental habits, include people of various ages and gender; who come in at all hours of the day, weekdays and weekends; who are married and single; and so on.

Analyzing the Findings. Having administered the survey questionnaire, analyze your findings. Compare the results with other research data you have collected and try to account for any major differences. Review your questions and sampling procedures to check for bias. If you have used the survey to gather statistical data, include information about various statiscal tests (validity, margin of error, and so forth) you have used to verify your results. As you incorporate the survey results in your research paper, include a description of the survey population and the procedures used to administer the questionnaire. Include a copy of the questionnaire in your paper's appendix.

Documenting the Survey

Make a working bibliography card as soon as you decide to conduct a survey. Since in most cases you will not be citing the name of a particular respondent to your survey or questionnaire, list yourself as the author. Figure 5.6 shows the bibliography card for a survey such as you might administer as part of your own research. No separate card is made for the survey questionnaire, since it is part of the survey itself.

NOTE: The information given here on surveys can produce excellent results for the kind of research topics and assignments usually undertaken by college undergraduates. If your research depends heavily upon extensive survey information that you collect yourself, consult a more thorough resource, such as Arlene Fink and Jacqueline Kosecoff's *How to Conduct Surveys: A Step by Step Guide* (Newbury Park, CA: Sage, 1985), available in paperback.

Randall, Steve.
Survey. Oct 11, 1990

FIGURE 5.6 A bibliography card for a self-administered survey

Speeches and Lectures

Listening to Community Speakers

One good way to gain more familiarity with your research topic is to listen firsthand to what others have to say about it. Watch local newspapers and community announcements for upcoming events related to your research topic. It is likely that such occasions will feature a presentation by a recognized authority or group of informed spokespersons. If you know of a particular organization that may be sponsoring a conference or public meeting, get its number from the telephone directory and call about future scheduled meetings and speakers.

Use your imagination about where to hear public speakers on your research topic. Remember that public speeches and addresses include everything from your minister's sermon about marriage to a city council member's harangue on taxes.

Attending Campus Lectures

Take advantage of the opportunities presented on your own or neighboring campuses. Consult the campus newspaper and college organizations about visiting scholars, faculty addresses, and club debates. Consult a course syllabus or ask a particular professor when he or she will be lecturing on your research topic. Remember that you may need permission to sit in on lectures for courses you are not enrolled in.

Documenting Speeches and Lectures

Using your research question as a focus, make a checklist of important points to listen for, and take careful notes on any lecture or public address. You may be able to use a tape recorder, or the presentation may be available on video tape later from the sponsoring organization. Check ahead of time about both possibilities.

In addition, be sure to record necessary information for a bibliography card about the event. Include the speaker's name and position and the date, place, and occasion of the presentation (see Figure 5.7). Follow the form shown in Chapters 10 and 11 if you later include the lecture or speech in the Works Cited list of your paper. If the information is not available when you hear a speaker, consult the sponsoring organization later for the documentation details you need.

NOTE: For historic speeches made by well-known individuals, consult the appropriate volume of *Speech Index* in your library. Speeches made as recently as last week are available from the *Public Affairs Information Service (PAIS) Bulletin* or the online database PAIS (see Chapter 2).

Rastall, Glen
"Is Clean Air Enough to Ask?"
Three Cities Conference
Denver, CO
6 Oct. 1990

FIGURE 5.7   A bibliography card for a speech

Radio and Television

Investigating the Past

Use radio and television programs to put your research in touch with people and events from the past, as well as the present. Many early radio and television productions, ranging from the nightly news to old radio dramas like *The Shadow* and popular television comedies like *I Love Lucy*, are commercially available today on tape or video.

One excellent source is the Vanderbilt Television News Archive, an outstanding video tape collection of major news broadcasts and documentaries since 1968. To find out what the Archive and other such sources hold, consult your library's copy of the *Television News Index and Abstracts* (Nashville, TN: Vanderbilt Television News Archives, Vanderbilt University, 1972–date. Monthly). You can use taped material to study historical events at the time they were first reported to the world over radio or television.

Researching Current News

Using current radio or television broadcasts as a basis for research requires both alertness and planning. Check the newspapers regularly or scan *TV Guide* to keep informed about weekly programs related to your research topic. In addition, a brief telephone inquiry to the local radio or television station may yield information about future programs to watch for. Even if you are unsure about a program's content ahead of time, make a checklist of the things you especially want to note for your research. The checklist will help you take notes and keep your attention focused.

Taping a Broadcast. A good deal of the time you will have little or no advance notice of a program airing. In these cases, listen or watch carefully, taking notes throughout the broadcast and checking them during commercial breaks. If you have the equipment, use a tape recorder to copy radio broadcasts or a video recording machine to tape a television program while you are tuned in and taking notes. You can review the tapes later, filling out your notes and taking down the bibliographic information for a preliminary citation card. If you cannot get all the information you need during a program, check its listing in the newspaper or, for television broadcasts, consult the recent weekly issues of *TV Guide* or *Facts on File* at the library.

Using Transcripts. Anytime you miss a radio or television show completely or need to study its contents more closely, you may be able to send for a *transcript,* a printed copy of the broadcast. Transcripts of news broadcasts, documentaries, interviews, talk shows, and even some entertainment programs are often available upon request from major radio and television stations. Issue-oriented television programs—like *60 Minutes, CBS Reports,* or those produced by Public Broadcasting Service (PBS)— offer program transcripts on a regular basis. Transcript availability is usually announced during a radio and television broadcast, but you can always call the station to make sure. For transcripts of past radio programs, consult your library's set of *Summary of World Broadcasts by the British Broadcasting Corp.* (microform, 1973–date) or for television, a source like *CBS News Television Broadcasts* (microform, 1963–date).

For information about publications and broadcasts for radio and television, as well as for a complete listing of radio stations and their addresses in the United States, the *Gale Directory of Publications and Broadcast Media* is a useful source. The full title and other bibligraphic information is given here to show the range of material it provides:

> *Gale Directory of Publications and Broadcast Media: An Annual Guide to Publications and Broadcasting Stations, Including Newspapers, Magazines, Journals, Radio Stations, Television Stations, and Cable Systems.* 2 vols. Detroit: Gale, 1990.

Documenting Radio and Television Programs

Make out a preliminary citation card for any radio or television program you intend to include in your research. Figures 5.8 and 5.9 show the information to include for each kind of source. If you include a radio or television program in your paper's list of Works Cited, follow the forms suggested in Chapters 10 and 11.

---

*"California and the State of U.S. Education." With
John Jameson.
NBC Radio. KNBC, Los Angeles
7 May 1991*

FIGURE 5.8 A bibliography card for a radio program

---

*"Where Is the Rest of the Universe?"
Prod. Peter R. Baker
Narr. Richard Chamberlain
PBS. KCET Los Angeles
15 April 1990*

FIGURE 5.9 A bibliography card for a television program

Public Print Sources

Printed information is everywhere in our society. Pamphlets, circulars, government documents, newsletters, posters, and advertisements tell us almost more than we want to know about our world. Though you will need to weigh the authority and objectivity of any such printed sources, you should not overlook the current information about people, events, or products they can provide for research.

Finding Materials

The Vertical File. The vertical file collection of your campus or community library is a good place to start finding such materials as pamphlets (see Chapter 2), or you may collect a variety of public print items by visiting offices, laboratories, factories, zoos, museums, or other locations related to your research topic (see "Observing Onsite," earlier in this chapter).

Public print items not found in a library or by directly visiting a source may be available by mail. Your library's copy of the *Vertical File Index: A Subject Guide to Selected Pamphlet Material* (1935–date) will provide information about what products exist and how to order directly from the publishers. Though hardly able to list every pamphlet, poster, or brochure distributed, the *Vertical File Index* provides a comprehensive and up-to-date list of such materials. Publishers' addresses are included, as well as each item's cost, so you can send away for anything you want to use for your research.

If you decide to order something from the *Vertical File Index,* do so promptly. Pamphlets and similar materials are not permanently stocked. Also, your order may take several weeks to arrive.

U.S. Government Publications.   As the nation's largest publisher, the United States government yearly produces thousands of publications: documents, brochures, pamphlets, posters, guidebooks, directories, photographs, and newsletters. The various branches of government annually publish current information on thousands of subjects, including cities, people, roads, lakes, diseases, housing, agriculture, education, technology, employment, and wildlife.

Some 1,400 academic, law, and public libraries across the nation are depositories for most documents printed by the United States government. In addition, nearly every state also has at least one such library designated as a Regional Depository Library to receive and store *all* publications distributed by the Government Printing Office (GPO). Any librarian can tell you which libraries near you receive government documents and which may be Regional Depositories, or you can consult a helpful guide to information sources, such Matthew Lesko's *Information U.S.A.* (New York: Viking-Penguin, 1986).

To find out about published government pamphlets and related materials, consult the *Monthly Catalog of United States Publications* (1895–date) or the *Public Affairs Information Service (PAIS) Bulletin* (1915–date) at a library or online through a computer database like DIALOG (see Chapter 2). If the material you want is not at your library, you can usually get it through interlibrary loan.

Documenting Public Print Sources

Make out a bibliography card for any public print sources you intend to use in your research (see Figure 5.10). If you include an item in your paper, list it in the Works Cited section.

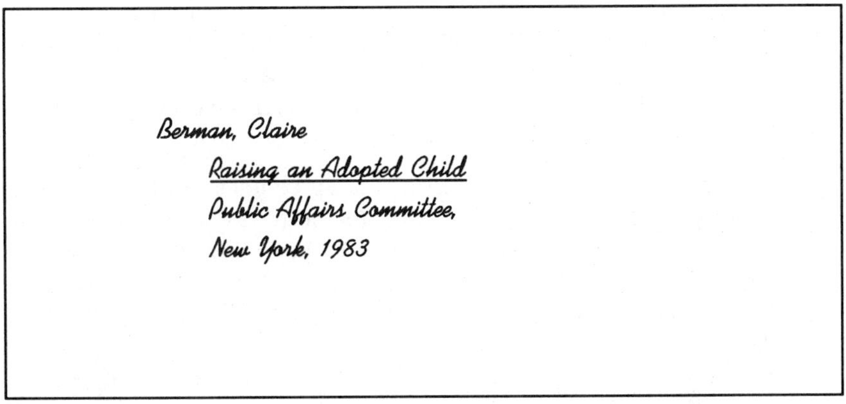

Berman, Claire
    Raising an Adopted Child
    Public Affairs Committee,
    New York, 1983

FIGURE 5.10   A bibliography card for a pamphlet on raising an adopted child

WORKING WITH OTHERS

Educational research shows that some of the most effective learning takes place among a community of learners. Take advantage of that fact: Let your friends and classmates know when you intend to investigate sources beyond the campus library. More than likley, you will find that they can share in your efforts or at least increase your enthusiasm with their own fresh insights and enjoyment of the topic. If you do team up with a classmate to do research beyond the campus or community library, consider the following suggestions ahead of time.

- Before visiting a research location with someone else, decide about sharing transportation, how long you will stay, and roughly what each of you hopes to accomplish.

- Share the responsibilty of finding out about local private libraries, businesses, hospitals, or other sites that may be of value to you and others. Make a list of such places, and divide the work of telephoning or visiting in person to get information needed before deciding on a site visit together.

- Make checklists of the specific activities each of you expects to accomplish for any onsite visit. Discuss these lists together, checking for any omissions and ensuring that your plans do not conflict.

- If your topics overlap in any way, you may be able to work together on an interview or in conducting your own survey. (If your topics do not overlap, it may still be possible to poll people about more than one issue with a single survey instrument.) Work together on setting up and conducting the interview or survey. Formulate questions and analyze results together to make sure that each of you gets the information you need.

- Attend public presentations together or agree ahead of time that one of you will go and take careful notes for both. (Be sure your instructor allows you to use another's notes as part of your own research, however.) You can do the same with radio and televison programs by deciding ahead of time who can most conveniently listen to or record a particular broadcast. Prepare a checklist and take good notes for any of these kinds of activities, especially if the notes will be used by another.

- You and your collaborator may find it convenient to collect pamphlets or other material for each other onsite or to order certain material together from the *Vertical File Index*. Talk about your individual needs to see what kinds of material you can work toward acquiring together.

CHAPTER SIX

Reading and Recording Information

An accurate understanding and interpretation of sources is integral to the value of your research paper's content. Conduct your research to make the most efficient use of your own time and the resources available. Careful reading, accurate notetaking, and thoughtful evaluation as you examine a source will ensure good results.

Planning Your Reading

Avoid putting the time and thinking about your topic at the mercy of haphazard reading. Once you have established a working bibliography, use the work's title, publication information, author's name, or the source's length to estimate its place in your research needs. Naturally, you cannot always know in advance what a source contains, but planning your reading will make the best use of sources and time.

The following suggestions will help you plan an efficient use of reading time:

1. Review the working bibliography to consult general sources first: magazine articles, histories, and other broad discussions. This will allow you to organize your research of available materials.

2. When selecting sources to read, consider their intended audience, as well as your own purposes. Popular magazines will be your best resources when you need general ideas, current opinions, or recent developments; turn to more scholarly journals and books for detailed studies and recognized authorities on the topic.

3. Once familiar with a topic through reading general sources, move next to those sources that treat the topic specifically or in detail. It is best to work in such sources as soon as you can do so comfortably. This way, you avoid having to read through general ideas that are repeated throughout several different sources.

4. Plan your reading to examine no more than one or two related aspects at a time. This will organize notetaking and focus your thinking on the material. For example, Anne Kramer made a point to read first a journal article and then a book that specifically addressed Mark Twain's use of regional dialects. Take care to keep your bibliography and your reading balanced. Consulting different viewpoints will enhance your understanding of the topic and allow for comparing opinions as you read.

5. Finally, you can waste a lot of valuable time and energy running back and forth from the periodical room to the book stacks or from one campus library to another. When possible, organize your reading activities around types of sources and their locations. This will prevent your omitting a potentially valuable source because you don't have time to go back for it.

Types of Reading

Skimming

Skimming is a way of reading quickly to find out what is said. Rather than read everything in a selection, look for key words, main ideas, subheadings, illustrations, or other features related to your research question. The goal in skimming a source is not to read it thoroughly. Rather, find out if it has the kind of information you seek, and if it does, determine what to read more closely.

Skimming Books.   Before spending time on a close reading, first skim a book to evaluate its possible usefulness. Use the book's major components to determine its contents and scope.

1. *Start with the title.*   A main title alone may be too general to indicate a book's subject, or it may not accurately reflect the book's focus. Main titles such as *Lucy's Child* or *Mark Twain,* for example, give no hint of the books' respective contents. The full titles of these works, however, more completely suggest their subjects:

> *Lucy's Child: The Discovery of a Human Ancestor*
> *Mark Twain: The California Experience*

Attention to a complete title can tell you if a particular book is something you want to examine more closely, put off reading until later, or ignore altogether.

2. *Consult the table of contents.* Here, you will find a list of chapters included in the book and the pages on which they begin. A quick examination of the table of the contents and of any promising chapters will tell you whether to return to the book later for more detailed study.

Let's say, for example, that you were interested in researching the topic of animal intelligence. A general bibliographic source, such as the *Essay and General Literature Index,* might refer you to a work titled *Through a Window,* anthropologist Jane Goodall's account of her studies of chimpanzees in the Gombe region of East Africa. The table of contents

Contents

FIGURE 6.1 A table of contents listing a book's chapters

Source: From Jane Goodall, *Through a Window: My Thirty Years with the Chimpanzees of Gombe,* p. vii. Copyright (c) 1990 by Soko Publications Limited. Reprinted by permission of Houghton-Mifflin Company. All rights reserved.

(see Figure 6.1) for Goodall's book lists at least one especially relevant chapter, "The Mind of the Chimpanzee." Skim this chapter first to assess its usefulness, and then examine others whose titles also suggest they might address your topic or research question. If your skimming indicates any chapters merit further study, make out a bibliography card for the book so you can return to it later.

3. *Search the index.* In case small segments of information on your topic also appear in other places than the chapters you consult, turn next to the index located at the back of the book. Most nonfiction books include an index, an alphabetical list of the topics, subtopics, ideas, places, and names mentioned in the book. The page numbers after each entry tell where to find the item listed. In addition to looking for a topic by name in the index, also search for it under a major term. In Jane Goodall's book on chimpanzees, for example, the index lists "mind, brain, intelligence, 12–23, 206–9" under the term "chimpanzees."

Sometimes you need to look for a topic under a synonym or closely related term. If you found no entries in a book's index under "alcoholism," let's say, you should next look under related terms, such as "substance abuse," "addiction," "drinking," or "encounter group."

In addition to skimming a book's table of contents and index, also look for other useful features:

- The *preface* or *introduction* to a book may give an overview of the subject or suggest that particular book's approach to it.
- An *appendix* (plural *appendices*) provides additional information on topics discussed in the book and may include maps, graphs, charts, or other helpful material.
- A *glossary* lists special terms and their definitions as they relate to the book's subject.
- A book's *bibliography* may guide you to other books or resources to use in your research.

If you do not read closely and take notes from a book when you first skim it, use the working bibliography card to record the author and title, as well as a brief note on what you found and the relevant page numbers. Return to the book later when you know more about what you need from it.

Skimming Periodical Articles.   You can usually skim articles in magazines, journals, and newspapers more quickly than books. Titles of periodical articles are usually more specific than book titles, and they often include subheadings to label and organize content for the reader. Articles in most scholarly science journals, such as *Journal of Marine Research* and *Journal of Applied Psychology,* are organized according to guidelines recommended by the American Psychological Association (APA). Articles in APA form are often divided into major sections boldly labeled as Abstract, Introduction, Method, Results, Discussion, and References. Use these headings to skim such journal articles for the information you seek, as well as to organize and label any notes.

To skim any periodical article, scan it quickly, paying attention to features such as bold-faced headings, subsections, and illustrations. Skim the first sentence of each paragraph or subsection to identify its main idea. You may want to read the last paragraph or two closely for the author's conclusions. If you think the article is worth reading more thoroughly later, make a note on the back of the bibliography card to review it.

Close Reading

Close reading requires careful attention to all the words and sentences in a selection to understand its full meaning. After you have skimmed a source and decided to read all or part of it closely, you read carefully to comprehend ideas and to record information. While these two purposes can undoubtedly overlap, awareness of them as separate activities will help focus your notetaking and organize your thinking as you read.

Reading for Meaning. Reading to comprehend meaning involves recognizing main ideas, as well as making inferences about what you read. As you read any material, pay attention to key ideas and statements that support an overall point.

The Thesis or Summary Statement. In most articles or chapters in books, you will recognize a thesis or summary statement that explains the author's major point. (Review the discussion of thesis statement in Chapter 3.) The main point usually appears near the beginning of a discussion but not necessarily. Wherever it occurs, the main point dominates the text. All the other ideas, sentences, paragraphs, and examples relate to it. Make a habit of identifying the main point of any material you read. As you read and take notes, consciously relate the main point to the other ideas in the text.

Topic Sentences. The topic sentence contains the paragraph's major idea, the concept that all other elements in the paragraph support or explain. Supporting ideas for a thesis may occur as the topic sentence stated at the beginning, middle, or end of a paragraph. In the following paragraph, the topic sentence occurs in the first sentence. Notice how all other sentences help to build upon the idea stated in the topic sentence:

Topic sentence **Examples support** **the topic sentence** **Transition word** **signals *additional*** **details**	Regular cocaine users put up with many unpleasant drug effects. Restlessness, irritability and apprehension are common. Users tend to become suspicious and even display paranoid symptoms—frequently changing locks and phone numbers, doubting friends and showing inappropriate anger or jealousy. All this derives from cocaine's impact on the sympathetic nervous system—the network that controls "flight or fight" responses to fright. In addition, even at fairly low doses cocaine may cause tremors, cold sweats, and grinding of teeth. At higher doses, vomiting and nausea may result, along with muscle pains, a disoriented feeling and dizziness—followed, in some cases, by life-threatening seizures. —Ira Mothner and Alan Weitz, *How to Get Off Drugs: Everything You Should Know to Help Someone You Love Get Off—and Stay Off—Drugs, Including When to Seek Help and Where to Find It* (New York: Simon and Shuster, 1984) 75.

When reading this paragraph for ideas, note particularly the main idea stated as the topic sentence. Use the main idea to focus your attention on the examples and details that develop the topic sentence further.

Implied Topic Sentences.   Sometimes the main idea in a paragraph is implied rather than stated directly. In these cases, the author feels that the point of the paragraph is obvious, and it is up to the reader to understand the central meaning. This paragraph by Annie Dillard, for example, avoids stating in an outright topic sentence that a jungle is crowded with unusual and somewhat threatening varieties of life:

> Unseen in the jungle, but present, are tapirs, jaguars, many species of snake and lizard, ocelots, armadillos, marmosets, howler monkeys, toucans and macaws and a hundred other birds, deer, bats, peccaries, capybaras, agoutis, and sloths. Also present in this jungle, but variously distant, are Texaco derricks and pipelines, and some ofthe wildest Indians in the world, blowgun-using Indians, who killed missionaries in 1956 and ate them.
> —Annie Dillard, "In the Jungle," *Teaching a Stone to Talk: Expeditions and Encounters* (New York: Perennial-Harper, 1988) 57.

You should read such paragraphs as you would any other, paying attention to how the ideas and information fit together to present an overall picture or main idea. When reading paragraphs with implied main ideas, always sum up the main point in your own words, and make it a part of your notes.

Taking Effective Notes

You will need to take good written notes on all the information collected during your research. The notes will help to organize your thinking about what you investigate, as well as provide general ideas, quotations from authorities, and specific data when you write the paper. Since you cannot remember everything you discover about a topic, develop and follow a consistent system of notetaking that will help you select, organize, and record information.

What to Take Notes About

Your research notes will be more useful if you recognize in advance what to record from your reading. Certain information needs to be written down each time you take any kind of notes about a source:

1. The title and author of the source. (You will also need to include the publisher's name, as well as the place and date of publication, if you have not made a working bibliography card for each source consulted during your research.)
2. The page number(s) from which the material is taken.
3. The content you want to record.

Note Format

Arrange the note information any way that is convenient and makes for easy reference. Consistency in the way you record page numbers, identify direct quotations, or add your own commentary is essential for accurate interpretation of the notes later.

Figure 6.2 shows a typical arrangement of essential note material on one of Anne Kramer's notecards. Anne labeled the card with the heading "*HF* in the Classroom" and used it for notes on an article titled "Scholars and *Huck Finn:* A New Look." Notice that only the source's author, identified by a first initial and last name, is needed on the notecard. Anne had previously recorded the author's complete name, the full title of the source, and all relevant publishing information on a separate bibliography

HJ in the Classroom

B. Chambers —

Chaired a conference on teaching HJ.

quote   *"A number of conference participants later said they had experienced, in their own education, the lack of strategies to teach about Twain's stereotypic portray of Black people." (2)*

Yet those same instructors said they continued to teach the novel because it "had so much going for it" (2) from a literary point of view.

mine   *They all admit that teaching the novel is a problem — but it's too important to leave out.*

FIGURE 6.2 A sample notecard with marginal notations ("quote" and "mine")

card. In order to make her notes clearly understandable later, Anne punctuated quoted material clearly and indicated her own analysis with the notation "mine" in the margin. She used parentheses to separate and identify page numbers.

Note Content

Using your research question as a guide, you will find that a good deal of your notetaking will be based on evolving intuition: As a preliminary thesis or response to the research question begins to form from your reading, you will start to recognize what things to record in your notes. Taking more notes, you will also begin to recognize how the pieces of collected information fit together to support one or more major ideas that may form an answer to the research question or the basis of a preliminary thesis for the paper. The further you progress in your research, the more you will recognize with increasing certainty what material to record.

Before starting research, review the sample papers in Chapter 9 and Appendix A. Examine them to acquaint yourself with the kinds of ideas and information that make up a research paper. Naturally, you will not know all the information needed from your research sources until you begin writing the paper; however, your increasing sense of what you will eventually say about the topic should help identify material for notes. Depending upon your topic and your own knowledge of the subject, the contents of the notes will include a wide variety of information.

1. Take notes to record background information that you need to understand the research topic better. If you are investigating welfare fraud, you may first need to learn about the extent of the problem, existing laws, facts about the history of state assistance programs, or the legal definitions of terms. Eventually, your reading and notes on such material will supply the broad understanding necessary to research and write effectively on the topic. Expect the background notes on any subject to decrease as you learn more about it and begin focusing on supporting a preliminary thesis.

2. Take notes to summarize general ideas supporting your preliminary thesis statement. Your preliminary thesis will probably shift in focus or change completely as you pursue your research. Groups of major ideas will emerge from your reading, changing your thinking or the emphasis of the preliminary thesis.

You will find it easier to organize your notes on such ideas by listing them under subtopic headings. As Anne Kramer did her reading research on *Adventures of Huckleberry Finn,* for instance, she recorded her notes under headings such as Historical Reactions, Twain's Comments, Black Critics' Views, and Value of *HF.* As Anne gathered additional ideas about her topic, she added more headings, discontinued a few, and eventually merged others under new headings. This process gave Anne a way to organize her notes and to begin to identify categories of ideas she could plan to include in her paper (see Figure 6.3).

3. Take notes on explanatory information such as histories, definitions of terms, plot summaries, biographical data, or other material that you may need to provide for the paper's reader. For a paper about former Soviet President Mikhail Gorbachev, you may need notes about the form of the Soviet government, background on the 1991 coup attempt, or the other highlights of Gorbachev's political career. A paper on cocaine use would need notes for defining terms such as *crack* and *freebasing.* The sample paper by student Ron Bonneville includes a brief overview of U.S. trade deficits to inform readers of conditions that enable the Japanese to hold so much real estate and other investments in the United States.

4. Take notes to record quotations, examples, or anecdotes that will illustrate or support your ideas in the paper. Quoting an eloquently stated opinion or the words of a recognized expert lends interest as well as authority to your own discussion (see "Using Quotation," Chapter 8). You can use specific examples from an interview with an expert on computer

viruses. A paper on problems faced by new U.S. immigrants might include an anecdote about someone's first attempt to register for school or to apply for a job.

5. Take notes on little known facts or questionable and controversial ideas about your topic. Even if accurate, facts and opinions that are not commonly known or may seem questionable to your paper's reader need to be carefully recorded and supported by documentation. Selected research may suggest people can actually lose weight by *thinking* themselves thin, but your reader may not accept this assertion or may believe you have misunderstood the facts. To prevent losing credibility, take good notes to describe the research fully and indicate an authoritative source for it in your paper. (See Chapters 9–11 on citing such sources.)

6. Take notes to record statistical figures, such as percentages, weights, amounts of money, ratios, and dates that are not commonly known, as well as the sources in which you found them. Your readers may need to know that Americans throw away 160 million tons of trash each year or that 55% of American women in 1987 worked outside the home. Figures like these can add precision to your paper's discussion, as well as convincingly support and illustrate your ideas. Take notes on all such figures related to your research question. The frequency with which you come across such statistics in your research will determine whether or not they are commonly known or need to be documented. (See Chapter 9 about documenting figures.)

The notes from material such as that mentioned here will shape your thinking during the research stage. Expect to take more notes than you will actually need, and do not hesitate to write down anything you think may be of importance later. Eventually, you will combine the material from your notes with your own ideas, as well as those of others you cite in the research paper.

Figure 6.3 shows Anne Kramer's notecards for a discussion of Jim, the slave who escapes with Huckleberry Finn down the Mississippi. Notice how Anne used her notes on the original source material to illustrate and support a paragraph's main idea in her paper:

Original from source	It is significant that although the Negro, Jim, has some human dignity, essentially he fulfills all the requirements of the prevailing stereotype. He is ignorant and superstitious and his loyalty to Huck is one more instance the of childhood dream common to American writing. Above all he violates our conception of adult maleness. —Charles H. Nichols, "Color, Conscience, and Crucifixion: A Study of Racial Attitudes in American Literature and Criticism," *Jahrbuck für Amerikastudien* 6 (1961): 37–47.

Characterization of Jim

C. Nichols — "Color"

Jim and Huck have a close friendship, but Jim still "fulfills all the requirements of the prevailing stereotype." (41)

Jim is "ignorant and superstitious" (41).
His loyalty is part of American tradition in literature.

"Above all he violates our conception of adult maleness." (41)

Cites Leslie Fiedler, white critic, who agrees.

FIGURE 6.3 A notecard on the characterization of Jim

Notes as used in the paper

Despite our final impression of his character, however, most black critics agree that Jim is demeaned by his representation as the stereotypical "good nigger." Jim may indeed be shown to possess a noble character, but Twain also portrays him as an ignorant and superstitious black man "who violates all our conceptions of adult maleness" (Nichols, "Color" 41). Whatever nobility Jim has is not merely contrasted with his treatment by whites.

Where to Record Notes

While everyone has his or her own method for taking notes, some are more useful for preparing a research paper than others. Again, *consistency* is the key to any successful notetaking. Decide early on a system that you will follow. A regular routine for storing notes and registering information will keep them from getting lost and prevent omissions that may cause extra work later.

Record your notes in a legible and accurate fashion. It is easy to become confused later about note contents. Be consistent about listing or marking bibliographic data, source summaries, quotations, page numbers, and your own comments. (See Chapter 8 on how to punctuate quotations and quote accurately.) Mark your notes in a way that clearly separates and identifies each. Notations such as "Mine," "quote," "summary," and so forth can keep note content clearly identified (see Figure 6.2).

Decide how or on what you want to store your notes. There are plenty of options. Notecards, a notebook, photocopies, or a computer are common preferences. You will probably vary your method from time to time to suit certain kinds of information, but using one medium throughout your research is most efficient. In general, the best method is one that consistently fits your work habits and meets the needs of your research materials.

Notecards.   Keeping your notes on cards offers the greatest flexibility and convenience. Notecards can be arranged or shuffled to suit any order you need, and you can easily add or take out cards as your research progresses. Use a card large enough to record plenty of information. Large 5" x 8" cards provide ample space for recording notes, commentary, and bibliographic information. Use a separate card for each source. Include subtopic headings to categorize your notes (see Figures 6.2 and 6.3) and to group cards in the same categories later. Keep the cards bound with a rubber band, and carry them with you when doing research.

A Research Notebook.   For some topics, especially those requiring extensive notes or columns of figures, recording all your research ideas in a single notebook is also a good idea. Notebook pages allow plenty of room for adding your own extensive commentary or other remarks to your notes, and a bound notebook keeps all your work together for easy use. If you have been keeping a research notebook, use a major part of it to record reading notes. This will make other research materials (research schedule, observations, survey questions, etc.) more accessible for review when working with your notes or their sources. You can cut and paste various sections of the notebook pages together for easy reference when you start to write your paper.

Photocopies.   Photocopied materials are not notes but the basis for notes. Nonetheless, considerations of length, complexity, availability, or your need for precise data may make it necessary to photocopy portions of printed research sources. Photocopying is a valuable aid to any researcher, though overreliance on it can become expensive and doubly time consuming: You will still have to reread the contents of photocopied materials and make notes on them before writing your paper.

Figure 6.4 shows the kind of notes Ron Bonneville made on a photocopy of material about Japanese financial power in the United States. Ron decided to photocopy the page rather than record notes from it because of the many statistics it included and his uncertainty about which ones he might want later for his paper. In this way, Ron used the photocopied material to supplement his notetaking, not replace it.

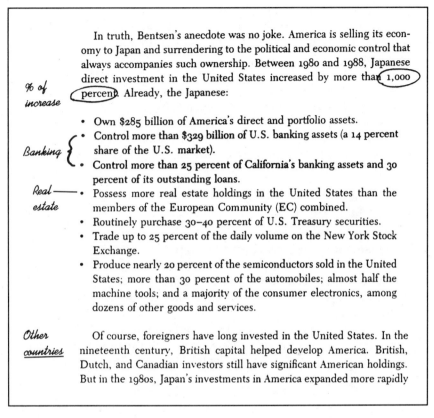

In truth, Bentsen's anecdote was no joke. America is selling its economy to Japan and surrendering to the political and economic control that always accompanies such ownership. Between 1980 and 1988, Japanese direct investment in the United States increased by more than 1,000 percent. Already, the Japanese:

% of increase

- Own $285 billion of America's direct and portfolio assets.
- Control more than $329 billion of U.S. banking assets (a 14 percent share of the U.S. market).
- Control more than 25 percent of California's banking assets and 30 percent of its outstanding loans.

Banking

Real estate

- Possess more real estate holdings in the United States than the members of the European Community (EC) combined.
- Routinely purchase 30–40 percent of U.S. Treasury securities.
- Trade up to 25 percent of the daily volume on the New York Stock Exchange.
- Produce nearly 20 percent of the semiconductors sold in the United States; more than 30 percent of the automobiles; almost half the machine tools; and a majority of the consumer electronics, among dozens of other goods and services.

Other countries

Of course, foreigners have long invested in the United States. In the nineteenth century, British capital helped develop America. British, Dutch, and Canadian investors still have significant American holdings. But in the 1980s, Japan's investments in America expanded more rapidly

FIGURE 6.4 A photocopy with marginal notes

Source: Excerpt from *Agents of Influence* by Pat Choate. Copyright (c) 1990 by Pat Choate. Reprinted by permission of Alfred A. Knopf, Inc.

On Computer. Computers can make storing and using research notes both easier and more difficult. Storing research notes on a computer allows you to revise them with follow-up commentary, to reorganize them according to developing subtopics, and to merge them once you get to the writing stage. A separate file for sources listed in the working bibliography is also a good idea: You can update and alphabetize the list as you need, adding it to the paper when you have finished writing the text. If your computer software program has outlining features, you can use the topic headings from notecards to create a working outline.

Unless you have regular access to a computer and are in the habit of working consistently with one for your academic needs, however, you may need to use an additional method of notetaking, as well. Remember that you will not always have a computer available wherever you do research, and you will regularly have to transcribe handwritten notes and other collected data into the computer almost daily. Unless your computer program does it for you, you will also need to make back-up copies of all your material on a regular basis to prevent loss due to a machine or program malfunction.

Too many methods of storing information results in misplacing notes and wasting time trying to consolidate results. For all your notetaking, avoid using loose sheets of paper, more than one notebook, or too great a mixture of ways to store your research notes. Choose a means of storing notes that prevents loss while still allowing flexibility, organization, and ease of use.

Types of Notes

Your notes are a literal record of what you learn about the research topic. In addition to recording your findings, taking notes prompts you to read sources critically. In the act of reading and taking notes, you organize and reinterpret information for yourself, thereby understanding it better. (A drawback to photocopying materials is that it postpones this important critical process.)

Different research sources and your individual responses to them will require varying kinds of notes. Though books and periodicals will supply the majority of your note content, notetaking will also be important for recording what you learn from other kinds of sources: Onsite observations; pamphlets and other literature; responses to interview questions; films, radio, and television broadcasts; and public speeches or lectures will also require good written notes. While your way of recording information will vary with each kind of source, the following methods are basic to all notetaking:

- Summary
- Paraphrase
- Direct quotation
- Combination notes

As this lists suggests, the majority of your notes will represent a condensation of information. You should know the differences among these major kinds of notes and how to use them effectively in your research, including giving proper acknowledgment to your sources.

Summary. Summary reduces what is originally said in a source by restating it more briefly in your own words. You summarize original material by eliminating unimportant ideas and condensing essential ones to a single statement or two. Since your goal is to reduce without distorting meaning, you must understand the original well before attempting to summarize it.

How much you summarize from a source depends upon your purpose. You may summarize large portions of a work, such as the action of a novel, the development of a scientific theory, or the content of a journal article. To summarize large amounts of content, read the whole piece closely, at least twice. Take notes as you read, looking for main ideas or subdivisions of the content (see "Close Reading," earlier in this chapter). Then combine your notes by reducing their content into a few sentences that summarize the whole. Read your summary carefully several times. Add or delete content until you have condensed the original without distorting or leaving out important parts.

In summarizing any entire work or large portions of it, your aim is to reduce the whole piece by including only the main ideas. Smaller portions of a work are summarized in much the same way, though you can be more selective about what you summarize. In most research notetaking, you need to condense and record only the information most relevant to your topic, research question, or thesis. This could mean summarizing only a few sentences or a single paragraph if that is all the information relevant to your research.

Ron Bonneville used such selective notetaking to summarize part of a *Newsweek* magazine article ("18 Holes, Low $$ Price," 7 Dec. 1990: 45) about Japanese acquisition of American golf courses. Since most of the article discussed information he already knew, Ron used only the following paragraph from the article to supplement his research:

> The Japanese have a passion for American golf courses. They love to play them—and buy them. Japan has 12 million golfers, and the price and difficulty of getting a tee time on their crowded courses has driven hundreds of thousands to U.S. resorts in recent years. Inevitably, familiarity breeds investment. In September, Minoru Isutani, a confessed golf nut, paid $800 million for Pebble Beach, one of the two most admired courses in the United States. Two years earlier, Sports Shinko paid $250 million to add the exquisite La Costa Resort & Spa near San Diego to the company's string of golf clubs in Japan. Riviera Country Club, the Los Angeles course Ben Hogan made famous, went for $108 million.
> —"18 Holes, Low $$ Price," *Newsweek* 7 Dec. 1990:45.

Ron recorded his summary of this paragraph on a notecard with the heading "Japanese Ownership—Golf Courses." Notice that the summary (which follows) omits irrelevant information from the paragraph, including the names of Japanese buyers and the approximate dates when the golf courses were purchased:

> 12 million golfers--hard to get a tee in Japan.
> Japanese are buying up America's golf courses, includ-
> ing Pebble Beach (for $800 million) and La Costa Sport
> & Spa (for $250 million). Even the reknown Riviera
> Country Club, where golf legend Ben Hogan played, has
> been taken over (for $108 million) ("18 Holes").

Ron saved time and kept his notes more readable by selectively recording only the information he needed from the article and the paragraph. His summary was effective enough, in fact, for him to use in the final version of his research paper (see Appendix A).

While the purpose of a summary is to condense an original, it should not be so abbreviated as to lose its usefulness later. Ron's summary also included a subheading (U.S. Ownership Abroad) as well as the title and page number from the original. Other data he would need for recording the source in his paper was listed on a separate bibliography card (see Chapter 4). Like Ron, you may occasionally want to summarize information with a fragmentary phrase—"12 million golfers. Hard to get a tee in Japan"—or your own shorthand way of reducing language. It is best, however, to write your summary in complete sentences. This helps you to grasp the content better and keep notes understandable.

Paraphrase. Good paraphrase clarifies a source's content by recasting it into your own words. Whereas a summary seeks to condense or eliminate length, paraphrase restates the original almost line by line. The result is that a paraphrase is usually about the same length as the original, but the words are your own. Remember that proper citation of the source must always accompany any paraphrase.

Paraphrase whenever the language or content of the original cannot be adequately summarized. This often happens with technical and scientific material, where the detailed content or language may be unsuitable for condensing to notes or for use in your paper. At other times, you may paraphrase by combining original details and language with your own wording in order to shorten the content. In general, use paraphrase whenever doing so will make your notes more useful and the information clearer to your paper's reader.

The following excerpt demonstrates material suitable for paraphrase. The example is from an article published in *TESOL Quarterly,* a journal written for linguists and (as the title acronym indicates) "Teachers of English to Speakers of Other Languages" (TESOL). The paragraph summarizes research on the relationship between notetaking and learning by students who are native and nonnative speakers of English.

There appears, in other words, to be a need to rehearse information noted down rather than just to take notes on information imparted via lecture format. Incorporating a review-of-notes condition into the present design might have yielded quite different results and might have tested the delayed effect, not just the immediate effect, of the encoding hypothesis. In sum, results of the present study suggest that note taking without opportunity for review of notes is of questionable utility for either American or international lecture attendees.

—Patricia Dunkel, Shitala Mishra, and David Berliner, "Effects of Note Taking, Memory, and Language Proficiency on Lecture Learning for Native and Nonnative Speakers of English," *TESOL Quarterly* 23 (1989): 547.

The language and content in this excerpt may be appropriate for the author's intentions and the journal's audience. For the purposes of note-taking, however, and for better understanding by your paper's reader, the passage should be paraphrased.

A good paraphrase effectively recasts original language for better clarity and readability. Poor paraphrase simply changes the words of the original or mixes the original with rephrased material. Compare the following paraphrase with the original paragraph above:

There seems, then, to be a necessity for rehearsing note content instead of just taking notes on lecture information. Including a note review in the current plan may have given different results and tested not only the immediate effect but also the delayed effect of the encoding hypothesis. In summary, the findings of this study suggest that taking notes without the chance to review them has questionable usefulness for American or foreign lecture students ("Effects of Note Taking" 547).

This is a poor paraphrase. It merely substitutes new words for the language of the original. Good paraphrase, on the other hand, translates the *meaning* of the original by effectively recasting its language into clearer form.

Students need to review lecture notes rather than simply write down information presented in lecture. If this research study had included the practice of reviewing notes, the delayed as well as the immediate effect of notetaking on learning might have been tested.

```
Overall, however, it seems that notetaking alone,
without the practice of reviewing notes, may have
little value for any lecture student, whether native or
nonnative speaking ("Effects of Note Taking" 547).
```

Because you are adding your own wording and sentence structures, a good paraphrase should also sound like your own writing. This does not mean that you take credit for the paraphrased material, however. Notice that the paraphrase above correctly cites the title (shortened for convenience) and page number of the original. Be sure to record the page number of any paraphrased original on your notecard, and cite the source for any paraphrase when it appears in your paper.

Direct Quotation.   Use quotation when you need to record a source's precise language, whether spoken or written. The emphasis here is on *need:* You quote because the original language is necessary or the sense cannot be conveyed by other words. You may need to use quotation for the following purposes:

1. *To capture individual authority or interest—*An authority, well-known person, or another individual should be quoted when his or her own words would be more important or more interesting to your reader.

```
According to Barbara Bush, "Having a literate America
would help almost everything" ("A First Lady Who
Cares" 43).
```
—Barbara Kantrowitz and Ann McDonald, "A First Lady Who Cares," *Newsweek* 7 July 1989: 43.

```
Dr. Robert Webber, head of research for the New York
Cancer Institute, says a person's attitude "can
influence susceptibility to disease more than most of
us realize" (102).
```

```
"I got my father to let me ride the mule to school one
day. As I came over the hill toward the schoolhouse, a
cub black bear came out of the bushes behind us. The
mule turned and saw the bear, gave a sort of loud
snort, and took off! I could hardly hold on, but I did.
The next thing I knew, the mule and me had raced
through the front door of the schoolhouse and landed
smack in the middle of a geography lesson" (Satler, 129).
```

Used in appropriate amounts to illustrate a point or demonstrate character, direct quotations from individuals add liveliness and credibility to your paper's discussion.

2. *To ensure accuracy*—Exact language is often needed to define special terms, describe conditions, or report results. The precise language that scientific, medical, and technical sources rely upon for accuracy cannot always be preserved in a summary or paraphrase. In these cases, it is usually best to use direct quotation:

> A complex number in trigonometry can be represented on a two-dimensional diagram: "The horizontal axis is the real axis and the vertical axis is the imaginary axis. The number $a + bi$ is represented by a point drawn a units to the right of the origin and b units up" (Glenn 82).

> "Ibuprofen is one of several nonsteroid anti-inflammatory drugs used to reduce inflammation, relieve pain, or reduce fever. All nonsteroid anti-inflammatory drugs share the same side effects and may be used by patients who cannot tolerate Aspirin" (Simon and Silverman 317).

Legal discussions may require quotation to ensure strict interpretation or adherence to a given law:

> Our Constitution states that "No person shall be convicted of treason unless on the testimony of two witnesses to the same overt act, or on confession in open court" (III, 3).
> —U.S. Constitution, Art. III, sect. 3.

> The court decreed that, in cases of divorce, an *indignity* is any "affront to the personality of another or a lack of reverence for the personality of one's spouse" (Gifis 284).
> —Steven H. Gifis, *Law Dictionary* (New York: Barton's, 1984) 284.

In instances such as these, you may need quotation to ensure precise meaning or to emphasize the accuracy of your own understanding of the material.

3. *To illustrate unique language*—Sometimes language is more important for its uniqueness or emotional power than its ability to convey meaning. In discussing a literary work, quotation demonstrates the author's use of language to create meaning and tone. You might quote an example like the following from John Steinbeck's *Grapes of Wrath* to illustrate how he describes the onset of the great drought that created the "dust bowl" conditions of his novel's setting:

> "The dawn came, but no day. In the gray sky a red sun
> appeared, a dim circle that gave a little light, like
> dusk; and as that day advanced, the dusk slipped back
> toward darkness, and the wind cried and whimpered over
> the fallen corn" (Steinbeck 2-3).
> —John Steinbeck, "The Grapes of Wrath" (New York: Viking, 1939) 2–3.

In other instances, a memorable phrase or a particularly telling remark can often reveal more than any paraphrase could capture:

> Those of us who are well fed may find it difficult to
> understand that the homeless are grateful for whatever
> is available. As Benjamin Franklin once said, "Hunger
> never saw bad bread" (40)
> —Benjamin Franklin, *Poor Richard's Almanac*, 1773 (Philadelphia: Rosenbach, 1977) 40.

> As government cutbacks in social and educational
> programs increase, the need for volunteers becomes even
> greater. We should remember the words of John F.
> Kennedy, who said, "Ask not what your country can do
> for you—ask what you can do for your country."
> —John F. Kennedy, Inaugural Address, Washington, DC, 21 Jan. 1961.

> Who had the right to sign memos for the president in
> his absence? "Everybody and nobody," according to one
> White House source (*Newsweek* 84).

These examples demonstrate situations in which direct quotation would be appropriate and effective. Remember, however, that too much quotation dilutes the quality of your discussion. A dependency on quotation instead of paraphrase decreases your analysis of the material during notetaking; too much quotation in your paper can bury ideas and make the reader do all the thinking. Avoid excessive quotation by summarizing and paraphrasing whenever possible. If quotation adds something that paraphrase or summary cannot, be sure it fits one of the situations described here.

Whenever you use quotation, be sure to quote all words and punctuation *exactly as they appear in the original.* Mark your notecard clearly to indicate that the material is a direct quotation and to show all necessary punctuation and page numbers. Notice that each of the examples given above cites the source for the quoted material. Such citation is an absolute requirement any time you use quotation in your paper.

Combination Notes.   Combining summary, paraphrase, and quotation in your notes or the paper itself allows for adapting source material to your own style and fitting it into a discussion. When combining notetaking methods, take care to identify for yourself which notes are summary, paraphrase, or quotation so as not to misrepresent the material later in your paper.

Plagiarism

Unfortunately, beginning writers of research papers sometimes fall into committing *plagiarism,* using another person's language or ideas without acknowledgment. Some plagiarism results from borrowing from a source and consequently forgetting to acknowledge its author in the paper. At other times, plagiarism occurs because the student writer purposely wishes to take credit for the words or ideas of another. Intentional or not, however, all plagiarism is theft: It is taking what belongs to someone else and using it dishonestly.

To avoid commiting plagiarism in your research paper, make sure any notes you take are complete and accurate and that you will be able to acknowledge their sources later. As you write the paper, remember that any time you use someone else's words, expressions, or ways of thinking about something, you commit plagiarism if you do not give credit to the source.

Acknowledging a Source.   To acknowledge a source, you name it at the same time you present its words or ideas in your paper. Whether the language presented is your own or the source's makes no difference. The idea is as important as the words used to express it. Notice how sources are named directly within the text in each of these examples:

MLA (Modern Language Association) Style
The first life forms probably began appearing about
3,000 million years ago in a kind of "prebiotic soup of
organic molecules" (Gregory 233).

People who argue for legalizing drugs believe that they are not really as dangerous as we think or that truly unsafe drugs would never be widely used (Nadelmann 56).

APA (American Psychological Association) Style

While classification of children's drawings shows some similarity among individuals (Kellog, 1970), Golomb (1981) emphasizes the difficulty of interpreting development by comparisons with models.

Number-Reference Style

If we assume that phobic neuroses can be effectively treated by desensitization,[1] there still remains the problem of treating multiple afflictions. Roth's work in this area suggests several useful approaches.[2]

(See Chapters 10 and 11 for instruction on documentation following these various styles.)

In addition, each source you cite in the text of the paper must be listed on the Works Cited or References page. If you fail to acknowledge your sources in these ways, you are guilty of plagiarism, which can have such serious consequences as a failing grade on the research paper, failing the course, or even being expelled from college.

Avoiding Plagiarism. Because of the ethical and practical seriousness of plagiarism, give scrupulous attention to avoiding it throughout your research. Following these guidelines will keep you from making mistakes that might result in unintentional plagiarism:

1. *Understand and use correct notetaking methods.* Know the difference between summary, paraphrase, and quotation, as well as when and how to use them correctly. (See the preceding discussion for the proper use of these methods.)

2. *Take accurate and legible notes.* Record page numbers clearly for any material you summarize, paraphrase, or quote, as well as for any figures or uncommonly known facts you borrow. Annotate your notes by adding comments such as "my words," "quoted," "summary," "her idea," and so forth (see Figure 6.2). Remember that faint periods and ambiguous quotation marks are easily overlooked or misread. Use heavy, bold punctuation, especially for quotation marks and any punctuation included within a quotation.

3. *Know what to document.* You must cite in your paper's text and document in the Works Cited or References page(s) the source for any words, expressions, ideas, organization of ideas, facts, or lines of thinking you borrow or adapt. This means that your notes will always need to include the title, author's name, and publication facts about the source, as well as specific page number(s) for any information you record. (See Chapter 4 on what to record on a bibliography card for books and magazines.)

Whenever you quote directly, for example, or even paraphrase what another writer has said, you must cite the source for that material. Similarly, if you state in your paper that "three-fourths of the American public favor raising the tax on cigarettes," tell where you got such information. If you rely particularly upon one source for your extended description, let's say, of how a typical nuclear power plant operates, give credit to that source. In each of these cases, make sure that your notes include specific page numbers and other documentation information you will need in the paper. (Chapters 10 and 11 describe necessary documentation information and forms for various kinds of sources.)

Your paper will not need to document information that is *common knowledge*—ideas or facts that are generally well known or basic to a field of study. Understandably, you may not be able to judge what information is considered common until you have done a fair amount of research on your topic. Thus, when beginning research on dinosaurs, for example, you may not know that they lived during what is called the Mesozoic Era. Similarly, when first investigating the topic heroin, you may not know that the main effects of this narcotic occur in both the nervous and digestive systems. After you have consulted three or four sources on your topic, however, you will be able to recognize what information is common knowledge.

It is always a good idea, of course, to record complete documentation for any information you find. Do so during initial reading and notetaking until you have a sense of what is common knowledge for your subject. As you later write the paper, however, remember that you should not cite sources for commonly known facts and ideas.

4. *Make a bibliographic card for every note source.* You cannot give credit to a source if you lack the information to do so. Fill out a bibliography card for each source you take notes from, and *consistently* record the title, author's name, publishing date, and other data necessary to acknowledge the work in your paper. (See Chapter 4 on what to record for various sources.)

5. *Acknowledge sources in your paper.* Follow the correct form for citing sources in the body of your paper, as well as for listing them on the Works Cited or References pages (see Chapters 10 and 11).

A final word: Do not underestimate the potential problem of plagiarism, but do not let it distort your perception of the research paper, either. You are encouraged to use and build upon the work of others—though naturally, your paper should not simply become a patchwork quilt of other people's words and ideas. Borrow and always acknowledge when you must, but remember that your own ideas are the most important ingredient of the paper.

Evaluating Sources

The critical evaluation of source materials will continue throughout your research. As your understanding of the topic changes, so, too, will your estimation of your sources. In turn, your opinion of each source's value or authority will shape the way you think about the topic and read or take notes.

Consequently, evaluation of sources should not come only after your research has been completed but before and during your reading, as well. This is because in thinking judgmentally about a source, you also think critically about its content. You may decide not to bother reading a source at all or to take entirely different kinds of notes because of what you decide about its value. By consulting the opinions of others about a source, you can learn which ideas are considered important or what others have found controversial. You can study the sources more efficiently because you know what to look for as you read and take notes.

Developing Judgment

In part, your judgment of a source's authority and value to your research will develop out of your own reading in the field. The more you learn about your subject, the more perceptive you will become about sources. Some that were impressive at the start of your research may eventually seem inadequate; the importance of others will emerge only as your research itself becomes more complete. As you grow familiar with a topic, you will recognize particular authors and works that repeatedly crop up in your reading; you will also learn the publishers and journals that are most prestigious in the field; and you will gradually come to value works that treat your topic comprehensively over those providing only general introductions.

Consulting Other Opinions

Because you cannot read everything written on your research topic, you will want to consult those sources with the greatest authority or whose ideas are most valuable to your discussion. While your own broad reading on a topic will help judge the expertise and usefulness of some sources, you may also need opinions from others more familiar with the field. Having located a particular source, such as a book or a scholarly journal article, use your library's general reference sources to find out how others reacted to it.

Using Book Reviews.   Critical discussions like those published in the *New York Times Book Review,* the *Times Literary Supplement,* or scholarly journals give you the opinions of experts about a work's strengths or weaknesses. Book reviews can help you learn more about a topic, as well as about the book and its author's standing in the subject field.

The most useful resource for general book reviews is *Book Review Digest (BRD)* (New York: H. W. Wilson, 1905–date). Drawing upon reviews published in nearly a hundred general periodicals and scholarly journals, *BRD* summarizes a book as well as any reviews written about it (see Figure 6.5). Because *BRD* usually includes several reviews for each work listed, use it to avoid having to consult multiple sources to learn about a book or its author. If you need more information than summarized versions provide, use *BRD* to locate the complete reviews in their original publications.

In addition to *Book Review Digest,* reviews of scholarly books and articles are available in most of the specialized indexes discussed in Chapter 3. The following indexes are also useful for general and scholarly works:

> *Book Review Index.* New York: H. W. Wilson, 1905–date.
> *Current Book Review Citations.* New York: H. W. Wilson, 1976–date.
> *Index to Book Reviews in the Humanities.* Williamston, MI: Thomson, 1960–date.
> *Technical Book Review Index.* New York: Willis, 1961–date.

Using Citation Indexes.   The number of times an author has published in a field, which journals have carried his or her work, and how others have valued it are all important considerations in evaluating a source. Computer-produced periodical indexes such as *Arts & Humanities Citation Index, Science Citation Index,* and *Social Science Citation Index* provide information such as the following:

- What other current and past works an individual has authored
- What other authors have cited the work, as well as where and when
- Where a work has been reviewed
- Where follow-up studies, corrections, or applications have been described
- Where the article is summarized as as abstract in the major journals for the field

SEWELL, DAVID R., 1954-. Mark Twain's languages:
discourse, dialogue, and linguistic variety. 188p $22 1987
University of Calif. Press
 813 1. Twain, Mark, 1835-1910
 ISBN 0-520-05702-3 LC 86-32632

"In the following chapters I shall trace an often contradic-
tory movement from one characterization of language to
another as it develops in Mark Twain's works. Chapter
2 examines Twain's relation to . . . the authority of
standard grammar and usage, which Twain never consciously defied. . . . Chapter 3 examines Twain's embodiment
in The Gilded Age of a premise that descended to him
from Emerson through the essayist Richard Grant White:
corrupt language means a corrupt society. The remainder
of the book focuses on Twain's encounter with variety:
the shock of foreign languages, the heteroglossic mix of
dialects and idiolects along the Mississippi seen in Huckleberry Finn, the role of language as a divisive tool of
power in the racially divided society of Pudd'nhead Wilson.
The final chapter documents Mark Twain's journey toward
representing dialogue as mutual incomprehension." (Introduction) Bibliography. Index.

"[This] should prove to be one of the most significant
books on Mark Twain published in this decade. It is
a tight, cogent study, extremely useful in its command
and application of sophisticated language theory as a critical
tool to examine the dynamics of Mark Twain's fiction.
Sewell is well-versed in contemporary socio-linguistic theory,
and establishes the parameters of his discussion in clear,
jargon-free prose. Especially influential is Mikhail Bakhtin,
whose theories about language Mark Twain anticipated.
. . . Through a detailed review of the fiction, letters,
essays, and notebooks, Sewall demonstrates that not only
was language Mark Twain's life-long preoccupation but
that his attitudes toward and struggles with it prove to
be a key to more comprehensive thematic concerns. .
. . Sewell strikes a nice balance between delineation of
socio-linguistic theory, survey of historical and biographical
background, and close reading of primary texts. . . . Although
Sewell shows familiarity with the range of Mark Twain
scholarship, he penetrates far beyond what others have
done on this crucial subject."
 Am Lit 60:298 My '88. James D. Wilson (700w)

"Building on the work of Henry Nash Smith's MarkTwain:
The Development of a Writer [BRD 1963] and Richard
Bridgman's The Colloquial Style in America [BRD 1966,
1967], but going beyond them, Sewell's study of Twain's
languages makes it possible to see more completely not
only the major works like Huckleberry Finn but also
the minor works like The Gilded Age, Tom Sawyer Abroad,
and 'The Celebrated Jumping Frog' as well. Sewell traces
Twain's increasing awareness that language confuses as
often as it clarifies, that in the end we may be incom-
prehensible to each other. One of the best studies of
Twain in the last several years, Sewell's book goes far
in helping us better understand both Twain the man and
his works. Highly recommended for undergraduates and
graduate students."
 Choice 25:625 D '87. E. Suderman (170w)

SEXUAL UNDERWORLDS OF THE ENLIGHTEN-
MENT; edited by G.S. Rousseau and Roy Porter. 280p
il $35 1988 University of N.C. Press
 306.7 1. Sexual behavior 2. Europe—Social conditions
 ISBN 0-8078-1782-1 LC 87-27893

"The editors of this second volume in a projected trilogy
on Enlightenment sexuality (the first was Paul-Gabriel
Boucé's Sexual Life in Eighteenth-Century Britain, 1982)
. . . have chosen ten essays that [focus on] . . . aspects
of eighteenth-century sexology, medicine, prostitution, law,
pornography, homosexuality and culture. While the emphasis is on England, contributors are British, American
and French." (Times Lit Suppl) Index.

FIGURE 6.5 Sample entries from *Book Review Digest*

Source: Entries from *Book Review Digest*, 1989. Copyright (c) 1989, 1990 by The H. W.
Wilson Company. Reprinted by permission of the publisher.

Available in print or online, citation indexes can supply information to help judge a work's originality, authority, and application. Citation indexes list mainly journal articles, but some books are included, as well. Remember that citation indexes are usually organized into three different volumes: *permuterm index, source index,* and *citation index.* Using key words from a work's title or the name of an author, you can use any one of the indexes to locate information. (See Chapter 4 on citation indexes and how to use them.)

Evaluation Criteria

While it is essential to consult the work of recognized authorities in order to integrate their ideas with your own thinking, not all your research information will come with identifiable credentials. In general, a source will be useful to your research if it meets one or more of the following criteria:

1. It was written by a reliable authority whose methods and reasoning appear valid. Not everything you use in your research has to (or should) be written by someone with a Ph.D., but the author's education, experience with the topic, and reputation should play a major part in your evaluation and use of a work.
2. It offers facts and ideas other sources do not.
3. It sets forth facts and ideas that do not contradict known concepts or other works without good evidence.
4. It demonstrates knowledge and consideration of other viewpoints and research in the field. Look for discussion of opposing ideas, as well as the application and citation of others' works.
5. It is current in terms of both its publication date and its information. Remember that knowledge changes more rapidly in some fields than in others. Ideas in the humanities, for example, tend to remain consistent longer than those in the sciences, where constant research and new technology change existing knowledge daily.

Apply these criteria as you begin to take notes from your research sources, as well as when you begin writing your paper and integrating source material into the text.

WORKING WITH OTHERS

The diligence required for reading and taking notes can seem less demanding when you share your progress and results with others. As often as possible during this period, take time to discuss your work with a friend, or compare your reading and notetaking with a classmate's. Telling others about what you have read will give you a better perspective on what you have done so far. Consider these suggestions as you share your research reading and notetaking with another.

- Compare your techniques for skimming and close reading with those used by a classmate. What differences can you identify that may suggest ways to improve your own approaches? Can you provide the other person with any tips?

- Discuss the notes you take and compare your method of notetaking with that of your classmate. Does a comparison reveal you are taking the right kind of notes? Are you taking too few? Too many?

- Find out how someone else stores his or her research notes. Can you suggest any ways to improve upon your friend's method or your own? What problems have you each had with notetaking? Were you able to solve them?

- Show the person you are working with a sample of how you record quotation or paraphrase in your notes. Does your method seem adequate? Discuss the concept of plagiarism. Do you both understand plagiarism? What has your instructor said about it?

- Compare your evaluations of the sources from which you have both read and taken notes. Have you used the same criteria to evaluate such sources? Are there others that would also be useful?

- Using *Book Review Digest* or library citation indexes can be difficult. Discuss these sources with your collaborator to make sure you both understand their benefits and how to use them.

Sharing your thoughts about your reading will help you to understand and to evaluate your sources more thoroughly than thinking about them alone. Continue discussing these and any other aspects of your research with a classmate or friend.

Planning Your Paper

You should no sooner write a research paper without having a plan than you should build a house without having a blueprint. Depending upon your writing skills and the way you prefer to work, a plan can range from a rough sketch of your major ideas to a detailed outline. Planning the paper will get you started writing and help direct your efforts any time you are unsure of how next to proceed. Rather than simply plunge into the act of writing your research paper, take the time now to organize your ideas and plan the best use of your research. Once you have a plan, you will be prepared to adapt your writing methods to carrying it out.

Using Your Research Notes

Plan your paper by first reviewing notes you recorded from library materials or other research sources. Your goal at this point is to get an overall view of your topic as represented in the notes. Reviewing the notes will also show what you have to work with in terms of ideas and information for the paper.

Arranging and Studying Your Notes

Read carefully through the notes several times, studying their contents and noting subheadings or other clusters of information. Relate the contents of each set of notes to the information in other sets as you proceed. The goal here is to see how your notes, all the pieces of information

147

you have collected, fit together. What picture do they make in terms of answering the research question?

You may find it useful to merge separate groups of notes with previously different subheadings or to arrange the notes into a particular order, such as a chronological or cause-effect sequence. (Having notes on cards makes such rearranging easy, as does having them on computer. If you use a notebook to record notes, cut out each section so you can rearrange the notes as needed.) In your review of the notes, look for examples, anecdotes, quotations, or statistics that appear particularly useful or striking. Consider how these and other content relate to your research question or a preliminary thesis statement.

Reviewing the Research Question

Although the planning stage is not the place to begin a new research topic, you may need to modify the focus of your research question and its answer before proceeding further (see Chapter 3). After reviewing your research notes, take time to consider what research question and answer they best support. If you began your research by asking What effect does early fame have upon the adult lives of child stars? a review of your notes may suggest a different approach: What factors contribute to successful adult lives for child stars? A slight change such as this may promote fuller use of your research material and help you frame a more precise final thesis statement.

Reviewing the Preliminary Thesis Statement

The preliminary thesis statement you devised earlier to guide your research may still be sufficient, or it may need to be revised to reflect your note material and any modification in the original research question (see Chapter 3). Write the research question and thesis statement at the top of a notebook page or other sheet of paper. Underneath, list the topic headings from your notecards. As you do so, include under the various headings the major ideas or examples that should be part of the paper. Do not worry too much whether you list information in some final order or if it will indeed be part of your paper. At this stage, you simply want to see how major ideas relate and how accurately the thesis statement describes the note material. As you compare the research question, note material, and preliminary thesis, consider the extent to which they relate. Modify the preliminary thesis as needed to match the research question, as well as the ideas and information on the notecards.

Devising a Final Thesis Statement

The thesis statement asserts the main idea controlling your paper's content and organization. In turn, every part of the paper's content supports the thesis statement by explaining it further or offering evidence and examples that show it is accurate. Your thesis will grow out of the thinking you do about the research topic and from deciding on a focus for the information collected from your sources.

A good thesis statement is not devised quickly. It will probably be revised several times before and during the writing of the paper so that it conforms to the evolving content. You may also need to add or delete content during the writing stage in order to support the thesis statement more closely. Good planning of the thesis before you write can help you avoid making too many alterations later.

Writing an Effective Thesis Statement

State the thesis statement as a single sentence, perhaps as two, if necessary. Your goal is to convey your main point concisely but fully. That will help the reader recognize the relationship of ideas and the emphasis of your paper.

The thesis statement should state your conclusions about the research question in an argumentlike fashion:

```
Americans should view the expansive Japanese presence
in the United States as a positive example of this
country's new global development.
```

```
Black readers feel the language and characterization in
Huckleberry Finn demeans them and consequently
undermines the literary value of the novel.
```

```
Recent prevention programs have resulted in significant
reductions among gay and bisexual men of behavior that
transmits the HIV virus, which causes AIDS.
```

A good thesis invites the reader's interest. Rather than state the obvious, it should promise a discussion worthy of the time needed to read the paper. Avoid weak thesis statements that only summarize known facts and conditions, that are too general to state a clear argument about the topic, or that state an intention:

Weak (summarizes known facts)	AIDS is a usually fatal disease in which the body's immune system fails to resist infection.
Better	AIDS victims should have legal access to promising new drugs without having to wait for their approval by the U.S. Food and Drug Administration.
Weak (too general)	The drug problem is something we need to solve.
Better	Antidrug campaigns are most effective when designed and targeted for specific local populations.
Weak (intention only)	This paper will show that the moral content of children's cartoons is too ambiguous to present acceptable behavior models.
Better	The moral content of children's cartoons is too ambiguous to present acceptable behavior models.

As the "Better" examples above demonstrate, a good thesis statement focuses the paper's discussion on a central idea. In most cases, you will need to experiment several times to find the exact wording for the thesis, and you may need to reword it again during or after writing the paper. The more focused you can make the thesis when planning the paper, the easier writing the body of the paper will be.

Reviewing Your Paper's Purpose

The overall purpose of your paper is determined by what you plan to tell your audience and your strategy for presenting information on the topic. Research papers that primarily intend to persuade a reader of the author's viewpoint about a topic have an *argumentative* purpose; those that minimize expression of the author's ideas and seek mainly to present information for the reader's benefit are *informative*. In order to organize your discussion material effectively, you should plan your paper with one of these two major purposes in mind.

An Argumentative Purpose.   In an argumentative paper, remember to keep your position on the topic consistent and clearly related to the thesis throughout. Your thesis *statement,* or a form of it, should appear more than once in the introduction and perhaps only once again in the conclusion of the paper. The thesis *idea,* expressed in varying ways to match the context, should be a continuous concept that runs more or less explicitly through each section of the argumentative paper. An argumentative paper about the challenges of raising an adopted child, for example, would emphasize the thesis throughout the discussion:

Introduction leads into thesis	. . . Raising an adopted child can pose unexpected problems for even the most loving of parents.
Topic sentence restates thesis idea	One difficulty adopting parents have to overcome is an often unrecognized desire that the adopted child is actually theirs. "I feel like she is one of my own" is a warm expression of closeness, but it may also reflect the wish that the adopted child <u>had</u> been born into the family. . . .
Successive paragraphs develop the thesis further	Raising a child of another race presents adopting parents with additional and sometimes overwhelming challenges. Experts, in fact, are divided over the wisdom of transracial adoptions. . . .
	Becoming the parent of an adopted child can get even more difficult when there are other biologically parented children in the family. . . .
Thesis statement idea is continued	The difficulties of raising an adopted child are certainly real, but they are not insurmountable. When parents learn ahead of time . . .

An Informative Purpose.   In an informative paper, the thesis will receive less emphasis than the information you provide the reader. Keep the content focused on information rather than issues, and maintain a reasonable balance in the material you provide about each subject discussed. To avoid stuffing an informative paper with unneeded material, create topic sentences that control the content and focus of each paragraph.

Notice how the following discussion blurs its informative purpose by introducing facts and issues (here, shown italicized) not related to the topic sentence or the writer's purpose:

Informative topic sentence	Several studies document sustained changes in sexual behavior within the gay male population residing in various U.S.
Irrelevant facts and issues	cities. *Researchers had difficulty gathering certain kinds of data because some gay men are hesitant to share information or identify themselves as gay, evidence that social disapproval is still a concern for many gay males in our society.* Anti—AIDS programs seem to be working, as shown by contrasting the results of a 1984 study of San Francisco men with those found more recently in a New York study showing an even greater decline in risk—related activity.

Which Purpose Is Appropriate?   Deciding whether your paper's purpose is argumentative or informative depends upon your research assignment, your research material, and how important your own interpretation, viewpoint, or evaluation is to the discussion. Your research material will determine, for example, whether you are prepared to argue for or against allowing females to serve in U.S. combat forces (argumentative paper) or should instead report on the growth of opportunities for women in the armed services today (informative paper).

Comparing the Purposes of Sample Papers

Because it seeks to persuade readers of her research conclusions, Anne Kramer's paper on Mark Twain's *Adventures of Huckleberry Finn* has an argumentative purpose. Similarly, Ron Bonneville's paper on foreign proprietorship in the United States argues that Americans should view the expansive Japanese presence in the United States as a positive stage in this country's global development (see Appendix A). Both of these writers recognized that their topics provided enough unsettled questions or controversy to call for further discussion and reasoned conclusions from them. The sample research paper reviewing the current literature on AIDS prevention programs, on the other hand, is an informative paper that seeks to inform its readers more than convince them of any particular viewpoint (see Appendix A).

Using Your Paper's Purpose for Planning

Unless your assignment requires a particular purpose for your paper, decide whether it will be more effective as an argumentative or as an informative paper. Keep your purpose in mind as you construct an outline for the paper.

Working with an Outline

An outline is a tool to assist in your organization and writing of the paper. You will understand and appreciate the use of an outline best by keeping certain principles in mind:

- An outline assists you by organizing material and providing a pattern to follow as you write. It gives your reader an overview of the paper's discussion and major ideas.
- Outlines are both informal and formal. You may wish to use the informal type for your own writing needs, perhaps using it later to create a formal outline of the paper. Formal outlines are more effective for planning a paper, especially a longer one, but they also take more preparation.
- Some writers work best by drafting a working plan or outline before they write and making changes as needed. Others prefer to complete the outline after the paper is finished, using it as a means to check the paper's organization and emphases. You should follow the practice that works best for you.
- Since writing is a creative and recursive process, the outline and the paper's content will necessarily change at times to consistently reflect each other.

Both informal and formal outlines are discussed in the following pages. Which type you work with depends upon your writing preferences and the requirements of your research assignment.

An Informal Outline

If you are not required to make a formal outline for your research paper, you may want to work from an informal one. Though such an outline is informal and intended for your use only, it still requires careful planning to be useful.

Begin by writing your paper's title at the top of a work page, with the final thesis right below it for easy reference. After reviewing your notecards, list the major categories of ideas for the paper in a logical sequence, perhaps under headings such as Introduction, Body, and Conclusion to get started or until more specific major headings occur to you. It will probably help if you number the categories and leave enough space between them to add supporting material from notes later.

Since the informal outline is solely for your own use, make notations, additions, or deletions as you need while organizing and writing the paper. Under the proper subheadings, include important facts, dates, or examples that you want to include in the paper. Feel free to write full sentences: At some point, you may want to add them directly to the paper.

Figure 7.1 shows the informal outline for Anne Kramer's paper on black readers' responses to *Adventures of Huckleberry Finn.* Though Anne was required to submit a formal outline with her paper, she felt more comfortable beginning with her own loosely structured plan. She followed her informal outline to write most of the paper and then used it later to construct a formal topic outline (see later in this chapter). Anne found her informal outline helpful to her writing, but she also recognized that the form and structure required by a formal topic outline demonstrated the organization of ideas in the paper better. In fact, she used the formal topic outline as a guide when she revised her paper's first draft. A comparison of the informal outline in Figure 7.1 with the final topic outline (see Appendix to Chapter 9) shows the changes, additions, and deletions Anne made when she wrote the paper.

A Formal Outline

A formal outline differs from an informal one by following a standard format and organization. The formal outline subdivides categories of information, designating each category by different letters and numbers and by separate headings. The degree of importance or inclusiveness of each heading is shown in the outline by successive indentation; that is, the less important a category, the more it is indented under more significant categories:

The Response of Black Readers to Mark Twain's
Adventures of Huckleberry Finn

Thesis: The response of black readers to Huckleberry
  Finn centers not only upon the work's language and
  characterization but on its consequent value as
  literature, as well.

Introduction
  —HF followed The Adventures of Tom Sawyer
  —first published in England
  —banned in Concord as "trash"
  —criticism of Victoria Earle Matthews

Body
1. Language and dialects
   —linguists say dialect use is authentic (King 13)
   —see Twain's preface to the novel
   —"illusion of accuracy makes the art" (Hill xxii)
   —variety establishes separate identities of
     characters (Huck, Jim, duke)
2. Jim's character
   —Twain: dialect is carefully researched (preface)
   —Jim is not given dignity (Nichols 15)
   —"exaggerated," reinforces stereotype (Ford 434)
3. Critical opinions
   —Hemingway: "best book we've had"
   —Smith: "great . . . with defects" (vi)
   —Nichols: "indispensable" (14)
   —flawed ending--Tom Sawyer, delayed saving of Jim
   —Use of nigger a problem
   —Jim's character--realistic but negative
   —Hill: American realism
4. Black responses to HF
   —offended by use of nigger
   —Margot Allen's experience and controversy
   —Black critic responses divided
   —student responses--Professor Corderman
   —characterization of Jim negative

Conclusion
Value as literature
   —"trigger to outrage" (Smith)
   —moral drama about conscience and humanity
   —Corderman quotation?

FIGURE 7.1 Anne Kramer's informal research paper outline

```
I. Major heading
   A. Minor heading
      1. Detail heading
         a. Example heading
         b. Example heading
            (1) Minor example heading
            (2) Minor example heading
      2. Detail heading
   B. Minor heading
      1. Detail heading
      2. Detail heading
   C. Minor heading, etc.
```

Subdivisions within headings can continue even further than shown here, though most rarely need to go beyond the level of example headings (a, b, etc.).

As the above example demonstrates, the headings within a formal outline are each part of a whole. If you subdivide a topic heading, it must have at least two parts. That is, every I will have at least a II, every A a B, every 1 a 2, and so on:

```
I. National Parks
   A. Size
      1. Public-use areas
      2. Primitive areas
   B. Types
      1. Recreation
      2. Preservation
```

Outlines for papers and articles written for the sciences or business may use a decimal outline, in which decimal divisions indicate successive headings:

```
1. Major heading
   1.1 Minor heading
       1.1.1 Detail heading
       1.1.2 Detail heading
             1.1.2.1 Example heading
             1.1.2.2 Example heading
```

```
  1.2  Minor heading
       1.2.1  Detail heading
       1.2.2  Detail heading
2.  Major heading, etc.
```

Types of Outlines

The Topic Outline. Each heading in a topic outline is worded as a noun (College) or nounlike phrase (Applying for Admission, To Enroll in Classes). Keep all headings brief and clearly related to the major heading.

A topic outline can appear easy to compose, but be aware that its level of generality can cover up weaknesses in organization or content. The advantage to a topic outline is that it is brief and identifies the main points of discussion quickly:

```
 I.  Reduction of the rain forests
     A. Questionable benefits
        1. Increased farm land
           a. Cleared forest
           b. New farmers
        2. Timber for export
        3. Intracontinent trade
        4. Modernization
           a. New roads
           b. Hydroelectric dams
     B. Environmental effects
        1. Failure of land to support farming
        2. Loss of plant and animal species
           a. Numbers
           b. Potential uses
        2. Extermination of primitive cultures
           a. Relocation
           b. Modernization
           c. Disease
        3. Disruption of major rivers
        4. Increase in the greenhouse effect
II. International response
```

The Sentence Outline. A sentence outline requires more planning and writing than the topic form, but its completeness will prove more useful when you begin to write the paper. You can incorporate complete sentence from the outline into the paper as topic sentences for successive paragraphs:

I. Despite progress in utilizing the Amazon more productively, development is producing disastrous results with worldwide consequences.
  A. The eight nations through which the Amazon runs have had high expectations that its development would prove beneficial.
    1. The Amazon forest has been cleared to provide increased farm land.
      a. Some 20% of the state of Rondonia is under development.
      b. Farmers receive free land.
    2. The exportation of rare hardwoods has increased since restrictions have been removed.
    3. The building of roads and clearing of the Amazon River have increased the possibility for intracontinent travel and trade throughout Amazonia.
    4. The changes have helped modernize many primitive areas of the Amazon.
      a. Dams and roads are making it possible for Amazon people to reach new areas to live.
      b. Electricity has improved living conditions.
  B. Attempts to utilize the Amazon's rich forest and land, however, are having devastating effects on the the region.
    1. The nutrient-poor soil will not support farm crops.
    2. Hundreds, perhaps thousands, of valuable plant and animal species have already been lost because of development.

      a. A four-mile area of forest may
         support over 1,500 different species of
         life.
      b. Many of these have valuable uses in
         medicine or industry.

The Paragraph Outline. A paragraph outline provides a summary of the main parts of the outline. You should be careful to develop each paragraph fully as a unit. Remember, however, that since the paragraphs in such an outline represent an entire section, they are not developed enough to fit directly into the paper:

I. Reduction of the rain forest

   A. The elimination of millions of acres of Amazon
      rain forest has provided many Amazonians with
      the opportunity of clearing and owning their
      own farms. In the western state of Rondonia,
      some 20% of the land has been been cleared to
      provide new farm land for those who will settle
      there. Exports of hardwood have increased
      significantly from the massive reduction of the
      forest, and modern roads have allowed increased
      travel and trade. New hydroelectric dams
      provide electricity for hospitals and other
      modern advantages.

   B. Attempts to utilize the Amazon's rich forest
      and land, however, are having devastating
      effects upon the region. Since the nutrient-
      poor soil will not sustain crops, clearing
      millions of acres of forest to provide new farm
      land has proven dismally unsuccessful. Worse
      yet, hundreds, perhaps thousands, of valuable
      plant and animal species have already been lost
      because of development. A four-mile area of
      forest may support over 1,500 different species
      of life, many of which have valuable uses in
      medicine or industry.

Creating Your Own Outline

To begin the outline for your paper, start by arranging your notecards or other materials into main categories, assigning each a major heading designation indicated by a roman numeral. For example, an outline from notecards for a paper on current research findings about drug addiction might begin this way:

   I. Definition   **Major headings**

  II. Causes

 III. Effects

 IV. Treatment

Next, review the note material included in each major heading category. If you have enough material for at least two minor categories, add them as subdivisions. The number or letter identifier of each new level of subdivision should align with the text portion of the preceding level. Note that the "A." below aligns on the preceding entry, "Definition." Follow this style:

   I. Definition

     A. Problem of defining   **Minor headings**

     B. Use and abuse

     C. Prevalent types

  II. Causes

     A. Social factors   **Minor headings**

     B. Psychological needs

     C. Genetic origins

 III. Effects

     A. Physiological   **Minor headings**

     B. Psychological

     C. Societal

 IV. Treatment

     A. Chemical substitutes   **Minor headings**

     B. Clinical therapy

     C. Support groups

Now examine the note material included within each of the minor categories to determine whether you have enough material to subdivide into at least two detail headings. If so, include them in the outline, using arabic numerals (1, 2, 3, etc.) and aligning them on the appropriate indent (as explained earlier):

```
I. Definition
   A. Problem of defining
      1. APA definition              Detail headings
      2. WHO definition
   B. Use and abuse
      1. Stable addiction            Detail headings
      2. Unstable addiction
   C. Prevalent types
      1. Physiological               Detail headings
      2. Psychological
II. Causes
   A. Social factors
      1. Alienation                  Detail headings
      2. Drug availability
   B. Psychological needs
      1. Personality disorders       Detail headings
      2. Stress and trauma
   C. Genetic origins
      1. Neurologic vulnerability    Detail headings
      2. Alcoholism
```

Most outlines do not require extensive enough development to need example headings. If you wish to include them, however, repeat the processes described above, using small letters (a, b, c):

```
II. Causes
   A. Social factors
      1. Alienation
         a. Familial                 Example headings
         b. Economic
      2. Drug availability
         a. Cocaine                  Example headings
         b. Alcohol
```

B. Psychological causes
   1. Personality disorders
      a. Antisocial behavior   Example headings
      b. Low self—esteem
   2. Stress and trauma
      a. Overachievers   Example headings
      b War veterans

Guidelines for the Formal Outline

■ Although not always necessary, it is a good idea to include the thesis statement at the top of the outline for a research paper (see the outline for the sample research paper in Chapter 9).

■ Align each new level of subentry below the previous-level entry (see above).

■ Align headings of the same degree at the same margins. Do so by aligning the periods following the number or letter identifiers:

I. _____
   A. _____
      1. _____
      2. _____
II. _____
   B. _____
III. _____

■ Word headings to maintain the same parallel forms, generally as noun phrases (*Addiction*) or nounlike phrases such as gerund phrases (*Treating addiction*) or infinitive phrases (*To treat addiction*). Which form you use will depend upon the grammatical parallelism of your outline:

Unparallel Headings

I. Defining addiction
   A. Difficult to define
   B. Some uses and abuses
   C. Prevailing types
II. Causes of addiction
   A. Societal
   B. Your own personality
   C. Genes also contribute

Parallel Headings

I. Definition

    A. Problem of defining

    B. Use and abuse

    C. Prevalent types

II. Causes

    A. Social factors

    B. Psychological needs

    C. Genetic origins

Once you have completed a satisfactory outline for the paper, write your final thesis statement at the beginning of the outline, as well. The thesis statement and outline will direct your writing and help to keep the content and main idea consistent.

A Review of
Basic Patterns of Development

Planning the organization and exposition of your paper's content should include considering the standard patterns that underlie most people's thinking about a subject. Writers employ these patterns to provide a structure for their ideas and for developing a discussion. Narration, description, definition, and analogy are minor patterns that can sustain brief discussions or whole paragraphs in long works. The major patterns—argumentation, comparison-and-contrast, classification, and cause-and-effect—are useful structures for longer compositions like the research paper. These four major patterns can support a paper's purpose by providing logical methods for organization, development, and expression.

The patterns of development described below may be used as outline structures for your research paper or combined with other outline models. They may also serve as development patterns for smaller sections of the outline and the paper.

Argumentation

Arguing a position requires presenting opposing viewpoints and refuting or qualifying each reason for opposition to your argument. The structure for arguing a position is often determined by the nature of the pro and con arguments discussed. The following outline demonstrates a typical argument pattern:

```
   I. Thesis
      A. Background
      B. Thesis position
  II. Ideas opposing thesis
      A. First reason
      B. Second reason
 III. Support for thesis (refutation)
      A. First reason
      B. Second reason
  IV. Conclusion
```

Another argumentation pattern might take this form:

```
   I. Introduction
      A. Background to the problem
      B. Thesis statement
  II. Body
      A. Opposing viewpoint
         1. Reason
         2. Reason
      B. Thesis position (refutation)
         1. Reason
         2. Reason
      C. Solution proposal
 III. Conclusion
```

Comparison-and-Contrast

Although it is possible to write an entire paper that either compares or contrasts two or more things, a more common practice is to combine the two approaches into a comparison-and-contrast pattern.

One method of comparison-and-contrast examines each subject separately in terms of selected features:

```
   I. Japanese education     Subject 1
      A. Levels              Feature 1
      B. Access              Feature 2
      C. Standards           Feature 3
```

```
II.  U.S. education              Subject 2
     A. Levels                   Feature 1
     B. Access                   Feature 2
     C. Standards                Feature 3
III. Conclusion
```

A second method compares and contrasts subjects directly by examining the same features:

```
I.   Education levels            Feature 1
     A. Japan                    Subject 1
     B. U.S.                     Subject 2
II.  Access                      Feature 2
     A. Japan                    Subject 1
     B. U.S.                     Subject 2
III. Standards                   Feature 3
     A. Japan                    Subject 1
     B. U.S.                     Subject 2
IV.  Conclusion
```

Classification

The process of classification is similar to that for comparing and contrasting: identifying the qualities that put things into the same category or distinguish one category from another (e.g., drug therapy programs: Behavior versus encounter). Begin by identifying the principle by which items will be classified (e.g., types of children's toys, kinds of legal statutes, ways to purchase a car). Next, designate the categories to which the items belong. Your discussion of the topic would then describe the items in such a way as to differentiate them from other items and categories:

```
I.   Principle of classification: Types of therapy
II.  Categories of classification
     A. Behavior therapy
        1. History
        2. Examples
     B. Encounter therapy
        1. History
        2. Examples
```

```
C. Gestalt therapy
   1. History
   2. Examples
D. Interactional approach
   1. History
   2. Examples
III. Conclusion
```

Cause-and-Effect

Cause-and-effect patterns are useful for showing how one event or circumstance causes another event or circumstance (e.g., how sulfur emissions from factories destroy lake life through acid rain). Direct and indirect causes may be discussed, as well as recommendations for any problem or condition they have created:

```
  I. Problem or condition: Acid rain
 II. Causes
     A. Direct: Nitric and sulfuric acid
     B. Indirect: Exhaust from cars and factories
III. Effects
     A. Direct: Destruction of fish and plant life in
               lakes and streams
     B. Indirect: Loss of recreation and natural
                 resources
     C. Indirect: Threat to human health
 IV. Solution (recommendation)
```

APA and Scientific Patterns

A paper following the guidelines of the American Psychological Association (APA) or one discussing research, methodology, and conclusions for a scientific study may be organized as follows:

```
  I. Introduction
 II. Methodology
III. Results
 IV. Discussion
  V. References
```

Creating a Title

Many writers prefer to create a title after the paper is finished so that it accurately reflects the content and focus. Others create the title along with the thesis statement and outline as an additional reminder to themselves during the writing stage of the paper's focus. Whichever you prefer, take the time to devise a title that indicates (1) what the paper is about and (2) what approach you have taken toward the subject. The following titles meet these criteria:

```
A Critical View of Tax Shelters

Why New York Is America's Best-Loved City

Families: Do They Really Exist Any More?
```

Use subtitles when they provide additional focus:

```
Teen Music: Can Mean Lyrics Hurt You?

Sleaze T.V.: Viewers Are Saying No
```

Avoid vague, high-sounding, or cute titles that hide the paper's content and approach:

Vague	`Youths at Risk`
Overblown	`A Brief Examination of the Cause-and-Effect Relationship of Lower-Than-Average Grades among College Transfer Students`
Cute	`The "Purrrfect" Pet: Cats as Support Animals`

Remember: Do not underline or use quotation marks around the title of your own paper unless it is named in your text. (See Chapter 12 for guidelines on placement and spacing when typing the title.)

WORKING WITH OTHERS

The more completely you plan the research paper at this point, the more smoothly you will proceed with the writing. Planning the paper with the help of a friend or classmate will ensure that you are actually ready to write and that the logic of the paper's organization is apparent to others.

Take the time to share your research material and to discuss the following major points from this chapter with someone else.

- Review the research question and your notes with another person to be sure you have enough material to support a thesis statement. Point out the examples you intend to include in the paper.

- Does your friend or classmate feel there are enough examples in the notes to support your thesis? Discuss any quotations you plan to include in the paper, as well as your reasons for doing so.

- Ask the person you are working with to state the final thesis statement in his or her own words. How could the thesis be stated more effectively?

- Ask whether the paper seems to be informative or argumentative in its purpose. Can the other person offer any advice on which one of these approaches might work best for your paper? If you are working with a classmate, what purpose will his or her paper support?

- Look over the outline for the paper together. Does it meet the requirements of the assignment? Do the proposed contents support the thesis? Is the organization of material logical and effective? Should any headings be changed, moved, or deleted? Is the form for the outline correct?

- What pattern of development is best for this paper? Briefly summarize the approach the paper will take. Decide together whether that approach seems appropriate for your thesis and purpose.

- Evaluate the proposed title for the paper. Does it clearly indicate the paper's subject and the author's position? Can the two of you think up any other appropriate titles together?

If possible, share your writing preparation with more than just one person, especially if you have lingering questions about any particular aspects of the paper. Be sure to ask others to review their plans with you, also. You will find that discussing another's plans for writing the research paper will provide valuable insights about your own readiness.

CHAPTER EIGHT

Writing Your Paper

Once you have completed a carefully planned outline, the writing of your paper should proceed fairly smoothly. Plan to write the paper over a period of several days, expecting to make changes, to run up against writer's block for short periods, or even to make another visit to the library. But do not despair: Such hurdles are always overcome. They rarely prevent a paper from getting written if the author has been working diligently up to this point.

Reviewing Your Preparation for Writing

Before actually starting to write, take time to review what you have prepared so far to support the composing process:

- A final thesis statement
- A clear purpose (argumentative or informative)
- Notecard material
- An outline of the projected paper

You will need to draw upon all of these as you write the paper. Keeping your purpose, thesis, outline, and notecards nearby as you work will help generate ideas and keep the paper organized.

Preparing to Write

Progressing in Stages

Your paper will undoubtedly go through several versions before it is completed. It is usually helpful to work from successive drafts, though writers vary in the way they like to proceed with any paper.

Revising as You Write. Some writers prefer to write, revise, and finalize each part of the paper fairly thoroughly before moving on to the next part. This system works well when you have a strong outline and need to have a sense of completion before moving on to the next part of writing. A drawback is that you can get bogged down finetuning a single section: You may spend so much time trying to get one part just right that you lose momentum for writing.

Revising a Whole Draft. A more practical method of writing is to create the paper in three draft stages, usually in rough, revised, and final forms.

1. In the *rough draft,* aim to get as much of the paper's content written down as you can. Do not worry much about spelling, copying whole quotations, or even fully documenting sources.
2. In the *revised draft,* review the writing style, make improvements in the order of ideas, add supporting details, and check to see that you have fully developed and supported the thesis statement.
3. For the *final draft,* check spelling and punctuation closely, make sure all documentation is accurate in form and content, and generally check the paper to see that it conforms to the standards of the research paper assignment.

Whether you revise as you write, prefer to work with whole drafts, or use a combination of approaches is really up to you. The important thing is to write consistently, following the outline you prepared or changing it when necessary to maintain organization and focus in the paper.

Determining an Appropriate Style

Before you begin to write, decide how you want to sound to your paper's audience. The semiformal style and language you use for most college papers is also appropriate for the research paper; however, because the research paper is not a personal essay, pay particular attention to matters of voice and tone, qualities that influence how your writing affects the reader.

Voice. Avoid using the personal pronoun *I*, since in most cases, the paper is not about you but about your research findings and conclusions. Avoid saying *I think* . . . or *I found that* . . . unless you are reporting your own efforts and they are relevant to the immediate subject under discussion. For instance: *Though Cranston and others have argued for changing the law,* **I found** *most police personnel in favor of the current statute.* In most cases, express your ideas in a third-person voice that remains objective and allows focus on the subject: *Though Cranston and others have argued for changing the law,* **most police** *personnel favor the current statute.*

Tone. Throughout the paper, write in a tone that is consistent with the paper's purpose, subject, and audience. *Tone* is the writer's attitude toward the subject and the audience. It can be formal, serious, humorous, sarcastic, ironic, or any other quality evoked by the language and style of expression. Which tone you adopt for your paper will depend upon the subject and your attitude toward it. Obviously, some subjects require a certain tone just because of their nature. The subject of AIDS would undoubtedly require a serious tone, for example. A sarcastic or humorous tone would be unusual for a research paper, though some subjects might be effectively handled in one of these ways (a paper about designer clothing for pets, for example).

Considering the Audience

Since most readers will not share your familiarity with the paper topic, anticipate what they will need to understand to follow the paper's discussion most easily. Be alert as you write to include necessary information and definitions that will assure the clarity and effectiveness of your discussion.

Defining Unfamiliar Terms. Review your topic to identify unfamiliar names, terms, and concepts that you should identify for the reader. Make sure you understand such items yourself, and be prepared to define them for your audience. Unless they are the subject of your discussion, you normally will not define common terms (e.g., *nuclear reactor, Pentagon, dolphin*) unless they are the specific subject of a discussion. Brief mention of well-known individuals seldom requires further identification, but explain any persons, terms, or concepts that may be unfamiliar to your reader:

Individual identified

> At this point, Madison turned to his friend Elbridge Gerry for support. Gerry was also a member of the Democratic-Republican Party, and he later became Madison's vice-president. Madison had hoped . . .

Major term defined

> The "Electra complex," which Sigmund Freud first identified, is today defined as a normal emotional crisis in females resulting, at an early stage of psychosexual development, from sexual impulses toward the father and jealousy of the mother (Heber 112). This is the "Electra complex" that Sylvia Plath once stated the speaker of her poem "Daddy" was attempting to resolve.

Note that Sigmund Freud is not identified, since readers would be familiar enough with his name to understand this brief mention. The same is not true for Elbridge Gerry.

Using Appositives.   When possible, keep definitions and explanations from interrupting the text by using *appositives,* which are descriptive words or phrases that qualify or rename the terms that precede them. Notice that appositives are usually connected by a comma to the term they identify:

> At this point, Madison turned for support to his friend Elbridge Gerry, also a *Democratic-Republican and later Madison's vice-president.*

> The poem can be understood in the context of Freud's theory of an "Electra complex," *a normal emotional crisis in females resulting, at an early stage of psychosexual development, from sexual impulses toward the father and jealousy of the mother* (Heber 112).

Simplifying Difficult Terms. Avoid overdefining terms or defining those that may be simply sophisticated or unfamiliar to you. Use simple terms when possible, especially if a more complex term is going to show up only once in the paper. Thus, rather than burden the reader with a term like *microcom networking protocol* when discussing computer functions, use instead *a method for detecting and correcting errors in data transmissions.* Your reader will also probably follow a discussion about the human immune system more easily if you refer to *erythrocytes,* for example, simply as *red blood cells.*

Explaining Special Uses of Common Terms. Familiar terms that you use with special meaning in the paper or that are used synonymously with other familiar terms may require clarification. When Anne Kramer prepared her paper on black reader responses to *Adventures of Huckleberry Finn,* for instance, she at first felt she needed to define such terms as *dialect, vernacular, ironic,* and *black.* While some of these were initially unfamiliar to Anne, she later decided that most readers would probably know them or could check any dictionary for their meaning. She recognized, however, that the term *black* had several popular alternatives and could carry special implications for many readers. Since Anne used *black* to denote what her sources called by various names—*African-American, Black,* and *Negro*—she decided to define in a note what she meant by the term and why she used it in the paper (see the Chapter 9 Appendix).

In general, sensitive consideration of your audience will help you decide which terms need defining and which do not. As you prepare to write the paper, be sure to have on hand the information you may need to provide any necessary definitions or explanations.

Writing the Paper

The Introduction

The introduction announces the paper's topic, presents the thesis statement, and engages the reader's interest in what the paper will say. There are no rules as to how long an introductory section should be. An overly lengthy introduction, however, can lose the paper's focus and eventually cause the reader to wonder what you are getting at. How you go about introducing the paper's topic and thesis will depend upon your own writing preferences and the material you need to include before moving to the body of the paper.

Starting with an Anecdote. Introduce the paper with an anecdote (a brief account of an incident) when it helps to illustrate or lead into the topic. Ron Bonneville's paper on Japanese ownership of U.S. properties opens with a humorous anecdote directly relevant to his paper's topic and leading into the statement of the paper's thesis (which is italicized in all examples):

> When President George Bush attended the funeral of the late Japanese Emperor Hirohito in January 1989, comedian Jay Leno quipped that "as President of the United States, [Bush] figured he should meet the owners" (Holger 39). Leno's remark demonstrates the extent to which the American public is both aware of and nervous about the amount of Japanese ownership in the United States. . . . While the concerns expressed are justified, however, *Americans should view the expansive Japanese presence in the United States as a positive stage in this country's global development.*

Introducing the Topic's Significance.   Point out the importance of a topic by demonstrating its widespread effect or important consequences:

> The crack and cocaine epidemic in America has gone beyond killing the users to addicting children even before they are born. All across America today, doctors are delivering babies whose symptoms range from all-out dependency on crack or heroin to major brain and organ damage due to the mother's use of drugs. The problem is so great that next year, more babies born in the United States will die from drug addiction than in any other country in the world (Keeler 23). *Though federal and state programs to educate the young have reduced their numbers, drug-dependent pregnancies seem destined to continue in this country for some time.*

Offering Statistics.   Statistics provide a quick and concrete way to interest a reader in the topic:

> Americans today throw away 160 million tons of garbage and trash a year, roughly 3.5 pounds a day apiece. That is enough to spread 30 stories high over 1,000 football

fields. The average family of 3 sends 29 bags of trash
to the dump every month, but in 5 years, a third of our
present landfills will be full ("Buried" 57). The
question facing America today is: Where will we bury
all the mountains of garbage and trash in the future?
Right now, no one has an answer, but *states are
scrambling to resolve a problem that, if not settled
soon, literally threatens to bury us in trash.*

Quoting an Authority. Quoting an authority allows you to agree or
disagree with the opinion expressed, or the quotation can emphasize the
importance of the paper's topic. Anne Kramer's paper opened with this
quotation by Nobel Prize–winning author Ernest Hemingway:

"All modern literature comes from one book by Mark
Twain called <u>Huckleberry Finn</u>," wrote Ernest Hemingway
in 1935. "It's the best book we've had" (22). Although
most literary critics and scholars, as well as the
general reading public, would agree with Hemingway's
assessment, Mark Twain's <u>Adventures of Huckleberry Finn</u>
is also one of the most controversial classics on
American bookshelves. Banned and denounced as "the
veriest of trash" by the Concord Library Committee when
it was first published in America (Rule 10),
<u>Huckleberry Finn</u> has borne a long history of staunch
criticism and debate, first over what white audiences
viewed as its common vulgarity and, increasingly in
this century, over what many perceive as its racist and
demeaning portrayal of black character. *The result has
been a concerned, often outraged black response to
<u>Huckleberry Finn</u> that centers not only upon the work's
language and characterization but upon its consequent
value as literature, as well.*

Reviewing a Controversy. If your paper is taking a position on or
examining a controversy, you may want to review general issues before
discussing the major arguments in depth:

The American public's long-standing debate over gun
control has taken on new urgency of late because of
the widespread availability and use of assault-style
weapons. Gun-control advocates fear that awesome,
rapid-fire weapons like the Uzi and AK-47 are giving
drug lords and other criminals the ability to outgun
the police. They want these kinds of weapons banned,
but gun enthusiasts say that would mean the end of
their right to own such guns, too. Pro-gun advocates
argue that the Constitution guarantees them the right
to bear arms, including Uzis and AK-47s. *The recent
debate has set off a flurry of political reactions that
seem to have upset everyone but the criminals it
originally centered upon.*

Summarizing the Literature. A summary of the recent literature
presents an overview of issues related to the paper's topic. The introductory summary below focuses on the positions of black critics on the issue
of the literary value of *Adventures of Huckleberry Finn* and the question
of banning the novel:

Black critics of Mark Twain's <u>Adventures of
Huckleberry Finn</u> continue to define the novel's
strengths and weaknesses along both literary and racial
lines. Kenny J. Williams, for example, recognizes
several flaws in characterization and plot but ends by
calling the novel a "classic." Richard K. Barksdale
sees the novel as great because of its ironic rather
than simply positive view of black and white
friendships. David L. Smith finds that . . . . *The one
point on which each of these critics agree, however, is
that Twain's <u>Adventures of Huckleberry Finn</u> is too
important a book to go unread by any generation of
Americans.*

Providing Background Information. Set the stage for a discussion
by providing the reader with background information on the topic:

Though the first airplane flight by the Wright brothers
in 1903, as well as the early rocket experiments of Dr.
Robert Goddard, certainly laid the foundations for
space flight today, the real leap in progress came in
1957 when the Soviet Union launched the first orbiting
satellite. That success was followed by several more
Soviet firsts: the first long space flight, the first
man in space, the first woman in space, and the first
walk in space. The United States began catching up to
the Soviets in the early 1960s with President John F.
Kennedy's promise to land a man on the moon before the
end of the decade. *When the first moon landing did take
place in 1969, it changed America's commitment to space
exploration in ways no one had expected.*

Defining a Key Term.   Define a central term, and explain its relationship to the discussion:

The "Electra complex," which Sigmund Freud first
identified, is today defined as a normal emotional
crisis in females resulting, at an early stage of
psychosexual development, from sexual impulses toward
the father and jealousy of the mother (Heber 112). This
is the "Electra complex" that Sylvia Plath once stated
the speaker of her poem "Daddy" was attempting to
resolve. *An examination of the Electra complex theory,
in fact, reveals the psychosexual sources for the basic
structure and major images of Plath's remarkable poem.*

The Body

The body of the paper develops the thesis statement according to the
sequence of ideas planned in the outline. You should write the body of
the paper as if it were an unfolding discussion, advancing one major idea
at a time. Each paragraph should state a main idea, which is developed by
supporting discussion and examples and followed by the next logical point
for development. Your goal is to examine the topic fully while integrating
your research material to support and develop the thesis statement.

Writing Effective Paragraphs.   As you compose the body of the paper, avoid writing paragraphs that amount to little more than a collection of other writers' ideas and examples. Each paragraph in the paper should contain at least one idea of your own, usually expressed as the topic sentence. The paragraph should gain development from further discussion and supporting examples, with your own analyses and commentary weaving the various parts together.

Transitions show the relationship between words, sentences, or paragraphs. Use transitions (italicized in the following example) to give your writing *coherence*, which is the logical flow and connection of ideas:

> We cannot blame the activities of humans entirely for acid rain, *however*. Volcanic eruptions and forest fires, *for example*, release substantial amounts of sulfur and nitrogen compounds into the air. *In addition*, microbial processes in oceans and coastal mud flats the world over generate constant amounts of gaseous sulfur compounds. *Finally*, nitrogen oxides in the air result *not only* from the action of soil bacteria *but also* from the heat produced by lightning. Studies indicate, *in fact*, that natural emissions of sulfur and nitrogen are roughly equal to those produced by humans (Cordova 258).

The above paragraph also demonstrates *unity* because the content relates to the single idea expressed in the topic sentence: *We cannot blame the activities of humans entirely for acid rain.* Everything in the paragraph's examples and discussion directly relates to the topic sentence.

Writing in the Appropriate Tense.   In discussing a work of literature, use the present tense to write about what is said or to describe actions or events occurring within the context of the work:

> Examples of Twain's portrayal of Jim as the stereotypical "darkey" denounced by Victoria Earle Matthews abound in <u>Adventures of Huckleberry Finn,</u> as when Huck tricks Jim into believing that he had only dreamed of losing Huck on the river (118–121) or when the duke dresses Jim in a King Lear gown and paints his face blue (203).

In discussing other kinds of subjects, use tenses appropriate to the events described. Note how the tense shifts in this paragraph—from past to present—as the discussion moves from the past to the present:

> Three years ago, the small, economically depressed town
> of Blytheville wanted a Japanese steel firm to build
> its new 500-acre steel mill there instead of elsewhere.
> To convince the Japanese of the town's potential,
> citizens invited corporate officials to visit, even
> hosting dinners and community sports events in their
> honor ("Blytheville"). In a similar manner, American-
> owned microchip manufacturers are today busily courting
> Sony, Hitachi, NEC, and Mitsubishi in hopes of gaining
> much-needed Japanese assistance in technology and
> production costs.

Integrating Sources.   The paper's content is a discussion of what your research has led you to understand about the topic. You will need to draw upon your research sources for examples, authority, certain kinds of facts, and effective expressions. Rather than simply add these to the paper, however, you should blend your research into the discussion as part of your own way of understanding the topic. The research material should fit logically and linguistically into the paper's discussion. Irrelevant material, no matter how interesting or otherwise important, should be omitted.

The following discussion uses source material without integration, preventing the voice of the paper's author from coming through:

> Twain's "explanatory" preface shows he
> was concerned about how his readers would
> react to the dialects in <u>Huckleberry</u>
> <u>Finn.</u>

Use of period isolates quotation from writer's discussion

> In this book a number of
> dialects are used, to wit: the
> Missouri negro dialect; the
> extremest form of the backwoods
> South-Western dialect; the

Overquoting obscures writer's point

> ordinary "Pike-County" dialect;
> and four modified varieties of

this last. The shadings have
not been done in a haphazard
fashion, or by guess-work; but
pains-takingly, and with the
trust-worthy guidance and
support of personal familiarity
with these several forms of
speech. (2)

Twain's accurate use of dialects in
the novel has been highly praised.
Linguist James N. Tidwell points out that
"Twain includes only two Negro features
in Jim's speech" but says Twain is
"accurate in presenting the low
colloquial, Southern and Negro features
of Jim's speech. . ."(qtd. in Bell 17).
In the opinion of Hamlin Hill, Twain's
use of dialects signals the "liberation"
of the vernacular in American literature
(xii). Henry Nash Smith thinks Twain's
use of dialect makes the novel
technically and artistically great
(xxiv), while Matthew Kern calls the
dialect use "brilliant" (34).

Sources not integrated

The following version shows a better integration of sources and clearer expression of the writer's own ideas:

Twain himself calls attention to the
dialects of <u>Huckleberry Finn</u> in the
"explanatory" preface to the novel.
Assuring readers that the possibly
awkward-sounding speech of his characters
is both authentic and intended, he
explains that the book uses several
different vernaculars, including "the

*Use of selected
quotations and
paraphrase
condenses
material
and keeps
writer's ideas
prominent*

Missouri Negro dialect" and others with
which he has "personal familiarity" (2).
Modern linguists have in fact vouched for
the accuracy of the regional dialects in

Discussion of dialect is moved to a content note

the novel[4], and literary critics today
praise Twain's "liberation" of the
vernacular voice in American literature

Source material condensed

(Hill xii) as constituting the novel's
technical and artistic greatness (cf.
Smith xxiv).

As this second example demonstrates, you should weave source material into your own commentary and explanation, pruning quotation to highlight important ideas.

Using Quotations. Use direct quotations to give examples and lend authority or whenever a summary would forfeit precision or lose the effectiveness of the original. Except as explained below, maintain the exact wording, spelling, and punctuation of the original any time you quote.

Quotation Marks. Quotation marks separate your own words from those of another. In general, include all quoted words, phrases, or sentences of less than four lines between quotation marks. The following example demonstrates the integration and clear indication of quoted material with the writer's own sentences:

The speaker in Plath's "Daddy," for example, expresses
her seething bitterness over the men in her life who
have failed to return her love. Thus she claims her
father is "a devil" and her husband "a vampire" who
"drank my blood." Though the speaker says at the end of
the poem that she is "through" with anguishing over her
father's death and lost affection, her words seem more
insistent than certain. As Carol Langer points out,
"The poem's intensity of tone and imagery suggest there
is yet more grief than has found words" (45).

Note that titles of short poems such as "Daddy" are also included between quotation marks.

Selection. Since few statements from your sources will require full presentation, omit unnecessary words when you quote. Rather than quote whole sentences, integrate fragments of the original into your own sentences:

Original	"A book so clearly great, yet with such evident defects, poses a difficult critical problem." —Henry Nash Smith, introduction, *Adventures of Huckleberry Finn* by Mark Twain (Boston: Houghton-Riverside, 1958), v.
Integrated quotation	Almost since its first appearance, readers have been divided over the work literary historian Henry Nash Smith describes as "a book so clearly great, yet with such evident defects" (v).
Original	"The genesis of speech is not to be found in the prosaic, but in the poetic side of life: the source of speech is not gloomy seriousness, but merry play and youthful harmony." —Otto Jespersen, *Language: Its Nature, Development and Origin* (London: Allen and Unwin, 1922) 154.
Integrated quotation	Though Jespersen holds that the origins of speech are "not to be found in the prosaic" or in "gloomy seriousness" (154), language is nonetheless a practical medium before it is anything else.

Exceptions to Quoting Exactly. In most cases, a quotation must reproduce words, phrases, and sentences exactly as they appear in the original. Occasionally, however, a quotation may be made clearer or used more effectively with slight alteration of grammar or wording. While some changes are permissible, remember that they must be made in accordance with accepted practices as well as with care not to distort the original meaning of the quotation. Follow these guidelines:

■ *Initial capital letters.* You may change an initial capital letter to fit quoted material grammatically into your own:

Original	"There is a little bit of Huck Finn in all of us" (Gilman 20).
Quotation integrated	Gilman says that "there is a little bit of Huck Finn in all of us" (20).

or

Since "there is a little bit of Huck Finn in all of us" (Gilman 20), we should understand Huck's loyalty to Tom Sawyer, too.

However, if the quoted sentence follows an introduction and is set off by punctuation, the original capital letter must remain:

Gilman says, "There is a little . . .

or

Huck's character should be understood by every reader, insists Gilman: "There is a little . . .

■ *Ending punctuation.* You may change or omit the ending punctuation of the original when the quoted material is added to your own sentence.

Gilman (20) says, "There is a little bit of Huck Finn in all of us," but that explanation still leaves us wondering about Huck's later irresponsibility toward Jim.

or

Though Gilman (20) claims that "there is a little bit of Huck Finn in all of us," we cannot overlook Huck's later irresponsibilty toward Jim.

Though the original sentence ended with a period after *us,* it is understood that the punctation in these examples may have been changed to fit grammatically with the second writer's own sentence structure.

Other than the two cases discussed here and following, you must indicate all other changes in the original material with the use of brackets or ellipses.

■ *Brackets.* Square brackets may be used to change or add to the original wording of a quotation. If your typewriter does not have square brackets, leave spaces for them as you type the paper and add brackets later in ink. Do not confuse brackets [ ] with parentheses ( ).

As with ellipses (discussed below), alter original wording sparingly to avoid interrupting your text with cumbersome punctuation or explanatory material. Use brackets only as needed for the following purposes:

1. To alter a quotation for grammatical accuracy:

Original
> "As President of the United States, he
> figured he should meet the owners."
>
> —Jay Leno, as quoted in Jenson Holger, "A Record Year for U.S. Buys: The Hostility Rises in America," *Macleans* 8 Aug. 1989: 39.

Quotation
altered
> When President George Bush attended the
> funeral of Japanese Emperor Hirohito in
> January 1989, comedian Jay Leno quipped
> that "as President of the United States,
> [Bush] figured he should meet the owners"
> (Holger 39).

2. To enclose the term *sic* (meaning "thus" or "so") to reassure the reader that you have quoted accurately despite an error in the source:

> "When Twain's <u>Adventures of Huckleberry Finn</u> appeared
> in 1875 [sic], Americans were faced with a new kind of
> hero, one many of them considered unfit for that role,"
> says Talbert (11).

Adventures of Huckleberry Finn was published in 1885, not 1875. The addition of *sic* in brackets acknowledges the error in the original.

3. To clarify a quotation's meaning:

> As Alan Shears argues in <u>The Dollar Abroad,</u> "These
> fluctuations [in the value of the dollar] are not just
> economically important. They can make or break world
> peace efforts" (34).

4. To add material between parentheses:

> Yates manages to tell us a number of intriguing details
> about the members of Sylvia Plath's family (e.g., "Otto
> [Sylvia's father] grew up speaking German and Polish"
> [126]).

5. To explain added emphasis:

> Smith argues that the greatness of Huck's character
> lies in his "<u>integrity of emotion</u> [my emphasis], not in
> intellectual acuteness" (xxii).

An alternate method that avoids interrupting the text is to follow the quotation with explanation of the change in parentheses:

> Smith argues that the greatness of Huck's character
> stems from his "<u>integrity of emotion</u>, not in
> intellectual acuteness" (xxii; emphasis added).

■ *Ellipses.* Omit unnecessary material from a quotation or show that it is part of another sentence in the original with the use of three spaced periods (. . .), called *ellipsis points.* Ellipses can indicate the omission of words, phrases, or sentences, but their use should never misrepresent the meaning or context of the original material.

The guidelines below demonstrate uses of ellipses to quote from the following sample passage:

> Mark Twain's emergence as author, rather than as
> celebrity or legend, was slow but continual during the
> years after his death. And Huck tagged along with him
> as he rose in stature. Several factors ensured their
> ultimate admission into the pantheon of American
> classics.
>
> —Hamlin Hill, introduction, *Adventures of Huckleberry Finn*, Centennial Facsimile Edition (New York: Harper, 1987) x.

1. To omit material from within a sentence:

> Hill points out that "Mark Twain's emergence as
> author . . . was slow but continual during the years
> after his death" (x).

Note that this use of ellipses calls for a space before and after each of the periods.

2. To omit beginning material:

```
As Twain's reputation as an author grew, explains Hill,
". . . Huck tagged along beside him as he rose in
stature" (x).
```

Though the above method is acceptable, avoid cluttering your sentences with unnecessary ellipses. Instead, introduce the quoted material using the word *that*, with no punctuation between it and the quotation:

```
As Twain's reputation as an author grew, Hill explains
that "Huck tagged along beside him as he rose in
stature" (x).
```

3. To place omitted material at the end of a sentence:

```
Hill (xi) writes that after Twain's death in 1910, his
"emergence as author, rather than as celebrity or
legend, was continual. . . ."
```

Note that this use, with the source page citation included *before* the quotation, requires three spaced periods for the ellipsis, plus a fourth period to end the sentence (closed to the last word). Another method is to give the source page citation *after* the quotation. The final period is then separate from the three spaced ellipsis points:

```
Hill writes that, after Twain's death in 1910, his
"emergence as author, rather than as celebrity or
legend, was continual . . ." (x).
```

4. To omit sentences in the middle of a quotation:

```
Hill states that "Mark Twain's emergence as author,
rather than as celebrity or legend, was slow but
continual during the years after his death. . . .
Several factors ensured [his] ultimate admission into
the pantheon of American classics" (x).
```

Note that there is no space before the period ending the first sentence, but there are spaces before and after the ellipsis points that follow it. The inclusion of the bracketed *his* in this example keeps the quotation grammatical without distorting its meaning.

5. To omit paragraphs from a long quotation, using a continuous line of spaced periods to indicate the ellipsis:

> Mark Twain's emergence as author, rather than as celebrity or legend, was slow but continual during the years after his death. And Huck tagged along with him as he rose in stature. Several factors ensured their ultimate admission into the pantheon of American classics.
>
> . . . .
>
> Critical interpretations of <u>Huckleberry Finn</u> became more complex, finding more elaborate patterns and themes than merely the colorful panorama of Mississippi life. A major social theme became belatedly apparent: <u>Huckleberry Finn</u> was about freedom as opposed to slavery or, more universally, about freedom as opposed to social restraint and coercion. (x)

Do not indent the first line of a single paragraph when you quote it, even though it may have been indented in the original. But note that when quoting *two or more* paragraphs that were indented in the original, you must indent the first line of each paragraph three spaces, as shown in the above example.

6. To omit lines of poetry from a quotation:

> You stand at the blackboard, daddy,
> In the picture I have of you,
>
> . . . .
>
> I was ten when they buried you.
> At twenty I tried to get back, back to you.
> I thought even the bones would do. (Plath 53)

—Lines from "Daddy" by Sylvia Plath from *The Collected Poems of Sylvia Plath,* edited by Ted Hughes. Copyright (c) 1963 by Ted Hughes. Reprinted by permission of Harper Collins Publishers.

Long Quotations. Any quotation that is longer than four typed lines should be set off as a block and indented 10 spaces from the left margin. Introduce the quotation with a complete sentence and a colon (unless the context calls for some other kind of structure and punctuation):

Other critics, like Hamlin Hill, for
instance, point out that Huck Finn was
simply not the kind of fictional hero
nineteenth—century parents wanted their
children to read about:

A colon introduces
quotation after
complete sentence

> The problem was that Huck lied,
> stole, and spoke inelegant
> vernacular language; he smoked,
> was disrespectful toward his
> elders, and lived in a lower—
> class environment that was
> distressingly vulgar. Huck was
> "common," and even more
> outrageous, he seemed to enjoy
> his shabby condition and
> outcast level in society. (vii)

The Conclusion

The conclusion to your research paper is as important as every other part, possibly even more so. Here is where you will summarize, evaluate, restate for emphasis, place in perspective, and finally drive home the major ideas and lasting impressions you want a reader to take away from the paper. Don't disappoint your audience with an ending that does no more than restate what has already been said. Make the conclusion of your paper as interesting and insightful as possible, something worth the reader's further consideration.

Devising an Effective Conclusion. While there is no single way to conclude any research paper effectively, two guidelines need to to be observed:

1. Reemphasize the thesis statement without repeating it word for word.
2. Be sure the last paragraph clearly signals a conclusion about what has been said.

Avoid the temptation to introduce new issues or list unanswered questions in the conclusion. Instead, offer your reader content that brings the discussion to a logical close.

The following examples demonstrate common approaches to concluding a research paper discussion. You will notice that some closings combine more than one approach.

Reemphasizing the Thesis Statement. Make certain your reader grasps the main point of your paper by emphasizing the paper's thesis again in the conclusion. Rather than simply repeating the thesis statement word for word, emphasize key words and concepts that represent the thesis in the context of the conclusion itself. The final paragraph of Ron Bonneville's paper on Japanese ownership in America, for example, echoes the paper's thesis that expansive Japanese presence in the United States is a positive stage in this country's global development:

> Americans need to recognize that the Japanese presence
> in this country is a reflection of the "new order" of
> which Secretary Baker speaks. If Rockefeller Center in
> New York is a symbol of America, the fact that it is
> now Japanese owned is also a symbol of America's new
> relationship with the world. Properly viewed and
> understood, it is a beneficial relationship for the
> United States, one which, as ex–Ambassador to
> Japan Mansfield predicts, "holds the promise of well–
> being for nations and peoples around the world"
> ("Mansfield" A12).

Presenting a Quotation. An eloquent or particularly striking comment by another voice than your own can effectively sum up your position or significantly affect your reader's awareness. Anne Kramer, for example, felt she wanted her readers to recognize that the conflicting concerns surrounding *Adventures of Huckleberry Finn* were rooted in its power as a great literary work. For this reason, her conclusion returned to the quotation from Ernest Hemingway that appeared at the beginning of the paper:

> The majority of black readers today would agree that,
> properly taught and understood, Mark Twain's <u>Adventures
> of Huckleberry Finn</u> can serve as what black writer
> Charles H. Nichols calls an "indispensable part of the
> education of black and white youth" ("A True Book" 14).
> Certainly, <u>Huckleberry Finn</u> has come a long way from

what made it the "veriest of trash" for white audiences
in the nineteenth century. Today, the book acts for
black as well as white readers as what another black
writer, David L. Smith, calls "a trigger to outrage"
(5), a classic work of art that stirs reflection and
humanity in all of us. In this sense, <u>Adventures of</u>
<u>Huckleberry Finn</u> is perhaps, after all, just what
Ernest Hemingway insisted, "The best book we've had."

Providing Direction or Offering Solutions. If your paper has explored a problem or traced its effects, provide your audience with a direction for action or point out realistic solutions. An informative paper dealing with new developments in the treatment of AIDS might conclude with the following suggestions for further action:

The fact that AIDS victims are living longer because of
recent medical advances places new responsibilities
upon the rest of us. Now we must not only do what we
can to prevent the spread of this deadly disease, but
we must also learn how to aid its victims in surviving
with AIDS. As actress Whoopi Goldberg says, we can all
learn to do something: "If you're a carpenter, you
could build a ramp that would allow more mobility for
someone in a wheelchair. A good cook could provide hot
meals for someone living nearby" (43). What can you and
I do to help? Start by finding out about state-
sponsored AIDS projects or other concerned groups in
your community. Join them. Take part. You'll find you
have more to offer in the war against AIDS than you
ever thought possible.

Evaluating Results. Use the conclusion of your paper to evaluate significant effects or to describe and analyze results. A research report on experiments to identify color preferences among different ethnic groups, for example, might conclude with an analysis of major problems encountered and their influence on the project results. The following paragraph concludes a research paper discussing attempts by world governments to preserve threatened species and environments through international agreements:

As these cases demonstrate, international treaties
alone cannot overcome worldwide threats to fragile
ecosystems and endangered species. As we have seen,
ecosystems and wild animals do not necessarily stay
within national protective boundaries. Even when they
do, the Third World countries in which threatened
entities are found are often too debt ridden to enforce
agreements, preserving instead what are referred to as
"paper parks" that exist only in writing (Golob and
Brus 349). Written global agreements to save wetlands
or threatened plants and animals will never be enough,
however, without the recognition of people everywhere
that nature is neither ours to control nor to destroy.
Without such recognition, human beings themselves may
become the most endangered species on the planet.

Providing a Broader Perspective.   Just as the paper's introduction
has led your reader to a closer examination of the topic, so, too, should
the conclusion lead away from it to a broader perspective. An examination
of a historical event, for example, would conclude by discussing its relationship to later events or its relative significance today. In a literary study,
move from discussing the work itself to seeing it in the context of the author's life or other works:

Sylvia Plath was nearing her thirtieth birthday in the
month that she composed "Daddy" and several other of
her strongest poems. As her marriage to poet Ted Hughes
began falling apart during this time, Plath used her
anger and pain as catalysts to transform her earlier
dependency on male authority figures into spiteful,
creative independence. It is no surprise that "The
Jailer," "Fever 103°," "Ariel," and "Lady Lazarus" all
echo "Daddy" in their vivid images of rebirth and
purification mixed with angry renunciation of males.
The speaker of "Lady Lazarus" rises "out of the ash"
the way the poet's genius itself seemed to rise out of
her own suffering and spiritual rebirth. Plath's

suicide four months after writing "Daddy" and these
other late poems only adds a further, harsh validity
to the psychological and spiritual complexity of all
her work.

Other Backmatter

The concluding section of your research paper will be followed by a
separate page(s) of content notes (see Chapter 9) and a separate Works
Cited page(s) (see Chapter 10), in that order. Documentation of sources
cited in the paper (see Chapter 9) will appear both in the body of the text
and in the Works Cited page(s).

Preparing a Final Draft

By now, your research paper should have a well-developed introduction,
body, and conclusion, followed by any necessary content notes or footnotes and the Works Cited page(s). What you have written at this point
will most likely represent 95% or more of the paper's final content. Any
remaining material will come through performing three important last
steps: revising, editing, and proofreading. These steps understandably often overlap during the process of revision. Conscientiously following
through on each of them, however, will ensure that nothing is left out of
the paper and that everything done so far is in its most effective and final
form.

Revising

Few papers can be written thoroughly with only a first draft. You will
undoubtedly need to make some revisions in the arrangement of the paper's major parts to ensure its general readability, to be certain that it
forms a whole, and to know that everything is in the right order. Since up
to now, you have no doubt been deeply engrossed in the act of writing the
paper, set it aside for a another day or two. When you return to it, you will
read it through with a fresh eye.

Begin your revision by looking at the overall paper as an investigation
and discussion of the research subject. Does the content develop a
smoothly connected *discussion* rather than an assemblage of quotation
and paraphrase? Does the paper exhibit unity and coherence as a whole
and in the development of its paragraphs? Look for transitions that make
the writing clear and flowing.

Review each part of the paper as follows:

1. Reread the *introduction.* A good introduction will arouse a reader's interest in the subject and the discussion that follows. The thesis statement should be clearly stated and follow logically from the introductory material itself.

2. Is the *body* of the paper developed sufficiently? Is there a logical progression of ideas among the individual paragraphs? Remember that the thesis statement idea should be prominent throughout the paper. Check each paragraph for its relationship to the thesis.

3. The *conclusion* should be worth reading. Make sure it offers sufficient content without beginning or alluding to a new subject of discussion. The paper's thesis statement should be emphasized again in the conclusion, but avoid just repeating it word for word.

Revise the paper by rearranging large parts of the content as needed. You can accomplish this by drawing arrrows or making notes on the draft itself, or you can cut and paste various parts in the desired order. If you are writing on a computer, use the "move" functions of your writing program to rearrange text. How much you need to revise depends upon what you recognize is needed, but do not fall into the trap of starting the paper all over again. If you have followed your outline and provided logical connections between the major parts of the paper, rearranging some parts or editing others should be sufficient to prepare for the final typing.

Editing

Editing involves making changes to the text in order to strengthen the content and writing style. Here is when you will need to improve the paper's language or edit sentences and paragraphs for weak style or development.

1. Reread each paragraph to see that it has a topic sentence related to the paper's thesis. Be alert to noticeably long paragraphs that may need trimming or division. Paragraphs that are surprisingly short may need to be combined with others or developed more with examples. At the same time, check for paragraphs that may be "stuffed" with research information irrelevant to the thesis. Edit such paragraphs out of the paper, or revise them as needed. Be sure that each paragraph offers examples and that these support or explain the topic sentence.

2. Edit the paper's language to sharpen vocabulary. Be sure that all central terms are defined for the reader and that any complex terms are used

only when necessary. Avoid the passive voice where possible, and use strong, active verbs in place of weaker constructions. Vary your paper's style and vocabulary to avoid repetition and to add precision; weave paraphrase and quotation into your own sentence structures:

> As Brewer *points out*, "Though certainly admirable,
> Twain's stylistic versatility could sometimes become a
> major weakness" (66).

> Brewer (66) *says* that Twain's versatility was at times
> also a great weakness.

> Brewer *has argued* that Twain's versatility was at times
> also a great weakness (66).

> Other critics *agree* with Brewer (66) that Twain's
> versatility was at times also a great weakness.

A dictionary or thesaurus can provide alternatives for any words that may get frequently repeated in the paper.

3. Also edit to avoid sexist language, wording that discriminates against males or females by inaccurately portraying them in stereotypical ways. The following sentence, for example, demonstrates erroneous sexual stereotyping of male and female roles:

> A nurse's salary can improve a great deal once she has
> two or three years of experience. A doctor, however,
> has to complete his residency requirement in a hospital
> before he sees much increase in income.

Language such as this is sexually biased because it implies that all nurses are female and all doctors are male. Using *he or she* in place of the single pronouns may eliminate some of the bias, but such use can sound awkward if repeated. A better way is to construct sentences using plural nouns and pronouns:

> Salaries for *nurses* can improve a great deal once *they*
> have two or three years of experience. *Doctors*,
> however, have to complete *their* residency
> requirements in a hospital before *they* see much
> increase in income.

Another way to avoid bias is to omit the use of pronouns altogether:

```
Salaries for nurses with two or three years' experience
can improve a great deal. Doctors, however, have to
complete residency requirements in a hospital before
seeing much increase in income.
```

Also edit to remove language that discriminates against groups of various ages, ethnicities, sexual preferences, and so on.

Proofreading

Proofread you paper several times to make minor corrections in spelling, punctuation, and typing. Do not make the mistake of relying upon others to proofread for you. Even if someone else has typed the final version, you will find that your own acquaintance with the research material is an essential safeguard against misspellings or omissions of content.

Correct small typing mistakes and other errors neatly by hand, using correcting fluid and ink. If there are very many such corrections, however, preserve the paper's neatness by retyping some sections. After you have carefully read the final version several times and made necessary corrections, share the paper with others who can proofread it again for you with a fresh view of the content.

WORKING WITH OTHERS

Rather than wait until the entire paper is completed, discuss your efforts with others throughout the planning and writing stages. If it helps, set up a regular meeting time at two- or three-day intervals to discuss your progress. Such a pattern will help to keep your writing on schedule.

You'll find that talking over your progress with others during the writing stage of the research paper can help you get over writer's block and test the paper's effectiveness as you work. Having someone else review the final draft of the paper for revision and editing purposes is always a good idea.

After you have proofread the paper yourself, ask a friend or classmate to look it over, too. Listen carefully as he or she responds to these or any additional concerns about which you have questions or would value a response.

- Often another person's immediate reaction or interest in a paper can be a measure of how well it is written. Ask your friend or classmate how he or she responds to the paper. Is it readable? Is the discussion interesting?

- How effective does your reader feel the paper's introduction, body, and conclusion are? What areas are particularly strong? Do any weak parts need more development or revision?

- Does the paper have a clear, logical organization? Is the thesis supported throughout?

- Proofread the paper together. If you are working with a classmate, take turns reading each other's papers. Indicate any mistakes with a small check in pencil in the paper's margin. Discuss the checked places together to be sure about any changes to the paper.

- Next to your instructor, a classmate is probably the best judge of the paper's use of sources and their proper citation. Ask his or her opinion on these matters, and be prepared to follow through with any you feel important to the paper's total effectiveness.

As you discuss your paper with others during the writing and revision stages, listen carefully and take notes whenever you can. Try not to hurry this important sharing session. The more time you spend reviewing each other's papers, the more confident you can be of the paper's strengths. While working with other classmates during this time, remember to offer the same serious attention to their papers as you have asked for yours.

CHAPTER NINE

Acknowledging Sources
Intext Citation and Content Notes (MLA Style)

In addition to the discussion of the research topic, your completed paper will also include documentation of the sources you have cited and, in some cases, content notes that provide further information about your research. You must always give credit in the paper for any ideas and language you borrow directly or adapt from another source, although you should not cite sources for information that is common knowledge. (See the discussion of plagiarism and common knowledge in Chapter 6.)

Following a Standard Documentation Format

Generally speaking, entries in the Works Cited section at the end of the paper tell the reader what sources you have borrowed from in writing the paper's content. Such general acknowledgments, however, do not tell the reader precisely what was taken from a source and where or show how it was used in the paper's discussion. Consequently, documentation formats used in writing for various disciplines also include either intext citation of sources or endnotes or footnotes to convey this kind of precise acknowledgment of sources.

This chapter describes the methods of documentation recommended by the Modern Language Association (MLA), a nationwide association of teachers and scholars that sets standards for publishing papers about English and modern and classical languages. Documentation formats used by writers in other disciplines are discussed in Chapter 10.

MLA Documentation

MLA documentation style requires up to three methods of acknowledging sources in a research paper: (1) parenthetic intext citation of sources, (2) full documentation in the Works Cited page(s), and when appropriate to the paper, (3) content notes. All sources cited in text or mentioned in the content notes must also appear in the Works Cited page(s). These methods of documentation are preferred by the MLA, though some schools and journals still use footnotes or endnotes. Which documentation method you use may depend upon your subject and the format your instructor wants you to follow. (If your instructor wants you to use endnotes or footnotes, see the discussion of *Chicago* style in Chapter 11.)

Using Intext Citation

Intext citation means identifying the source of any borrowed material immediately as it appears, right in the text of the paper. (An intext citation is only the first such acknowledgment you will give your sources; the Works Cited section of your paper will list each source again, giving complete publication information.) Intext citation requires the minimum information a reader would need to find the item in the Works Cited page(s) of your paper or in the cited material itself. In most cases, this means giving the author and page number(s) for the source you are crediting:

Author	According to Berman, adopted children "want to be connected with a past heritage or a genealogical history"
Page number	(119).

This example demonstrates intext citation form for a single author. Note, however, that no citation is needed when you refer to an author's entire work rather than a part of it:

Alice Walker's <u>The Color Purple</u> examines people's hopes and dreams with great sensitivity.

For citing authors, titles, and other kinds of information, follow the guidelines given below.

Placement of Items.   When the identity of an author is important for purposes of clarity, emphasis, or authority, include the name in your text as you introduce a quotation or paraphrase. Place page number(s) of the source in parentheses at the end of the borrowed material:

Author cited with quotation	Henry Nash Smith argues that the Huck Finn of the novel's last chapter is "decidedly inferior to the character who had been capable of such a profound loyalty to his friend Jim in the middle section" (xxii).
Author cited in paraphrase	According to Henry Nash Smith, Huck's character diminishes in the last chapter when he proves to be less of a friend to Jim than before (xxii).

When your major emphasis is on the content of the borrowed material, however, include the author's name in parentheses with the page number(s):

It's clear that by the last chapter Huck is "decidedly inferior to the character who had been capable of such a profound loyalty to his friend Jim in the middle section" (Smith xxii).

Huck's character clearly diminishes in the last chapter when he proves to be less of a friend to Jim than before (Smith xxii).

NOTE: Be certain that you do *not* place a comma between the author's name and the page number(s). MLA citation form calls for listing the author's name and the page numbers *without punctuation,* as in the preceding examples. In addition, never use *p.* or *pg.* before the page number(s).

An author's name should appear only once in any intext acknowledgment. Include the author's name in the text or in the parentheses following, but not in both:

Incorrect: **Author named** **in both text** **and parenthetic** **citation**	Ex–ambassador to Japan Mike Mansfield believes that the relationship between Japan and the U.S. "holds the promise of well–being for nations and peoples around the world" (Mansfield A12).

Citing an Author, Editor, or Corporation.   In general, treat individuals, editors, corporate authors, and others who would normally be considered responsible for producing a work as its author. Note that the intext citation form for an author and editor does not distinguish between their roles. In the Works Cited section of the paper, however, the designation *ed.* (for *editor*) differentiates between them for your reader. The following examples demonstrate alternative techniques for placement of author names:

Single author	Despite the current international squeeze on U.S. markets, the Bush administration has at least managed to lower the huge trade imbalance by a significant fraction and strengthen export growth at the same time (Kennedy 528).
Single editor	As Robert J. Slater insists, "If we can't learn from the Japanese, it's because we don't really want to" (77).
Corporate author	According to a recent survey, most Americans now agree that foreign ownership of U.S. properties is "bad for the country" (Smick–Medley 8–9).
	The American Commission on Economic Development has documented that foreign investors own the majority of prime real estate holdings in many U.S. cities, including New York and Los Angeles (15).

In a case such as this, where the name of the source is long or perhaps similar to that of another source, the MLA suggests citing the name in the text discussion rather than within a parenthetical citation. Long intext citations, as well as other parenthetical material, break up the content and impair the reader's concentration.

Citing More Than One Author. Cite both authors by their last names if there are two, but cite only the first author's last name followed by *et al.* ("and others") if there are three or more authors:

■ Two authors:

Authors introduced in text	Naisbitt and Aburdene claim we are approaching the day when "virtually all women will work except for a few months or years when they are raising children full-time" (7).
Parenthetic citation of authors	We are approaching the day when "virtually all women will work except for a few months or years when they are raising children full-time" (Naisbitt and Aburdene 7).

■ Three or more authors:

Authors introduced in text	According to studies by Mathers et al., AIDS is decreasing only in specifically targeted areas of the country (72).
Parenthetic citation of authors	We know that AIDS is decreasing only in very narrow, specially targeted areas of the country (Mathers et al. 72).

Citing Multiple Works by the Same Author. When listing more than one source by the same author in the Works Cited page(s), give the author's name in the citation, followed by a comma, followed by the name of the source and the page number(s):

Sylvia Plath's poetry has long been recognized as exhibiting a "good deal of disturbance with proportionately little fuss" (Alvarez, "Poetry" 26).

Entries for Alvarez's work would appear in alphabetical order by title in the Works Cited page(s). After the first entry, additional works listed would show three unspaced hyphens for the author's name:

> Alvarez, A. "Poetry in Extremism." <u>The Observer</u>
>   14 March 1963: 26–33.
> ---. "Sylvia Plath." <u>Tri-Quarterly</u> 7 (1966): 65–74.

Citing Titles.   Cite titles of sources only when (1) there is no author's name provided or (2) you need to distinguish between one source and another by the same author (*The Sun Also Rises* and *The Old Man and the Sea,* by Ernest Hemingway, for example). In both cases, use recognizable, shortened versions of the title when it is cited: *Sun* for *The Sun Also Rises; Huck Finn* for *Adventures of Huckleberry Finn,* and so on. (See Chapter 12 for common abbreviations for literary titles.)

1. If there is no author to cite, describe the issuing magazine, newspaper, agency, or other authority when you introduce the borrowed material:

> A recent article in <u>Newsweek</u> magazine claims Japanese
> corporations who buy Hollywood studios have no
> intentions of getting involved in actual production
> decisions ("Next Stop" 48).

> A weekly news magazine recently claimed that Japanese
> corporations who buy Hollywood studios have no
> intentions of getting involved in actual production
> decisions ("Next Stop" 48).

The Works Cited entry would look like this:

> "Next Stop, Tinseltown." Newsweek 20 Mar.
>   1989: 48–49.

2. To distinguish between material taken from different sources by the same author, cite page number(s) and shortened titles in parentheses, as follows:

> The strongest of Hemingway's male characters embrace
> rituals of disciplined courage as a part of their roles

in life. We see this in the fine, respectful precison
of the great Belmonte when he enters the "territory of
the bull" (<u>Sun</u> 135) and again when the old fisherman
vows to "be worthy of the great [Joe] DiMaggio who does
all things perfectly even with the pain of the bone
spur in his heel" (<u>Old Man</u> 68).

Citing Indirect Sources.　Though it is always best to consult a source
directly for any material you adapt from it, you may not always be able to
do so. In cases when you cannot locate the original source of a quotation,
cite the source you have, preceding it with *qtd. in* ("quoted in"):

As two ex–Secretaries of State, Henry Kissinger and
Cyrus Vance, warned in a recent <u>Foreign Affairs</u>
article, "America's ability to influence events
abroad . . . will be determined in a large part by
how rapidly we get our economic house in order"
(qtd. in "Fitting" 80).

The inclusion of *qtd. in* with the source citation indicates that the
writer did not take the quotation from the actual *Foreign Affairs* article by
Kissinger and Vance, but instead got it from an article with the shortened
title "Fitting." The Works Cited entry for this citation would include only
the indirect source, not the *Foreign Affairs* article by Kissinger and Vance:

"Fitting into a Global Economy." <u>U.S.</u>
<u>News & World Report</u> 26 Dec. 1989: 80–82.

Citing Multiple Sources.　If you borrow an idea mentioned in more
than one source, give credit in the paper to all sources. Always cite multiple sources parenthetically. Separate the sources with a semicolon:

It is clear that Huck is too conditioned by his white
upbringing to think of Jim's future or even his
precarious freedom at the end of the novel (Nilon 23;
Jones 31-32).

Each source would then appear in the paper's Works Cited section in
the normal manner.

NOTE: Citing multiple sources parenthetically in text is cumbersome and may interfere with your reader's concentration. Cite multiple sources in text sparingly and only when necessary. If you need to list more than three, cite the sources in a note rather than parenthetically in the text (see "Using Content Notes," later in this chapter).

Citing Volume and Page Numbers.   For a work in more than one volume, cite the volume number followed by a colon, followed by a space and the page number(s):

```
Freud believed in a process he called "free
association" to uncover the hidden meaning of
dreams (V: 221).
```

Citing Page Numbers of Classical Works.   A classical work remains in demand long after its author's death. Once its copyright has expired, such a work may be published in several editions by different publishing houses. Classical works such as *Adventures of Huckleberry Finn* or *The Scarlet Letter,* for example, appear in several editions, each published by a different publisher and each bearing the same material but on differently numbered pages. Since your reader may have an edition with different pagination than yours, give the page number for your source, followed by a semicolon and the chapter, book, section, or other parts abbreviated and numbered, as well:

```
Twain satirizes monarchies by having Huck give Jim a
brief lesson about kings and dukes (130; ch. 22).

The main character in Dostoyevsky's Crime and
Punishment tries to convince himself that he has
"killed a principle" rather than another human being
(271; pt. 3; sec. 6)
```

When discussing a classic poem such as *Paradise Lost* or *Canterbury Tales,* line numbers will also be more useful to your reader than page numbers of an edition he or she may not have. Omit page numbers, and cite the work by divisions such as canto, book, part, line(s), scene, or act. Use abbreviated or shortened titles (see Chapter 12), followed by numbers separated with periods to represent the work's divisions. Thus PL *2.428–29* would indicate part 2, lines 428–29, of John Milton's *Paradise Lost:*

Reference
to a poem

> Milton's Satan exhibits "monarchal
> pride/Conscious of highest worth"
> (<u>PL</u> 2.428-29) when speaking early in the
> poem. Later, however, he is described as
> "Squat like a toad, close at the ear of
> Eve" (4.799-800).

Similarly, discuss a drama (such as Shakespeare's *Macbeth*) by providing line, scene, and act numbers: Mac. *3.2.25-38*. Roman numerals, instead of arabic as shown here and above, are acceptable if they appear in the source or if your instructor prefers them. (See Chapter 12 on numbers.)

Citing Nonprint Sources.   Nonprint sources such as an interview, recording, or television or radio speech have no page numbers. Cite these kinds of sources by giving the author's name in the text or parenthetically. The author's name in the Works Cited list will key readers to the type of work referred to:

Text entry

> Governor Barrington said he would be
> sorry to see opponents of the bill "use
> the law to fight against justice."

Works Cited
entry

> Barrington, Alan. Personal interview. 18
> Oct. 1990.

Text entry

> As one critic complained, "Twain never
> had a good explanation of Huck's behavior
> at the end of the novel, so why should
> we?" (Carter).

Works Cited
entry

> Carter, Andrew. Address. "Huck
> Finn--Again." National Literature
> Conference. Boston, 20 May 1989.

Citing Multiple Page References to the Same Work.   When discussing a short story, novel, long poem, or play throughout the paper, do not repeat the author's name for each reference. In general, name the author and title once, and cite only page numbers after that.

When discussing a prose work, for example, omit the author's name after the first page citation:

```
In The Old Man and the Sea, Hemingway's fisherman
believes firmly in his own courage, of being "worthy of
the great DiMaggio" (68). He recalls days when, much
younger, he felt he could "beat anyone if he had to"
(70). Though he eventually loses his great fish, the
old man insists that "man is not made for defeat"
(103), and the novel ends with his "dreaming about
the lions" (127).
```

```
The old fisherman believes firmly in his own courage,
of being "worthy of the great DiMaggio" (Hemingway 68).
He recalls days when, much younger, he felt he could
"beat anyone if he had to" (70).
```

To allow a reader to find quoted material in any edition of a prose work, include the chapter number after the page number, separated by a semicolon:

```
The old fisherman believes firmly in his own courage,
of being "worthy of the great DiMaggio" (Hemingway 68;
ch. 4).
```

Using Content Notes

Content notes differ from the documentation appearing in footnotes or the Works Cited page(s) of your paper. You may find such notes helpful in providing additional commentary or explanations that are not immediately relevant to your paper's discussion. Be aware, however, that you should use such notes sparingly. Make a point to include important material in the main text of your paper. Reserve content notes for the addition of *necessary* qualification or explanations when their inclusion in the main text would otherwise interrupt your discussion.

To include content notes in your paper, follow these guidelines:

1. Refer your paper's reader to a content note by means of a superscript numeral, a raised arabic number immediately following the material to which the note refers:

```
                    Until the 1950s, the United States was
                    the only country in the world with a
                    manufacturing base sufficient to control
```

worldwide production and leadership
(Neale 34). By the 1960s, other
countries, including Japan, had begun to
achieve the same or a higher level of
production skills, with greatly cheaper
labor costs to make them significantly

Content note   competitive.[4] Hence, the weakening value
of the American dollar today is also
symbolic of the decline of American
dominance in world manufacturing and
trade.

2. Type superscript numerals, such as the numeral [4] shown above, by turning the typewriter roller up so that the typed number appears about a half space above the text, usually at the end of the sentence to which it refers, as here[2]. If you are writing on a computer, type the superscript numeral by using the appropriate function keys or commands for your word-processing program.

3. Do not space between the superscript number and any word or punctuation that precedes it.

4. Remember that superscript numbers for content notes should appear in numerical sequence throughout the text, regardless of what page they appear on.

5. Place all content notes on a separate page(s) with the centered title Notes appearing at the top. (See the Notes page of the sample research paper at the end of this chapter.) Content note entries should appear immediately below, each preceded by a raised number indicating the text material to which it corresponds. The following content note, for example, refers to the correspondingly numbered material in the preceding paragraph example:

[4]Japan's rise as a world power in business and
technology, of course, has been due to more than just
the availabilty of cheap labor. Peters and Waterman
(37-39) point to Japan's management structure and, like
Naisbitt and Aburdene (278), to the culturally dominant
social and business ethics that underlie its great
success.

6. Any source you mention in a content note must also appear with complete documentation in the Works Cited page(s) of the paper. For instance, you would need to include the authors mentioned in the preceding example (*Peters and Waterman,* etc.) in the Work Cited page(s) even if you did not also cite them in the paper's text.

Content notes can be used for a variety of purposes:

- To elaborate on matters not strictly relevant to the text discussion

> [1]Twain himself seems to have felt that Huck's struggle with his conscience over helping a runaway slave was central to the book's message. In an apparent attempt to be more explicit about the meaning of Huck's decision to help Jim, Twain made several careful notes and revisions to the published version of the book prior to reading it aloud to tour audiences. See Smith (260).
>
> [2]Sacks (149) points out that there has also been a parallel shift in the public's attitude toward the deaf. He claims the change from perceiving the deaf as pathetic victims to viewing them as uniquely empowered is demonstrated in two popular films: The Heart Is a Lonely Hunter (1975) and Children of a Lesser God (1986).

- To add clarification

> [3]Scholars and others who comment on the frequency of "nigger" in Huckleberry Finn vary in their count, however. For Williams (39), it occurs between 160–200 times; Bell (10) says 150 times. My own count totaled 156.
>
> [4]Not all biologists agree with Wilson's estimates. Lugo (81–90) argues that a slight shift in assumptions would predict a loss of only 9% of threatened species by the year 2000. If Lugo is correct, however, even a

9% loss from 5 million species would result in 450,000 extinct species.

[5]This is not to say that Asians and Europeans consider all U.S. exports inferior. American–made clothing--especially denim jeans--and Hollywood films are still top–rated exports everywhere (Dorn 33).

■ To evaluate or compare sources

[6]Published in 1910, Howells' <u>My Mark Twain</u> remains one of the most perceptive and personal contemporary accounts of Twain's personality.

[7]Keeler's study of underachieving college students is based on interviews with college students and professors. A more persuasive viewpoint is expressed in Mike Rose's <u>Lives on the Boundary</u> (New York: Macmillan, 1989). Rose tells of his own under–privileged education and its relevance to his teaching and working with struggling minority students at UCLA.

■ To provide statistics

[8]Ravitch and Finn found that, of 8,000 17–year-olds sampled, more (68%) had read <u>Adventures of Huckleberry Finn</u> or at least knew its story (80.5%) than any other major work (89, 106). A recent survey by <u>U.S. News & World Report</u> of 696 college seniors found that 95% could name the author of <u>Adventures of Huckleberry Finn</u>, while only 62% could name the author of the next best known work, <u>Canterbury Tales</u>, by Geoffrey Chaucer ("Reader's Block" 89).

[9]Laboratory results over a six–week period showed a loss of 3.05 mg of potassium, with a corresponding 9% decrease in fluid volume. Density measurements were not recorded during the first cycle of testing but were found during the second cycle to be .07% higher.

■ To explain methods or procedures

> [10]I interviewed Robert Nelson with the assistance
> of an interpreter who conveyed my questions to him in
> American Sign Language (ASL), translating his responses
> orally to me. His "words," as quoted in this paper,
> are the verbatim answers provided to me and recorded on
> tape by the interpreter, Louise Ibarra.

> [11]Researchers induced three types of naturally
> occurring fungi--penicillium, acremonium, and
> uloclabium--into selenium—contaminated soil
> through addition of humus, regular aeration, and
> irrigation between 1983 and 1985. The fungi
> converted selenium to the less toxic gases
> dimethylselenide and dimethyldiselenide. See
> Golub and Brus (369).

■ To cite additional sources

> [12]For more information on Twain's private
> attitude toward blacks and other minorities, see
> Spiller (932); Gresham (114); and Pettit (140). Twain's
> acquaintance with other than American blacks is
> discussed in Coleman O. Parsons, "Mark Twain: Paid
> Performer in South Africa," Mark Twain Journal 19
> (1978): 2–11.

> [13]See also Sacks (42), Luria and Yudovich (121),
> and Church (63).

■ To shorten major source citations

> [14]All references and page number citations for
> Adventures of Huckleberry Finn are from the Centennial
> Facsimile Edition (Harper & Row, 1987).

> [15]Ernest Hemingway, The Old Man and the Sea.
> Future citations in the text will be to page numbers
> only.

■ To define an important term

> [16]For consistency and to reflect the most common usage today, throughout this paper, I have used the term <u>black</u> to refer to the people some of my sources have variously called <u>Negro</u>, <u>Black</u>, or <u>African-American</u>.

> [17]The term <u>phantasmal voices</u> refers to the sense of actually hearing speech, which the postlingually deaf may experience when they read lips. They do not, of course, actually "hear" speech. They instead translate the visual experience into an auditory correlate based on their memory of sound as they knew it before becoming deaf. See Sacks (6).

The sample research paper in the Chapter Appendix (see pages 213–232) demonstrates the use of content notes to clarify and add information pertinent to the author's discussion. As you examine this paper, note the way sources are used and given proper intext citation throughout.

WORKING WITH OTHERS

Check the accuracy of your paper's documentation by sharing the final draft with others. Seek advice about the effectiveness of any content notes, and encourage readers to make suggestions. The following suggestions may also be helpful.

■ Ask your reader to note the placement and accompanying punctuation for all intext citations as they appear in the paper. Check for complete parentheses, with periods following the parentheses whenever they appear at the end of a sentence. Be sure that no comma separates the author's name and the page number citation, as in this correct example: (Smith 65).

■ Point out any unusual intext citations that you want your reader's opinion about. For example, look especially at multiple-author entries, works cited only by title, or different authors with the same last name. Are these cited correctly in the paper?

- Discuss your rationale for each of the paper's content notes. Does your reader feel each note serves a useful purpose? Should any be reduced or rewritten?

- Use the sample paper that follows (see the Chapter Appendix) to compare your own and your reader's final drafts. Discuss major differences, as well as any intext citations or content notes you have questions about.

APPENDIX

A sample student research paper follows on pages 213–232. Review the annotations throughout for guidelines on a variety of subjects. Consult the cross-references given for more information.

Center
paper's
title, your
name, and
course
information
on title page

The Response of Black Readers
to Mark Twain's
<u>Adventures of Huckleberry Finn</u>

by
Anne Kramer

English 101
Professor Jeanne Corderman
December 14, 1990

Kramer ii

Outline

Thesis: The black response to <u>Huckleberry Finn</u> centers not only upon its demeaning language and negative portrayal of black character but upon its consequent value as literature, as well.

I. Introduction: Reputation of the novel

II. Language and characterization
   A. Criticism of Victoria Earle Matthews
      1. Black dialect
      2. Characterization of blacks
   B. Twain's realism
      1. "Explanatory" note
      2. Accuracy of dialects
      3. Jim's dialect contrasted with Huck's
   C. The use of "nigger"
      1. Twain's purpose
      2. Uses in the text

III. Characterization of Jim
   A. Seen as stereotype
   B. Used by Huck and others
   C. Effect on readers

IV. Value of <u>Huckleberry Finn</u>
   A. Jim's overriding humanity
   B. The novel as a moral "trigger to outrage"

Margin annotations:

Write thesis at beginning of outline

Use standard outline form

This outline is organized by topics

Include running head; use lowercase roman numerals for preliminary pages and arabic numerals for text pages

The Response of Black Readers
to Mark Twain's
<u>Adventures of Huckleberry Finn</u>

Repeat title on first page of text

Opening paragraph begins with a quotation

"All modern literature comes from one book by Mark Twain called <u>Huckleberry Finn</u>," wrote Ernest Hemingway in 1935. "It's the best book we've had" (22). Although most literary critics and the general reading public would agree with Hemingway's assessment, the novel he and many others have so highly praised is also one of the most controversial classics on American bookshelves. Banned and denounced as "the veriest of trash" by the Concord Library Committee when it was first published in America (Rule 10),

Cite sources parenthetically in text

Mark Twain's <u>Adventures of Huckleberry Finn</u> has borne a long history of staunch criticism and debate, first over what white audiences viewed as its common vulgarity and, increasingly in this century, what many perceive as its racist and demeaning portrayal of black character. The result has been a concerned, often outraged black[1] response

Use short title for discussing work

to <u>Huckleberry Finn</u> that centers not only upon the work's language and characterization but upon its consequent value as literature, as well.

Raised numeral refers reader to Notes page(s)

Thesis concludes introductory section

Kramer 2

The concerns of black audiences over
language and characterization in
Huckleberry Finn date back at least to
1896 with the outspoken criticism of
Victoria Earle Matthews, the first
national chairperson of the National
Association of Colored Women. Addressing
the Association that year, Matthews
openly criticized "the Negro-hating Mark
Twain" (Robinson 190) along with other
white novelists whose works she felt
misrepresented "people of African descent
in the United States" (Matthews 170). She
advocated a new "race literature," which
would more positively portray people of
color and eliminate "the traditional
Negro in dialect, the subordinate, the
servant" so familiar to readers of the
day (173). Anticipating the resentment
future generations would feel over Jim's
characterization in Huckleberry Finn,
Matthews further spoke against the stream
of current literature portraying every
black character as the representative
"Darkey" (176).

    Such criticism of Twain and other
white novelists of the age identified
what black readers today view as the
central issues surrounding Huckleberry

Preceding
author
citation
allows for
citing page
numbers
alone here

Kramer 3

Type dash as two unspaced hyphens

Finn--the demeaning portrayal of black character and dialect. Twain himself calls attention to the dialects of Huckleberry Finn in the "explanatory" preface to the novel. Assuring readers that the possibly awkward-sounding speech of his characters is both authentic and intended, he explains that the book uses several different vernaculars, including "the Missouri Negro dialect" and others with which he has "personal familiarity" (2).[2] The success of Twain's efforts to create characters through natural, realistic speech has been highly praised, with linguistic authorities of today vouching for the accuracy of the many regional dialects he presents.[3] In fact, what critic Hamlin Hill and others have praised as the "liberation" of the vernacular voice in American literature (Twain xii) is something most critics agree constitutes the novel's technical and artistic greatness (cf. Smith, xxvii).

Use common academic abbreviations such as *cf.* "compare"

Despite such present-day praise, however, contemporary black readers and critics--like Victoria Earle Matthews, cited earlier--find Twain's thoroughness in presenting "the Missouri Negro

Lowercase roman numerals indicate preliminary pages in source

Kramer 4

dialect" spoken by Jim and other black
characters in <u>Huckleberry Finn</u>
nonetheless demeaning. Thus, when Huck
and Jim discuss the biblical King
Solomon, Huck's language may be cast in
the vernacular, but it is also clearly
superior to Jim's stereotypical "Darkey"
way of speaking:

> [Huck:] "Well, but he <u>was</u> the
> wisest man, anyway; because the
> widow she told me so, her own
> self."
> [Jim:] "I doan k'yer what de
> widder say, he <u>warn't</u> no wise
> man, nuther. He had som er de
> dad—fetchedes' ways I ever see.
> Does you know 'bout dat chile
> dat he 'uz gwyne to chop in
> two?" (111)

Such contrasting styles of speaking
give Huck, Jim, and the novel's other
characters distinctive identities, but
they also emphasize racial differences
among characters. Black writer Nick Aaron
Ford feels that Jim's "inconsistent,
exaggerated, comic dialect" in the novel
reinforces the reader's belief in the
inability of blacks "even to come close
to mastering the language patterns of the

The author integrates quotation with her own sentence structures

Brackets enclose material not included in original

Separate dialogue with quotation marks and paragraphing between speakers' remarks

Indent long quotations 10 spaces from left margin. Do not indent a single quoted paragraph.

Kramer 5

dominant culture" (434). Another black
writer, Charles H. Nichols, points out
that Jim's "absurd dialectical speech"
robs not only him but also other black
characters in the novel of their dignity
and separate identities as individuals
("A True Book" 15).

Nowhere, however, is the charge of
insensitivity and linguistic racism in
<u>Huckleberry Finn</u> more heatedly focused
than upon the liberal use of the word
<u>nigger</u>, spoken by Huck and others
throughout the novel and appearing some
150-200 times or more.[4] Black as well as
white critics are divided on Twain's
reason for using the term, as well as
upon its overall effect upon readers.
Some agree that the term was the common
and most authentic word Twain could have
used in <u>Huckleberry Finn</u> and that
employing any other would have seriously
jeopardized the book's integrity (Rule
17). It is clear from Twain's own
writings that he consciously moved away
from using the word in his later works
and even before creating <u>Huckleberry Finn</u>
(Petitt 91). That fact gives support to
the view of several critics, black as
well as white, that Twain may have been

Margin notes:

Cite both titles and page numbers to distinguish several works by same author

Underline word discussed in text

Kramer 6

using the word <u>nigger</u> ironically in the
novel as a way of making white readers
more self-conscious about it (Rule 17;
Nichols "A True Book" 15).

    In Twain's own time, <u>nigger</u> was
already considered demeaning to blacks
(Rule 17), and it seems clear that even
Huck recognizes the word's negative
senses, as when he talks about sinning
and going to hell for helping a <u>nigger</u>
rather than a <u>slave</u> or <u>runaway</u>. The term
appears consistently in a variety of
contexts whenever anyone mentions someone
who is black. Jim, for instance, is
introduced in Chapter 2 as "Miss Watson's
big nigger, named Jim" (22); Huck tells
us "you can't learn a nigger to argue"
(114), and the doctor who treats Tom
Sawyer assures others that Jim "ain't a
bad nigger" (356). In one much debated
exchange, Aunt Polly asks Huck if anyone
got hurt when the cylinder head of the
boat he was supposedly on blew up. Huck
answers, "No'm. Killed a nigger," to
which she replies, "Well, it's lucky;
because sometimes people do get hurt"
(280).

    Black critics generally agree that
in this scene, Huck is not speaking for

Separate
multiple
citations
with
semicolons

Kramer 7

his own view of black people but only
attempting to make his lie more
successful, playing upon Aunt Sally's own
"glib and conventional bigotry" (David
Smith 5) in order to expose it to the
reader. Charles H. Nichols, in fact,
interprets the scene as carrying out
Twain's purpose of satirizing "racist
self-righteousness" throughout the novel
("Color" 41).

Give both
first and
last names
when two
authors
have same
last name

The difficulty black as well as
white readers today have adjusting to
Twain's use of <u>nigger</u> in the novel is
matched by the general reaction to the
characterization of Jim. Critics agree
that Twain too often debases him at the
hands of Huck and other white characters.
Black critics especially feel that Jim
may indeed be noble, but in addition to
being demeaned through the book's
language, he is also presented as the
stereotypical "good nigger," ignorant and
superstitious, a boy-man who "violates
all our conception of adult maleness"
(Nichols, "Color" 41). Black novelist
Ralph Ellison views Jim even more
harshly, describing him as no more than
"a white man's inadequate portrait of a
slave" (qtd. in Bell 13).

Kramer 8

Examples of Twain's portrayal of Jim
as the stereotypical "Darkey" denounced
by Victoria Earle Matthews abound in the
novel, as when Huck tricks Jim into
believing that he had only dreamed of
losing Huck on the river (118–121) or
when the duke dresses Jim in a King Lear
gown and paints his face blue (203). The
ultimate example of Jim's debasement, of
course, occurs in the final chapters,
when Tom and Huck use Jim to carry out
their game of freeing him from a castle.
Scenes such as these are intended to be
humorous, but both white and black
critics agree that they succeed only by
demeaning Jim (cf. Spiller 933; Nichols
410). Black readers, especially young
ones, says Hank Aaron Ford, find such
scenes especially disturbing:

> It is embarrassing . . . to see
> a member of their race,
> fictional or real, become an
> object of fun and condescending
> laughter to members of the
> white majority, as is the case
> with Jim. In such a situation
> the [reader] identifies with
> Jim and thus suffers a painful
> loss of dignity and self—
> respect. (436)

Ellipsis
indicates
omission
of original
material

Cite source
for long,
indented
quotation
at the end,
following
final
period

Use
brackets to
indicate
alteration
of original
material in
quotation

Kramer 9

Indeed, for black audiences
generally, the potential value of reading
<u>Adventures of Huckleberry Finn</u> as a work
of significant literature continues to be
seriously undermined by the novel's
seeming mockery of blacks and the
insensitivy of whites to their feelings
about the novel's racist implications.
Recalling her feelings when reading
<u>Adventures of Huckleberry Finn</u> in a
predominantly white school, for instance,
Margot Allen describes her own reactions
to the constant appearance of the term

Use colon to introduce long quotation

<u>nigger</u> as follows:

> I need not tell you I hated the
> book! Yet, while we read it, I
> pretended that it didn't bother
> me. I hid, from my teacher and
> my classmates, the tensions,
> discomfort and hurt I would
> feel every time I heard that
> word or watched the class laugh
> at Jim and felt some white
> youngster's stare being
> directed my way. . . . ("Huck
> Finn: Two Generations" 9)

As a result of her early experience with
the book, Allen feels that there is a
heavy cost to pay in reading <u>Huckleberry</u>

<u>Finn</u>. It is a cost, she says, "borne in
large part by young Black students who
may experience a complex range and mix of
feelings from indifference to anger, from
insult to humiliation" (12).

Despite such feelings by Allen and
others, a majority of black and white
readers defend not only the novel's being
taught in school but also insist upon its
value as great literature. Many view
Twain's use of realistic racial epithets
like <u>nigger</u> as having a positive, ironic
effect upon the general reader's
attitudes towards racism itself. Black
writer David L. Smith feels Twain's use
of the term <u>nigger</u> is "neither to offend
nor merely to provide linguistic
authenticity" (5). Rather, he says, Twain
uses the term to establish "a context
against which Jim's specific virtues may
emerge as explicit refutations of racist
presuppositions" (6). In Smith's opinion,
Jim's humanity wins all readers over to
seeing blacks as worthy human beings, so
much so that applying the term <u>nigger</u> to
Jim or anyone else seems wrong.

Such a view of the word's
effectiveness in this way is echoed by
the experience of Professor Jeanne

Kramer 11

Corderman, who has taught <u>Adventures of
Huckleberry Finn</u> to black and white
college students for several years.
According to Professor Corderman, both
black and white students react negatively
to the novel's use of <u>nigger</u>, though for
different reasons:

> Black students seem to resent
> the term because they view it
> as echoing the racial prejudice
> they already see in our
> society. White students, on the
> other hand, <u>grow</u> into resenting
> the term because they learn
> though reading the novel how
> inhumanely Jim and other slaves
> are treated and how truly
> unjust a derogatory term like
> <u>nigger</u> is to them.

Professor Corderman points out that
the term's use leaves both white and
black students feeling ambiguous about
the novel. Black as well as white
students, she says, are torn: They
condemn Huck for hesitating about saving
Jim and later delaying his freedom,
though they admire Huck as an individual
and respect his struggle to break with
the laws of his society (Corderman).

The response that readers of
Huckleberry Finn have to Jim, in fact,
underlies a good deal of the controversy
surrounding the novel. For many, so
strongly and positively is Jim's
character represented that he "excels
even Huck in fidelity and innate
manliness, to emerge as the book's
noblest character" (Spiller 932). Though
black critics resent Jim's manipulation
by Huck and other whites, many also view
Twain's depiction of Jim's behavior as
realistic for the times. Most see Jim's
submissiveness, in fact, as a condition
of prewar slavery (Doughty 57) or as a
practical necessity for existing as a
runaway (Barksdale 17). Despite his final
criticism of Twain's portrayal of Jim,
black writer Ralph Ellison also feels
that, in a literary sense, Jim is a
complex character "fitted into the
outlines of the minstrel tradition," from
which emerge his "dignity and human
capacity" (qtd. in Bell 10). Black critic
Bernard W. Bell states that it is "sad
but true for many black readers that
Twain's 'Nigger' Jim is the best example
of the humanity of black American slaves"
that nineteenth-century white American
fiction can offer (17).

Use *qtd. in*
to indicate
indirect
source

Kramer 13

The complicated, sometimes
conflicting attitudes of blacks toward
Jim's character and the novel's language
have challenged the novel's position as a
classic to be taught in public schools.
Most black readers agree that the book
should be taught but also argue that it
is more suitable for older readers of
high school and college age (Allen 12;
Chambers 13) and that teachers need more
sensitive training and preparation
whenever they teach the novel (Nichols
434-36). Michael Meyers, assistant
director of the National Association of
Colored People (NAACP), says, "Our
position is that you don't ban Huck Finn;
you explain Huck Finn ("On Huck" 3).

The majority of black readers today
would agree that, properly taught and
understood, Mark Twain's Adventures of
Huckleberry Finn can serve as what black
writer Charles H. Nichols calls an
"indispensable part of the education of
both black and white youth" ("A True
Book" 14). Certainly, Mark Twain's
Huckleberry Finn has come a long way from
being what made it the "veriest of trash"
for white audiences in the nineteenth
century. Today, the book acts for black

Use
paraphrase
to summarize
source's
content

Place familiar
abbreviations
of
organizations
in
parentheses
after first
citation of
name

Kramer 14

as well as white readers as what another
black writer, David L. Smith, calls a
"trigger to outrage" (5), a classic work
of art that stirs reflection and humanity
in all of us. In this sense, <u>Adventures
of Huckleberry Finn</u> is perhaps after all
just what Ernest Hemingway insisted, "The
best book we've had."

**Page number
for this
quotation
is cited
earlier
in text**

Kramer 15

Notes

Title the
list of
notes
Notes

Explains author's use of major term

[1]For consistency and to reflect the most common usage today, I have throughout this paper used the term black to refer to the people some of my sources have variously called Negro, Blacks, or African-Americans.

[2]Hereafter, all quotations from Twain's Adventures of Huckleberry Finn will be followed by page numbers only.

Explains citation method and short title for work under discussion

Provides additional evidence and relevant commentary

[3]Black writer Bernard W. Bell (17) points out that Twain's representation of Jim's dialect has been described as "competent" and "accurate" by linguist James N. Tidwell in "Mark Twain's Representation of Negro Speech," American Speech 17 (1942): 174-76. See also The Story of English, by Robert McCrum, William Cran, and Robert MacNeil, pp. 261-62.

Comments on controversy; may also clarify apparent discrepancy in text

[4]Interestingly, scholars and others who comment on the frequency of nigger in Huckleberry Finn vary in their count of the word's appearance. For Williams, it occurs between 160-200 times (39); Bell (10) says 150 times. My own count comes closer to Bell's—156 times.

Kramer 16

Works Cited

Allen, Margot. "Huck Finn: Two
    Generations of Pain." <u>Interracial
    Books for Children Bulletin</u> 15.5
    (1984): 9–12.

Bell, Bernard W. "Twain's 'Nigger' Jim:
    The Tragic Face Behind the Minstrel
    Mask." <u>Mark Twain Journal</u> 22.2
    (1984): 10–17.

Chambers, Bradford. "Scholars and Huck
    Finn: A New Look." <u>Interracial Books
    for Children Bulletin</u> 15.4 (1984):
    12–13.

Corderman, Jeanne. Personal interview.
    14 Nov. 1989.

Crum, Robert, William Cran, and Robert
    MacNeil. <u>The Story of English</u>.
    Elisabeth Sifton Books Ser. New
    York: Viking, 1986.

Ford, Nick Aaron. "<u>Huckleberry Finn</u>: A
    Threat and a Challenge." <u>Teachers
    College Record</u> 70.5 (1969): 429–40.

Hemingway, Ernest. <u>Green Hills of Africa</u>.
    New York: Scribner's, 1935.

Matthews, Victoria Earle. "The Value of
    Race Literature." Speech delivered
    at the First Congress of Colored
    Women of the United States, 1895.
    Afterword and bibliography by Fred
    Miller Robinson. <u>Massachusetts
    Review</u> 27 (1986): 169–91.

Marginal annotations:

Alphabetize entries by authors' last names

Title the reference list *Works Cited*

Form for personal interview

Form for work in series

Form for listing three authors

Form for book title included in title of periodical article

Kramer 17

Nichols, Charles H. "'A True Book with Some Stretchers': <u>Huck Finn Today</u>." <u>Mark Twain Journal</u> 22.2 (1984) 13–16.

---. "Color, Conscience and Crucifixion: A Study of Racial Attitudes in American Literature and Criticism." <u>Jahrbuch für Amerikastudien</u> 6 (1961): 37–47.

"On <u>Huck</u>, Criticism and Censorship." Editorial. <u>Interracial Books for Children Bulletin</u> 15.1-2 (1984): 3.

Robinson, Fred Miller. Afterword. "The Value of Race Literature." By Victoria Earle Matthews. Speech delivered at the First Congress of Colored Women of the United States, 1895. <u>Massachusetts Review</u> 27 (1986): 169–91.

Rule, Henry B. "A Brief History of the Censorship of <u>The Adventures of Huckleberry Finn</u> [sic]." <u>Lamar Journal of the Humanities</u> 12 (1986): 9–18.

Smith, David L. "Huck, Jim, and American Racial Discourse." <u>Mark Twain Journal</u> 22.2 (1984): 4–12.

Smith, Henry Nash. Foreword. <u>Adventures of Huckleberry Finn</u>, by Mark Twain. Boston: Houghton Mifflin, 1958.

Include the issue number (2) when only year-date is given in source

Use three unspaced hyphens to represent author's name when multiple works listed by same author

Form for editorial with no author

Form for entry with an afterword

Use *sic* in brackets to indicate error in original

Form for edition with foreword

Kramer 18

Spiller, Robert E., et al., eds. <u>Literary</u>   Form for
     <u>History of the United States</u>. 3rd   revised
     ed., rev. London: Macmillan, 1963.   edition
Twain, Mark. <u>Adventures of Huckleberry</u>
     <u>Finn</u>. Introduction by Hamlin Hill.
     Centennial Facsimile Ed. New York:
     Harper, 1987.

Documenting Sources

The Works Cited List (MLA Style)

The Works Cited list follows your paper's Notes section (or the paper's text if there are no notes), its pages numbered consecutively with those preceding it. Although often informally referred to as a *bibliography* (which is a broad list of *available works* on a subject), the Works Cited section is actually more precise: It is a summary listing each of the *sources named in the text.* For this reason, the Works Cited section of the paper reflects the focus and breadth of your discussion, and it serves as an aid to the research others may do on the subject.

What to Include

When compiling the list of sources for the Works Cited page(s), be certain to include every source you have mentioned in the paper but no others. List each source from which you (1) borrowed ideas or (2) quoted material or that you (3) named in a note. Sources included in the first two categories will also have previously been cited parenthetically in the text. Works mentioned in your paper's Notes will have received previous citation there, as well. Only works included in the text or Notes should appear under the heading Works Cited.

This undoubtedly means some, perhaps several, works that contributed background information or common knowledge to your research will not be listed on the Works Cited page. You may have consulted 50 sources during your research and ended up paraphrasing, quoting, or naming only 10 of them in your research paper. Only those 10 sources will be listed under Works Cited.

Listing Works Cited Entries

In keeping with the MLA format, sources named on the Works Cited page should be listed alphabetically by the author's surname or, if no author is given, by the first word of a work's title. (If the title begins with the word *A, An,* or *The,* alphabetize by the second word in the title.) When listing more than one work by the same author, cite each work alphabetically by title, using three hyphens in place of the author's name after the first entry. (See the example for Claiborne in Figure 10.1.)

To prepare the list of entries, it is easiest to sort your bibliography cards into the desired order and then work directly from them. If you have entered the bibliography sources into a computer file, you may be able to utilize a program function to alphabetize the list for you.

Formatting the Works Cited Page

To type the initial Works Cited page, center the title *Works Cited* one inch down from the top of the paper. Begin the first line for each entry flush with the left margin. Indent the second and all other lines for each entry five spaces from the left margin. Double-space throughout, including between entries (see Figure 10.1).

Works Cited Entries

The Works Cited section should provide the paper's reader with enough information to locate any of the works listed. The three basic units of information included for any kind of source are author, title, and publication facts, in that order. Some sources require additional information or may be cited with a special focus. In order to save a reader time and to ensure accuracy, follow the standard forms and abbreviations recommended for the discipline in which you are writing. (See Chapter 11 on documentation forms for other disciplines.) The discussion and examples that follow in this chapter correspond to the documentation guidelines of the Modern Language Association (MLA).

Martin 14

Works Cited

Burke, James. <u>Connections</u>. Boston:
    Little, Brown, 1978.

Claiborne, Robert. <u>Our Marvelous English</u>
    <u>Tongue: The Life and Times of the</u>
    <u>English Language</u>. New York: Times,
    1983.

---. <u>The Roots of English: A Reader's</u>
    <u>Handbook of Word Origins</u>. New York:
    Times-Random, 1989.

Land, Sharon. "<u>It's</u> and Common Usage."
    <u>Contemporary Language</u> 22 (Oct.
    1987): 176-88.

Ogg, Oscar. <u>The Twenty-Six Letters</u>. Rev.
    ed. New York: Van Nostrand, 1983.

Skeat, Walter. <u>Concise Etymological</u>
    <u>Dictionary of the English Language</u>.
    New York: Capricorn, 1963.

"Spelling Was Never Easy, Says Expert."
    <u>New York Times</u> 17 Mar. 1987: B3.

Weekly, Ernest. <u>An Etymological</u>
    <u>Dictionary of Modern English</u>. Vol.
    2. Dover: New York, 1967. 2 vols.

Williams, Raymond. <u>Key Words: A</u>
    <u>Vocabulary of Culture and Society</u>.
    Rev. ed. New York: Oxford UP, 1976.

FIGURE 10.1 Sample Works Cited page

General Guidelines

A Works Cited entry for most sources will follow the standard order of author, title, and publication information. Note that the second and following lines of information for an entry are indented five additional spaces:

<table>
<tr><td>Book entry
form</td><td>Hirsch, E. D., Jr. <u>Cultural Literacy:
What Every American Needs to Know</u>.
Boston: Houghton, 1987.</td></tr>
<tr><td>Periodical
entry form</td><td>Greenberg, Donald P. "Computers and
Architecture." <u>Scientific American</u>
Feb. 1991: 104–09.</td></tr>
</table>

When the entry for a source requires additional kinds of information, follow these sequences:

For a Book:
1. Author(s)
2. Title of part of the book (in quotation marks)
3. Title of the book (underlined)
4. Editor, translator, or compiler
5. Edition
6. Number of volumes
7. Series title or number
8. Place, publisher, and date published
9. Volume number of this book
10. Page numbers for the part cited from this book (#2 above)

These elements would appear as follows in the Works Cited entry for a book:

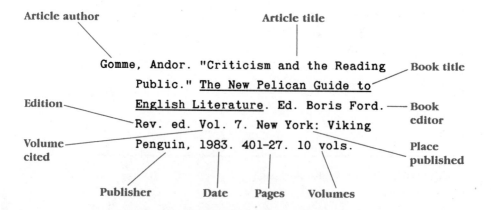

Article author

Article title

Gomme, Andor. "Criticism and the Reading Public." <u>The New Pelican Guide to</u>

Book title

Edition

<u>English Literature</u>. Ed. Boris Ford. —— Book editor

Rev. ed. Vol. 7. New York: Viking

Volume cited

Penguin, 1983. 401-27. 10 vols.

Place published

Publisher   Date   Pages   Volumes

For a Periodical:

1. Author(s)
2. Title of the article (in quotation marks)
3. Title of the periodical (underlined)
4. Series title or number
5. Volume number (and issue number, if there is one)
6. Date of publication
7. Page numbers of the article cited

These elements would appear as follows in the Works Cited entry for a periodical article:

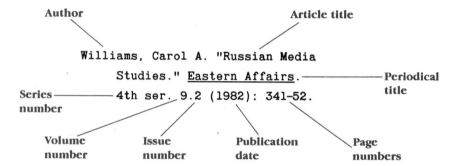

Author Names. A book, periodical, or other type of source may be written by one or several authors or an organization or group of some kind, or it may be the product of an editor, translator, or other type of compiler. Any one of these individuals or groups may be listed in the Works Cited section as the "author" of the work.

To list a source in the paper's Works Cited section, follow these general practices:

1. Cite the work alphabetically by the author's last name:

Cowley, Malcolm. <u>A Second Flowering: Works and Days</u>
    <u>of the Lost Generation</u>. New York: Viking, 1956.
Gibbs, Nancy. "Starving the Schools." <u>Time</u> 15 April,
    1991: 32–33.
Naisbit, John, and Patricia Aburdene. <u>Re–inventing the</u>
    <u>Corporation</u>. New York: Warner, 1985.
Newman, Charles, ed. <u>The Art of Sylvia Plath</u>.
    Bloomington: Indiana UP, 1971.
Resources for the Future. <u>United States Energy</u>
    <u>Policies: An Agenda for Research</u>. Michigan: Books
    on Demand, 1968.

If no author is given, list the work by the first word of the title (see "Titles," following).

2. Provide the author's name exactly as it is stated on the book's title page. Do not substitute initials for names when names are given (not *R. L. Atwood* instead of *Robert L. Atwood*). Do not omit initials when they are given (not *Carolyn Maitland* instead of *Carolyn M. Maitland*). Omit titles such as *Ph.D.* and *M.D.*:

Forster, E. M. <u>A Passage to India</u>. New York: Harcourt,
    1985.
Gergen, David R. "The Politics of Sound Bites." <u>U.S.</u>
    <u>News and World Report</u> 12 Sept. 1988: 76.
Harding, R. S. O., and G. Teleki, eds. <u>Omnivorous</u>
    <u>Primates</u>. New York: Columbia UP, 1981.

3. List multiple works by the same author in alphabetical order by title. Do not repeat the author's name with each work. Instead, substitute three unspaced hyphens and a period in place of the author's name after citing the first work (see *Hemingway*, below). But if that author writes a work with another person, list that work as a new entry (see *Daiches*):

Daiches, David. <u>The Novel and the Modern World</u>.
    Chicago: U of Chicago P, 1984.
Daiches, David, and John Flower. <u>Literary Landscape of</u>
    <u>the British Isles: A Narrative Atlas</u>. New York:
    Penguin, 1981.
Hemingway, Ernest. <u>Death in the Afternoon</u>. New York:
    Scribner's, 1932.
---. <u>A Farewell to Arms</u>. New York: Scribner's, 1929.
---. <u>The Old Man and the Sea</u>. New York: Scribner's,
    1983.
Keillor, Garrison. <u>Leaving Home: A Collection of Lake</u>
    <u>Wobegon Stories</u>. New York: Viking, 1987.

Editors, Compilers, and Translators of Books. A work that is an anthology or collection is usually the product of an editor or compiler. List such persons alphabetically by their last names, followed by the abbreviation *ed.* (plural *eds.*) or *comp.*:

Lewin, Roger, ed. <u>Thread of Life: The Smithsonian Looks</u>
    <u>at Evolution</u>. Washington, DC: Smithsonian, 1982.

Leach, Maria, and Jerome Fried, eds. <u>Funk and Wagnall's</u>
  <u>Standard Dictionary of Folklore, Mythology, and</u>
  <u>Legend</u>. New York: Crowell, 1980.

Scarlett, Kirk R., comp. <u>Anecdotes of Shame: Stories</u>
  <u>from the White House Staff</u>. Boston: Samuels, 1981.

For editors or translators of another writer's work, cite the person
first whose work you are focusing upon in your paper.

Emphasis upon editor or translator	Gibson, James, ed. <u>The Complete Poems of</u> <u>Thomas Hardy</u>. New York: Macmillan, 1976.
	MacIntyre, C. F., trans. <u>French Symbolist</u> <u>Poetry</u>. Berkeley: U of California P, 1971.
Emphasis upon original author	Hardy, Thomas. <u>The Complete Poems of</u> <u>Thomas Hardy</u>. Ed. James Gibson. New York: Macmillan, 1976.
	Laforgue, Jules. "Complaints des Pianos." <u>French Symbolist Poetry</u>. Trans. C. F. MacIntyre. Berkeley: U of California P, 1971. 88–92.

(For citing the writer of an introduction, foreword, preface, or afterword,
see section 30 at the end of this chapter.)

Titles. List the title of a work exactly as it appears on the work itself.
For a book, consult the title page, and include a subtitle if one is given.
For the title of a periodical article, locate the first page of the article itself
or check the periodical's table of contents for the exact title. Since punctuation between the main title and subtitle of a work is not usually shown,
you may need to supply it. Always use a full colon followed by a single
space to separate the main title and subtitle. Underline the title of a book
or periodical in full; place the title of a periodical article between quotation marks:

Book with subtitle	Hall, Donald. <u>Remembering Poets:</u> <u>Reminiscences and Opinions</u>. New York: Harper, 1978.

Magazine article
subtitle   Severy, Merle. "Iraq: Crucible of
                              Civilization." <u>National Geographic</u>
                        May 1991: 102–115.

(For the title of a work included in another work's title, see section 18 at
the end of this chapter.)

   Place of Publication, Publisher, and Date.   Since publishers for periodicals, unlike those for books, remain standard and are not essential to
locating periodical material, do not include the name of the publisher and
the place of publication for periodical entries on the Works Cited page.
   For a book, consult the title page or the copyright page for publication facts. Give the place of publication first, followed by a colon, the
name of the publisher, and the publication date:

Miller, Sue. <u>Inventing the Abbots and Other Stories.</u>
     New York: Dell, 1987.

   Place of Publication.   Give the name of the city in which the book
was published. If the city may be unfamiliar to your readers, add the postal
abbreviation of the state or country (Englewood Cliffs, NJ; Darwin, Aus-
tral.):

Duff, Charles. <u>The Basis and Essentials of Spanish.</u>
     Totowa, NJ: Littlefield, 1972.
Palmer, Eve. <u>The Plains of Camdeboo: The Classic Book
     of the Karoo.</u> Rev. ed. Johannesburg, S. Afr.:
     1986.

When more than one city of publication is listed, give only the name of the
first city mentioned.

   Publisher's Name.   Give the publisher's name in shortened form,
omitting articles, business abbreviations (Inc., Co., Ltd.), or descriptions
(Publishers, Library, & Sons):

Dutton	E. P. Dutton
Harcourt	Harcourt Brace Jovanovich, Inc.
Harper	Harper and Row Publishers, Inc.
Houghton	Houghton Mifflin Co.
McGraw	McGraw-Hill
Norton	W. W. Norton and Co. Inc.
Prentice	Prentice-Hall
Simon	Simon and Schuster, Inc.

For university presses, abbreviate *University* as *U* and *Press* with *P*. Do not use periods after either letter:

Cambridge UP   U of Chicago P
Oxford UP   UP of Florida

(See Chapter 12 for other examples and further guidelines for shortening publisher names.)

Page Numbers. When citing part of a complete work (such as a chapter in a book or an article in a periodical), give the continuous page numbers on which the cited material is located. Do not use any abbreviation such as *p.*, *pp.*, or *pg.* with page numbers.

For entries included in a book, give the page number(s) after the period following the work's publication date:

Holroyd, Michael. "The Wrong Turning." <u>Lytton Strachey:</u>
    <u>A Critical Biography</u>. Vol. 1. New York: Holt,
    1967. 1: 425-60. 2 vols.
Wlliams, William Carlos. "Shakespeare." <u>Selected</u>
    <u>Essays</u>. New York: New Directions, 1954. 55-56.

When listing periodical articles, give the inclusive page numbers for the entire article cited, listing the first page reference exactly as it is given in the source: *221-32; B2-4; Nov/6*. When the article does not appear continuously on consecutive pages (e.g., appearing first on page 2 and then skipping to page 8), give only the first page number and a plus sign:

Genscher, Hans-Dietrich. "Germanys: Toward a New
    Transoceanic Partnership." <u>Los Angeles Times</u>
    15 Apr. 1990: M2+.
Martz, Larry. "Into a Brave New World." <u>Newsweek</u>
    25 Dec. 1989: 40+.

For periodicals issued on a daily, weekly, or monthly basis, include the day and month published when these are given. Abbreviate all months except May, June, and July:

Emery, David. "Too Late for Court, Says Reagan." <u>New</u>
    <u>York Times</u> 16 May 1989 natl. ed.: A8.
Harrington, Spencer P. M. "The Looting of Arkansas."
    <u>Archaeology</u> May/June 1991: 23-30.

Index to
Works Cited Forms

The rest of this chapter outlines standard MLA forms for sources listed in the Works Cited section of a research paper. Use the list below as a quick index to these forms when compiling and editing your own paper.

Books

1. A Book by One Author
2. More Than One Book by the Same Author
3. A Book by an Author Whose Name Includes Initials
4. A Book by an Anonymous Author
5. A Book by a Pseudonymous Author
6. A Work by a Classical Author
7. A Book by Two or Three Authors
8. A Book by More Than Three Authors
9. More Than One Book by the Same Multiple Authors
10. A Book with an Editor
11. A Book with Two or Three Editors
12. A Book with More Than Three Editors
13. A Book by a Corporation, Committee, Institution, or Other Group
14. The Proceedings of a Conference or Meeting
15. A Book in Multiple Volumes
16. A Single Volume Included in a Multivolume Work
17. A Part of a Volume Included in a Multivolume Work
18. A Book That Is Included in Another Book
19. A Book That Is Part of a Series
20. A Book That Is an Anthology or Collection
21. A Work Included in an Anthology or Collection
22. A Work Cross-Referenced to an Anthology or Collection
23. A Book That Is a Second or Later Edition
24. A Book That Has Been Revised
25. A Book That Has Been Reprinted
26. A Book Printed by a Division of a Publisher
27. A Book Printed before 1900
28. A Book Published in a Foreign Language
29. A Book That Has Been Translated
30. A Book with an Introduction, Preface, Foreword, or Afterword
31. The Bible
32. A Published Dissertation
33. An Unpublished Dissertation

34. A Dissertation Abstract
35. A Government Publication
36. A Legal Citation

Magazines and Journals

37. An Article in a Journal with Continuous Yearly Pagination
38. An Article in a Journal with Pagination by Issue
39. An Article with No Author Named
40. An Article in a Weekly Magazine
41. An Article in a Monthly Magazine
42. An Article in a Series
43. A Published Interview
44. A Review in a Magazine or Journal
45. An Article Title That Includes Another Title
46. A Letter, Comments, or Notes in a Journal or Magazine

Newspapers

47. Standard Form for a Newspaper Article
48. An Unsigned Article in a Newspaper
49. Citing the Edition of a Newspaper
50. Citing the Pagination of a Newspaper

Other Sources

51. An Interview
52. A Public Address, Speech, or Lecture
53. A Letter
54. A Pamphlet
55. A Bulletin
56. A Work in Microform
57. Mimeographed Material
58. An Advertisement
59. A Manuscript or Typescript
60. An Unpublished Paper
61. Computer Software
62. Material from a Database
63. A Work of Art or a Photograph
64. An Illustration, Table, Chart, or Map
65. A Cartoon
66. A Film, Video Tape, Video Disc, or Slide Program
67. A Television or Radio Program
68. A Recording

Works Cited Forms

Books

1. A BOOK BY ONE AUTHOR

> Tan, Amy. <u>The Joy Luck Club</u>. New York: Putnam, 1989.
>
> *Parenthetic citation form:* (Tan 45).

2. MORE THAN ONE BOOK BY THE SAME AUTHOR

Give the author's name in the first entry only. Use three hyphens followed by a period to replace the name in each subsequent entry. List works alphabetically by title.

> Faulkner, William. <u>Absalom! Absalom!</u> New York: Random, 1951.
>
> ---. <u>Light in August</u>. New York: Random, 1968.
>
> ---. <u>The Sound and the Fury</u>. New York: Cape and Smith, 1929.
>
> *Parenthetic citation form:* (Faulkner, <u>Light</u> 112).

3. A BOOK BY AN AUTHOR WHOSE NAME INCLUDES INITIALS

Always use the same form for an author's name as given on the title page of the work.

> Auden, W. H. <u>Collected Shorter Poems: 1927–1957</u>. New York: Random, 1964.
>
> Fitzgerald, F. Scott. <u>Tender Is the Night</u>. New York: Scribner's, 1951.
>
> *Parenthetic citation forms:* (Auden 21); (Fitzgerald 91).

While it is not necessary to provide the full names of well-known authors, you may supply the full name in brackets if you wish:

> Auden, W[ystan] H[ugh]. <u>Collected Shorter Poems: 1927–1957</u>. New York: Random, 1964.

4. A BOOK BY AN ANONYMOUS AUTHOR

> <u>Beowulf</u>. Trans. E. Talbot Donaldson. Ed. Joseph F. Tuso. New York: Norton, 1975.
>
> *Parenthetic citation form:* (<u>Beowulf</u> 6).

5. A BOOK BY A PSEUDONYMOUS AUTHOR

Molière. <u>Le Misanthrope and Other Plays.</u> Trans.

    Donald M. Frame. New York: NAL, 1968.

To indicate the real name of an author published under a pseudonym, use square brackets followed by a period:

Molière [Jean Baptiste Poquelin]. <u>Le Misanthrope and</u>

    <u>Other Plays.</u> Trans. Donald M. Frame. New York:

    NAL, 1968.

Parenthetic citation form: (Molière 51).

6. A WORK BY A CLASSICAL AUTHOR

Sophocles. <u>Oedipus the King</u>. Trans. Stephen Berg and

    Clay Diskin. London: Oxford UP, 1989.

Virgil. <u>The Aeneid</u>. Trans. Robert Fitzgerald. New York:

    Random, 1983.

Parenthetic citation forms: (<u>Oed</u>.3.115–18); (<u>Aen</u>. 1.61).

7. A BOOK BY TWO OR THREE AUTHORS

Cite the name of the first author in reverse order, separated by commas, and follow it with the other authors' names in normal order. Use *and* before the last author's name.

Ravitch, Diane, and Chester E. Finn. <u>What Do Our</u>

    <u>Seventeen-Year-Olds Know?</u> New York: Harper, 1987.

Whitfield, Philip, Peter D. Moore, and Barry Cox. <u>The</u>

    <u>Atlas of the Living World</u>. Boston: Houghton, 1989.

Parenthetic citation forms: (Ravitch and Finn 121);
(Whitfield et al. 80).

8. A BOOK BY MORE THAN THREE AUTHORS

Cite only the first author for works written by more than three persons. Use the abbreviation *et al.* (meaning "and others") preceded by a comma to stand for the names of additional authors.

Guerin, Wilfred, et al. <u>A Handbook of Critical</u>

    <u>Approaches to Literature</u>. New York: Harper, 1979.

Parenthetic citation form: (Guerin et al. 45).

9. MORE THAN ONE BOOK BY THE SAME
   MULTIPLE AUTHORS

Cite all works alphabetically by title, listing authors fully in the first citation only. Use three hyphens followed by a period in place of all authors' names in succeeding entries.

Leakey, Richard E., and Roger Lewin. <u>Origins: The
    Emergence and Evolution of Our Species and
    Its Possible Future</u>. New York: Dutton, 1977.
---. <u>People of the Lake: Mankind and Its Beginnings</u>.
    New York: Avon, 1979.

Parenthetic citation form: (Leakey and Lewin, <u>Origins</u>, 102).

10. A BOOK WITH AN EDITOR

To focus on the work of the editor:

Lathem, Edward C., ed. <u>The Poetry of Robert Frost</u>. New
    York: Dodd, 1977.
Moore, Geoffrey, ed. <u>Portrait of a Lady</u>. By Henry
    James. New York: Penguin, 1984.
Newman, Charles, ed. <u>The Art of Sylvia Plath</u>.
    Bloomington: Indiana UP, 1971.

Parenthetic citation forms: (Lathem 33); (Moore 144);
(Newman 13).

To focus on the work of the author:

Frost, Robert. <u>The Poetry of Robert Frost</u>. Ed. Edward
    C. Lathem. New York: Dodd, 1977.
---. "Stopping by Woods on a Snowy Evening." <u>The Poetry
    of Robert Frost</u>. Ed. Edward C. Lathem. New York:
    Dodd, 1977. 28.
James, Henry. <u>Portrait of a Lady</u>. Ed. Geoffrey Moore.
    New York: Penguin, 1984.
Sexton, Anne. "The Barfly Ought to Sing." <u>The Art of
    Sylvia Plath</u>. Ed. Charles Newman. Bloomington:
    Indiana UP, 1971. 174–81.

Parenthetic citation forms: (Frost, "Stopping" 28);
(James ii); (Sexton 180).

11. A BOOK WITH TWO OR THREE EDITORS

> Doherty, William, and Macaran Baird, eds. <u>Family</u>
>> <u>Centered Medical Care: A Clinical Casebook</u>.
>> New York: Guilford, 1987.
> Temoshok, Lydia, Craig Van Dyke, and Leonard S. Zegans,
>> eds. <u>Emotions in Health and Illness</u>. New York:
>> Grune, 1983.
>
> *Parenthetic citation forms:* (Doherty and Baird 12);
> (Temoshok, Van Dyke, and Zegans 51).

12. A BOOK WITH MORE THAN THREE EDITORS

> Spiller, Robert E., et al., eds. <u>Literary History of</u>
>> <u>the United States</u>. London: Macmillan, 1969.
>
> *Parenthetic citation form:* (Spiller et al. 443).

13. A BOOK BY A CORPORATION, COMMITTEE, INSTITUTION,
OR OTHER GROUP

> Council on Environmental Quality. <u>The Global Two</u>
>> <u>Thousand Report to the President: Entering the</u>
>> <u>Twenty-First Century</u>. New York: Penguin, 1982.
> National League for Nursing. <u>Toward Excellence in</u>
>> <u>Nursing Education</u>. New York: National League, 1983.
> Shiner History Book Committee. <u>History of Shiner Texas</u>.
>> Dallas: Curtis, 1986.
>
> *Parenthetic citation forms:* (Council 11); (National 84);
> (Shiner 22).

These coporate author names have been shortened to avoid lengthy parenthetic citations that might interrupt the reader's attention to the text. See additional guidelines for avoiding extended parenthetic citations for government authors, following (section 35).

14. THE PROCEEDINGS OF A CONFERENCE OR MEETING

Include the place, date, and nature of the conference or meeting if these are not provided in the title.

> Federal Bar Association Staff. <u>Conference on</u>
>> <u>Advertising Law: Proceedings of the Federal Bar</u>
>> <u>Association, Conference, September, 1980</u>.
>> Washington, DC: Federal Bar Assoc., 1980.

<u>Meeting the Challenge of Reality: Proceedings</u>. 23rd
International Communications Conference,
Washington, DC, May 1976. Washington, DC:
Society for Technical Communications, 1976.

Parenthetic citation forms: (Federal 237); (<u>Meeting</u> 58).

15. A BOOK IN MULTIPLE VOLUMES

Hasegawa, Nyozekan. <u>The Japanese Character: A Cultural
Profile</u>. 10 vols. Westport: Greenwood, 1989.
Shakespeare, William. <u>The Complete Works of William
Shakespeare</u>. Ed. David Bevington. 6 vols.
New York: Bantam, 1990.

Parenthetic citation forms: (Hasegawa, vol. 2);
(Shakespeare, <u>Ham</u>. 3.220-26).

16. A SINGLE VOLUME INCLUDED IN A MULTIVOLUME WORK

Follow this form to cite an entire volume in a multivolume work:

Blair, Hugh. <u>Lectures on Rhetoric and Belles Lettres</u>.
Ed. Harold F. Harding. Vol. 2. Carbondale:
Southern Illinois UP, 1965. 2 vols.

Parenthetic citation form: (Blair 2: 112-19).

17. A PART OF A VOLUME INCLUDED IN A MULTIVOLUME WORK

To cite a part of a volume in a multivolume work, give the volume
number of the part you are citing before the place of publication (as
shown above). Cite the inclusive page numbers of the material after the
publication date, and follow the page numbers with the total number of
volumes.

Blair, Hugh. <u>Lectures on Rhetoric and Belles Lettres</u>.
Ed. Harold F. Harding. Vol. 2. Carbondale:
Southern Illinois UP, 1965. 116. 2 vols.
Lincoln, Abraham. "Autobiography Written for John L.
Scripps." <u>The Collected Works of Abraham Lincoln</u>.
Ed. Roy B. Basler. Vol. 4. New Brunswick, NJ:
Rutgers UP, 1953. 60-63. 8 vols.

Parenthetic citation forms: (Blair); (Lincoln 4: 61).

18. A BOOK THAT IS INCLUDED IN ANOTHER BOOK

Do not underline the title of a complete book when it is included within another work's title.

> Lynn, Kenneth S. The Scarlet Letter: <u>Text, Sources,</u>
> <u>Criticism</u>. New York: Harcourt, 1961.

Parenthetic citation form: (Lynn 30).

19. A BOOK THAT IS PART OF A SERIES

Include the series name and number (when given) before the place of publication.

> Botta, Paul Emile. <u>Observations on the Inhabitants of</u>
> <u>California, 1827–1828</u>. Trans. John Francis Bricca.
> Early California Travel Ser. 5. Los Angeles:
> Glen Dawson, 1952.
>
> Ray, G. Carleton, and M. G. McCormick–Ray, eds.
> <u>Wildlife of the Polar Regions</u>. Wildlife Habitat
> Ser. New York: Abrams, 1981.

Parenthetic citation forms: (Botta 19); (Ray 68).

20. A BOOK THAT IS AN ANTHOLOGY OR COLLECTION

> Baym, Nina, et al., eds. <u>The Norton Anthology of</u>
> <u>American Literature</u>. 3rd shorter ed. New York:
> Norton, 1989.
>
> Stevens, Wallace. <u>Collected Poems</u>. New York: Random,
> 1982.

Parenthetic citation forms: (Baym 332–33); (Stevens 237).

21. A WORK INCLUDED IN AN ANTHOLOGY OR COLLECTION

Give the name of the author for the work you are citing, followed by the work's title in quotation marks or underlined, depending upon how it is regularly indicated. Next give the title of the anthology or collection, followed, if appropriate, by the editor's or translator's name in normal order preceded by *Ed.* or *Trans.* After the publication information, give the page numbers where the work appears in the anthology or collection.

> Crane, Stephen. "The Open Boat." <u>The Norton Anthology</u>
> <u>of American Literature</u>. Eds. Nina Baym, et al. 3rd
> shorter ed. New York: Norton, 1989. 1569–84.

Stevens, Wallace. "The Palm at the End of the Mind."
Collected Poems. New York: Random, 1982. 237.

Twain, Mark. Adventures of Huckleberry Finn. The Norton
Anthology of American Literature. Eds. Nina Baym,
et al. 3rd shorter ed. New York: Norton, 1989.
1170-1358.

Parenthetic citation forms: (Crane 1574-75); (Stevens 237);
(Twain 1334).

22. A WORK CROSS-REFERENCED TO AN ANTHOLOGY OR COLLECTION

When you cite two or more works from the same anthology or collection, cross-reference them to the editor of the larger work, which you must also cite separately. Give only the editor's surname after the name of the author and title of the work you are citing. Use no punctuation between the editor's name and the page numbers for the cited work. Omit *ed.* or other descriptive words in the cross-reference.

Baym, Nina, et al. eds. The Norton Anthology of
American Literature. 3rd shorter ed. New York:
Norton, 1989.

Faulkner, William. "That Evening Sun." Baym 2005-16.

Wright, Richard. "The Man Who Was Almost a Man." Baym
2118-26.

Parenthetic citation forms: (Baym 142-44); (Faulkner 2007);
(Wright 2125).

23. A BOOK THAT IS A SECOND OR LATER EDITION

Abernathy, Glenn. The Right of Assembly and
Association. 2nd ed. Columbia: U of South
Carolina P, 1985.

Old, R. W., and S. B. Primrose. Principles of Gene
Manipulation. 3rd ed. Palo Alto, CA:
Blackwell, 1985.

Parenthetic citation forms: (Abernathy 77); (Old and
Primrose 15).

24. A BOOK THAT HAS BEEN REVISED

Use the abbreviation *Rev. ed.* when a book has been revised by someone other than the author.

Abernathy, Glenn. <u>The Right of Assembly and</u>
<u>Association</u>. Rev. ed. Columbia: U of South
Carolina P, 1985.

Fowler, H. W. <u>Modern English Usage</u>. Rev. Ernest Gowers.
2nd ed. New York: Oxford UP, 1965.

Parenthetic citation forms: (Abernathy 33); (Fowler 28).

25. A BOOK THAT HAS BEEN REPRINTED

Use the abbreviation *rpt.* and give the date of original publication after the title of the work.

Lang, Edith, and George West. <u>Musical Accompaniment of</u>
<u>Moving Pictures</u>. Rpt. of 1920 ed. Salem, NH:
Ayer, 1989.

Parenthetic citation form: (Lang and West 86).

26. A BOOK PRINTED BY A DIVISION OF A PUBLISHER

Paperback versions of cloth-bound editions are often reprinted by divisions of the main publisher. If the title or copyright page carries a publisher's special imprint, list the division first, joined by a hyphen to the name of the main publisher.

Carver, Raymond. <u>Where I'm Calling From</u>. New York:
Vintage–Random, 1989.

Parenthetic citation form: (Carver 116).

27. A BOOK PRINTED BEFORE 1900

Cite early books as you would any other, but omit the publisher's name.

Melville, Herman. <u>Redburn</u>. London, 1849.

Parenthetic citation form: (Melville 200).

Note that the lengthy and descriptive subtitle common to many older books is usually shortened. The full title of Melville's *Redburn*, for example, is *Redburn: His First Voyage, Being the Sailor-boy Confessions and Reminiscences of the Son-of-a-Gentleman, in the Merchant Service.*

28. A BOOK PUBLISHED IN A FOREIGN LANGUAGE

Maintain capitalization, spelling, and punctuation of names and titles exactly as in the original. Include any special symbols (e.g., accent marks, umlauts) required by the respective foreign language.

Hansen, Klaus P. <u>Die retrospektive Mentalität:</u>
<u>europäische Kulturkritik und amerikanische Kultur</u>
<u>(Cooper, Melville, Twain)</u>. Tübingen, W. Ger.:
G. Narr, 1984.

Parenthetic citation form: (Hansen 177).

29. A BOOK THAT HAS BEEN TRANSLATED

To focus on the translator:

Garnet, Constance, trans. <u>War and Peace</u>. By Leo
Tolstoy. New York: Modern Library, 1931.

Parenthetic citation form: (Garnet iv).

To focus on the original author:

Tolstoy, Leo. <u>War and Peace</u>. Trans. Constance Garnet.
New York: Modern Library, 1931.

Parenthetic citation form: (Tolstoy 140; ch. 5).

30. A BOOK WITH AN INTRODUCTION, PREFACE,
FOREWORD, OR AFTERWORD

To focus on the author of the introduction: If the author of the supplementary material is also the author of the book, give only the last name
of the author after *By* (see the *Dickey* entry, below). List the page numbers
of the part of the book you are focusing upon, unless you are citing the
entire work (see the entry for *Bell*, below).

Bell, Quentin. Introduction. <u>The Diary of Virginia</u>
<u>Woolf</u>. Ed. Anne Oliver Bell. Vol. 2. New York:
Harcourt, 1977. xiii–xxviii. 4 vols.

Dickey, James. Preface. <u>Babel to Byzantium: Poets and</u>
<u>Poetry Now</u>. By Dickey. New York: Farrar,
1968. ix–x.

Haynes, Renee. Afterword. <u>The Roots of Coincidence: An</u>
<u>Excursion into Parapsychology</u>. By Arthur Koestler.
New York: Vintage–Random, 1973. 141–49.

Hill, Hamlin. Introduction. <u>Adventures of Huckleberry</u>
<u>Finn</u>. By Mark Twain. Centennial facsim. ed.
New York: Harper, 1987. vii–xviii.

Kermode, Frank. Foreword. <u>The Romantic Agony</u>. By Mario

    Praz. Trans. Angus Davidson. London: Oxford,

    1970. v-ix.

Parenthetic citation forms: (Bell xx); (Dickey ix); (Haynes
143); (Hill viii); (Kermode vi).

If you have referred to both the work's author and the writer of the
supplementary material in your paper, you will need to cite them both
separately under Works Cited (see below).

To focus on the author of the work:

Koestler, Arthur. <u>The Roots of Coincidence: An</u>

    <u>Excursion into Parapsychology</u>. Aftwd. Renee

    Haynes. New York: Vintage-Random, 1973.

Praz, Mario. <u>The Romantic Agony</u>. Fwd. Frank Kermode.

    London: Oxford, 1970.

Twain, Mark. <u>Adventures of Huckleberry Finn</u>. Introd.

    Hamlin Hill. Centennial facsim. ed. New York:

    Harper, 1987.

Parenthetic citation forms: (Koestler 67); (Praz 20);
(Twain 58; ch. 7).

31. THE BIBLE

Unless your paper uses more than one biblical source, no listing of
the Bible is necessary under Works Cited if you use the King James Version. Cite other versions of the Bible as you would a book with an anonymous author, but do not underline the title.

The Bible. Revised Standard Version.

New American Bible: Revised New Testament. Grand

    Rapids: Christian UP, 1988.

The Revised English Bible with Apochrypa. London:

    Oxford UP, 1990.

Parenthetic citation form: (Gen. 2: 11).

32. A PUBLISHED DISSERTATION

Use the abbreviation *Diss.* for *Dissertation* after the title of the dissertation and before the name of the degree institution. Include the year in
which the degree was granted after the institution name, followed by
standard publication information (place, publisher, date).

Struve, Wilson. <u>Picasso, Cubism, and Deconstructionist</u>
<u>Literature.</u> Diss. U of Kansas, 1986. Austin, TX:
Republic, 1987.

Parenthetic citation form: (Struve 12).

33. AN UNPUBLISHED DISSERTATION

For an unpublished dissertation, cite the title in quotation marks,
followed by the degree institution and date.

Rowland, William Gordon. "Writers against Readers:
English and American Romantic Writers and the
Nineteenth—Century Reading Public." Diss. U of
Virginia, 1988.

Parenthetic citation form: (Rowland 55).

34. A DISSERTATION ABSTRACT

Depending upon your source, include the abbreviation *DA* for *Dissertation Abstracts* or *DAI* for *Dissertation Abstracts International,* followed
by the volume number and then the date in parentheses. Give the page
number on which the abstract appears, including the series letter (*A* de-
notes humanities and social sciences; *B,* the sciences; *C,* European dissertations). The name of the degree institution ends the citation.

Graham, Albert. "A Study of Vocabulary Recall among the
Elderly." <u>DA</u> (1970): 2111A. U of Nebraska.
Stanley, D'Lisa Ann. "The Relationship between Roommate
Rapport and Social Skills Development of First
Semester Female College Freshman." <u>DAI</u> 34 (1988):
2435A. Texas Tech U.

Parenthetic citation forms: (Graham); (Stanley).

35. A GOVERNMENT PUBLICATION

Government agencies generate a multitude of documents in varying
forms. The citation examples shown here are representative of the most
common types. Observe these guidelines:

a. In most cases, treat the major agency as the author, followed succes-
sively by subagencies. For United States government documents, it
helps to remember that *departments* (e.g., Department of Health and

Human Welfare, Department of Justice) oversee *bureaus, administrations, offices,* and the like (e.g., National Bureau of Standards, Maritime Administration, Office of Justice Programs).

b. Note the standard abbreviations for certain items when citing U.S. government publications: The *Congressional Record* is abbreviated *Cong. Rec.*; its page numbers begin with *H* or *S* to stand for the *House* or the *Senate* sections of the publication. Most United States government materials are printed by the *Government Printing Office,* abbreviated *GPO.*

c. If you list more than one entry by the same agency, do not repeat the agency name. Use three hyphens followed by a period for each successive entry by the same agency/author. The example below uses hyphens to stand for *United States* and *Dept. of Commerce* as given in the previous entry:

Cong. Rec. 17 Mar. 1989. S2966. Florida State. Joint
      Committee on Language Education. Standards for
      Elementary Grades Language Instruction. Tampa:
      Greydon, 1988.

United Nations. General Assembly. Resolutions and
      Decisions. 42nd sess. 15–21 Dec. 1987. New York:
      United Nations, 1988.

United States. Dept. of Commerce. Bureau of the Census.
      1987 Census of Retail Trade: Pennsylvania.
      Geographic Area Ser. Washington: GPO, 1989.

---. ---. Bureau of Economic Analysis. Selected Foreign
      Investment Fluctuation: Analysis. Washington:
      GPO, 1986.

---. President. Public Papers of the Presidents of the
      United States. Bk. 2. July 4–Dec. 31, 1987.
      Washington: GPO, 1989.

Parenthetic citation forms: Although you may cite the author of a government publication parenthetically—e.g., (United Nations, General Assembly 65–81)—it is best to avoid interrupting the reader with a lengthy parenthetic citation. Whenever possible, name the author in the text and cite page numbers in parentheses:

The report from the United Nations General Assembly
shows worldwide crop yields have changed dramatically
in the last seven years (225).

36. A LEGAL CITATION

Citations for sections of the United States Constitution, federal and state codes, as well as court cases are usually heavily abbreviated. If your paper requires several such citations, you may want to consult *A Uniform System of Citation*, published by the Harvard Law Review Association (1986).

The following examples demonstrate common practice. Use these for comparison with your own legal source and as a guide for citation.

    US Const. Art. 6, sec. 3.

    12 US Code. Sec 2283. 1973.

    Federal Financing Bank Act of 1973. 96 Stat. 879.
        Pub. L. 97-255. 1982.

    New Jersey. Const. Art. IV, Sec 6.

To cite a court case, give the name of the case, using the abbreviation *v.* for *versus* and ending with a period. Next list the volume and page number in the work cited, the kind of court that decided the case, and the year:

    People v. Keith. 741 F 2d 220 DC CA 3d 1984.

The entry shows that the case of People *v.* Keith was decided in the Third District Court of Appeals in 1984. The case is described in volume 741 of the *Federal Reporter,* second series, page 220.

Note that the name of a court case should be underlined in your paper or in a parenthetic note, but not in the Works Cited list.

Parenthetic citation forms: See the guidelines above for citing government authors and their works.

Magazines and Journals

37. AN ARTICLE IN A JOURNAL WITH CONTINUOUS YEARLY PAGINATION

    Elley, Warick B. "Vocabulary Acquisition from Listening
        to Stories." Reading Research Quarterly 24 (1989):
        221-29.

Parenthetic citation form: (Elley 223).

38. AN ARTICLE IN A JOURNAL WITH PAGINATION BY ISSUE

Page numbers alone will not locate a work in a publication bearing new page numbers for every issue of the same yearly volume. For journals with separate pagination for each issue, give the issue number after the volume number (e.g., *16.3*):

Frederiksen, Norman. "The Real Test Bias: Influences of
Testing on Teaching and Learning." <u>American
Psychologist</u> 39 (1984): 193-202.

Gray, Andrew. "On Translating Wagner." <u>The Opera
Quarterly</u> 6 (1988): 532-52.

Poague, Leland, and William Cadbury. "The Possibility
of Film Criticism." <u>The Journal of Aesthetic
Education</u> 23.4 (1989): 5-22.

Parenthetic citation forms: (Frederiksen 202); (Gray 533);
(Poague and Cadbury 14-16).

39. AN ARTICLE WITH NO AUTHOR NAMED

"No Hope for Antarctica." <u>Mosaic</u> 4.2 (1988): 34-37.

Parenthetic citation form: ("No Hope" 35).

40. AN ARTICLE IN A WEEKLY MAGAZINE

Palmer, Robert. "The Fifties." <u>Rolling Stone</u> 19 Apr.
1990: 44+.

Parenthetic citation form: (Palmer 48).

Use a plus sign (+) after the first page number to indicate that an article does not appear continuously on consecutive pages. Thus, the pagination for an article beginning on page 12, skipping to page 14, and reap-
pearing on pages 17-19 would be indicated by 12+, followed by a period
to end the entry.

41. AN ARTICLE IN A MONTHLY MAGAZINE

McDermont, Jeanne. "Some Heartland Farmers Just Say No
to Chemicals." <u>Smithsonian</u> Apr. 1989: 114+.

Parenthetic citation form: (McDermont 117-18).

42. AN ARTICLE IN A SERIES

If the article in the series has the same title and author in each issue
of a publication, list all bibliographic information, including serial publication dates, in one entry:

Dendam, Karl H. "The Artist's Only Muse." <u>Fine Arts
Journal</u> 14 (1990): 112-19; 15 (1990): 253-61,
293-96.

If the series articles have different titles in various issues, list each separately. You may include a brief explanation at the end of the entry to indicate that the article is part of a series:

Varry, Joan. "Prisons." <u>Stateside</u> Dec. 1989: 55–67.
　　Pt. 2 of a series.

Parenthetic citation forms: (Dendam 14: 118); (Varry 56).

43. A PUBLISHED INTERVIEW

Nixon, Richard. Interview. "Paying the Price." <u>Time</u> 2
　　Apr. 1990: 46–49.

Parenthetic citation form: (Nixon 46).

(For listing other sources of interviews, see 52, below.)

44. A REVIEW IN A MAGAZINE OR JOURNAL

Leithauser, Brad. "A Nasty Dose of Orthodoxy." Rev. of
　　<u>Flannery O'Connor: Collected Works</u>, ed. Sally
　　Fitzgerald. <u>The New Yorker</u> 7 Nov. 1988: 154–58.

Parenthetic citation form: (Leithauser 157).

45. AN ARTICLE TITLE THAT INCLUDES ANOTHER TITLE

Put the title of the periodical article you are citing in quotation marks and underline any titles it includes of whole works. Included titles that are usually written in double quotation marks should be written with single quotation marks, as in the first example:

Cohen, Jane. "Keats's Humor in 'La Belle Dame sans
　　Merci'." <u>Keats–Shelley Journal</u> 17 (1968): 10–13.
Rampersad, Arnold. "<u>Adventures of Huckleberry Finn</u> and
　　Afro–American Literature." <u>Mark Twain Journal</u> 22
　　(1984): 47–52.

Parenthetic citation forms: (Cohen 10); (Rampersad 50).

46. LETTERS, COMMENTS, OR NOTES IN A JOURNAL OR MAGAZINE

Harris, Angela. Letter. <u>Harper's</u> May 1989: 9.
Rossman, Gary. "Frost's 'Desert Places'." <u>The</u>
　　<u>Explicator</u> 27.3 (1987): 21–22.
Walsh, Thomas, and Natasha Walsh. "Patterns of <u>Who/Whom</u>
　　Usage." <u>American Speech</u> 64 (1989): 284–86.

Parenthetic citation forms: (Harris); (Rossman 22);
(Walsh 284–85).

Newspapers

47. STANDARD FORM FOR A NEWSPAPER ARTICLE

For all newspaper articles, provide the name of the author, the article title (in quotation marks), and the newspaper title (underlined), as well as the publication date, section (if appropriate), and page numbers. If the place of publication is not part of the title, supply it in square brackets after the newspaper name.

> Hawk, Steve. "Air Force Takes Wraps Off Stealth
> Bomber." <u>Orange County Register</u> 23 Nov. 1988: A13.
> Rollins, Fred. "Teachers Say Yes to Parents in the
> Classroom." <u>Newsday</u> [Garden City, NY] 9 July
> 1989: 2+.

Parenthetic citation forms: (Hawk); (Rollins 6).

48. AN UNSIGNED ARTICLE IN A NEWSPAPER

> "Dolphin Wars Hit the Beaches." <u>Boston Globe</u> 22 Aug.
> 1987: A2.

Parenthetic citation form: ("Dolphin").

49. CITING THE EDITION OF A NEWSPAPER

When it is given, designate the edition (*morning ed., Barton County ed.,* etc.) after the date:

> "Bus Strikers Wait It Out." <u>New York Times</u> 22 Sept.
> 1991, natl. ed.: B5.
> "Gorbachev to Meet with Lithuanian Leaders."
> <u>Los Angeles Times</u> 16 Mar. 1989, late ed.: A1+.
> Kalette, Denise. "Poll: 83% Fear for Environment." <u>USA
> Today</u> 13-15 Apr. 1990, weekend ed.: A1.

Parenthetic citation forms: ("Bus Strikers");
("Gorbachev" A3-4); (Kalette).

50. CITING THE PAGINATION OF A NEWSPAPER

Newspapers vary in pagination forms, and some even change the paginating format for different editions of their own publication. Follow the forms below as they apply to each newspaper you cite.

a. Pagination separate for each lettered section:

> "Air Controllers Face Long-Standing Problem." <u>USA Today</u>
> 10 Feb. 1989: 2A+.

Lesker, Stanley. "Freeways Aren't So Free Anymore."
    <u>Los Angeles Times</u> 9 May 1989: C5.

b. Section designation not included in page number:

Dahlberg, John. "Was Reagan Only Kidding?"
        <u>New York Times</u> 12 Jan. 1988, early ed.,
    sec. 3: 1.
"Tennis Packs 'Em In." <u>Dayton Sun News</u> 27 Aug. 1989,
    sec. C: 4.

c. Pagination continuous, no section designations:

"Benson Ready and Waiting for Finals." <u>USA Today</u> 3 Nov.
    1989: 34.
Rogers, Anne L. "Bottle Collecting Is Big Business for
    Some Folks." <u>Wall Street Journal</u> 15 Dec. 1988,
    eastern ed.: 9.

Parenthetic citation forms: ("Air Controllers" 2A);
(Lesker); (Dahlberg); ("Tennis"); ("Benson"); (Rogers).

Other Sources

51. AN INTERVIEW

For an interview you have conducted yourself, list the name of the interviewee first. Indicate the type of interview, and give the date on which it was conducted.

Nguyen, Phan. Personal interview. 10 Nov. 1989.

Tomlinson, David. Telephone interview. 7 Jan. 1990.

To list a published or recorded interview, start with the name of the interviewee, followed by *Interview* (unless a title makes it obvious). If there is a title for the interview, include it in quotation marks:

Edwards, Robbie. "Let's Talk with Robbie Edwards."
        <u>Profile</u> 12 July 1986: 34.
Abdul-Jabbar, Kareem. Interview. <u>The Larry King Show</u>.
    WGCI Chicago. 2 Apr. 1990.
Nixon, Richard. Interview. "Paying the Price." <u>Time</u>
    2 Apr. 1990: 46–49.

Parenthetic citation forms: (Nguyen); (Tomlinson);
(Edwards); (Abdul-Jabbar); (Nixon 47).

52. A PUBLIC ADDRESS, SPEECH, OR LECTURE

If the presentation has a title, place it in quotation marks and provide information about the occasion, place, and date of the presentation. For any presentation without a title, provide a descriptive phrase after the speaker's name.

Adams, Hazard. "The Dizziness of Freedom; or, Why I
Read William Blake." Ninth Annual Faculty Lecture.
U of Washington, 5 Nov. 1984.

Thoc, Van. "On Student Access." English Council of
California Two-Year Colleges Annual Statewide
Conference. San Diego, CA, 22 Oct. 1988.

Whitson, Carol. Address. City Council Meeting.
Branning, MI, 24 July 1987.

Parenthetic citation forms: (Adams); (Thoc); (Whitson).

53. A LETTER

For a letter published in another work, cite the letter's author first, followed by the descriptive title of the letter in quotation marks. Following this, add the date of the letter and, if the editor has assigned one, its number. After including standard information about the source in which the letter is reprinted, include the page numbers for the letter.

Freud, Anna. "Letter to A. A. Brill." 27 Dec. 1939. In
Anna Freud: A Biography. By Elisabeth Young-
Bruehl. New York: Summit, 1988. 241.

Greenough, Alexander. "To Jackson King." 12 Nov. 1913.
Letter 84 in Letters to Buffalo: The
Correspondence of Alexander Greenough. Ed. John
Silverman. Boston: Lang, 1934. 33-34.

For an unpublished letter, describe the material, including the date written, the collection in which it was found (if any), and the letter's location.

Eliot, T. S. Letter to Bertrand Russell. [4] Jan. 1916.
Mills Memorial Library. McMaster University,
Hamilton, OH.

A letter written to you should be cited as follows:

Cheney, Sharon. Letter to the author. 4 Feb. 1990.

Parenthetic citation forms: (Freud); (Greenough 34);
(Eliot); (Cheney).

54. A PAMPHLET

Pamphlets are listed the same as books:

Berman, Claire. <u>Raising an Adopted Child</u>. New York:
     Public Affairs Committee, 1983.

U.S. Public Health Service. <u>What About AIDS Testing?</u>
     Washington, DC: GPO, 1988.

<u>Your Cat and You</u>. Millpark, MI: Newsway, 1987.

Parenthetic citation forms: (Berman 20);
(U.S. Public Health 61); (<u>Your Cat</u> 4).

55. A BULLETIN

Energy Resource Commission. <u>Intra–State Waste</u>
     <u>Management Ordinances</u>. Department of Energy,
     Bulletin JRB–5. 3 Sept. 1986. Washington:
     GPO, 1986.

Harding, Frederick. <u>Marital Status and Employee</u>
     <u>Benefits</u>. Bulletin 43. Sacramento, CA: State Dept.
     of Employment, 1987.

Parenthetic citation forms: (Energy Resource Commission 36);
(Harding 102).

56. A WORK IN MICROFORM

List any work on microfilm or microfiche in its regular format (book,
article, etc.), but add the description *Microfilm* or *Microfiche* after the
title.

Trillin, Calvin. "Uncivil Liberties." Microfilm. <u>The</u>
     <u>Nation</u>. 17 May 1986: 686.

Parenthetic citation form: (Trillin).

57. MIMEOGRAPHED MATERIAL

Eisen, Carol O. <u>Paradigms for Thinking</u>. Mimeographed.
     Seattle, 1990.

Parenthetic citation form: (Eisen).

58. AN ADVERTISEMENT

Give the title, heading, or first words of an advertisement in quotation
marks. Include the word *Advertisement,* followed by a period. Add the rest
of the regular information about the source that carried the advertisement:

"It Wouldn't Be Christmas Without Chanel."
Advertisement. <u>Connoisseur</u> Dec. 1989: 37.

Parenthetic citation form: ("It Wouldn't").

59. A MANUSCRIPT OR TYPESCRIPT

Bradley, Frederick. "Art and Science in the Nuclear
Age." Unpublished essay, 1981.

Hadley, Joyce. Notebook 7, ts. Hadley Collection.
Trinity Coll., Hartford.

Joyce, James. "Penelope." Ts. Huntington Library,
Pasadena, CA.

Parenthetic citation forms: (Bradley 4); (Hadley 23); (Joyce).

60. AN UNPUBLISHED PAPER

Brenner, William G. "The Good, the Wise, and the Ugly
in Faulkner's World." Unpublished paper, 1988.

Parenthetic citation form: (Brenner 2).

61. COMPUTER SOFTWARE

List the author (if known) and underline the title (including the version—e.g., *Displaywrite 3*) of a commercially produced computer program first, followed by the description *Computer software.* Next list the publisher's name, shortened (e.g., *Tandy,* not *Tandy, Inc.*), followed by a comma and the date of publication. Add other information that would indicate operating requirements, such as the computer type, memory units, operating system, and the form of the program.

Close, Arnold. <u>Checkbook Manager</u>. Computer software.
Houser, 1988. 32KB, cartridge.

<u>Vellum</u>. Computer software. Ashlar, 1989. Apple
Macintosh SE/30, Apple 6.0.2, 4MB, disk.

<u>Zork I</u>. Computer software. Infocom, 1982. IBM, 48K.

Parenthetic citation forms: (Close); (<u>Vellum</u>); (<u>Zork I</u>).

62. MATERIAL FROM A DATABASE

List the item information the same as you would other printed material, but also include the name of the vendor and any access numbers or codes.

"Mark Twain." <u>Academic American Encyclopedia</u>. 1981 ed.
Compuserve, 1983. Record n. 1874.

Matthews, Victoria Earle. "The Value of Race
     Literature." Rpt. of speech delivered at
     the First Congress of Colored Women of the
     United States, 1895. <u>Massachusetts Review</u> 27.2
     (1986): 169-91. Dialog file 38, item 892902
     25A-06084.

Parenthetic citation forms: ("Mark Twain"); (Matthews 170).

63. A WORK OF ART OR A PHOTOGRAPH

Give the name of the artist when known, followed by a period and the title; underline the title if the work is a painting or sculpture. For any art you view personally, list the proprietary institution and, if not indicated in the institution's title, the city where the work is found.

Duchamp, Marcel. <u>Nude Descending a Staircase</u>.
     Philadelphia Museum of Art.
Rodin, Auguste. <u>The Thinker</u>. Metropolitan Museum of
     Art, New York.

Cite photographs or other reproductions of a work of art the same as above, but also add publication information about the source of the reproduction.

Moore, Henry. <u>Recumbent Figure</u>. Illus. 842 in <u>History</u>
     <u>of Art</u>. By H. W. Janson. 2nd ed. Englewood Cliffs,
     NJ: Prentice-Hall, 1977.
Van Gogh, Vincent. <u>Self-Portrait</u>. The Louvre, Paris.
     Illus. in <u>Vincent by Himself</u>. Ed. Bruce Bernard.
     Boston: Little, Brown, 1985. 279.

Parenthetic citation forms: (Duchamp); (Rodin); (Moore);
(Van Gogh). These forms are acceptable, but you should normally name the artist and work in the text.

64. AN ILLUSTRATION, TABLE, CHART, OR MAP

"Arctic Settlement." Illus. in <u>Past Worlds: The Times</u>
     <u>Atlas of Archaeology</u>. Maplewood, NJ: Times Books,
     1988. 271.
<u>Birds of Ohio</u>. Chart. Toldeo: Green Tree, 1987.
<u>Mexico</u>. Map. Chicago: Rand, 1985.

Parenthetic citation forms: ("Arctic"); (<u>Birds</u>); (<u>Mexico</u>).

65. A CARTOON

> Trudeau, Gary. "The Far Side." Cartoon. <u>Washington Post</u>
> 29 Jan. 1990. D8.
>
> Vietor, Dean. Cartoon. <u>New Yorker</u> 7 Nov. 1988: 51.

Parenthetic citation forms: (Trudeau); (Vietor).

66. A FILM, VIDEO TAPE, VIDEO DISC, OR SLIDE PROGRAM

For a film, list the title, underlined, followed by the name of the director, distributor, and the year, in that order. Add other information you feel is relevant. To focus on one person's involvement, cite that individual first, followed by a description of his or her role.

> Spielberg, Stephen, dir. <u>Raiders of the Lost Ark</u>. Prod.
> Frank Marshal. With Harrison Ford and Karen Allen.
> Paramount/Lucas Film, 1981.
>
> <u>Star Trek: The Motion Picture</u>. Dir. Robert Wise.
> Paramount, 1979. Metrocolor. 132m.

Parenthetic citation forms: (Spielberg); (<u>Star Trek</u>).

For a video tape, slide program, or filmstrip, include the medium after the title:

> <u>All's Well That Ends Well</u>. Video tape. By William
> Shakespeare. Prod. Jonathan Miller. New York:
> Time—Life, 1981. 166 min. VHS.
>
> <u>Climbing the Rockies</u>. Slide program. By James Mitchell.
> Boston University, Boston. 14 Sept., 1986.
> 48 slides.
>
> <u>The Greehouse Effect</u>. Sound filmstrip. Prod. Viewpoint
> Productions. Science Library, 1984. 125 fr., 16 min.

Parenthetic citation forms: (<u>AWW</u> 3.1.76–81); (<u>Climbing</u>);
(<u>Greenhouse</u>).

For a video disc, include the format, such as CAV or CLV, focusing on relevant additional information as you would for a film or film video.

> Brown, J. Carter, host. <u>National Gallery of Art</u>. Video
> disc. Champaign: U of Illinois, 1989. CAV.
>
> <u>Children at Play and Work</u>. Videodisc. New York: Chart,
> 1988. CLV.

Parenthetic citation forms: (Brown); (<u>Children</u>).

67. A TELEVISION OR RADIO PROGRAM

<u>Gone With the Wind: Pt. 1</u>. By Margaret Mitchell. Adapt.
John Newcomb. Dir. Pat Larson. NBC. KNBC
Los Angeles, 17 Jan. 1976.

Parenthetic citation form: (<u>Gone</u>).

68. A RECORDING

London, Jack. <u>The Call of the Wild and Other Stories</u>.
Audio tape. Read by Arnold Moss and Jack Dahlby.
Listening Library, CXL 517. 1987.

Tchaikovsky, [Peter Ilyich]. <u>The Nutcracker</u>. Cond.
Leonard Slatkin. Saint Louis Symphony Orchestra.
RCA, D216 A3. 1985.

Parenthetic citation forms: (London); (Tchaikovsky).

WORKING WITH OTHERS

As with intext citations and the content notes for the paper, you will appreciate another reader's assurance that the Works Cited section is done
correctly. Share the final draft of your paper with a friend or classmate in
these ways.

- Ask your reader to assist in checking to see that every work cited intext or in the Notes section of the paper is also represented on the
  Works Cited page(s). An easy way to do this to list each author or
  work as you read the draft and then compare the list with the entries
  on the Works Cited page(s).

- Draw your reader's attention to any unusual entries, such as multiple
  works by the same author, single artist performances, or video discs.
  Check these entries together to see if they appear in correct form.

- If you are working with a classmate, compare his or her Works Cited
  entries with your own. Note any differences in the way you have each
  listed similar kinds of sources, and discuss them. Make changes as
  necessary.

- Finally, encourage your reader to look for omissions of underlining,
  quotation marks, colons, or periods in the Works Cited entries. Make
  corrections before you type the final version of the paper.

CHAPTER ELEVEN

Alternative Documentation Styles

Author-Year (APA),
Number-System (CBE),
and *Chicago* (Footnote/Endnote)

Research papers written for most college English courses follow the Modern Language Association (MLA) author-page documentation style discussed in Chapters 9 and 10. Papers for other subjects, however, often require different documentation formats. Writers in the social, biological, medical, and applied sciences; education; fine arts; and humanities (excluding literature) follow formats recommended by their own professional associations or leading journals. Documentation in these disciplines differs from MLA style in the way sources are cited in the text and the reference section.

In general, papers that do not use the author-page, MLA style of documentation follow one of three other basic formats:

1. *Author-year, or APA (American Psychological Association), style.* Sources are cited parenthetically in the text by the author's last name and the work's publication date:

```
The changes that Kilner (1963) traced demonstrate
further patterns of simplification and reduction
(Shore, 1990).
```

All sources cited in the text are fully documented in a References section at the end of the paper.

2. *Number-system reference, or CBE (Council of Biology Editors), style.* Raised superscript numerals in the text—like this[5]—refer to numbered sources listed at the end of the paper in a References, Literature Cited, or References Cited section.

3. Chicago (The Chicago Manual of Style), *or footnote or endnote style.* Raised superscript numerals in the text refer to notes and documented sources appearing either at the bottom of the page as footnotes or as endnotes at the end of the paper in a Notes section.

Understanding Various Styles

The various documentation formats discussed in this chapter and preceding ones provide emphases for writers and readers in what are often specialized fields of study. As bewildering as the variety of styles can often seem, however, try not to be intimidated by their differences. After all, you need only master one documentation style to write your own paper. Familiarity with different documentation styles, on the other hand, can aid you in locating and taking accurate notes from a variety of sources—or even in documenting your own paper. If necessary, use your knowledge of a particular documentation style to change your paper's intext citations and reference list to conform to any of the formats used by other disciplines. Naturally, which documentation style you follow for your paper will depend upon its subject, the example of a particular journal, or the requirements of your instructor. As you pursue your research and writing, take care not to confuse variant forms appearing among discipline journals with the guidelines given here.

Author-Year Documentation

The author-year style of documentation is so named because it includes an author's last name and the year of publication whenever a writer *cites* a source:

```
Hall (1987) points to a lack of adequate research data
as the primary hindrance to acid-rain legislation.
Other writers (Keene & Wilson 1990), however, stress
economic concerns.
```

Intext citations such as these direct the reader to more complete descriptions of the named authors' works in the paper's References section.

Placed at the end of the paper, the References list each source cited in the text alphabetically by the author's last name (or by a work's title when no author is given). In addition to the author's name, each entry also provides the work's title and publication information.

APA Style

Author-year documentation style is the form adapted by the American Psychological Association (APA) and recommended in its guide, *Publication Manual of the American Psychological Association*. Because it provides efficient intext citations of other researchers' work, APA documentation style predominates in papers for the social sciences and several other disciplines, including anthropology, biology, business, education, economics, political science, psychology, and sociology. Though they often practice slight variations, writers and journals in these disciplines follow basic APA style for intext citations and for listing sources in the paper's References sections.

Abstracts

Papers written according to APA style or other formats for the sciences or social sciences often include an *abstract,* which is a short 100- to 150-word summary of the paper. (Abstracts for theoretorical papers are usually briefer, 75 to 100 words.) The abstract should state the purpose (thesis), findings, and conclusion of your research without commenting on or evaluating the paper itself. Put the abstract on a separate page, titled Abstract, after the title page. Use lowercase roman numerals for page numbers. The sample abstract for Ron Bonneville's paper in Appendix A provides a model.

Headings

Headings function like brief titles to emphasize certain content and to indicate the main sections of the paper. Like an outline, textual headings indicate the organization of the paper's content and emphasize the importance of each section. Use indentation, upper- or lowercase letters, and underlining to show the level of importance of each heading (i.e., the hierarchy, as in an outline). Topics with the same level of importance have the same type of heading throughout the paper.

Many articles in APA journals use standard headings—such as Purpose, Method, Procedure, Results, and Conclusions—to organize the discussion. Most student research papers, however, use headings that reflect the paper's subject, as these sample headings for a paper on drug testing illustrate:

1st level—Type   Rationale for Drug Testing
the heading
centered, upper-
and lowercase

    <u>Procedures</u>   2nd level—Type the heading flush left,
                                upper- and lowercase, and underlined

        <u>Testing methods.</u>
            3rd level—Indent the heading five spaces from the left.
            Capitalize the first letter only; underline the heading;
            end it with a period. The text begins on the same line,
            allowing a space after the period.

Although a paper may have as many as five levels of headings, student research papers seldom need more than two or three, if any. Check with your instructor as to the suitability of headings for your paper and his or her requirements for heading levels.

Intext Citation

APA form documents a paper's sources by both citing them in the text and describing them bibliographically in the paper's References list. When the work's author is named in the text, the publication date follows in parentheses:

Ramirez (1989) has pointed out the disadvantages of
postponing counseling until depression begins to
curtail normal activities.

When the author is not named in the text, cite the name parenthetically, *followed by a comma* and the year of the work's publication:

Decorative items found at the Sungir burial sites
demonstrate the early existence of social hierarchies
(Harlan, 1989).

NOTE: You may find during your research that some journals omit the comma between the author's name and the publication date, such as

(*Gross 1988*). APA style, however, requires punctuation. Unless your instructor approves omitting the comma, be sure that you include it.

The following method of citing a source is also acceptable:

```
Sark's 1988 study has shown that early humans switched
to meat eating much earlier than previously thought.
```

As the above examples demonstrate, intext citation allows acknowledgment of a source with the least interruption of the reader's attention to the paper's content. You give immediate credit to an authority whose work you have drawn upon and support your own arguments in doing so. Including a work's publication date in the citation is also important. Because information changes rapidly in some disciplines, such dates allow the reader to assess the relevancy of data and to make comparisons.

The guidelines here and on the following pages conform to the *Publication Manual of the American Psychological Association,* 3rd ed. (Washington, DC: APA, 1983).

AUTHORS

1. CITING AN AUTHOR, EDITOR, OR CORPORATE AUTHOR

Treat individuals, editors, corporate authors (e.g., associations, committees, and departments), and others who would normally be considered responsible for producing a work as its author. Cite personal authors or editors intext by their surnames only:

Individual author	According to Butler (1988), active group participation is another effective route to indirect self-assessment.
Editor	The list of recognized AIDS-related infections has grown every year since the disease was first identified (Rossman, 1990).

Spell out the name of each corporate author for the first intext citation, and cite its abbreviated form in brackets following: (*American Psychological Association [APA], 1983*). Thereafter, use the abbreviated form (*APA, 1983*) if it will be readily recognized by the reader and if the source will be easily found in the References list (where it should be fully spelled out). If the name is short or would not be readily understandable as an abbreviation, spell out the full name in all citations:

Corporate author
(first citation)

```
Founded in 1892, the American
Psychological Association promotes the
advancement of psychology as a science
and profession, as  well as a means
toward the betterment of human welfare
(American Psychological Association
[APA], 1983).
```

Corporate author
(subsequent
citation)

```
. . . toward the betterment of human
welfare (APA, 1983).
```

2. CITING TWO AUTHORS WITH THE SAME LAST NAME

Differentiate between two authors with the same last name by including their initials in the running text or in the parenthetic citation. Cite the authors in alphabetical order by their initials:

```
M. Street (1990) and W. R. Street (1989) identify major
lunar provinces yet to be be explored by satellite.
```

```
At least two experts (Street, M., 1990; Street, W. R.,
1989) identify major lunar provinces yet to be explored
by satellite.
```

3. CITING WORKS BY THE SAME AUTHOR, PUBLISHED THE SAME YEAR

Proceeding alphabetically by title, assign individual works by the same author and published in the same year a lowercase letter (*a*, *b*, *c*, and so forth) after the publication date: (*Navarro, 1989a*) or (*Navarro, 1989a, 1989b*). Also add the assigned letters to the publication date of each work as it appears alphabetically by title in the References section of the paper (see "Authors" section later in this chapter).

4. CITING A WORK WITH NO AUTHOR

Cite the work by its title, using the first two or three key words in place of an author's name:

```
One 20-year study found a significant correlation be-
tween the way individuals behaved in high school and
later as adults (Study of Adults, 1989).
```

Full title

```
A Study of Adults Exhibiting Stable Behavioral
Patterns over a Twenty-Year Period
```

U.S. exports to Japan hit a new high of $48.2 billion
in 1989 ("Trade War," 1990).

Full title   "The Trade War Gets Personal"

List such works alphabetically by full title in the paper's reference section.

NOTE: Cite a work's author parenthetically as *Anonymous* only if that is how the author is named in the source. The intext citation will look like this:

The cost of such programs (Anonymous, 1986) may account
for . . .

If you do cite an anonymous source, also list the work alphabetically, with *Anonymous* as author, in the References section of the paper.

5. CITING MORE THAN ONE AUTHOR

Separate multiple authors' names with *and* when the names are part of the running text. When you cite names parenthetically, separate them with an ampersand (*&*), not *and*:

Names in
running text
Wing and Gould (1979) have shown a
correlation between autism and low scores
on intelligence tests.

Gourdet, Ringly, Howland, and Lin (1989)
found that picture dependency decreases
as children improve their reading
skills.

Names cited
parenthetically
Other studies (Wing & Gould, 1979) have
shown a correlation between autism and
low scores on intelligence tests.

Picture dependency decreases as children
improve their reading skills (Gourdet,
Ringly, Howland, & Lin, 1989).

NOTE: Do not be confused by journal articles that use other ways to separate author names for intext citations. You may also find such parenthetic forms as (*Wells and Shorter, 1990*), (*Behrman; Rankin 1989*) and (*Davis, Graton, 1989; Li, Brennan, Kohler, 1990*) used in journals you research. Unless your instructor tells you otherwise, follow the APA forms shown here.

6. CITING UP TO SIX OR MORE AUTHORS

For works with two authors, use both names in every citation. For works with more than two authors but fewer than six, mention all names in the first reference:

Running text (first citation)	Greggio, Walters, Shore, and Ballen (1990) studied mitochondrial DNA to trace the global divergence of humans back 250,000 years.
Names cited in parentheses	One study (Greggio, Walters, Shore, & Ballen, 1990) used mitochondrial DNA to trace the global divergence of humans back 250,000 years.

After the first citation, give only the first name followed by *et al.* (not underlined) and the year:

Greggio et al. (1990) studied mitochondrial DNA . . .

One study (Greggio et al., 1990) used mitochondrial DNA . . .

All of the authors' names should be spelled out in the References.

When a work has more than six authors, cite only the first author's name, followed by *et al.*, for the first and succeeding intext citations. Spell out the names of all authors when listing them in the References.

NOTE: The phrase *et al.* comes from *et alii*, Latin for "and others." Since *al.* is an abbreviation for *alii*, it must always be written with a period after it. Do not underline *et al.* or put quotation marks around it in your paper.

7. CITING AUTHORS OF TWO OR MORE SEPARATE WORKS TOGETHER

Cite the works parenthetically only, beginning in alphabetical order with the first author's last name. Separate the citations with semicolons:

The privileged classes, for instance, have the luxury of time for long-term education and career planning (Breit, 1989; Lovett & Anderson, 1986; Wertham, 1990).

Each source should be listed fully in the References section of the paper.

QUOTATIONS AND SPECIFIC PARTS
OF SOURCES

APA documentation style uses the abbreviations *p.* or *pp.* for the words *page* and *pages, ch.* for *chapter,* and *sec.* for *section.* Use these or other standard abbreviations (see "Abbreviations" in Chapter 12) when citing specific parts of a work and whenever you use direct quotation or paraphrase. The following examples demonstrate common practice:

> Shepard and Chipman (1970) found that people can rotate mental images but only at a limited rate (cf. Ferguson, 1977, pp. 827-36).

> According to Beach (1987, esp. ch. 3), perceptual distortions can be both physiological and cognitive.

> Horne (1988) concludes that one primary function of sleep may be "to repair the cerebral cortex from the wear and tear of consciousness" (p. 41).

> If we interpret dreaming as "an analogue to our artistic yearnings" (Sheah, 1986, p. 207), we are still left with no explanation of its physiological importance beyond the cases made by Randall (1985, sec. 1) and Horne (1988).

LONG QUOTATIONS

Quotations of 40 words or more should be typed double-spaced and indented five spaces from the left margin. Indent the first line of each quoted paragraph five additional spaces. Place the page number of the source in parentheses after the period ending the quotation:

> Gregory (1987) explains these effects as follows:
> Sleep-deprivation causes sleepiness. It is difficult to keep awake someone who has been deprived of sleep for 60 hours. Such a person has frequent "microsleeps" and recurrently fails to notice, being unable to sustain a high level of attention. Sometimes visual illusions or hallucinations are experienced or the individual becomes paranoid. (p. 719)

LEGAL REFERENCES

Include the date of a court case in parentheses with the name; if the case is mentioned in the text, put the date in parentheses immediately after the case name:

```
Fletcher v. Peck (1810) established the right
of the U.S. Supreme Court to declare a state
law unconstitutional.

The U.S. Supreme Court established its right to
declare a state law unconstitutional more than a
hundred years ago (Fletcher v. Peck, 1810).
```

To cite a statute, give the name and year. Do not underline the name:

```
The Securities Exchange Act (1934) was designed to
protect the public from fraud or manipluation in the
sale of securities.

Federal law requires the regulation and registration
of securities exchanges (Securities Exchange Act,
1934).
```

PERSONAL COMMUNICATIONS

Unpublished letters, memos, telephone conversations, interviews, and such are personal communications. Since they are not available to other researchers, cite such information sources *only in the text*, not in the References for your paper. Give the last name and initials of your personal source, as well as the nearest exact date:

```
The Institute's chairperson, Dr. A. M. Reyes (personal
communication, September 4, 1990), thinks our society
celebrates childhood almost effortlessly but has
difficulty dealing with the changes that appear in
adolescence.

Some forestry personnel are now beginning to regret all
the media attention given to the new park proposal
(Charles May, personal communication, November 4,
1990).
```

References

Except for personal communications (such as letters, personal interviews, and the like), the References includes each of the sources cited in the paper's text. Include no other works, no matter how useful they may have been to you at some point in the research. This means that the References will undoubtedly not include some, perhaps several, works that contributed background information or common knowledge to your research. You may have consulted 50 sources during your research and ended up paraphrasing, quoting, or naming only 10 of them in your paper. Only those 10 will be listed as references.

The following pages provide guidelines and sample entries for works included in the References section of an APA-style research paper. Note that APA form calls for indenting the second and succeeding lines of each entry *three* spaces instead of the five required by MLA style. (See the References pages of Ron Bonneville's paper in Appendix A for an example.)

AUTHORS

1. CITING AUTHORS, EDITORS, AND CORPORATE AUTHORS

Treat the names of editors and corporate authors (i. e., associations, committees, corporations, councils) and editors the same as author names. Cite corporate authors by name, alphabetically. List personal authors and editors alphabetically by surname, followed by the initials of their first and (if given) middle names. For editors, use *Ed.* or *Eds.* in parentheses, followed by a period, after the name. Use an ampersand (&) between names of joint authors; the names are separated by commas. Follow these examples:

Single author	Alejandro, R. (1984). <u>The flavor of Asia</u>. New York: Beaufort Books.
Single editor	Barnes, L. A. (Ed.). (1982). <u>Advances in pediatrics</u>. Vol. 29. Chicago: Year Book Medical.
Joint editors	Dickstein, L. J., & Nadelson, C. (Eds.). (1988). <u>Family violence</u>. Washington, DC: American Psychiatric Press.
Two authors	Mintz, E., & Schmeidler, G. (1983). <u>The psychic thread: Paranormal and transpersonal aspects of pyschotherapy</u>. New York: Human Science Press.

Corporate
author

Smick—Medley & Associates. (1988).
<u>Foreign investment: A Smick—Medley and
Associates public opinion survey of
U.S. attitudes</u>. Washington, DC:
Author.

Parenthetic citation forms: (Barnes, 1982),
(Dickstein & Nadelson, 1988), (Smick—Medley, 1988)

NOTE: In the last example, the corporate author also published the work. The word *Author* should be used in place of the publisher's name to show this.

2. CITING A WORK WITH NO AUTHOR

Cite a work with no author alphabetically by title. Include the articles *a, an* and *the* at the begining of a title, but ignore them when ordering titles alphabetically:

Carnoy, M. (1980). <u>The state and
political theory</u>. Princeton, NJ:
Princeton University Press.

Book cited
by title

<u>A course for the 90's</u>. (1990). Austin,
TX: Four Square.

Del Polito, C. M., & Barresi, J. G.
(Eds.). (1982). <u>Alliances in health
and education: Serving youngsters with
special needs</u>. Laurel, MD:
Ramsco Publishing.

Newspaper article
cited by title

Higher health costs hit all sectors,
U.S. says. (1991, January 10).
<u>The Wall Street Journal</u>,
p. A2.

Parenthetic citation forms: ("Course," 1990);
("Higher," 1991)

NOTE: When a source provides no author's name, do not use *Anonymous* unless that term is actually given in the source. If the author is named as *Anonymous* in the source, list the work alphabetically under that term.

3. CITING WORKS PUBLISHED BY THE SAME AUTHOR(S)
   IN THE SAME YEAR

Proceed alphabetically by title, and assign lowercase letters (*a, b, c,* and so on) after the publication date. List works in the alphabetical order of the letters assigned:

> Giroux, H. (1988a). <u>Schooling and the struggle for public life: Pedagogy in the modern age</u>. Philadelphia: Temple University Press.
>
> Giroux, H. (1988b). <u>Teachers as intellectuals: Toward a critical pedagogy of learning</u>. South Hadley, MA: Bergin & Garvey.

Parenthetic citation forms: (Giroux, 1988a); (Giroux, 1988b); *or* (Giroux, 1988a, 1988b)

4. CITING MULTIPLE WORKS BY THE SAME AUTHOR(S)

List the works in chronological order of publication. Include each author's last name(s) and first and middle initial (if given) in each entry:

Single editor
> Jones, D. G. (Ed.). (1978). <u>Private and public ethics: Tensions between conscience and institutional responsibility</u>. Lewiston, NY: E. Mellen.
>
> Jones, D. G. (Ed.). (1982). <u>Business, religion, and ethics: Inquiry and encounter</u>. Westin, MA: Oelgeschlager.

Joint authors
> Leakey, R., & Lewin, R. (1977). <u>Origins: The emergence and evolution of our species and its possible future</u>. New York: Dutton.
>
> Leakey, R., & Lewin, R. (1978). <u>People of the lake: Mankind and its beginnings</u>. New York: Avon.

Parenthetic citation forms: (Jones, 1978); (Jones, 1982); (Leakey & Lewin, 1977); (Leakey & Lewin, 1978)

5. ORDERING SINGLE- AND JOINT-AUTHOR ENTRIES

Give the name of the first author in each entry. List personal works before edited works, single-author entries before multiple-author entries. Put joint-author entries in alphabetical order by the second and succeeding authors' names:

Author
> Lave, L. B. (1981). The strategy of social regulation: Decision frameworks for policy. Washington, DC: Brookings Institute.

Editor
> Lave, L. B. (Ed.). (1983). Quantitative risk assessment regulation. Washington, DC: Brookings Institute.

Joint authors
> Lave, L. B., & Omenn, G. S. (1981). Clearing the air: Reforming the Clean Air Act. Washington, DC: Brookings Institute.
>
> Lave, L. B., & Upton, A. C. (Eds.). (1987). Toxic chemicals, health and the environment. Baltimore, MD: Johns Hopkins University Press.

Parenthetic citation forms: (Lave, 1981); (Lave, 1983); (Lave & Omenn, 1981); (Lave & Upton, 1987)

For ordering multiple works published under the same name(s), follow the guidelines in 4 above.

DATES OF PUBLICATION

Place the work's publication date in parentheses, followed by a period, after the author's name. For magazine or newspaper articles, give the month and date of publication in parentheses after the year, separated by a comma. Do not abbreviate the month. Follow these examples:

Journal article
> Bandura, A. (1977). Self-efficacy: Toward a unifying theory of behavioral change. Psychological Review, 37, 122–147.

Newspaper article	Cash, R. (1990, September 14). Banks look for economic rainbow. <u>Los Angeles Times</u>, p. C5.
Magazine article	Karmin, M. W. (1990, April 16). The chip makers: Let's tango, not tangle. <u>U.S. News & World Report</u>, p. 40.
Book	Stern, D. N. (1985). <u>The interpersonal world of the infant</u>. New York: Basic Books.

Parenthetic citation forms: (Bandura, 1977); (Cash, 1990); (Karmin, 1990); (Stern, 1985)

TITLES

1. BOOKS

Capitalize only the first word of a work's title, the first word of a subtitle, and all proper nouns. Underline the complete title:

Lundgren, U. (1983). <u>Between hope and happening: Text and context in curriculum</u>. Geelong, Australia: Deakin University Press.

Palmer, B. (1984). <u>The 25-year war: America's military role in Vietnam</u>. New York: Da Capo Press.

Parenthetic citation forms: (Lundgren, 1983); (Palmer, 1984)

2. PERIODICALS

As with book titles, capitalize only the first word, the first word of a subtitle, and all proper nouns in the title of a magazine article. Do not underline the title or put it in quotation marks. Give the full names of newspapers, followed by a comma and the page number(s) of the article. Type the name of a journal, newspaper, or magazine in upper- and lowercase letters, and underline the name:

Anyon, J. (1979). Ideology and United States history textbooks. <u>Harvard Educational Review</u>, 49: 361-386.

Egan, J. (1989, January 30). After Tokyo, all the world's a bargain. <u>U.S. News & World Report</u>, pp. 58-59.

Parenthetic citation forms: (Anyon, 1979); (Egan, 1989)

PERIODICAL VOLUME AND ISSUE NUMBERS

For a journal, give the volume number, underlined, after a comma following the journal title. Indicate the issue number in parentheses immediately after the volume number (no space) whenever each issue of the journal begins with page 1. Indicate page numbers with *p.* or *pp.* for articles in magazines or newpapers but not for articles in journals. Follow the punctuation and spacing shown in these examples:

Journal, volume only	Anthi, P. R. (1983). Reconstruction of preverbal experiences. <u>Journal of the American Psychological Association</u>, <u>31</u>, 33–58.
Journal with issue number	Cherryholmes, C. (1983). Knowledge, power, and discourse in social studies education. <u>Journal of Education, 165</u>(4), 341–358.
Magazine article	Lemonick, M. D. (1989, September 18). What can Americans do? <u>Time</u>, p. 85.

Parenthetic citation forms: (Anthi, 1983); (Cherryholmes, 1983); (Lemonick, 1989)

PAGE NUMBERS

Use *p.* or *pp.* before the page number(s) for parts of books or articles in magazines but not for journal articles. Give inclusive page numbers in full: 361–382; 130–133. Separate discontinuous page numbers with a comma. Follow these examples:

Magazine article	Bartusiak, M. (1990, August). Mapping the article universe. <u>Discover</u>, pp. 60–63.
Chapter in volume	Burke, R. E. (1979). Election of 1940. In A. M. Schlesinger, Jr. (Ed.), <u>History of presidential elections, 1789–1968</u> (Vol. 4, pp. 2917–3006). New York: McGraw-Hill.
Chapter in book	Gregory, R. L. (1987). Consciousness. In <u>The Oxford Companion to the Mind</u> (pp. 160–164). Oxford: Oxford University Press.

Newspaper
article

Wright, R. (1991, January 9). Baker to
stress peaceful options. <u>Los Angeles
Times</u>, pp. A1, A11.

Parenthetic citation forms: (Bartusiak, 1990);
(Burke, 1979); (Gregory, 1987); (Wright, 1991)

AN EDITION OR REVISION OF A BOOK

Indicate an edition or revision of a book in parentheses after the title
of the work:

Herzfield, E. E. (1988). <u>Iran in the ancient East</u>
(repr. of 1941 ed.). New York: Hacker.

Hess, B. B., & Markson, E. W. (Eds.). (1985). <u>Growing
old in America</u> (3rd ed.). New Brunswick, NJ:
Transaction.

Wilson, M. (1983). <u>Managing a work force</u> (rev. ed.).
Brookfield, VT: Gower.

Parenthetic citation forms: (Herzfield, 1988);
(Hess & Markson, 1985); (Wilson, 1983)

A VOLUME IN A MULTIVOLUME WORK

Give the number of the volume(s) you consulted in parentheses after
the title. Use *Vol.* or *Vols.* before the volume number:

Grouws, D. A., & Cooney, T. (1989). <u>Perspectives on
research on effective mathematics teaching</u> (Vol. 1.)
Hillsdale, NJ: L. Erlbaum.

Parenthetic citation form: (Grouws & Cooney, 1989)

If particular volumes are published over more than a one-year period,
indicate the dates:

Scammon, R. M., & McGillivary, A. V. (Eds.).
(1972–1979). <u>America votes: A handbook of
contemporary American election statistics</u>
(Vols. 9–13). Washington, DC: Elections Research
Center.

Parenthetic citation form: (Scammon & McGillivary,
1972–1979)

A WORK PUBLISHED IN AN EDITED BOOK

List the work by its author's last name, followed by first and (if given) middle initial(s). Give the title, followed by the editor's initials and last name, in that order. Include the volume number (if applicable), followed by a comma and the page number(s) for the included piece in parentheses:

Burke, R. E. (1979). Election of 1940. In A. M.
    Schlesinger, Jr. (Ed.), History of presidential
    elections, 1789–1968 (Vol. 4, pp. 2917–3006).
    New York: McGraw–Hill.

Parenthetic citation form: (Burke, 1979)

A BOOK IN A SERIES

Give the name or number of the series, including page number(s) if you are citing a particular section of the work:

Crump, D. J. (Ed.). (1978). Into the wilderness.
    (Special Publications Series 13, No. 2). Washington,
    DC: National Geographic Society.
Population Reference Bureau. (1975). Family size and
    the Black American. Population Bulletin (No. 4.
    p. 11). Washington, DC: Author.

Parenthetic citation forms: (Crump, 1978);
(Population Reference Bureau, 1975)

A TECHNICAL OR RESEARCH REPORT

List a published report the same as a book. If the issuing agency has assigned a number, include that number in parentheses after the title, with no punctuation preceding it:

Briggs, D. E. G. (1981). Relationship of arthropods
    from the Burgess Shale and other Cambrian sequences
    (Open File Report 81–743). Washington, DC: U.S.
    Geological Survey.
Olivas, M. (1982). The condition of education for
    Hispanics. In La Red [The Net] (Report No. 56). Ann
    Arbor, MI: University of Michigan, Institute for
    Social Science.

U.S. Congress. Office of Technology Assessment.
(1988). <u>Electronic delivery of public assistance
benefits:</u> <u>Technology options and policy issues</u>
(S/N 052-003-01121-2). Washington, DC: U.S.
Government Printing Office.

Parenthetic citation forms: (Briggs, 1981); (Olivas, 1982);
(U.S. Congress, 1988)

THE PROCEEDINGS OF A MEETING

For published proceedings, treat the work the same as a book:

De Vore, R. W., & Jackson, J. S. (Eds.). (1987).
<u>Proceedings of the Carnahan Conference on Security
and Technology</u>. Lexington, KY: University
of Kentucky.

For unpublished proceedings, cite when and where the meeting was held, as there is no publisher:

World Food Conference. (1976, June). <u>Proceedings of the
World Food Conference</u>. Conference held at Iowa State
University, Ames, IA.

Parenthetic citation forms: (De Vore & Jackson, 1987);
(World Food, 1976).

LEGAL SOURCES

Give the information needed for a reader to locate the source. Using the source itself or a referent to it as your guide, give the information indicated in the following examples. If your typewriter does not have keys for typing the symbol for *section* (§), use the abbreviation *Sec.* Note that you should not underline names of court cases in the References, but do underline them in the text citation. Do not underline the names of laws, acts, codes, or documents (such as the U.S. Constitution).

1. A FEDERAL DISTRICT COURT OPINION

Name	Volume	Source	Page	Region	Date

Hazard v. Kinola, 554 F. Supp. 927 (S.W. Ark. 1981).

This 1981 case was tried in federal district court for the Southwestern District of Arkansas. It appears in volume 554, page 927, of the *Federal Supplement*.

Parenthetic citation form: (Hazard v. Kinola, 1981)

2. A CASE APPEALED TO THE U.S. SUPREME COURT

Name   Volume   Source   Page   Date

Baker v. Carr, 369 U.S. 186 (1965).

This case was tried in 1965 before the U.S. Supreme Court. It appears in volume 369 of the *United States Reports*, page 186.

Parenthetic citation form: (Baker v. Carr, 1985)

3. A FEDERAL LAW

Name   Title number   Source   Section   Date

Voting Rights Act, 42 U.S.C. § 1973 (1965).

Passed into law in 1965, this act appears in title 42, section 1973, of the *United States Code.*

Parenthetic citation form: (Voting Rights Act, 1965)

Many federal laws are often cited by title number rather than by name. Note that the *United States Code* (cited above) may be abbreviated as U.S.C.:

15 U.S.C. sec. 221 (1978).

For more information about the form of legal references, see *A Uniform System of Citation* (Cambridge, MA: Harvard Law Review Association, 1986).

NONPRINT SOURCES

1. A FILM OR VIDEO

Give the principal contributors' names, followed by their function(s) in parentheses. Specify the medium in brackets after the title, followed by the location and name of the distributor:

Choate, H. R. (Producer), & Kimbel, M. M. (Director).
(1980). Marriage and commitment [Film]. Chicago:
Academy Productions.
Intercultural Relations Institute (IRA). (1982). Take
two [Video]. Palo Alto, CA: Author.

Parenthetic citation forms: (Choate & Kimbel, 1980);
(IRA, 1982)

2. A CASSETTE RECORDING

Give the principal contributors' names, followed by their function(s) in parentheses. Specify the medium in brackets after the title. If a recording number is given on the source, include that information with the medium specification—(*Cassette Recording No. 71*). List the publisher's location and name last:

Peterson, R. T. (Ed.), & Walton, R. K. (Narrator).
(1990). Birding by ear [Cassette recording].
Columbus, OH: Ohio State University.

Parenthetic citation form: (Peterson & Walton, 1990)

Sample Reference List: Psychology

Though variations occur among some journals, the author-year style recommended by the American Psychological Association (APA) predominates in papers in psychology, education, and a number of other fields. The following examples conform to the guidelines discussed above and the recommendations of the *Publication Manual of the American Psychological Association,* 3rd ed. (Washington, DC: American Psychological Association).

References

Book/single author	Bruner, J. (1986). Actual minds, possible worlds. Cambridge, MA: Harvard University Press.
Book/joint authors	Cantor, N., & Kihistrom, J. (1987). Personality and social intelligence. Englewood Cliffs, NJ: Prentice Hall.
Journal article/ volume number	De Gramont, P. Language and the self. Contemporary Psychoanalysis, 23, 77–121.
Multiple works by same author (book & journal entries)	Edelson, M. (1984). Hypothesis and evidence in psychoanalysis. Chicago: University of Chicago Press.

Edelson, M. (1986). Causal explanation in
science and psychoanalysis:
Implications for writing a case study.
Psychoanalytical Studies of Children,
41, 89–127.

Edited and translated selection in multivolume work

Freud, S. (1957). Repression. In J.
Strachey (Ed. and Trans.), The
standard edition of the complete
psychological works (Vol. 19,
pp. 3–66). London: Hogarth Press.
(Original work published in 1915)

Journal article volume & issue numbers

Gecas, V., & Bower, Schwalbe, M. L.
(1983). Beyond the looking-glass self:
Social structure and efficacy-based
self-esteem. Social Psychology
Quarterly, 46(2): 77–88.

Book/editor

Gregory, R. L. (Ed.). (1987). The Oxford
companion to the mind. New York:
Oxford University Press.

Published report

John-Steiner, V., & Osterreich, H.
(1975). Learning styles among Pueblo
children (Final report HEW: NEG–000–3–
0074). Albuquerque, NM: University of
New Mexico.

Magazine article

King, P. (1989, May). The pretended self.
Psychology Today, pp. 60–61.

Selection in another work

Loewald, H. (1976). Perspectives of
memory. In M. M. Gill and P. S.
Holzman (Eds.), Psychology versus
metapsychology (pp. 298–325). New
York: International University Press.

Journal/joint authors

Pearlin, L. I., Menaghan, E. G., Lieber-
man, M. A., & Mullan, J. T. (1981).
The stress process. Journal of Health
and Social Behavior, 22, 337–356.

| Report/Corporate author | Psychiatry and the Community Committee. (1986). A family affair: Helping families cope with mental illness (GAP Report: No. 119). New York: Bruner-Mazel. |

Discipline Practices—APA Variations

Disciplines that follow APA, author-year documentation cite sources in the text, as described earlier in this chapter. For entries in the References list, however, many of these disciplines employ variations of APA form, modifying punctuation, spacing, capitalization, and other details. You may discover that adapted versions of APA references forms are common in papers or journals written for agriculture, anthropology and archaeology, the biological sciences, business and economics, education, geology, and home economics. Many papers in linguistics follow LSA style, a version of APA recommended by the Linguistics Society of America. In political science and sociology, writers often use APSA style, a variation of APA adopted by the American Political Science Association. (See the section on "Discipline Style Manuals" near the end of this chapter for guides on LSA and APSA documentation.)

Be alert to modifications of APA style (or any other major documentation style) as you read and record notes from all your research sources. Make sure such notes are accurate and that your own paper follows precisely the documentation style recommended by your instructor.

Number-System Documentation

The majority of authors, editors, and journals in the applied sciences (chemistry, computer sciences, mathematics, and physics) as well as the medical sciences employ the number-system style of documentation. This style uses arabic numerals in the text to cite sources correspondingly numbered and listed in the References section of the paper.

Intext Citation

The intext citation numerals appear in the text either (a) between parentheses, (b) between brackets, or (c) as raised superscript numerals, as shown here:

a. Harland (3) has shown that traditional comparisons of cigarette smoke yields have been reliable. On the other hand, it is important to remember that the chemical composition of nontobacco cigarette smoke is very different from ordinary tar (4,5).

b. Despite the endorsement of Nobel laureate Paul Berg [3], some scientists [1,7,12] maintain that the genome project is unnecessary or that it will produce only what Ayala [4, p. 10] calls "indecipherable junk."

c. Oxygen affects yeast viability and is essential to any yeast ethanol production process.[4-6] The Pasteur effect[12] demonstrates the influence of oxygen and respiration on the ability of the cell to produce ethanol.

(See the instructions for typing brackets and superscript numerals in Chapter 12.)

As these example show, it is not unusual for a citation to refer to more than one source at a time with the number-system method. In addition, note that the citation numerals do not necessarily appear in sequential order. Numeral sequence depends upon the method by which each discipline or publishing journal prefers to list and number sources in the paper's References.

References

For ordering sources in the References section, papers that employ the number-system style follow one of two widely used methods:

1. Numbering sources listed in the References section by their order of appearance in the text
2. Numbering sources according to their alphabetized order in the References

Disciplines and journals vary as to their practices. Which numbering method you use will depend upon the discipline or journal you are following or upon the directions of your instructor.

1. NUMBERING SOURCES BY ORDER OF APPEARANCE IN THE PAPER

In this method, citation numbers proceed sequentially throughout the text (1, 2, 3, and so on) until they are repeated when a source is cited again. Corresponding sources in the References section are listed and numbered in the order they are cited in the paper rather than alphabetically by author or title:

Parenthetic citation form

```
Fish use chemical signals to identify individual
members of a species, as well as to distinguish status
(3). Among certain fishes, color changes indicate
success or defeat in battle (4, 5).
```

References

```
3. Thomas, L. A long line of cells. New York: Viking
   Penguin; 1974.
4. Levine, J. S. Coral reef fishes use riotous colors
   to communicate. Smithsonian 21(8):98–103; 1990.
5. Webb, P. W.; Weihs, D. (Eds.). Fish biomechanics.
   New York: Praeger; 1983.
```

The changing order of sources during the draft stages of a paper using the number-by-appearance method can be troublesome. It is usually easiest to put the author's name in parentheses as you write the draft. Once the paper has been completed in draft form, with all sources entered and in final order, you can substitute numbers for the authors' names. The numbering of citation sources by order of appearance in the References is common for papers written in computer science, engineering, mathematics, and nursing.

NOTE: Titles of sources are not underlined or italicized in number-system style.

2. NUMBERING SOURCES BY ALPHABETIZED ORDER

Begin by alphabetizing all sources for the paper according to the author's last name (or the work's title if there is no author given). Next, number each source sequentially, as shown below:

Literature Cited entries

```
1. Cohen, S. Red sea diver's guide. Tel Aviv, Israel:
   Red Sea Divers; 1975.
2. Levine, J. S. Coral reef fishes use riotous colors
   to communicate. Smithsonian 21(8):98–103; 1990.
```

3. Randall, J. E. Red sea reef fishes. London: Immel
   Publishing; 1983.
4. Thomas, L. A long line of cells. New York: Viking
   Penguin; 1974.
5. Webb, P. W.; Weihl, D. (Eds.). Fish biomechanics.
   New York: Praeger; 1983.

As you write the paper, cite these sources parenthetically by number (or raised superscript) as they appear in the text. Remember that a number should be repeated in the text whenever the source it designates is cited more than once.

Parenthetic citation form

Fish use chemical signals, for example, to identify
individual members of a species, as well as to
distinguish status (4). Among certain fishes, color
changes indicate success or defeat in battle (2,4,5).

Note that sources are *not* cited in numerical order. The references above to Thomas (4), Levine (2), and Webb & Weihl (5), for example, correspond to the order in which those authors appear in the Literature Cited section.

Listing reference sources aphabetically by their author's last name and then numbering citations accordingly is the usual method for papers in biology, mathematics, and psychology.

Other Features

ABSTRACTS

A paper following the number-reference style generally includes an abstract, or brief summary, of the paper. (Reviews of the literature, however, do not include an abstract.) The abstract informs the reader of the paper's contents and serves as a useful review once the paper has been read. If your instructor wishes you to include an abstract with your paper, see the general discussion on "Abstracts" earlier in this chapter.

HEADINGS

Headings serve as short titles for various sections of the paper. They are helpful in organizing the discussion and emphasizing important ideas for the reader. See the discussion on "Headings" earlier in this chapter if you plan to include headings in your paper.

JOURNAL ABBEVIATIONS

Disciplines following the number-system style of documentation consistently abbreviate titles of journals listed in the paper's References section. The exceptions to this practice are journals whose titles contain only a single word (e.g., *Biochemistry, Geology, Science*). While such one-word titles should not be abbreviated in your paper, you will need to abbreviate others.

Make certain the abbreviations you use conform to accepted practices for the discipline you are writing about. The major source for all discipline abbreviations is the *American National Standard for Abbreviation of Titles of Periodicals, Z39.5-1969* (New York: American National Standards Institute, 1974).

Standard abbreviations for journals common to specific disciplines are also given in the following sources:

Biological Sciences

Bibliographic Guide for Editors and Authors. Washington, DC: American Chemical Society, 1974.
Biological Abstracts (published annually each January).
Chemical Abstracts Service Source Index (CASSI). Washington, DC: American Chemical Society, 1984 (online).

Chemistry and Related Fields

ACS Style Guide: A Manual for Authors and Editors. Washington, DC: American Chemical Society, 1986.
Chemical Abstract Service Source Index (CASSI). Washington, DC: American Chemical Society, 1984 (online).

Mathematics

Abbreviation of Names and Serials. Providence, RI: American Mathematical Society, 1985.
Bibliographic Guide for Editors and Authors. Washington, DC: American Chemical Society, 1974.

Medical Sciences

Index Medicus (any current issue).

Physics

AIP Style manual. 4th ed. New York: American Institute of Physics, 1990.

CBE Style

The number-system style of documentation established by the Council of Biology Editors (CBE) is recommended for papers in anatomy, genetics, physiology, and zoology. Though several journals in these and other scientific disciplines follow a form of APA style, CBE format also provides the general standard for number-system documentation in the sciences and in technology generally. In addition to using it for your own paper, becoming familiar with CBE documentation form will enable you to understand and adapt the number-reference styles used by other disciplines throughout the applied and physical sciences.

Intext Citation

Cite sources parenthetically by number as they are mentioned in the text or according to the number of their alphabetized source in the Reference list, as explained earlier. Place citation numerals between parentheses or brackets or use raised superscript numbers.

Parenthetic citation form

Reference list/ Order of source citation	Pair bonding among certain organisms increases reproductive efficiency (1), and some studies suggest it also decreases competitive behavior (2,3).
	Pair bonding among certain organisms increases reproductive efficiency [1], and some studies suggest it also decreases competitive behavior [2,3].
Reference list/ Alphabetical order by author names	Pair bonding among certain organisms increases reproductive efficiency,[14] and some studies suggest it also decreases competitive behavior.[1,6]

References

Title the list Literature Cited, References, or References Cited. List and number sources in the order they are cited intext. Note the following important practices:

1. Separate multiple authors' names with semicolons.
2. Capitalize words in titles according to the style followed in the source (e.g., on the title page).
3. Do not underline or put quotation marks around titles.
4. Abbreviate journal titles, but do not abbreviate single-word titles.
5. Give the publication date last, following a semicolon.
6. Type the second and following lines flush with the left margin of the first line.

Sample Reference List

Literature Cited

Author listed as *Anonymous*
1. Anonymous. Birds of prey area opposed. Audubon Leader 21:1; 1979.

Journal article
2. Axelrod, C.; Hamilton, W. D. The evolution of cooperation. Science 211:1390–1396; 1981.

Edition
3. Barnes, R. D. Invertebrate zoology. 4th ed. New York: Holt; 1980.

Work in a series
4. Brooks, P. G. Cambrian arthropods of the Burgess Shale. Paleontology. Ser.3, 16:332–38; 1981.

Joint authors
5. Cox, C. B.; Moore, P. D. Biogeography. 4th ed. Oxford, England: Blackwell Scientific Publications; 1985.

Corporate author
6. Council for Science and Society. Companion animals in society. London: Oxford University Press; 1988.

Volume
7. Dodd, B. E. Blood group topics. Vol. 3. Chicago: Year Book Medical Publishers; 1978:23–34.

Abbreviated journal title
8. Deem, A. W.; Thorp, F. Jr. Toxic algae in Colorado. J. Am. Vet. Med. Assoc. 95:542; 1986.

Single author
9. Hay, D. A. Essentials of behaviour genetics. Melbourne, Australia: Black-well Scientific Publications; 1985.

NOTE: Many standard reference works are better known and may be cited by their titles rather than an editor's name. If the editor's name is included, place it after the title:

1. Annual review of cell biology. G. E. Pallade, ed.
   Palo Alto, CA: Annual Reviews; 1987.
2. Dictionary of genetics. 3d ed. King, R. C. &
   Stansfield, W. D., eds. London: Oxford University
   Press; 1985.

Discipline Practices—CBE Variations

Like basic author-year (APA) style, number-system method documentation includes varying practices in both citation and references forms. Papers in the applied sciences—chemistry, mathematics, physics, and the medical sciences, for example—often follow documentation styles recommended by discipline associations. (See the list of style manuals for various disciplines near the end of this chapter.) By consciously noting such variations, you should have no trouble understanding the application of number-system documentation in scientific journals to your own research paper.

As you take notes during reading or prepare your own paper's references, do not confuse standard CBE documentation form with modified versions. Be certain that your own paper follows your instructor's requirements.

Chicago-Style Documentation

Writers in the fine arts (art, music, dance, and philosophy) as well as certain areas of the humanities follow a documentation system described in *The Chicago Manual of Style*, 13th ed. (Chicago: The University of Chicago Press, 1982) and consequently known as *Chicago* style. This system uses raised numbers—like this[7]—in the text to direct readers to listed sources and commentary appearing either at the bottom of the page as footnotes or at the end of the paper as endnotes. Though source notes fully list every work cited in the paper, a Works Cited or References section also sometimes follows the text or endnote section.

Note Numbering

The raised, or superscripted, numbers for *Chicago*-style documentation run consecutively ([1], [2], [3], etc.) throughout the text and in the note sections, without repetition. Note numbers *follow* all punctuation marks (except dashes); do not put them inside parentheses. Place the numbers near the material whose source(s) you are acknowledging or commenting on, usually at a punctuated pause or at the end of the sentence:

> Though so-called "glitter rock" had its share of critics,[3] such music could also include surprising innovation. Singer David Bowie, for example, drew upon West Indian reggae and African drums for new sounds and rhythms.[4]

Superscript numbers like those above refer the reader to correspondingly numbered notes (comments or bibliographic listings of sources) at the bottom of the page or at the end of the paper. Such notes would have the same content whether they appear as footnotes or endnotes.

Note Form and Content

FIRST NOTATION OF A SOURCE

Many entries will require only the name of the author(s), full underlined title, and publication facts. When it is necessary to include other kinds of information, follow this sequence: author(s), editor(s), or translator(s); title; series, volume number, or edition; publication data; page(s). The following sample footnote for a work with two authors demonstrates the basic form for the first time you cite a source:

> 10. Jacob Epstein and Arnold L. Haskell. Sculptor Speaks: A Series of Conversations on Art, rev. ed. (Salem, NH: Ayer Company, 1990), 80.

EXTENSIVE REFERENCES TO ONE WORK

When you refer several times to the same work throughout your paper, document the source fully in a single note, with an explanation of how future references will be cited in the text of the paper:

> 11. Bruce Bernard, ed. Vincent by Himself: A Selection of Van Gogh's Paintings and Drawings Together

<u>with Extracts from His Letters</u> (Boston: New York Graphic
Society–Little, Brown, 1985), 21. Future references to
Van Gogh's paintings and letters in this paper will be
to this work, with page numbers given in the text.

    12. Unless otherwise stated, lyrics quoted in this
paper are from <u>Beatlesongs</u> (New York: Simon and
Schuster, 1989), by William J. Dowling.

CITING MULTIPLE SOURCES

Whenever you cite several works documenting the same material
within the text of the note, separate the entries with semicolons:

    13. On this point, see also Lloyd Goodrich, <u>The</u>
<u>Four Seasons: Paintings and Drawings by Andrew Wyeth</u>
(New York: Art in America, 1962), 93; Thomas Hoving,
<u>Two Worlds of Andrew Wyeth: Kuerners and Olsons</u>
(New York: Metropolitan Museum, 1976), 221; and
Fairfield Porter, "Andrew Wyeth," <u>Art News</u> 57
(December 1958): 13.

SUBSEQUENT NOTATIONS

A subsequent notation, one referring to a source that has already
been fully cited in an earlier note, should be shortened. Cite the author or
editor by last name only (but give the full name or initials if another author
or editor has the same last name). Give the relevant page number(s),
following a comma, after the name:

First note

    14. Jacques Barzun, <u>Music in</u>
<u>American Life</u> (Bloomington: Indiana
University Press, 1962), 42.

Subsequent note

    15. Barzun, 83–85.

NOTE: Some disciplines give a shortened version of the title after the
author's name in the subsequent note—*12. Barzun,* Music, *83–85*—even
when only one work by an author is documented. For cases when you
document more than one work by an author, see the guidelines that
follow.

MULTIPLE WORKS BY ONE AUTHOR

Whenever an author has more than one work mentioned in notes, a
shortened title *must* accompany the author's name:

First note for **this work**	16. Jacques Barzun, <u>Critical</u> <u>Questions: On Music and Letters, Culture</u> <u>and Biography, 1940–1980</u> (Chicago: University of Chicago Press, 1980), 61.
Shortened title	17. Barzun, <u>Critical Questions</u>, 93.
Previously cited work	18. Barzun, <u>Music</u>, 106.
Second work	19. Barzun, <u>Critical Questions</u>, 163.

USING *Ibid*

While repeating an author's name, as shown above, is usually clearest for most readers, you may also use the Latin abbreviation *Ibid.* (for *ibidem*, "in the same place") to stand for the name of the author and the title of the work cited *immediately preceding*. Do not use *Ibid.* with an author's name or a work's title, since it replaces both. Use *Ibid.* without page numbers if the pages are the same as in the preceding entry; include page numbers if they are different:

First notation	20. Jacques Barzun, ed. <u>Pleasures of</u> <u>Music: An Anthology of Writings about</u> <u>Music and Musicians from Cellini to</u> <u>Bernard Shaw</u> (Chicago: University of Chicago Press, 1977), 42.
Subsequent note/ **different pages**	21. Ibid., 83–85.
Same pages as **preceding note**	22. Ibid.
Different work	23. Barzun, <u>Critical Questions</u>, 19.

NOTE: The latinate abbreviations *loc. cit* and *op. cit* are no longer in use. When you want to draw the reader's attention to other sources, use the abbreviation *cf.* ("confer" or "compare") or the short directives *See* or *See also.*

COMMENTARY AND QUOTATIONS

Use commentary notes to explain documentation methods, to compare sources, or to supplement the text; however, do not use notes to include material that more properly belongs to or is important for understanding the text. The content of most notes, especially footnotes, should be written as a single paragraph. Longer notes are sometimes acceptable, but in general, avoid them. Document a quotation or other material included in a note by giving the source in parentheses after the material and before the final period. Use brackets to include publication data already between parentheses.

     24. The Chinese philosopher Confucius, however, stated the Golden Rule in negative terms: "What you do not want done to yourself, do not do to others" (W. L. Reese, <u>Dictionary of Philosophy and Religion: Eastern and Western Thought</u> [Atlantic Highlands, NJ: Humanities Press, 1980], 198).

Note Placement

Follow the requirements of your instructor about which type of notes to use for *Chicago*-style documentation. If you have a choice between footnotes or endnotes, however, you will find the latter preferable, since they are much easier to prepare. Footnotes, regardless of their length, must appear on the same page as their relevant text; consequently, they are often difficult to manage. A word-processing program that arranges them automatically is extremely helpful.

FOOTNOTES

The notes appear at the bottom of the page, separated from the text by triple-spacing or a 12-space rule (underline) beginning at the left margin. Indent the first line of the footnote five spaces. Type the footnote number on the line, not raised,[*] followed by a period. Be sure that the footnote number and content correspond to the superscripted numerals in the text and that the footnote numbers run consecutively throughout the paper. Single-space each footnote, but double space between individual notes.

ENDNOTES

Place the notes on a separate page, immediately following the last page of the paper's text, but after any appendix and before a bibliography, if these are included in the paper. Do not type a number on the first endnote page, but count it and number all other endnote pages. Center and type the title "Notes" two inches down from the top of the page; allow four blank lines between the title and the first note. Indent the first line of each note five spaces, with the second and succeeding lines typed flush with the left margin. Type endnote numbers on the line, not raised.[*] Double space the content of individual endnotes, as well as between them.

---

[*]Raised footnote and endnote numbers are also acceptable, but be consistent in the method you use. Type raised numerals with no space between the last number and the first word—[5]*David Jones* . . .

Sample Note Forms

Though footnotes and endnotes differ as to where they appear in the paper, the forms for individual entries, including punctuation, are the same (except that you double-space individual endnotes, as described above). The examples below demonstrate *Chicago*-style footnotes or endnotes for various types of sources and commentary. The entries conform generally to the guidelines of *The Chicago Manual of Style*, 13th ed. (Chicago: University of Chicago Press, 1982).

Book/ **single author**	1. Mortimer Adler, <u>Ten Philosophical</u> <u>Mistakes</u> (New York: MacMillan, 1985), 182.
Subsequent reference	2. Ibid., 136.
New book/ **same author**	3. Mortimer Adler, <u>Aristotle for</u> <u>Everybody</u> (New York: Bantam–Dell, 1983), 201.
Subsequent reference	4. Adler, <u>Ten Philosophical</u> <u>Mistakes</u>, 64.
Book/joint editors	5. J. T. Crump and William P. Maher, eds., <u>Chinese and Japanese Music</u> (Ann Arbor, MI: University of Michigan Press, 1975), 18–23.
Book/ **multiple authors**	6. Yuri Tsivian et al. <u>Silent</u> <u>Witnesses: Russian Films, 1980–1919</u> (London: British Film Institute and Edizioni Biblioteca dell'Immagine, 1982.
Subsequent reference	7. Crump and Maher, 97.
Selection in **edition**	8. Geoffrey Nowell–Smith, "Minelli and Melodrama," in <u>Home Is Where the</u> <u>Heart Is: Studies in Melodrama and the</u> <u>Woman's Film</u>, ed. Christine Gledhill (London: British Film Institute, 1987), 74.
Commentary **referring to** **other sources** **for comparision**	9. Musicians today tend to disagree with Menuhin. Cf. John Rahn, "Computer Music: A View from Seattle," <u>Computer</u> <u>Music Journal</u> 12 (Fall 1988): 18; Harold

Abelson and Gerald Jay Sussman, <u>Structure</u>
<u>and Interpretation of Computer Programs</u>
(Cambridge, MA: The MIT Press, 1985); and
William Kornfield, "Machine Tongues VII:
LISP," <u>Computer Music Journal</u> 4, no. 2
(Summer 1980): 6–12.

Subsequent reference   10. Nowell–Smith, 73.

Magazine article   11. Joan Acocella, "Baryshnikov Goes
Modern," <u>Connoisseur</u>, November 1990,
118–119.

Newspaper article   12. Marcia Dodson, "Korean Culture
Connection," <u>Los Angeles Times</u>, 9
January, 1991, B1, B7.

Discipline Style Manuals

As discussed earlier in this chapter, documentation practices between and
among discipline journals vary greatly. The most comprehensive guide is
The Chicago Manual of Style (13th ed.); however, it is written more for
professional writers and editors than for students working on course papers. The style manuals listed below recommend the basic documentation
forms for their respective disciplines. If you need more information than is
provided in this text about a particular discipline or journal documentation style, consult one of these sources.

Biological Sciences

Council of Biology Editors. *CBE Style Manual.* 5th ed. Bethesda, MD:
Council of Biology Editors, 1983.

Chemistry

Dodd, Janet S., ed. *The ACS Style Guide.* Washington, DC: American
Chemical Society, 1986.

Geology

United States Geological Survey. *Suggestions for Authors of the Reports of the United States Geological Survey.* 6th ed. Washington, DC: GPO, 1978.

Linguistics

Linguistics Society of America. *LSA Bulletin* Dec. issue, annually.

Literature and Languages

Achtert, Walter S., and Joseph Gibaldi. *MLA Handbook for Writers of Research Papers.* 3rd ed. New York: Modern Language Association of America, 1988.

———. *Style Manual.* New York: Modern Language Association of America, 1988.

Mathematics

American Mathematical Society. *A Manual for Authors of Mathematical Papers.* 7th ed. Providence, RI: American Mathematical Society, 1980.

Medical Sciences

American Medical Association. *American Medical Association Manual of Style.* 8th ed. Baltimore: Williams and Wilkins, 1989. Rev. ed. of *Manual for Authors and Editors,* 7th ed.

Physics

American Institute of Physics. *AIP Style Manual.* 4th ed. New York: American Institute of Physics, 1990.

Political Science

American Political Science Association. *Political Science* Fall 1985.

WORKING WITH OTHERS

The complex documentation forms for the various disciplines discussed in this chapter require close attention to details of form, punctuation, and spacing. Review the Notes and References page(s) of your draft with another person to see that you have handled such details correctly. A close review of the paper's documentation now will help you avoid errors and omissions when you prepare the final copy.

- Begin by asking a classmate or friend to review the the paper's notes for accuracy and correct form. Ask if each superscript numeral in the text has a correspondingly numbered note. Next, read the notes and the works named in them aloud while your classmate checks to make sure each work named is also included in the References list.

- Point out any unusual or complicated entries included in the References page(s). Ask your reader to verify the form and punctuation for entries such as multiple authors or editors, works included in a volume, and journal articles. Check such entries together to make sure they appear in correct form.

- Compare your reader's References list with your own. Note any differences in the way you each have listed similar kinds of sources, and discuss reasons for the differences. Make changes as necessary.

- Ask your reader to review the References list for omissions or unwanted inclusions of underlining, quotation marks, colons, or periods. Check to see that you have spaced correctly between volume and issue numbers. Also review any special formats required by your instructor or discipline.

CHAPTER TWELVE

Preparing the Final Manuscript

The thoughtful work you have done researching and writing the completed draft of your paper should continue through the preparation of the final manuscript. Plan time for production—including revising, editing, typing, and proofreading—of the final copy well in advance of the paper's due date. Your instructor undoubtedly views your taking responsibility for matters of correct formating and technical details as an important part of the research paper assignment. Careful preparation of the manuscript will enhance its contents and ensure his or her appreciation of your efforts.

Reviewing and Strengthening the Final Draft

Like most writers, you have undoubtedly made changes, additions, and deletions throughout developing several drafts of the research paper. Having now composed a final version, you should carefully review the draft before typing or printing a final copy. As you review, be prepared to (1) *revise* the paper as needed for overall focus and organization; (2) *edit* for style and correctness; and (3) *proofread* for omissions and other small errors.

Revising

Revise by making any necessary changes to the whole paper, taking into account such broad qualities as completeness, organization, unity, and purpose. Expect to add or delete content, but do not interpret *revision* as rewriting the paper. Your goal in revising is to assess the general flow of ideas and to rearrange content for more effectiveness.

How to Revise

Begin by carefully reading the draft several times to determine if the content flows smoothly and, on the whole, presents a complete discussion. Pay particular attention to and note any areas that appear underdeveloped, out of place, or irrelevant (see following). Mark changes right on the draft itself (see Figure 12.1), or use scissors and tape to rearrange sections to achieve the best order for the content. If you wrote the draft on a computer, work on a printed copy to provide a record of your changes. Use the computer's word-processing program later to add content and move or delete whole sections of text as needed.

What to Revise

As you review the draft for revision, follow these suggestions:

1. Make sure the paper's content is unified around a clearly stated main idea. The content of Ron Bonneville's paper in the Appendix, for example, develops and supports this thesis: While the concerns expressed are justified, Americans should view the expansive Japanese presence in the United States as a positive stage in this country's global development. Look for content in your draft that strays from the research topic or is not clearly related to the paper's thesis. You may need to change inappropriate content or, if it is a significant amount, revise the thesis statement to include it.

2. Identify the paper's introduction, body, and conclusion. Does the introduction state a thesis and introduce the paper topic effectively? Do paragraphs in the body of the paper illustrate and support the thesis? Study the conclusion of the paper to be certain that it clearly reasserts your positon and has developed logically from the rest of the paper.

3. If you made an outline of the paper during the planning stage, compare the outline with the final draft. Note any differences in content and organization, and determine whether they are appropriate.

4. Consider the flow of content in the paper to determine whether ideas proceed in a logical fashion. Does the content develop and support the paper's thesis? Look for recognizable patterns of development such as cause-and-effect, comparison-and-contrast, and chronological order. Are these patterns clear and handled effectively? If the content does not follow any of these patterns, should it be revised to do so?

5. Decide whether the discussion is complete. Do any significant ideas, arguments, supporting examples, or issues seem to be missing? Does the paper answer your original research question? Make any changes or additions necessary to ensure the completeness of the paper's discussion.

6. Determine whether your paper has achieved an argumentative or informative purpose (see Chapter 3). Would any changes in content or wording of the thesis accomplish your purpose more effectively?

Editing

Editing focuses upon details that influence the quality of a paper's content and expression. As in revising, the object here is not to rewrite the paper (though some additional writing may be called for) but to strengthen the paper's argument by sharpening expression and bolstering supporting evidence and documentation.

How to Edit

Work directly on the draft copy with a pen or pencil to add, delete, or modify the content and writing. Keep a dictionary at hand to check spelling. Consult a handbook as necessary for matters of grammar, punctuation, and style. If you write on a computer, you may be able to use a spell- or style-checking function to identify errors for editing. In most cases, however, careful reading of the draft, with pen or pencil in hand, will produce the best results, as well as a permanent record of the changes made.

Edit with an eye to improving the text rather than recreating it, but do not hesitate to eliminate weaknesses or outright errors. Figure 12.1 demonstrates common techniques as well as the thoroughness that may be required for effective editing.

---

wrote Ernest Hemingway ~~once wrote that~~ *in 1935,* "All modern literature comes from one book by Mark Twain called Huckleberry Finn/" ~~He claimed,~~ "It's the best book we've had" (22). Although ~~it appears that a large~~ ~~number of~~ literary critics and scholars, as well as the *general* reading public, would agree with Hemmingway's *assessment* ~~statement~~, Mark Twain's Adventures of Huckleberry Finn is also one of the most ~~debated and~~ controversial works on American bookshelves. ~~today.~~

FIGURE 12.1 An example of editing

What to Edit

As Figure 12.1 shows, editing occurs at the paragraph and sentence
level to correct spelling, grammar, and punctuation errors, as well as to
strengthen the paper's thesis support and documentation. In general, edit
the paper with close attention to these and the following matters of style
and correctness:

1. Edit the paper for redundant, repetitious, or ineffective word choices:

    Wordy   Several of the earliest and first settlers
               in the area made immediate friends with
               the Apaches.

    Edited   Several early settlers made friends with
               the Apaches.

    Vague   Some crimes are punished by very long
               sentences in prison.

    Edited   Capital crimes such as murder and kidnaping
               are punishable by life imprisonment
               or death.

2. Strengthen weak or faulty sentences. Reduce any that are too long to
    be effective by eliminating unnecessary words, clauses, and phrases:

    Too long   It is people who are victims of AIDS that
               are demanding more and more access to new
               treatments.

    Edited   Victims of AIDS are demanding increased
               access to new treatments.

3. Correct sentences that are incomplete or incorrectly punctuated:

    Sentence   Global warming will have varying effects.
    fragment   *Because of the changes it will create in*
    (italicized) *drought and rainfall frequencies.*

    Revised   Global warming will have varying effects
               because of the changes it will create in
               drought and rainfall frequencies.

Comma splice	Most of these ruins have been looted, even the villagers have helped themselves to saleable antiques.
Revised	Most of these ruins have been looted. Even the villagers have helped themselves to saleable antiques.

4. Eliminate discriminatory language. Stereotyping individuals by race, gender, age, nationality, or any other characteristic is as inappropriate in a research paper as it is in life. Avoid using language that perpetuates an inaccurate and unfair perception of any person or group of people. Writing a sentence such as *An airline pilot has to be a mechanic as well as a navigator if **he** wants to survive,* for example, implies that only men are airline pilots. Eliminate gender bias by rewriting such sentences:

Make pronoun unnecessary	An airline pilot has to be a mechanic as well as a navigator to survive.
Make subject and pronoun plural	Airline pilots have to be mechanics as well as navigators if they want to survive.

5. Examine each paragraph for a topic sentence or unifying idea that supports or develops the thesis statement. Check to see that the paragraph includes enough examples, reasons, or facts to support the topic sentence. Make sure that you have integrated your sources into the text in an effective way and that you present ideas of your own in each paragraph.

Technical Editing Guidelines

The following guidelines apply to research papers using the documentation style of the Modern Language Association (MLA). Certain subjects or the requirements of an individual instructor may call for variation. For conventions of manuscript preparation for APA-, CBE-, or *Chicago*-style papers, consult publication guidelines for the particular discipline (e.g., physics, history, or chemistry). (See the list of style manuals in Chapter 11.)

ABBREVIATIONS

The majority of abbreviations should appear in the paper's documentation to save space and add precision to the entries. In the paper's text, generally spell out all words except those commonly abbreviated between parentheses, such as *e.g.* ("for example") and *cf.* ("compare"). Otherwise, use abbreviations for major, recurrent terms in the paper only after first giving the full name in the text, with the abbreviation following in parentheses:

> Magnetic resonance imaging (MRI) offers several improvements over x—ray diagnosis. With MRI, for example, doctors can distinguish blood vessels from malignant tissue.

> One organization, Mothers Against Drunk Driving (MADD), has been particularly vocal on this issue. According to MADD, . . .

As these examples demonstrate, many abbreviations are written today without periods or other punctuation marks. Use periods or spaces in an abbreviation as common use suggests (in your sources, for example).

Avoid creating your own abbreviation for any term in the paper. When neccessary and useful, employ the standard abbreviations listed here for parenthetical comments in the text, for Works Cited (or References) entries, and for content notes, endnotes, or footnotes. Note the punctuation and use indicated for each abbreviation listed.

1. COMMON ABBREVIATIONS AND REFERENCE WORDS

Use the following abbreviations throughout your paper's documentation (Works Cited, References, and any notes), but employ them only parenthetically in the text:

abbr.	abbreviated, abbreviation
abr.	abridged, abridgment
acad.	academy
adapt.	adapted by, adaptation
anon.	anonymous
app.	appendix
assoc.	association
b.	born
bibliog.	bibliography, bibliographer, bibliographic(al)
biog.	biography
bk.	book
bull.	bulletin
c.	*circa* 'about' (with approximate dates: c. 1492)

cf.	*confer* 'compare'
ch.	chapter
col.	column
coll.	college
comp.	compiled by, compiler
cond.	conducted by, conductor
Cong.	Congress
Cong. Rec.	*Congressional Record*
Const.	Constitution
(contd.)	continued
d.	died
DA, DAI	*Dissertation Abstracts, Dissertation Abstracts International*
dir.	directed by, director
ed.	edited by, editor
e.g.,	*exempli gratia* 'for example' (See also the section on this term later in this chapter.)
et al.	*et alli* 'and others'
etc.	*et cetera* 'and so forth'
facsim.	facsimile
fig.	figure
fwd.	foreword, foreword by
GPO	Government Printing Office
HR	House of Representatives
i.e.,	*id est* 'that is'
illus.	illustrated by, illustration, illustrator
intl.	international
introd.	introduction
jour.	journal
LC	Library of Congress
ms., mss.	manuscript, manuscripts
narr.	narrated by, narrator
n.d.	no date of publication
n.p.	no place of publication; no publisher
n. pag.	no pagination
p., pp.	page, pages
perf.	performed by, performer
pref.	preface by, preface
prod.	produced by, producer
pseud.	pseudonym
pt.	part
rept.	reported by, report
rev.	revised by, revision, reviewed by, review

rpt.	reprint
sec.	section
sess.	session
sic	'thus, so' (See the discussion of this term later in the chapter.)
trans.	translated by, translator, translation
ts., tss.	typescript, typescripts
UP	University Press
vol., vols.	volume, volumes

2. ABBREVIATIONS OF TIME

Spell out the names of all months in the text. Except for May, June, and July, abbreviate the names of months in notes and documentation. Abbreviate some standard time designations—*a.m., p.m., BC, AD*—but spell out most other units of time—*minutes, hours, years*—when they appear in the text.

AD	*anno Domini* 'in the year of the Lord' (used before year date: *AD 1100*)
Apr.	April
Aug.	August
BC	Before Christ (used after year date: *65 BC*)
BCE	Before the Common Era
cent., cents.	century, centuries
Dec.	December
Feb.	February
hr., hrs.	hour, hours
Jan.	January
Mar.	March
min., mins.	minute, minutes
mo., mos.	month, months
Nov.	November
Oct.	October
sec., secs.	second, seconds
Sept.	September
wk., wks.	week, weeks
yr., yrs.	year, years

3. ABBREVIATIONS OF GEOGRAPHICAL LOCATIONS

Except for common abbreviations of some countries (*USA, UK*), spell out the names of cities, states, territories, provinces, and countries when they appear in the text. Abbreviate such locations in the paper's documentation, however. Designate American states by their ZIP code abbreviations: *AZ* for *Arizona; MA* for *Massachusetts; OH* for *Ohio.* A list of common abbreviations for other geographical locations follows. For places not given here, follow the practice of your research sources, an unabridged dictionary, or a standard atlas.

Aus.	Austria
Austral.	Australia
BC	British Columbia
Braz.	Brazil
Can.	Canada
DC	District of Columbia
Eng.	England
Gt. Brit.	Great Britain
Jap.	Japan
Isr.	Israel
Leb.	Lebanon
Mex.	Mexico
Neth.	Netherlands
Norw.	Norway
NZ	New Zealand
Pan.	Panama
PR	Puerto Rico
S. Afr.	South Africa
Sp.	Spain
Swed.	Sweden
Switz.	Switzerland
UK	United Kingdom
US, USA	United States of America

4. ABBREVIATIONS OF BOOKS OF THE BIBLE

Follow a quotation from a book of the Bible with parenthetical citation in the text, separating chapter and verse by a period with no space after it: *Acts 16.6* or *2 Kings 4.27.* Except for most one-syllable titles (*Job, Luke, Mark*), abbreviate books of the Bible when citing them in the text: *Eccles. 6.3, Matt. 11.12.* Do not underline the title of the Bible or place quotation marks around names of Biblical books (regardless of whether they are abbreviated).

A list of standard abbreviations for books of the Bible follows. For those not given here, devise unambiguous forms of your own, or consult a list of abbreviations at the front of most editions of the Bible.

Old Testament (OT)

1 and 2 Chron.	1 and 2 Chronicles
1 and 2 Sam.	1 and 2 Samuel
Dan.	Daniel
Deut.	Deuteronomy
Eccles.	Ecclesiastes
Esth.	Esther
Exod.	Exodus
Gen.	Genesis
Jer.	Jeremiah
Judg.	Judges
Lev.	Leviticus
Num.	Numbers
Prov.	Proverbs
Ps.	Psalms
Song Sol. (also Cant.)	Song of Solomon (also Canticles)

New Testament (NT)

1 and 2 Cor.	1 and 2 Corinthians
1 and 2 Thess.	1 and 2 Thessalonians
1 and 2 Tim.	1 and 2 Timothy
1 and 2 Pet.	1 and 2 Peter
Eph.	Ephesians
Jas.	James
Gal.	Galatians
Heb.	Hebrews
Matt.	Matthew
Phil.	Philippians
Rev. (also Apoc.)	Revelation (also Apocalypse)
Rom.	Romans

5. ABBREVIATIONS OF WORKS OF LITERATURE

Spell out the names of all sources, including literary works, listed in the Works Cited or References page(s) of your paper. You may abbreviate a work occurring frequently in the text or notes after first using the full title in the text, followed by the abbreviation in parentheses:

The Merchant of Venice (MV) is one of the earliest of
Shakespeare's attempts to mix comedy and tragedy.

For well-known authors and their works, use standard abbreviations, such as those listed below for Shakespeare. For other Shakespearian works or works by other authors, follow the practices of your research sources or devise easily understood abbreviations of your own: *GW* for *The Grapes of Wrath; SL* for *The Scarlet Letter; MD* for *Moby Dick,* and so forth.

Shakespeare

Ant.	*Antony and Cleopatra*
AWW	*All's Well That Ends Well*
F1	First Folio ed. (1623)
F2	Second Folio ed. (1632)
Ham.	*Hamlet*
1H4	*Henry IV, Part 1*
2H4	*Henry IV, Part 2*
H5	*Henry V*
JC	*Julius Caesar*
Lr.	*King Lear*
Mac.	*Macbeth*
MM	*Measure for Measure*
MND	*A Midsummer Night's Dream*
MV	*The Merchant of Venice*
Oth.	*Othello*
R2	*Richard II*
R3	*Richard III*
Rom.	*Romeo and Juliet*
Shr.	*The Taming of the Shrew*
TGV	*The Two Gentlemen of Verona*
TN	*Twelfth Night*
Tro.	*Troilus and Cressida*
WT	*The Winter's Tale*

ABSTRACTS

An abstract is not usually part of an MLA-style paper. Research papers in the sciences and social sciences, however, generally include an abstract as part of the paper's frontmatter. (If your instructor requires an abstract with your paper, see the discussions on "Abstracts" and "Headings" in Chapter 11.)

ACCENT MARKS

For both English and foreign words, include all accent marks necessary for accurate quotation and correct spelling (e.g., résumé, mañana, tête-à-tête). If your typewriter or word-processing program and printer do not have the necessary accent marks, write them in neatly by hand.

AMPERSAND

Do not use the ampersand symbol (&) to replace the word *and* in the text or in MLA-style citations. (Note that the ampersand is correct in APA-style papers only to cite authors in the text [*Harriston & Brown, 1989*] and in the References [*Harriston, R. M. & Brown, L. L.*].)

ANNOTATED BIBLIOGRAPHIES

If your instructor requires, you may annotate the paper's list of references by providing two or three descriptive sentences at the end of each entry in the Works Cited section. Characterize the work's subject, purpose, strengths or weaknesses, and general usefulness to the reader:

> Trenton, Patricia, and Patrick T. Houlihan. <u>Native</u>
> <u>Americans: Five Centuries of Changing Images</u>. New
> York: Harry N. Abrams, 1990. This work compares
> 500 years of historical information and artifacts
> with drawings, paintings, and photographs
> depicting Native Americans and their culture. The
> historical information provided is useful, but the
> book provides no art revealing how Native
> Americans have viewed themselves.

"BARS" (/)

Use the *virgule,* commonly known as a *bar* or *slash,* to indicate division or separation. When quoting up to three lines of poetry in the text, use this mark (with a space on each side) to show the original beginnings and endings of lines:

> William Blake's poem, "A Poison Tree," asserts the
> value of dealing openly with one's feelings: "I told my
> wrath. / My wrath did end," says the speaker.

Typed without a space before or after, the bar is also used to separate parts of a date expressed in digits *(3/12/91),* as well as fractions *(1/2, 1/3).* Avoid using expressions such as *and/or* and *his/her,* which require the bar and are generally too informal for precise writing.

CAPITALIZATION OF TITLES

For papers in MLA form, capitalize the main title and subtitle of all publications such as books, magazines, journals, and newspapers, as well as the titles of works (stories, essays, articles, chapters, appendixes, most poems, and plays) published in them. Capitalize the first and last words in such titles, as well as all other words except prepositions, conjunctions, articles, and the word *to* before a verb.

Follow these general examples even if a title's original capitalization differs (as when letters are variously capitalized for visual effect):

Books	<u>A Tale of Two Cities</u>
	<u>Zen and the Art of Motorcycle</u>
	<u>Maintenance: An Inquiry into Values</u>
Short stories	"A Rose for Emily"
	"I Stand Here Ironing"
Periodicals	<u>Modern Fiction Studies</u>
	<u>New York Daily News</u>
	<u>TV Guide Magazine</u>
Articles and essays	"Bush vs. Hussein—Again"
	"It Is Time to Stop Playing Indians"
	"Motherhood: Who Needs It?"
Short poems	"Theme for English B"
	"The Fish"
Plays	<u>A Midsummer Night's Dream</u>
	<u>Death of a Salesman</u>

When referring in the text to a poem without a title, use the first line as the name of the work. Do not alter the punctuation or capitalization of the original:

The imagery of Dylan Thomas's poem "Do not go gentle into that good night" suggests . . .

The last stanza of Dickinson's "I died for Beauty—but was scarce" compares . . .

The paper's reference list should cite the anthology or other work in which an untitled poem (usually short) appears.

Ordinarily, do not capitalize the initial articles in the name of a periodical (the *New York Times*). Nor should you write a title in all capital letters—except for the names of some journals when their titles include capitalized initials (e.g., *PMLA: Publications of the Modern Language Association of America*).

For disciplines following other than MLA style, see the examples in Chapter 11.

CONTENT NOTES

See the discussion and examples of content notes in Chapter 11.

COPYRIGHT LAW

Federal copyright law protects most published works and even unpublished manuscripts from commercial use or reproduction without permission. For the purpose of criticism or research, however, you may reproduce certain amounts of published or unpublished material without permission from the author or copyright holder. The amount you reproduce without permission cannot exceed *fair use,* that is, an amount considered reasonable for your purposes and in fair proportion to the copyrighted work as a whole. As long as your use is noncommercial and in an amount not exceeding fair use, you may copy or quote substantial amounts or even all of a chapter, a short story, article, short essay, short poem, or any drawing or illustration. Naturally, you must give credit in the paper to the source of any ideas or language you include in the text.

DATE OF PUBLICATION

Include the date of publication for each work listed in the Works Cited section of the paper. Dates for articles in magazines or journals usually appear on the cover or table of contents page. Locate the publication date of a book on the title page or the copyright page following it. If no printing date is given, use the latest copyright date. If there is no publication or copyright date given, use the abbreviation *n.d.* ("no date") in square brackets, as in *New York: Atlas, [n.d.].*

Whenever possible, get the publication date from the work itself. If you must learn the date of publication from another source, enclose the date in brackets: *[1974].* Place a *c.* (for *circa,* "around") before a date in brackets if you can only approximate the date: *[c. 1974].* Follow the date with a question mark if you are not certain of its accuracy: *[1974?].* (See Chapter 10 for the formats for listing publication dates of revised or reprinted material, as well as volumes published over a period of years.)

DATES

Use the same form throughout the paper for dates, that is, writing either *18 July 1982* or *July 18, 1982.* When the month and day precede the year, separate the day and year with a comma, as in the preceding example. An additional comma also follows the year if the date appears other than at the end of the sentence:

```
On July 7, 1982, Congress again approached the subject
of an Equal Rights Ammendment.
```

When the day is not included in the date, do not put a comma between the month and year; *July 1982.* To list daily, weekly, or monthly periodicals in the Works Cited section, abbreviate all months except May, June, and July, as in *4 Oct. 1988.*

Place the abbreviation *BC* after the year, but use *AD* before it: *450 BC,* but *AD 1100.* Write the names of centuries in lowercase letters—*the nineteenth century*—making certain to hyphenate them when used as adjectives—*nineteenth-century beliefs, seventeenth- and eighteenth-century poetry.* In general, write the names of decades without capitalization—*the sixties*—or use numbers—*the 1960s* or *the '60s.* Indicate a range of years with a hyphen, specifying full dates unless they are within the same century: *1794-1802* or *1951-53.*

DEFINITIONS

Define terms that are central to your topic and may not be familiar to your audience. At the same time, also avoid defining terms that may be unfamiliar only to you. Be consistent in the form for definitions.

Underline a word you are discussing as a word:

```
A periodical, as intended here, is a regularly
published magazine, journal, or newspaper.
```

Set off a technical term the first time you mention it with a definition by underlining; thereafter, use the term without underlining:

```
An iconic image is a visual pattern that persists in
the viewer's experience after the image source
terminates. The remarkable completeness of an iconic
image suggests . . .
```

NOTE: In this text, terms are not underlined but italicized, which is standard typographical format for most publications. The principles behind such treatment of terminology are the same as those outlined here, however. If you are following MLA style, you should underline, not italicize (see also "Underlining").

If you are translating a foreign term, underline the term, and place the definition between single quotation marks, with no intervening punctuation:

```
Gorbachev's defense of the new glasnost 'openness'
gained wide support in the West.
```

Use accurate terminology as required by your subject, but avoid overloading the paper with terms needing definition. In many instances, the substitution of a more common term or phrase may be just as effective. For example, use *ordered* rather than *enjoined* when describing instructions given by a court of law.

Also see the discussion about defining terms in Chapter 8.

e.g.

Use this abbreviation for *exempli gratia* 'for example' without capital letters and usually in parentheses to introduce an example: *e.g., as shown here*. Use a period after each letter, and do not space between the first period and the second letter. The term is set off by commas, *e.g.,* as here or set within parenthesis. Do not confuse *e.g.* with the abbreviation *i.e.,* which means "that is."

ENDNOTES

See Chapter 11 for instructions on the use of superscript numerals and notes placed at the end of the paper for documentation.

et al.

When referring to a single work by three or more authors, cite all of their names or that of the first author followed by *et al.* 'and others.' An intext citation would follow either of these formats: *(Cage, Andre, and Rothenberg 163)* or *(Cage et al. 163)*. In the Works Cited section, either of the following formats would be correct:

Cage, John, Michael Andre, and Erika Rothenberg.
    Poet's Encyclopedia. New York: Unmuzzled Ox,
    1980.

Cage, John, et al. Poet's Encyclopedia. New York:
    Unmuzzled Ox, 1980.

Although either format—citing all authors' names or using *et al.*—is correct according to MLA style, you should select one and use it consistently in your paper.

Note that *al.* is an abbreviation and must be followed by a period. No punctuation appears between the author's name and *et al.* (See also Chapter 11 for examples and use of *et al.* in other documentation styles.)

FOOTNOTES

See Chapter 11 for instructions on the use of superscript numerals and notes placed at the bottom of each page for documentation.

FOREIGN LANGUAGES

Indicate foreign words or phrases with underlining in the text:

Instead of the Zeitgeist, he discovered only la belle
dame sans merci.

For works published in a foreign language, follow the capitalization, spelling, and punctuation exactly as given in the original. (See also

"Accent Marks," earlier in this chapter.) If necessary for your particular audience, provide a translation of the title in brackets, along with the place of publication:

Sand, George. <u>La Petite Fadette</u> [Little Fadette].
Paris: Garnier-Flammarion, 1964.

ITALICS

Use underlining to show what would be printed in italics in most publications, such as titles and terms. (See "Definitions," earlier in this chapter, and "Underlining," later.)

NAMES OF PERSONS

State a person's full name the first time you use it in text—*Ernest Hemingway, Joyce Carol Oates, Percy Bysshe Shelley.* Thereafter, refer to the individual by last name only—*Hemingway, Oates, Shelley*—unless your paper mentions more than one person with the same last name, such as *Robert Browning* and *Elizabeth Barrett Browning.* Famous individuals may be referred to by their commonly known names rather than pseudonyms or seldom-used names—*Voltaire* instead of *Francois-Marie Arouet; Mark Twain* rather than *Samuel Clemens; Vergil* instead of *Publius Vergilius Maro.*

Do not use formal titles when referring to authors or other actual persons. Use *Ernest Hemingway* first and thereafter *Hemingway,* but not *Mr. Ernest Hemingway* or *Mr. Hemingway.* This also holds true for women: *Emily Dickinson,* then *Dickinson,* but not *Miss Dickinson.* Refer to characters in literary works by their fictional names: *Goodman Brown, Huck, Hester, Gatsby.*

NAMES OF PUBLISHERS

Use shortened forms of publishers' names for sources in the Works Cited or References page(s) and in content notes, footnotes, and endnotes. In general, shorten publishers' names by omitting the following elements:

- Articles (*a, an,* and *the*)
- First names (*Abrams* for *Harry N. Abrams, Inc.*)
- All but the first name listed (*Allyn* for *Allyn and Bacon*)
- Business abbreviations (*Inc., Co., Ltd.*)
- Descriptors (*Publishers, Library, Press, & Sons*)

For a university press, abbreviate *University* as *U* and *Press* as *P.* Do not use periods after either letter.

The following list provides examples of shortened names for many major publishers. For those not listed, devise abbreviated forms of your own following the guidelines and examples given here.

Abrams	Harry N. Abrams, Inc.
Allyn	Allyn and Bacon
Appleton	Appleton-Century-Crofts
Barnes	Barnes and Noble Books
Bowker	R. R. Bowker Co.
Cambridge UP	Cambridge University Press
Columbia UP	Columbia University Press
Dell	Dell Publishing Co., Inc.
Dutton	E. P. Dutton, Inc.
Feminist	The Feminist Press at the City University of New York
Harcourt	Harcourt Brace Jovanovich, Inc.
Harvard UP	Harvard University Press
Harvard Law Rev. Assoc.	Harvard Law Review Association
Houghton	Houghton Mifflin Co.
Harper	Harper and Row Publishers, Inc.
Holt	Holt, Rinehart and Winston, Inc.
Macmillan	Macmillan Publishing Co., Inc.
McGraw	McGraw-Hill, Inc.
NEA	The National Education Association
Norton	W. W. Norton and Co., Inc.
Oxford UP	Oxford University Press, Inc.
Prentice	Prentice-Hall, Inc.
Putnam's	G. P. Putnam's Sons
Simon	Simon and Schuster, Inc.
UMI	University Microfilms International
U of Chicago P	University of Chicago Press
UP of Florida	The University Presses of Florida

NUMBERS

In most cases and except as described here, use arabic numerals (1, 2, 3) rather than roman (iv, v, vi) for all numbers in your paper. The following general guidelines apply to most uses of numbers in an MLA-style research paper:

1. Write as words the numbers from one to nine: *six people, three restrictions.* Always write any number beginning a sentence as a word: *Nineteen hundred votes* . . . or *Three constellations* . . .

Use figures to express the number 10 and all higher numerals: *nearly 300 species, 88 pounds.* Also use figures to express any number requiring more than two words to write: *2 1/3, 3.477.*

2. To indicate count, place commas between the third and fourth digits from the right or, for larger numbers between the sixth and seventh, and so on: *4,000, 44,000, 81,723,000.* Do not use commas with figures that indicate line or page numbers, four-digit year numbers, or addresses, including ZIP codes: *lines 1037–67, page 1201, before 1990* (but *50,000 BC*), *25322 Shadywood Rd., Atlanta, GA 30304.*

3. Express related numbers in the same style: *four of the thirty-two students, less than 100 of the 3,000 men and women.* To indicate a range of numbers, give the second number in full when it is 99 or lower: *5–10, 12–21, 75–86.* For a number with three digits or more, give only the last two figures unless the third is needed for clarity: *91–102, 221–31, 998–1007, 5468–71, 5588–600.* Combine words and figures for very large numbers: *2.5 million, 150 billion.*

4. When typing numbers, do not substitute the small letter el (*l*) for the figure *1* unless your typewriter lacks the number key. Also, do not type the letter *O* for the figure zero (*0*).

(See related entries for other uses of numbers: "Dates"; "Percentages and Money"; and "Roman Numerals.")

PERCENTAGES AND MONEY

If your discussion includes only a few figures and they can be written in no more than two words, you may spell out numbers to indicate percentage and amounts of money: *six percent, one hundred percent, thirty-five cents, twelve dollars.* It is also acceptable to use numerals and the appropriate symbols to express such amounts: *4%, 85%, 18¢, $45.15, $3,670.* (See other guidelines in the section "Numbers.")

ROMAN NUMERALS

Use capital roman numerals whenever they are part of established terminology (*a Class III missile*), a name (*Elizabeth I, John Paul II*), or the heading for a formal outline (*IV. Major Influences*). Use small roman numerals to cite or to number the pages of a book or other printed source when those pages precede the text: *page vii.* Your instructor may also prefer that you use both capital and small roman numerals to designate acts and scenes of plays: Hamlet, *III.ii.*

Sic

Use the Latin word *sic* (meaning "thus," "so") to indicate that a quotation is accurate despite an apparent error in spelling, sense, or logic. Place the term, without quotation marks or underlining, between parentheses whenever it follows a quotation (as when included in your own

sentence) or between brackets whenever it must be added in the middle
of a quotation:

Following a
quotation

Rollins considers "the rascal Huckleberry
Fin" [sic] too resistant to authority to
be an acceptable role model for children
(12).

In the middle
of a quotation

Rollins insists that "the rascal
Huckleberry Fin [sic] is likely to be a
bad example for all children" (12).

Note that *sic* is not accompanied by a correction of the quotation.
Changes or corrections of a quotation should appear in brackets, without
sic. (See the discussion of *sic* later in this chapter and "Using Quotations"
in Chapter 8.)

SPELLING

Check the accuracy as well as the consistency of spelling throughout
the paper. Give extra attention to unfamiliar or complex terms, names of
individuals, and foreign words. If you use a computer program to check
spelling, do not overlook the need to proofread the manuscript carefully
yourself, as well. The spell-checking program will most likely not register
repeated or omitted words nor will it catch misused homonyms such as
it's and *its*.

If any words require accents or other marks for correct spelling, write
the marks in by hand if your typewriter or computer printer lack them (see
"Accents"). Use a complete, college-level dictionary to check words you
are unsure about. If more than one spelling is listed for a word, use the
first form given or the one with the more complete definition.

SUPERSCRIPTS

Use superscript numbers—like this[2]—for content notes and MLA
footnotes/endnotes. Avoid splintering a sentence with numerous superscript numerals or placing numerals where they interfere with reading the
text. As with text citations, place the numeral nearest the material to which
it refers. Note how the varying placement of superscript numerals in the
following examples might direct a reader to different commentary or
sources:

Several critics[3] have pointed out that Kaplan's
earliest work was realistic, a view that Davidson
apparently ignored.

Several critics have pointed out that Kaplan's earliest work was realistic,[3] a view that Davidson apparently ignored.

Several critics have pointed out that Kaplan's earliest work was realistic, a view that Davidson apparently ignored.[3]

Type superscript numerals a half space above the line by slightly turning the roll on the typewriter to move the paper up. Type the numeral, and return the bar to its original position. If you use a word-processing program, follow the procedures for typing superscripts. No punctuation or other marks should accompany superscript numerals. Type the numeral so that it follows all punctuation marks, like this.[2] Exceptions include dashes and parentheses when the superscript refers to material inside parentheses (such as here[4]).

TABLES AND ILLUSTRATIONS

Illustrative material included in your research paper should be genuinely helpful and presented as simply as possible. Use tables and illustrations to summarize, illustrate, simplify, or otherwise clarify the paper's content. Place such material as near the text referring to it as possible or in an appendix at the end of the paper.

1. *Tables.* Arrange information for a table in columns, and use the arabic-numbered label *Table 1* as a title (then *Table 2, Table 3,* and so on). Below the title, include a caption explaining the subject of the table. Type the caption and the title both flush left and above the table data. Immediately below the table, list the source and below it, any notes. Identify each note by a superscript letter (to distinguish the note from text). Double-space the title, caption, table data, source information, and notes throughout. Figures 12.2 and 12.3 provide models for most kinds of tables.

2. *Illustrations.* Nontabular material—such as drawings, graphs, charts, maps, and photographs—are considered illustrations. Label each illustration as *Fig.* (for *Figure*), and assign it an arabic number, as in *Fig. 3.* Number all illustrations consecutively throughout the text. Place the figure label, *along with a caption or title to explain the material,* below the illustration. Below the caption, give the source of the material. Begin all entries flush left, and double-space throughout the text accompanying the illustration. Figures 12.4 and 12.5 demonstrate models for various kinds of illustrations.

Always refer to specific tables and illustrations in the text by their labels: *Figure 2, Table 3, col. 1,* or *Fig. 4.* Sources for illustrations should be cited in the text like those for any other works (see the examples below), as well as fully documented in the Works Cited section of the paper.

Table 1
4th Week Student Enrollment Profile, 1987–91

Ethnicity	1987	1988	1989	1990	1991
Native					
American	208	209	220	227	233
Asian	2,220	2,245	2,472	2,860	3,164
Black	340	356	390	397	412
White	11,667	11,120	11,131	11,315	11,461
Hispanic	426	451	479	475	494
Filipino	49	58	61	88	99
Other	238	278	345	222	314
Unknown	2,774	2,338	1,463	1,110	901
Total	17,922	17,055	16,561	16,694	17,078

Source: Census System Files, Westfall Community College.

FIGURE 12.2 A sample table

Table 2
Student Responses[a] to Women Serving in Combat

Response	Women	Men	% of Total
1. Never	30	38	34.0
2. Only in emergencies	11	13	12.0
3. Only by volunteering	10	9	9.5
4. Only if not a parent	8	6	7.0
5. At any time	41	34	37.5

[a]One hundred female and one hundred male respondents.

FIGURE 12.3 A sample table

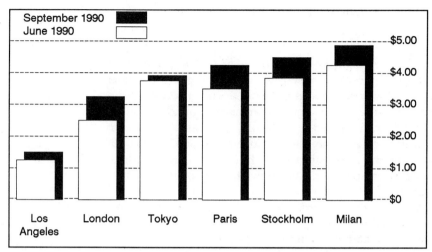

Fig 1. Price of Gasoline in Major World Cities During September 1990. Source: U.S. News & World Report 8 Oct. 1990: 63.

FIGURE 12.4 A sample illustration

Source: Adapted by permission from *U.S. News & World Report*, October 8, 1990, p. 63. Basic data: Runzheimer International.

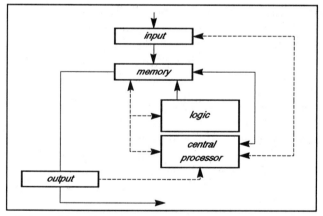

Fig. 2. Schematic diagram of a computer system. Dataflow is indicated by solid lines; signals are indicated by dashed lines. Source: Judith S. Levey and Agnes Greenhall, "Computer," The Concise Columbia Encyclopedia (New York: Columbia U P, 1983) 188.

FIGURE 12.5 A sample illustration

Source: Schematic diagram of a computer system from Judith S. Levey and Agnes Greenhall, *Concise Columbia Encyclopedia.* Copyright (c) 1983 Columbia University Press. Reprinted by permission.

TITLES

Other than the exceptions that follow, a title in an MLA-style paper should appear either between quotation marks or underlined. (See Chapter 11 for various forms for other documentation styles and disciplines.) A general rule is to use quotation marks around the title of a work not published or produced as a whole, such as a short story ("The Tell-Tale Heart") or an essay ("A Defense of Reason"). Also put quotation marks around the titles of chapters, short poems, unpublished works like dissertations or speeches, and individual episodes of radio or television programs.

The titles of works that are published independently should be underlined, including those of books (The Heart of Darkness), plays (Hamlet), and long poems (The Waste Land), as well as newspapers, magazines, journals, record albums, ballets, operas, films, and radio or television programs. Also underline the titles of works of art (Rodin's The Thinker) and names of ships, aircraft, and space vehicles (The Challenger). (See also "Underlining," following.)

An underlined title may include the name of a work that should normally be set in quotation marks: Twain's "Jumping Frog" and American Humor. Conversely, a work whose name is underlined may also be part of a title normally set in quotation marks: "The Sea in Virginia Woolf's To the Lighthouse." When a title that is normally set in quotation marks is part of another title in quotation marks, the included title appears within single quotation marks: "Another View of Twain's 'Jumping Frog'." Finally, when one underlined title includes another, the incorporated title appears with neither underlining nor quotation marks: Character and Art in Virginia Woolf's To the Lighthouse.

Do not underline or put quotation marks around titles of sacred writings (*the Bible, Genesis, New Testament, Koran, Talmud*) or the names of editions (*Centennial Facsimile Edition, New Revised Edition*), series (*American Poets Series*), societies (*The Thoreau Society*), or academic courses (*philosophy*, or *Philosophy 100*).

UNDERLINING

Show that a title should be printed in italic type (*like this*) instead of roman type with underlining (The Grapes of Wrath). A continuous underline is usually easier to read than a broken one, as well as faster and more accurate to type. Avoid separate underlining of words and punctuation to show titles. That is, avoid this: A Feast of Words: The Triumph of Edith Wharton.

WORD DIVISION

A word divided or hyphenated at the end of a line can make for ambiguous interpretation and interfere with the reader's concentration on the text. Rather than break up such a word at the end of a line, leave the line short. If you choose to hyphenate, consult a dictionary and break the word syllabically.

Producing the Final Manuscript

You may elect to type your paper or produce it using a computer and word-processing program. Whichever method you use, print the paper's contents on one side of the paper only. Follow the guidelines given here to prepare the final copy of the paper.

PAPER

Use standard 8-$^{1}/_{2}$- by 11-inch white paper between 16- and 20-pound weight, or thickness. Do not use onionskin or erasable paper, which often smudges. If you must use either of these for typing or printing the paper, submit a photocopy of the finished manuscript on plain, non-coated paper.

TYPE STYLE

Use a common, easily readable type size and style such as 10-point (elite) or 12-point (pica) throughout the manuscript. Use roman type; do not use script or italic for any material. If you wrote the paper using a computer, use a printer with letter-quality capability. Avoid printing the manuscript with a dot-matrix printer (although some 24-pin dot-matrix printers can produce good quality text). In general, a daisywheel or laser printer will produce the most readable and visually impressive manuscript.

RIBBON

Use a fresh black ribbon to type or print the paper. Watch for smudging or fading, and replace the ribbon if letters become difficult to read.

MARGINS

A one-inch margin at the top and bottom, as well as on both sides of the text, is standard for MLA-style papers.

SPACING

Except for footnotes, double-space the paper throughout, including the title, outline, indented quotations, captions, notes, appendixes, and Works Cited entries.

INDENTATIONS

Except for single-quoted paragraphs, indent each paragraph of text five spaces from the left margin. Indent quotations of four or more lines ten spaces from the left margin, but do not indent the first sentence of a single indented paragraph (even if it is indented in the original). When quoting two or more paragraphs, however, indent the first line of each paragraph an additional three spaces (a total of thirteen indented spaces; see Chapter 8, "Using Quotations").

To type entries in the Works Cited list, begin each flush left, but indent the second and succeeding lines five spaces. (See Chapter 11 for indentation requirements for APA, CBE, and other styles.)

For typing endnotes and footnotes, indent the first line five spaces, beginning with the raised superscript numeral. Type succeeding lines flush left.

PAGE NUMBERS

Except for the title page, number all pages preceding the first page of text consecutively with lowercase roman numerals (*ii, iii, iv,* and so on). Count but do not put a number on the title page if it appears as a separate page. If the title page is also the first page of text (as for a short paper), number it as page 1.

Following the preliminary pages numbered with roman numerals, begin on the first page of text to number all pages consecutively in arabic numerals (*1, 2, 3,* and so on) throughout the manuscript. Count and put a number on every page, including the first page of text. Place the page numbers one-half inch down from the top of the paper and one inch in from the right edge.

RUNNING HEADS

If your paper is in MLA style, begin on page 2 to include your last name, followed by a space, before each page number: *Kramer 2.*

MAKING CORRECTIONS

The finished paper should be submitted with as few errors or corrections as possible. After carefully proofreading the completely typed or printed paper, type any necessary corrections or revisions or add them by hand in ink. Place all corrections or additions above the text line, never below it or in the margins. Indicate where inserted words or punctuation marks should go in the line of text with a caret (^). Retype any page on which numerous revisions or corrections interfere with readability or the neat appearance of the paper. If you are writing on a computer, make the necessary additions, deletions, or corrections by rewriting and using the delete or text-moving functions of the word-processing program.

ORGANIZING AND BINDING

Organize the main parts of a completed research paper in this order:

1. Title page
2. Outline*
3. Abstract*
4. Text
5. Content notes
6. Appendix*
7. Works Cited

*Not always required.

Before turning the finished paper in to your instructor, make a photocopy for yourself in case the original gets lost or damaged.

Your paper needs no special cover or binding. Add a blank page at the front and back to help keep it neat. Secure all pages with a paperclip or staple in the upper-left corner. Do not put the paper in a folder or other type of cover unless your instructor approves.

WORKING WITH OTHERS

Many instructors believe students take more responsibility for revising, editing, and proofreading the final draft of a research paper when they perform these tasks by themselves. Before beginning to work with another person to review your own or each other's final drafts, check with your instructor about working cooperatively. If he or she agrees to your sharing the draft with others, use the following suggestions to guide you through this important final process.

- Before typing or printing a final version of the paper, exchange final drafts with another student in your class. Carefully read each other's drafts at least twice to share general impressions about the content and writing. Review the suggestions for revision, and offer helpful opinions about organization and unity of content. Check to see that the thesis statement is clearly stated or supported and developed throughout the paper's introduction, body, and conclusion. Is each of these sections effectively handled in the paper?

- Point out parts of your own draft that were improved by editing. Discuss the changes you made with your classmate. Ask his or her opinion about the effectiveness of the paper's sentences and use of language. If necessary, review the section on editing together.

- Without making corrections on the other person's draft, offer any helpful advice you can about problems in grammar, punctuation, or style. Encourage the author to review the draft to give these matters further attention. Point out any sentences in which the language may be discriminatory or sexist. Discuss these problems and ways to resolve them.

- Check general technicalities such as underlining and the use of numbers, abbreviations, and so forth in each other's draft. Identify anything that you may be unsure about, and discuss their use. Make changes or corrections as necessary.

- After you have printed or typed the final copy of the paper, exchange papers with your partner. Read to catch any glaring omissions or mistakes, and bring any problems to the attention of the author. Before turning the papers in to your instructor, take a few moments to congratulate each other on the work you have done.

Sample Research Papers

APA (Author-Year) and CBE (Number-System) Documentation Styles

Sample Paper 1:
APA (Author-Year)
Documentation Style

The following research paper, "Japan in America: The Meaning of Japanese Ownership of U.S. Properties," uses the author-year style of documentation recommended by the American Psychological Association (APA). The *Publication Manual of the American Psychological Association* (3rd ed., 1983) was written for authors intending to submit their papers for publication; it suggests that students alter guidelines as needed in order to meet the requirements of instructors. In a format consistent with other papers for college courses, for example, the title page of the sample research paper by Ron Bonneville does not include a running head, although APA style calls for one if the paper were intended for publication. All other features of the paper—including the abstract, intext citations, and entries in the References—conform to APA style.

Annotations in the margins of the paper describe important APA style features, which are discussed more fully in Chapter 11. Also consult your instructor regarding any special requirements he or she may have.

Japan in America

1   Number all
pages
consecutively
with arabic
numerals,
beginning
with the
title page

Type paper's
title
and other
necessary
information
double-spaced
and centered

Japan in America:

The Meaning of

Foreign Ownership of U.S. Properties

Ron Bonneville

American College

Check with
instructor
about citing
course
information

Professor Richard Braughn

English 117

December 15, 1991

Japan in America

2

Abstract

Recent acquisition by the Japanese of
such U.S. landmarks as Rockefeller
Center, Columbia Pictures, and CBS
Records has made the American public
fearful of what increased foreign
ownership of U.S. lands and businesses
may mean for this country's future. Many
Americans worry that extensive control of
major U.S. properties gives Japan too
much economic and political power, not
only abroad but in this country, as well.
Though these concerns may be justified in
some instances, the Japanese presence in
this country has also sparked a much
needed reevaluation by American
businesses and the federal government of
their own preparedness to meet the
challenges of worldwide economic
competition and global cooperation.
Rather than considering Japanese
ownership of U.S. properties as
potentially detrimental to their
interests, Americans should view Japanese
ownership of U.S. properties as part of
this country's growing involvement in a
world community.

Center
heading at
page top

Type abstract
as single
paragraph,
block format

For running head, use short title
or your last name, as instructed   Japan in America

                                                    3   First page
of text is
page 3

Center title
at top of page   Japan in America:

                        The Meaning of

            Japanese Ownership of U.S. Properties

                When President George Bush attended

            the funeral of Japanese Emperor Hirohito

            in January of 1989, comedian Jay Leno

            quipped that "as President of the United

Use square
brackets to
show change
in wording
of quotation   States, [Bush] figured he should meet the

            owners" (Holger, 1989). Leno's remark

            demonstrates the extent to which the

            American public is both aware of and

            nervous about the amount of Japanese

            ownership in the United States. There is

            no question that the Japanese are firmly

            established in America's business life,

            with such U.S. landmarks as New York's

            Rockefeller Center, Columbia Pictures,

            and CBS Records heading the list of just

            a few of their most recent acquisitions.

            The high visibility of Japanese

            investment in this country has prompted

            many Americans to worry more than ever

            before about what extensive foreign

            ownership really means for the United

            States. While the concerns expressed are   Thesis
statement
announces
paper's
main idea

            justified, however, Americans should view

            the expansive Japanese presence in the

            United States as a positive stage in this

            country's global development.

Japan in America

4

The size and rapidity of Japanese
investments in the U.S. is undeniably
great, including in 1988 over $100
billion in government securities, real
estate, and manufacturing plant
construction (Parton, 1989). Even a
partial list of recent acquisitions by
Japanese investors in the U.S. suggests
that they have taken over some of
America's most well-known and influential
properties--not to mention less
noticeable holdings such as warehouses,
skyscrapers, and retail complexes all
over America. Today, in New York City,
Japanese investors own at least 23 office
buildings, including such landmarks as
the Algonquin Hotel, the Citicorp Center,
and the Exxon Building (Glickman &
Woodward, 1989). In Washington, DC, at
least a quarter of the city's private
office space is owned by the Japanese
("Fitting," 1989).

Details
provide
convincing
examples

While recognizing Japan's role as a
major investor in the United States, we
should also remember that it is not the
first or necessarily the largest foreign
owner of U.S. properties. In fact,
America has a long history of foreign
acquisition, dating back to at least 1626

Japan in America

5

with the purchase of Manhattan Island,
New York, by the Dutch West India
Company's governor Peter Minuit. (He got
the Island from the Manhattan Indians for
the equivalent of about $24 in beads,
cloth, and trinkets.) Since that time,
foreign investment generally in the U.S.
has continued to grow, jumping from $83
billion in 1980 to over $262 billion by
1987 (Cooper, 1989). In 1988 alone, there
was a $68.5 billion (21%) increase in
foreign investment over the previous
year, with British, Canadian, and
Japanese takeovers accounting for three-
fourths of that figure (Holger, 1989). In
fact, so engrained has the tradition of
foreign ownership in the U.S. become that
today, 1 in every 14 Americans works for
a foreign employer ("Fitting," 1989).

   While the American public may have
quietly accepted the fact of foreign
ownership in the past, that attitude has
recently undergone a sharp change,
especially in regard to the Japanese. One
major reason is the resentment Americans
feel over the huge trade imbalance
existing between Japan and the United
States. Despite attempts by the Bush
administration to turn things around,

Use
parentheses
around less
significant
details

Japan in America

6

some $53 billion (44%) of the $119.8
billion U.S. trade deficit in 1989 was
with Japan ("Trade," 1990). Though the
reasons for the U.S.-Japan trade
imbalance are many, two basic causes are
most obvious: (1) The heavy consumption
of Japanese goods by the American public,
and (2) Japanese trade restrictions on
the sale of U.S. goods in Japan.

Critics of Japan's marketing control
point out that, when Americans buy more
Japanese goods than the Japanese buy
American products, the United States
comes out the loser economically and
politically worldwide. Too many U.S.
dollars in the hands of foreigners
weakens the dollar in purchasing value
against other foreign currencies like the
Japanese yen. The result is a United
States unable to influence world economic
and political events in a significant
way. As two ex-secretaries of state,
Henry Kissinger and Cyrus Vance, warned
in a recent Foreign Affairs article,
"America's ability to influence events
abroad . . . will be determined in large
part by how rapidly we get our economic
house in order" (qtd. in "Fitting," 1989,
p. 81). The extent of the problem has not

Ellipsis indicates that text has been omitted from original quotation

Citation form for quoting from indirect source

Japan in America

7

been lost on the American public, three—
fourths of whom now view the trade
deficit as a serious national security
problem, while over half see Japan as a
greater threat than the Soviet Union once

appeared ("Fitting," 1989).

Part of the American public's
uneasiness with Japan here and abroad
lies in the fact that the United States
has become the largest debtor nation in
the world, with Japan its major creditor.
The total U.S. trade deficit soared from
$19.3 billion in 1980 to a record $152.1
billion by 1987--mostly reflecting the
American public's heavy buying of
Japanese automobiles, radios, video
recorder units, and television sets
(Parton, 1989)[1]. Economists agree that,
if America's debtor status continues
along its current course, the Japanese
will hold the majority of the total U.S.
debt by the end of 1990 (Kennedy, 1989).

Such dependency scares many
Americans, particularly since it suggests
that the U.S. is no longer an independent
power in the world. While most Americans
recognize that our own spending habits
have put us into such debtor status, they
also resent the thought that the Japanese

Japan in America

8

are buying up America with devalued
dollars. To some politicians, like
Governor Richard D. Lamm of Colorado,
foreign investors represent a menace: "I
don't want the Arabs owning our banks or
the Japanese owning our means of
production. It terrifies me" (Tolchin &
Tolchin, 1988, p. 33).

Cite page number(s) with source of quotation

Americans who fear the extensive
presence of the Japanese and other
foreign investors in America feel they
may have too much influence on domestic
political issues. Many Americans dislike
the fact that scores of former
presidential advisors, exmembers of
Congress, military officials, and others
work in so-called "governmental
relations" (Choate, 1988, p. 2) offices
of foreign companies or for international
industry groups, many of them Japanese.

Opponents of foreign political clout
in America also resent Japanese and other
global investors' backing of Political
Action Committees (PACs), organizations
established by foreign-owned companies to
represent their interests in U.S.
politics. All together, PACs contribute
several millions of dollars to national
political campaigns every year—as much

Define key terms and identify abbreviations used

Japan in America

9

as $2.8 million in the 1987–88 U.S.
elections (Choate, 1990, p. 91).

Providing
page number
facilitates
locating
specific
information
in source

The influence PACs wield has
prompted Congress to seek clarification
of the legality of PACs under the Federal
Campaign Act of 1974. The act
specifically prohibits foreign nationals
from contributing to American political
campaigns, yet the foreign-owned U.S.
businesses themselves have a right to
support candidates and influence
legislation. The issue remains a cloudy
one legally and a sensitive one in terms
of international business (Glickman &
Woodward, 1989). Just how much influence
such lobbying groups have is open to
debate, though instances of Japanese-
owned companies getting preferential
treatment from both state and federal
agencies appear common (cf. Tolchin,
1988, p. 22; Choate, 1988).

The backlash of opinion against such
control of American business and politics
by the Japanese and others has been
strong. Most Americans now agree that
foreign ownership of U.S. properties is

Quote from
survey of
public
opinion

"bad for the country" (Smick-Medley,
1988, p. 8). Three-fourths also favor
heavy restrictions on foreign takeovers

Japan in America

10

of U.S. manufacturers, and a majority are
willing to support increased taxes on
imported goods to rebalance the trade
deficit with Japan and other countries
("Fitting," 1989). After a Japanese
investor bought $173 million in Hawaiian
housing, lawmakers considered a proposal
to ban all housing ownership by Japanese.
The ban proposal never passed (Egan,
1989), though the impetus behind it
demonstrates the extent to which
Americans fear losing their land to
foreign buyers.

Aware of the growing negative
feelings about their presence in the
U.S., the Japanese are beginning to
respond aggressively to change public
opinion. In 1989, the Keidanren, Japan's
most powerful business federation, made a
point of investigating the concept that
Americans have of "good corporate
citizenship" ("Charity," 1989, p. 41).
The federation's recommendation that
Japanese companies in America increase
their public service roles has resulted
in their getting involved with the United
Way and sponsoring summer math camps for
Native American students. In 1990,
Japanese companies will contribute $200

million to U.S. schools and charity
organizations, a 35% increase over the
previous year ("Charity," 1989). In
addition, Japanese—owned auto plants in
America are funding internships for
college students, providing plant tours
for other companies' employees, and
passing along helpful strategies to U.S.
employers about successful Japanese
business concepts (Parton, 1989).

The Japanese are also sensitive to
American fears about foreign control over
the U.S. businesses they have acquired.
To reassure the public, Japanese business
leaders make a point of insisting that
they do not intend to control American
businesses to the point of dictating
their operations. Japanese takeovers in
the film, record, and television
industries are a good example. Japan's
Sony Corporation emphasizes that it has
given the head of CBS Records a
completely free hand and will continue to
do so. JVC, a Japanese consumer
electronics corporation that has invested
$100 million to launch a new Hollywood
film—making company, also plans to leave
decisions up to veteran American
producers ("Japan Goes Hollywood," 1989).

Japan in America

12

As Shigeru Masuda, president of Zeron, a
Tokyo—New York based group putting up $20
million for a four-picture joint venture
in Hollywood, explains, "We won't
interfere creatively—-we are businessmen"
("Next Stop," 1989, p. 49).

The Hollywood experience with the
Japanese also illustrates an important
fact about the American economy: Like it
or not, the U.S. has also become
dependent upon Japan for the jobs of
thousands Americans right in their own
country. Japanese investors in U.S.
businesses poured over $100 billion
dollars into government securities, real
estate, and plant construction in 1988
alone ("Japan Basks," 1989). On the west
coast, the Japanese are welcomed in
Hollywood as providing fresh
opportunities for companies that have
recently lost financial backing to return
to production ("Japan Goes Hollywood,"
1989). Elsewhere in the U.S., Japanese
auto companies have created a virtual
"auto alley," stretching from Michigan to
Tennessee: Mazda of Michigan provides
jobs for 3,500 Americans; Toyota employs
3,000 people in Kentucky; Nissan in
Tennessee hires another 3,300; and Honda

Japan in America

13

in Ohio, 4,000 (Glickman & Woodward,
1989).

The benefits from Japanese ownership
in America, in fact, exist in nearly
every area of manufacturing and business.
In Tennessee, 30 Japanese companies--
giants like Nissan, Sharp, Toshiba, and
Bridgestone--have created more than 7,000
jobs and invested well over $1.25 billion
in manufacturing (Glickman & Woodward,
1989). In Arkansas, the impoverished town
of Blytheville worked hard and
successfully to convince the Japanese
steel firm Yamato Kogyo to build its new
500-acre steel mill there instead of
elsewhere ("Blytheville," 1989).
Meanwhile, American-owned microcomputer
chip manufacturers are gratefully
striking deals with Japanese firms like
Sony, Hitachi, NEC, and Mitsubishi to
share technology and production costs.
The trend reverses past practices when
the same companies not only competed
but when the help came from the U.S.
instead of the other way around (Karmin,
1990).

The Japanese, however, are giving
American business something more than
just money and providing American workers
with more than just jobs. Probably their

Japan in America

14

most important contribution has been the
impetus they have given Americans to
rethink their own business practices. In
the 1982 best-seller <u>In Search of
Excellence: Lessons from America's
Best-Run Companies</u>, authors Thomas J.
Peters and Robert H. Waterman stressed
that, in many important aspects, "the
excellent companies look very Japanese"
(p. 127). Because of the Japanese example
of success, American businesses have
learned to adopt new techniques and
standards, including such important
concepts as <u>TQC</u>, total quality control
(Glickman & Woodward, 1989, p. 105);
<u>global localization</u>, the practice of
putting design, engineering, and
production close to the final market; and
the <u>just in time</u>, or JIT, system, a
method of minimizing inventories and
cutting costs (Glickman & Woodward, 1989,
p. 225).

    Such concepts are starting to change
the way American manufacturers operate,
as well as helping to improve the quality
of what they produce. The inferior
quality of American-made goods has long
been recognized as the major block to
U.S. competition with Japan in the
domestic automobile and general

> Use italics or underlining for titles of books

> Since author and date are mentioned in text, cite only page number of quotation

Japan in America

15

electronics markets, as well as in
overseas exports. This was a point raised
by <u>In Search of Excellence</u> nearly 10
years ago and one which still holds true
today. Unfortunately for the U.S., the
rest of the world has turned toward the
products of Japan, Germany, Sweden,
Korea, and most of Europe as being not
only less expensive but also of better
quality than those from America ("Making
It Better," 1989).

The result is that foreign
businesses can outsell American producers
at home and abroad. They are rolling in
high profits and ready to buy up American
businesses in order to bypass import
restriction or to control supply flows
from the U.S. In the view of some
observers of the international business
scene, "the increasing presence of
foreigners shows just how weak the
economy has become: American companies
that once dominated the world economy are
now being outslugged on their own playing
fields!" (Glickman & Woodward, 1989, p.
20).

The lesson U.S. businesspeople have
learned and what the American public is
just starting to realize is that the role
of the United States in terms of economic

Japan in America

16

dominance in the world is changing. The
independence and consequent isolation
such dominance used to mean are being
transformed by international, global
movements, affecting everything from
business to the environment and world
peace. We are not powerfully alone
anymore but part of a global community.
Joint ventures between U.S. and Japanese
firms now include everything from
biochemicals to computers and, just
recently, the six billion dollar joint
agreement between the two governments to
produce the top—secret U.S. FSX jet
fighter. As John Naisbitt and Patricia
Aburdene insist in <u>Re—inventing the
Corporation</u> (1985), a recent examination
of American and worldwide business
trends:

Block indent long quotations of 40 words or more

> The interplay of economic
> developments in and between
> Japan and the United States is
> not only basic to the well—
> being of those two nations but
> is creating a degree of mutual
> economic cooperation and
> development unparalleled in
> world history. . . . Eventually
> people will come to speak of
> "U.S.A.—Japan, Inc." (p. 267)

Page number(s) for block quotation appear after ending punctuation

Japan in America

17

The relationship is not only
important financially but politically, as
well. As the world's second most
economically powerful nation, Japan has
the means to influence economic and
political development in the world as
much or more than even the U.S., with
loans to developing nations in 1989
totaling over $11 billion (Mansfield,
1989). Ex–U.S. Ambassador to Japan Mike
Mansfield believes that close cross–
commitments between the U.S. and Japan
"have expanded to include obligations to
the rest of the world community." In his
opinion, the United States and Japan,
because of their power and positions,
"influence the very structure of
international relations today"
(Mansfield, 1989, p. A2). In this same
vein, U.S. Secretary of State James
Baker, in recent trade talks with
Japanese leaders, stressed that the world
is forming "a new order" and asked Japan
to join the U.S. in creating a "Pacific
community reaching out to the rest of the
world" ("Free Trade," 1989, p. 48).

America and Japan are merging
cultures and economies faster than many
Americans can either appreciate or adjust

to with ease. It has become a fact of
modern life that McDonald's sells more
hamburgers in Japan than in New York City
("Japan Basks," 1989). Ads for one of
General Motors' newest made—in—Japan cars
confidently boasts, "Colt——It's all the
Japanese you need to know" ("Colt,"
1989).

What worries Americans today about
the Japanese is actually not their
presence in this country but what it
represents: The change of the United
States' role as the single most
independent and powerful country in the
world to one sharing that role in the
future with Japan and other developing
nations. In this sense, the Japanese
presence in America is a reflection of
the "new order" of which Secretary Baker
speaks. If Rockefeller Center in New York
is a symbol of America, the fact that it
is now Japanese—owned is also a symbol of
America's new relationship to the world.
Properly viewed and understood, it is a
beneficial relationship for the United
States, one which, as ex—Ambassador to
Japan Mansfield predicts, "holds the
promise of well—being for nations and
peoples around the world" (1989, p. A12).

Japan in America

19

References

Blytheville's bounty. (1989, June 5).
Time, p. 52.

Charity begins abroad. (1989, August 21).
Newsweek, p. 41.

Choate, P. (1988, July 19). Money talks:
How foreign firms buy U.S. clout.
Washington Post, pp. C1-4.

Choate, P. (1990). Agents of influence:
How Japan's lobbyists in the United
States manipulate America's political
and economic system. New York: Knopf.

Colt introduces two wagons for families.
(1989, April 3). Newsweek, p. 5.

Cooper, M. (1989, March 31). Foreign
investment in the United States.
Editorial Research Reports,
pp. 166-179.

Egan, J. (1989, January 30). After Tokyo,
all the world's a bargain. U.S. News &
World Report, pp. 58-59.

Fitting into a global economy. (1989,
December 26). U.S News & World Report,
pp. 80-82.

Free trade's double-header. (1989, July
10). U.S. News & World Report, p. 48.

Glickman, N. J., & Woodward, D. P.
(1989). The new competitors: How
foreign investors are changing the
U.S. economy. New York: Basic Books.

Begin
References
section
on separate
page;
center title

Form for
newspaper
article; list
multiple
works
by same
author in
chronological
order

Capitalize
first word
and all
proper nouns
of article
title; do not
enclose in
quotation
marks

Indent
second and
succeeding
lines of each
entry three
spaces

Japan in America

20

Holger, J. (1989, August 8). A record
year for U.S. buys: The hostility
rises in America. MacLean's,
pp. 38–39.

Japan basks in a 'Bush boom.' (1989,
January 9). U.S. News & World Report,
p. 53.

Japan goes Hollywood. (1989, October 9).
Newsweek, pp. 62–67.

Karmin, M. W. (1990, April 16). The chip
makers: Let's tango, not tangle. U.S.
News & World Report, p. 40.

Kennedy, P. (1989). The rise and fall of
the great powers: Economic change and
military conflict from 1500 to 200.
New York: Vintage–Random.

Making it better. (1989 November 13).
Time, pp. 78–81.

Mansfield, M. (1989, December 25).
Ambassador Mansfield talks to America.
U.S. News & World Report, pp. A2–12.

Naisbitt, J., & Aburdene, P. (1985).
Re–inventing the corporation:
Transforming your job and your company
for the new information society. New
York: Warner.

Next stop, Tinseltown. (1989, March 20).
Newsweek, pp. 48–49.

Single quotation marks appeared in original

Cite authors by last names; use initials for first and middle names

Capitalize first word and all proper nouns of book title

Use *p.* or *pp.* before periodical page numbers

Japan in America

21

Parton, R. L. (1989). <u>Japan in America:</u>
<u>The new Asian presence</u>. New York:
Lytle.

Peters, T. J. & Waterman, R. H. (1986).
<u>In search of excellence: Lessons from</u>
<u>America's best-run companies.</u> New
York: Harper.

Form for
corporate
author

Smick-Medley and Associates. (1988).
<u>Foreign investment: A Smick-Medley and</u>
<u>Associates public opinion survey of</u>
<u>U.S. attitudes</u>. Washington, DC:
Smick-Medley.

For more
than one
author, use
ampersand
(&) for *and*
before
last name;
separate all
names with
commas

Tolchin, M., & Tolchin, S. (1988). <u>Buying</u>
<u>into America: How foreign money is</u>
<u>changing the face of our nation</u>. New
York: Times Books.

The trade war gets personal. (1990, April
10). <u>U.S. News & World Report</u>,
pp. 38-40.

Japan in America

22

Notes

Begin notes on separate page; center title

[1]While we worry about Japanese investment in our own country, however, we should not ignore the fact that Japan is also a marketplace for U.S. investment and exports. Direct U.S. investment in Japan totaled $17 billion in 1988 (Mansfield, 1989), while U.S. exports to Japan hit a new high of $48.2 billion in 1989 ("Trade War," 1990). These figures underscore the mutual dependence both countries have come to share in the last 20 years of international growth and development.

Cite sources in note content when necessary

Sample Paper 2:
CBE (Number-System)
Documentation Style

The following research paper, a selected review of literature about AIDS-risk behavior, uses one form of number-system documentation recommended by the Council of Biology Editors (CBE) and described in its publication, the *CBE Style Manual* (1983). Note that sources in the References section of the paper are listed and numbered in alphabetical order by the authors' last names (or by title when no author's name was given in the source). Sources are cited parenthetically in text by their corresponding numbers and following any referenced content. Intext citations include page numbers after any quotation or whenever a source is lengthy. (See also the discussion of number-style documentation in Chapter 11.)

Annotations in the margin explain certain CBE stylistic and documentation features. Also consult your instructor regarding any special requirements he or she may have.

1

Reduction of AIDS–Risk Behavior
Among Gay Males and Other Populations:
A Selective Review of Literature, 1987–88

Center title,
your name,
and other
relevant
information

Daniel Fletcher
Psychology 202
May 10, 1991

Reduction of AIDS—Risk Behavior

2

Abstract

A selected review of AIDS—related
research published during 1987—88
suggests successful avenues for reducing
levels of high—risk sexual activity among
homosexual and other at—risk groups such
as black, Hispanic, nonurban, and
adolescent populations. The findings
recount successful efforts in reducing
high—risk sexual activity among gay males
and discusses factors that significantly
affect compliance or rejection of safe—
sex guidelines among such males, as well
as members of other groups. The research
provides a basis for continuing
educational programs and conducting
further research to prevent the spread of
AIDS.

Abstract
defines
paper's focus
and
summarizes
content

Running
head is
optional
unless paper
is to be
submitted for
publication;
use short
title or your
last name, as
instructed

Reduction of AIDS–Risk Behavior

3

Count title
and abstract
pages;
number with
arabic
numerals,
text begins
on page 3

No title on
first page of
text

Define key
terms and
abbreviations
used

Research published during 1987–88
demonstrates that prevention programs
instituted since the identification of
acquired immunodeficiency syndrome (AIDS)
six years earlier resulted in significant
reductions among gay men of behavior that
transmits the human immunodeficiency
virus (HIV) for the disease. Research in
psychology describes and evaluates
factors that inhibit (or sometimes
encourage) high–risk, AIDS–vulnerable
sexual activity; and social scientists
examine implications for extending AIDS–
prevention programs to other high–risk
groups, such as black, Hispanic,
nonurban, and adolescent populations.
Most importantly, such research
identifies successful efforts and basic
issues meriting continued study and
application in the fight against AIDS
today.

Introductory
paragraph
provides
overview
of paper's
focus and
discussion

Changes in Behavior

Decline in High–Risk Activity

Several empirical reports published
in 1987–88 and based on data collected
from self–identified gay men residing in
different U.S. cities document
significant, sustained changes in sexual
behavior within the gay population.

Second-level
heading is
set at margin,
with text
following
beneath

First-level
heading is
centered

Reduction of AIDS–Risk Behavior

4

Reflecting a decreasing rate of high–risk
behaviors identified in a 1984 study of
San Francisco men (10), a larger study of
gay men in New York City, for example,
identifies an even greater decline in
high–risk activity (8). These findings
are echoed in papers presenting research
showing that the rate of engagement in
unsafe sexual activities by gay and
bisexual males had dropped significantly
in Baltimore, Chicago, Los Angeles, and
Pittsburgh during the period 1985–1986
(5,7).

Contributing Factors. Based upon
these documented reductions in risk
behavior among large portions of the gay
population, research psychologists have
sought to determine what factors prompt
individuals to comply with or reject
safe–sex guidelines. A 1988 study (11)
interprets and correlates five such
factors: (1) knowledge of health
education guidelines; (2) drug and
alcohol use during sexual contact; (3)
individual beliefs regarding sex and
personal health; (4) personal efficacy;
and (5) knowledge of HIV antibody–testing
status.

The value of the first factor,
health education, in reducing high–risk

Source cited
by number as
it appears in
References

Form for
citing
multiple
sources at
same time

Third-level
heading is
indented and
followed by
period

Reduction of AIDS—Risk Behavior

5

sexual activity is challenged by research
finding familiarity with HIV risks to be
unrelated to risk behavior (1,12). Other
studies looking into the same factors,
however, identify variable changes in
sexual behavior as a "direct consequence
of health education" (3, p. 339;6).

Testing vs. Counseling. After
extensive evaluation of the literature
during this period, researchers conclude
that HIV virus testing alone is not as
effective in reducing high—risk behavior
as federal and state agencies hope.
Findings suggest that patterns of sexual
activity persist in many men regardless
of their status knowledge, with those who
decline testing or education remaining at
the greatest risk. The study recommends
that knowledge of antibody status should
be combined with quality counseling, and
more research should be done to
understand better the psychological
determinants of high—risk behavior (2, p.
864).

Population Models

Research demonstrating that high—
risk sexual activity among gay men has
continued to persist in areas of the U.S.
where AIDS is relatively rare suggests
the difficulty of determining consistent

Cite page
number(s)
after any
quotation

Reduction of AIDS-Risk Behavior

6

population models for study (6). By
looking closely at reduction and
nonreduction rates in high-risk sexual
activity, however, psychologists have
been able to formulate education and
prevention models for certain high-risk
populations. Mays and Cochran, for
example, examine factors associated with
risk perception and behavior changes in
black and Hispanic women. Their research
indicates that government agencies
providing education and prevention
programs should be sensitive to the
particular ethnic culture targeted, that
the health message should be structured
positively, that respected community
institutions ought to be engaged, and
that safe-sex practices need to be
translated into forms readily acceptable
to the target group (9).

Belief Systems

   Adolescent belief systems that
promote unsafe sex and leave that
population open to HIV infection were
studied and found to have significant
influence on high-risk sexual behavior
(13). Research by Flora and Thoresen
suggests that such systems threaten the
health safety of the adolescent
population and recommends that AIDS

Authors may be named in text; give number to facilitate locating source in References

Reduction of AIDS–Risk Behavior

7

prevention programs be modeled after
other successful health education
efforts, such as the antismoking and
antipregnancy campaigns (4, pp. 766–68).
In addition, research shows the need for
greater sensitivity to the diverse groups
within the adolescent population
threatened by AIDS--men, women, blacks,
and Hispanics. Because these are such
large populations and include the groups
"most at risk" in the U.S., the
researchers believe their needs for
changes in risk behavior should be
considered of primary importance in the
fight against AIDS (4, p. 968).

Conclusion summarizes paper's major ideas

Conclusion

The important research reviewed in
this selected study of literature for
1987–88 provides a basis for continuing
programs to prevent the spread of AIDS
among populations most at risk,
especially homosexual and other minority
groups. Evaluation of prevention
programs, further study of those factors
that promote or inhibit high–risk sexual
activities, and calls for the extension
of AIDS education programs to other
highly vulnerable groups in society
should continue by building upon this and
similar research.

Giving page numbers helps reader locate material in source

Reduction of AIDS–Risk Behavior

8

References

1. Calabrese, L. H.; Harris, B.; Easley,
   K. A. Analysis of variables impacting
   on safe sexual behavior among homosexual men in an area of low incidence for AIDS. Paper presented at
   the Third International Conference
   on AIDS. Washington, DC; 1987.

2. Coates, T. J.; Stall, R. D.; Kegeles,
   S. M.; Lo, B.; Morin, S. F.;
   McKusick, L. AIDS antibody testing:
   will it stop the AIDS epidemic?
   will it help people infected with
   HIV? Am. Psychol. 43:859–864;
   1988.

3. Emmons, C. A.; Joseph, J. G.;
   Kessler, R. C.; Montgomery, S.;
   Ostrow, D. G. Psychological
   predictors of reported behavior
   changes in homosexual men at risk for
   AIDS. Health Educ. Q. 13(4):331–345;
   1986.

4. Flora, J. A.; Thoresen, C. E.
   Reducing the risk of AIDS in
   adolescents. Am. Psychol. 43:965–970;
   1988.

Sources are listed in alphabetical order and numbered separately

Use authors' initials instead of first names

References section begins new page; center title at top

Reduction of AIDS-Risk Behavior

9

5. Fox, R.; Ostrow, D. G.; Valdiserri,
R.; Van Raden, B.; Polk, B. F.
Changes in sexual activities among
participants in the Multicenter AIDS
Cohort Study. Paper presented at the
Third International Conference on
AIDS, Washington, DC; 1987.

6. Jones, C.; Wasskin, H.; Gerety, B.;
Skipper, B. J.; Hull, H. F.; Mertz,
G. J. Persistence of high-risk
sexual activity among homosexual men
in an area of low incidence of the
acquired immunodeficiency syndrome.

Capitalize
first word
and all
proper nouns
in titles of
books and
articles

Sex. Transm. Dis. 14(2):79-82; 1987.

7. Joseph, J. G.; Montgomery, S.;
Kirscht, J.; Kessler, R. C.; Ostrow,
D. G.; Emmons, C. A.; Phair, J. P.
Behavioral risk reduction in
a cohort of homosexual men: two year
follow-up. Paper presented at the
Third International Conference on
AIDS, Washington, DC; 1987.

8. Martin, J. L. The impact of AIDS
on gay male sexual behavior
patterns in New York City. Am.
J. Public Health 77(5):578-581;
1987.

Do not use
italics or
underscoring
for journal
titles and
volume
numbers

Reduction of AIDS–Risk Behavior

10

9. Mays, V. M.; Cochran, S. D. Issues in the perception of AIDS risk and risk reduction activities by Black and Hispanic/Latina women. Am. Psychol. 43:949–957; 1987.

10. McKusick, L.; Horstman, W.; Coates, T. AIDS and sexual behavior reported by gay men in San Francisco. Am. J. Public Health 75:493–496; 1985.

11. Stall, R. D.; Coates, T. J.; Hoff, C. Behavioral risk reduction for HIV infection among gay and bisexual men. Am. Psychol. 43:878–885; 1988.

Format for listing paper presented at conference

12. St. Lawrence, J. S.; Kelly, J. A.; Hood, H. V.; Brasfield, T. L. The relationship of AIDS risk knowledge to actual risk behavior among homosexually–active men. Paper presented at the Third International Conference on AIDS, Washington, DC; 1987.

13. Strunin, L.; Hingson, R. Acquired immunodeficiency syndrome and adolescents: knowledge, beliefs, attitudes, and behaviors. Pediatrics 79:825–828; 1987.

Reference Sources for Selected Subjects

This appendix is comprised of lists of commonly found reference sources, first, by subject and next, within each subject, by type. Use these resources and others located near them in the library to find materials for general reading about a subject and for establishing a preliminary bibliography for research. Also consult the general reference sources listed throughout Chapter 4.

Index to Subjects

Reference Sources by Subject

Anthropology and Archaeology

Bibliographies, Guides, and Indexes
International Bibliography of the Social Sciences: Anthropology, 1985. Comp. International Committee for Social Science Information and Documentation Staff. New York: Routledge, 1989.

Encyclopedias, Dictionaries and Handbooks
The Cambridge Encyclopedia of Archaeology. Ed. Andrew Sherratt. New York: Cambridge UP, 1980.
Encyclopedia of Anthropology. Ed. David E. Hunter and Phillip Whitten. New York: Harper, 1976.
Heizer, Robert F., et al. *Archaeology: A Bibliographical Guide to the Basic Literature.* New York: Garland, 1980.
Student Anthropologist's Handbook: A Guide to Research, Training and Careers. Cambridge, MA: Schenkman, 1972.

Abstracts and Digests
Abstracts in Anthropology. Farmingdale, NY: Baywood, 1970–date. Quarterly.

Art and Architecture

Bibliographies, Guides, and Indexes
American Art Directory. New York: Bowker, 1952–date.
Applied and Decorative Arts: A Bibliographic Guide. Ed. Donald L. Ehresmann. Littleton: Libraries Unlimited, 1977.
Art Index. New York: Wilson, 1929–date. Quarterly.
Art Research Methods and Resources: A Guide to Finding Art Information. Ed. L. S. Jones. Dubuque, IA: Kendall, 1985.
Bibliographic Guide to Art and Architecture. Boston: Hall, 1977–85.
Contemporary Architects. 2nd ed. Chicago: St. James, 1987.
Fine Arts: A Bibliographic Guide. Ed. D. L. Ehresmann. 2nd. ed. Littleton: Libraries Unlimited, 1979.
Guide to the Literature of Art History. Comp. Etta Arntzen and Robert Rainwater. Chicago: ALA, 1981.
Illustration Index. Ed. Marsha Appel. 4th ed. Metuchen, NJ: Scarecrow, 1980.
Index to Art Periodicals. 11 vols. Boston: Hall, 1962. With supplements.

Encyclopedias, Dictionaries, and Handbooks
Dictionary of American Art. Ed. Matthew Baigell. New York: Harper, 1980.
Dictionary of American Painters, Sculptors, and Engravers. Ed. Mantle Fielding. New York: Editions, 1986.
Encyclopedia of American Art. New York: Dutton, 1981.
Encyclopedia of Twentieth-Century Architecture. Ed. Vittorio M. Lampugnani. Rev. ed. New York: Abrams, 1986.

Encyclopedia of Visual Art. Ed. Lawrence Gouring. Englewood Cliffs, NJ: Prentice Hall, 1988.

Encyclopedia of World Art. 15 vols. New York: McGraw, 1959–68.

McGraw-Hill Dictionary of Art. 5 vols. New York: McGraw, 1969.

Oxford Companion to Art. Ed. Harold Osborne. Oxford: Clarendon, 1970.

Oxford Companion to Twentieth-Century Art. Ed. Harold Osborne. Oxford: Clarendon, 1982.

Praeger Encyclopedia of Art. 15 vols. New York: Praeger, 1971.

Biographical Dictionaries and Directories

American Art Directory. 49th ed. New York: Bowker, 1982.

Afro-American Artists: A Bibliographical Directory. Ed. and comp. Theresa Cederholm. Boston: Boston Public Library, 1973.

Cumming, Paul. *A Dictionary of Contemporary American Artists.* 5th ed. New York: St. Martin's, 1988.

Marks, Claude. *World Artists 1950–1980.* 4 vols. New York: Wilson, 1982.

Who's Who in American Art. 17th ed. Ed. Jaques Cattell Press. New York: Bowker, 1986.

Databases

ARCHITECTURE DATABASE (RILA)
ART BIBLIOGRAPHIES MODERN
ART LITERATURE INTERNATIONAL

Biological Sciences

Bibliographies, Guides, and Indexes

Agriculture Index. New York: Wilson, 1916–63.

Bibliography of Bioethics. 8 vols. Detroit: Gale, 1975–date.

Biological Abstracts. Philadelphia: Biological Abstracts, 1926–date.

Biological and Agricultural Index. New York: Wilson, 1947–date. Monthly except August.

Botanical Bibliographies: A Guide to Bibliographical Materials Applicable to Botany. Monticello: Lubrecht, 1974.

General Science Index. New York: Wilson, 1978–date.

Guide to the Literature of the Life Sciences. 9th ed. Ed. R. C. Smith and W. M. Reid. Minneapolis, MN: Burgess, 1980.

Information Sources in the Life Sciences. Ed. H. V. Wyatt. Stoneham, MA: Butterworth, 1987.

Library Research Guide to Biology: Illustrated Search Strategy and Sources. Ann Arbor, MI: Pierian, 1978.

Encylopedias, Dictionaries, and Handbooks

American Men and Women of Science: Physical and Biological Sciences. 16th ed. 8 vols. Ed. Jaques Cattell Press. New York: Bowker, 1968.

Cambridge Encyclopedia of Life Sciences. E. Adrian Faraday and David S. Ingram. Cambridge: Cambridge UP, 1985.

CRC Handbook of Agricultural Productivity. 2 vols. Boca Raton, FL: CRC, 1981.

Dictionary of Botany. Ed. John R. Little and Eugene C. Jones. New York: Van Nostrand Reinhold, 1980.

Dictionary of the History Science. Ed. William F. Bynum et al. Princeton, NJ: Princeton UP, 1981.

Dictionary of Zoology. Ed. A. W. A. Leftwich. Princeton, NJ: Van Nostrand Reinhold, 1973.

Encyclopedia of Bioethics. 2 vols. New York: Macmillan, 1982.

Encyclopedia of the Biological Sciences. Ed. Peter Gray. 2nd ed. New York: Van Nostrand Reinhold, 1970.

Hammond Barnhart Dictionary of Science. Ed. Robert Barnhart. Maplewood, NJ: C. S. Hammond, 1986.

Larousse Encyclopedia of Animal Life. New York: McGraw, 1967.

McGraw-Hill Dictionary of the Life Sciences. Ed. Daniel N. Lapedes. New York: McGraw, 1984.

United States Department of Agriculture. *Yearbook of Agriculture.* Washington, DC: GPO, 1894–date.

Van Nostrand's Scientific Encyclopedia. Ed. Douglas M. Considine. 6th ed. New York: Van Nostrand Reinhold, 1982.

Abstracts and Digests
Biological Abstracts. Philadelphia: Biological Abstracts, 1926–date.

Databases
AGRICOLA
AGRIS INTERNATIONAL
AQUACULTURE
BIOSIS
LIFE SCIENCES COLLECTION
SCISEARCH
ZOOLOGICAL RECORD

Business

Bibliographies, Guides, and Indexes
Accountant's Index. New York: American Institute of Certified Public Accountants, 1921–date.

Brownstone, David, and Gorton Carruth. *Where to Find Business Information.* 2nd ed. New York: Wiley, 1982.

Business Index. New York: Wilson, 1958–date. Microfilm.

Business Periodicals Index. New York: Wilson, 1958–date. Monthly except August.

Daniells, Lorna M. *Business Information Sources.* Rev. ed. Berkeley: U of California P, 1985.

Encyclopedias, Dictionaries, and Handbooks
Ammer, Christine, and Dean Ammer. *Dictionary of Business and Economics.* Rev. ed. New York: Free Press, 1984.

Encyclopedia of Business Information Sources. Ed. Paul Wanerman. 4th rev. ed. Detroit: Gale, 1980.
Rosenberg, Jerry M. *Dictionary of Business and Management.* New York: Wiley, 1978.

Databases
ABI/INFORM
ACCOUNTANTS INDEX
D&B DUN'S FINANCIAL RECORD
D&B ELECTRONIC YELLOW PAGES
DISCLOSURE
ECONOMIC LITERATURE INDEX
LABORLAW
MANAGEMENT CONTENTS
MOODY'S CORPORATE NEWS
PTS F&S INDEXES
PTS PROMPT
STANDARD & POOR'S NEWS
TRADE AND INDUSTRY INDEX

Chemistry and Chemical Engineering

Bibliographies, Guides, and Indexes
Applied Science and Technology Index. New York: Wilson, 1958–date.
Chemical Industries Information Services. Ed. T. P. Peck. Detroit: Gale, 1978.
Chemical Publications. Ed. M. G. Mellon. 5th ed. New York: McGraw, 1982.
Chemical Titles. Easton: ACS, 1960. Biweekly.
Guide to Basic Information Sources in Chemistry. Ed. Arthur Antony. New York: Wiley, 1979.
How to Find Chemical Information: A Guide for Practicing Chemists, Teachers, and Students. Ed. Robert E. Maizell. 2nd. ed. New York: Wiley, 1987.
Selected Titles in Chemistry. 4th ed. Washington, DC: ACS, 1977.

Encyclopedias, Dictionaries, and Handbooks
Chemical Engineer's Handbook. 6th ed. New York: McGraw, 1984.
Condensed Chemical Dictionary. 10th ed. New York: Van Nostrand Reinhold, 1981.
CRC Handbook of Chemistry and Physics. Ed. Robert C. Weast. 69th ed. Boca Raton, FL: CRC, 1988.
Kirk-Othmer Encyclopedia of Chemical Technology. 3rd ed. 24 vols. New York: Wiley, 1978. Supplements.
Riegel's Handbook of Industrial Chemistry. 8th ed. New York: Van Nostrand Reinhold, 1983.

Abstracts and Digests
Annual Reviews of Industrial and Engineering Chemistry. Washington, DC: ACS, 1972–date.
Chemical Abstracts. Washington, DC: ACS, 1907–date.
General Science Index. New York: Wilson, 1978–date.

Databases
CA SEARCH
CHEMICAL ABSTRACTS
CHEMICAL INDUSTRY NOTES
CHEMIS
CHEMNAME
COMPENDEX
INSPEC
NTIS
SCISEARCH

Computer Science

Bibliographies, Guides, and Indexes

AMC Guide to Computing Literature. 1978–date. Annually.
Annotated Bibliography on the History of Data Processing. Ed. James W. Cortada. Westport, CT: Greenwood, 1983.
Applied Science and Technology Index. New York: Wilson, 1958–date.
Computer Literature Index. Phoenix, AZ: ACR, 1971–date.
Computer-Readable Bibliographic Data Bases: A Directory and Data Source-book. Washington, DC: ASIS, 1976–date.
Scientific and Technical Information Sources. Ed. C. Chen. Boston: MIT, 1987.
Zorkocsy, Peter. *Information Technology: An Introduction.* New York: Knowledge, 1983.

Encyclopedias, Dictionaries, and Handbooks

Computer Dictionary and Handbook. 4th ed. Indianapolis, IN: Sams, 1985.
Data Communications Dictionary. Ed. Charles J. Sipp. New York: Van Nostrand Reinhold, 1984.
Dictionary of Computing. New York: Oxford, 1986.
Encyclopedia of Computer Science and Engineering. Ed. Anthony Ralston. 2nd ed. New York: Van Nostrand Reinhold, 1983.
Encyclopedia of Computer Science and Technology. Ed. Jack Belzer. 20 vols. New York: Dekker, 1975–date.

Abstracts and Digests

Artificial Intelligence Abstracts. New York: Bowker, 1983–date. Annually.

Databases

BUSINESS SOFTWARE DATABASE
COMPUTER DATABASE
INSPEC
MICROCOMPUTER INDEX

Ecology

Bibliographies, Guides, and Indexes

Energy Information Guide. Ed. David R. Weber. Santa Barbara, CA: ABC-Clio, 1982–83.

Environment Index. Ed. M. Pronin. New York: Environment Information. Annual.
Environment Information Access. New York: EIC, 1971–date.
Environmental Periodicals Bibliography. Santa Barbara, CA: Environmental
Studies Institute, 1972–date.

Encyclopedias, Dictionaries, and Handbooks
Encyclopedia of Community Planning and Environmental Protection. Ed. Marilyn Schultz and Vivian Kasen. New York: Facts on File, 1983.
General Science Index. New York: Wilson, 1978–date.
Grzimek's Encyclopedia of Ecology. Ed. Bernhard Grzimek. New York: Van Nostrand Reinhold, 1977.
McGraw-Hill Encyclopedia of Environmental Science. Ed. S. R. Parker. 2nd ed. New York: McGraw, 1980.

Abstracts and Digests
Biological Abstracts. Philadelphia: Biological Abstracts, 1926–date.
Ecology Abstracts. Bethesda, MD: Cambridge Scientific Abstracts, 1975–date. Monthly.
Energy Abstracts for Policy Analysis. Oak Ridge, TN: TIC, 1975–date.
Environment Abstracts. New York: Environment Information Center, 1971–date.
Pollution Abstracts. Bethesda, MD: Cambridge Scientific Abstracts, 1970–date.

Databases
APTIC
BIOSIS PREVIEWS
COMPENDEX
ENVIRONLINE
ENVIRONMENTAL PERIODICALS BIBLIOGRAPHY
POLLUTION ABSTRACTS
WATER RESOURCES ABSTRACTS

Education
Bibliographies, Guides, and Indexes
Berry, Dorothea. *A Bibliographic Guide to Educational Research.* 2nd ed. Metuchen, NJ: Scarecrow, 1980.
Bibliographic Guide to Education. Boston: Hall, 1978–date.
Bibliographic Guide to Educational Research. Ed. D. M. Berry. 2nd ed. Metuchen, NJ: Scarecrow, 1980.
Current Index to Journals in Education. Phoenix, AZ: Oryx, 1969–date.
Education Index. New York: Wilson, 1929–date. Ten times a year with annual cumulations.
Education Journals and Serials. Ed. Mary E. Collins. Metuchen, NJ: Scarecrow, 1988.
Exceptional Child Education Resources. Reston, VA: CEC, 1968–date.
Philosophy of Education: A Guide to Information Sources. Ed. Charles A. Baatz. Detroit: Gale, 1980.

Resources in Education [formerly *Research in Education*]. Washington, DC: ERIC, 1956–date.
Subject Bibliography of the History of American Higher Education. Westport, CT: Greenwood, 1984.

Encyclopedias, Dictionaries, and Handbooks
Dictionary of Education. Ed. Carter V. Good. 3rd ed. New York: McGraw, 1973.
Encyclopedia of Education. Ed. Lee C. Deighton. 10 vols. New York: Macmillan, 1971.
Encyclopedia of Educational Research. Ed. Harold E. Mitzel. 5th ed. 4 vols. Washington, DC: Free Press, 1982.
Handbook of Research on Teaching. Ed. Merlin C. Wittrock. 3rd ed. New York: Macmillan, 1986.
Handbook of Research on Teacher Education. Ed. Robert Houston. New York: Macmillan, 1990.
Library Research Guide to Education. Ed. James R. Kennedy, Jr. Ann Arbor, MI: Pierian, 1979.

Abstracts and Digests
Digest of Educational Statistics. Washington, DC: United Sates Department of Education, National Center for Educational Statistics, 1962–date.
Education Abstracts. Paris: UNESCO, 1949–date.
Educational Documents Abstracts. New York: Macmillan, 1966–date.

Databases
AIM/ARM
A-V ONLINE
ERIC
EXCEPTIONAL CHILD EDUCATIONAL RESOURCES

Ethnic Studies

Bibliographies, Guides, and Indexes
Comprehensive Bibliography for the Study of American Minorities. Comp. Wayne C. Miller. 2 vols. New York: New York UP, 1976.
Ethnic Information Sources of the United States. Ed. Paul Wasserman and Alice E. Kennington. 2nd ed. 2 vols. Detroit: Gale, 1983.
Harvard Encyclopedia of American Ethnic Groups. Ed. Stephan Thernstrom et al. Cambridge, MA: Harvard UP, 1980.
Immigration and Ethnicity: A Guide to Information Sources. Comp. John D. Buenker and Nicholas C. Burckel. Detroit: Gale, 1977.
MLA International Bibliography. New York: MLA, 1921–date.
Oxbridge Directory of Ethnic Periodicals. New York: Oxbridge, 1979.
Social Sciences Index. New York: Wilson, 1974–date.

Abstracts and Digests
Sage Race Relations Abstracts. San Mateo, CA: 1976–date.
Sociological Abstracts. La Jolla, CA: Sociological Abstracts, 1952–date.

Asian-American Studies
Bibliographies, Guides, and Indexes
Chen, Jack. *The Chinese of America*. New York: Harper, 1982.
Melendy, Henry Brett. *Asians in America: Filipinos, Koreans, and East Indians*. New York: Hippocrene, 1981.
Wong, James I. *A Selected Bibliography on the Asians in America*. Palo Alto, CA: R and E, 1981.

Black Studies
Bibliographies, Guides, and Indexes
Afro-American Reference: An Annotated Bibliography of Selected Sources. Ed. N. Davis. Westport, CT: Greenwood, 1985.
Bibliographic Guide to Black Studies: 1987. Boston: Hall, 1988.
Black Access: A Bibliography of Afro-American Bibliographies. Comp. R. Newman. Westport, CT: Greenwood, 1984.
Black Resource Guide, 1990. Washington, DC: Black Resource, 1990.
Blacks in Selected Newspapers, Censuses and Other Sources: An Index to Names and Subjects. Ed. James de T. Abajian. 3 vols. Boston: Hall, 1977. First supplement 2 vols., 1985.
Fisher, Mary L. *The Negro in America: A Bibliography*. 2nd ed. Cambridge, MA: Harvard UP, 1970.
Index to Afro-American Reference Resources. Comp. Rosemary Stevenson. Westport, CT: Greenwood, 1988.
Index to Periodical Articles by and about Blacks. Boston: Hall, 1983–date. Annually.
The Negro in the United States: A Selected Bibliography. Comp. Dorothy B. Porter. Washington, DC: Library of Congress, 1970.
The Progress of Afro-American Women: A Selected Bibliography and Resource Guide. Comp. Janet Sims. Westport, CT: Greenwood, 1980.

Encyclopedias, Dictionaries, and Handbooks
Black American Reference Book. Ed. M. M. Smythe. Englewood Cliffs, NJ: Prentice Hall, 1976.
Dictionary of American Negro Biography. Ed. Rayford W. Logan and Michael R. Winston. New York: Norton, 1982.
Encyclopedia of Black America. Ed. W. A. Low. New York: McGraw, 1981.
Negro Almanac. Ed. H. A. Ploski and James Williams. 4th ed. New York: Wiley, 1983.
Who's Who Among Black Americans. Northbrook: WWABA, 1976–date.

Hispanic-American Studies
Bibliographies, Guides, and Indexes
A Bibliography of Criticism of Contemporary Chicano Literature. Comp. Ernestina N. Eger. Berkeley, CA: Chicano Studies Library Publications, U of California, 1982.
A Decade of Chicano Literature (1970–1979): Critical Essays and Bibliography. Ed. Luis Leal et al. Santa Barbara, CA: Editorial La Causa, 1982.

Dictionary of Mexican American History. Ed. Matt S. Meier and Feliciano Rivera. Westport, CT: Greenwood, 1981.
Hispanic American Periodicals Index. Los Angeles: UCLA Latin American Center, 1974–date.
Mexican Americans: An Annotated Bibliography of Bibliographies. Comp. Julio A. Martinez and Ada Burns. Saratoga, CA: R and E, 1984.
Selected and Annotated Bibliography for Chicano Studies. Comp. Charles M. Tatum. 2nd ed. Lincoln, NE: Society of Spanish and Spanish-American Studies, 1979.

Native American Studies
Bibliographies, Guides, and Indexes
American Indian Novelists: An Annotated Critical Bibliography. New York: Garland, 1982.
Guide to Research on the North American Indians. Ed. Arlene Hirschfelder. Chicago: ALA, 1893.
Indians of North America: Methods and Sources for Library Research. Hamden, CT: Library Professional, 1983.

Encyclopedias, Dictionaries, and Handbooks
Encyclopedia of North American Indian Tribes. Ed. Bill Yenne. New York: Crown, 1986.
Handbook of North American Indians. Ed. W. C. Sturtevant. Washington, DC: Smithsonian, 1978–in progress.
Reference Encyclopedia of the American Indian. Ed. T. M. Inge. 4th ed. Santa Barbara, CA: ABC-Cilo, 1986.

Databases for All Ethnic Studies
AMERICA: HISTORY AND LIFE
ERIC
P.A.I.S.
SOCIAL SCISEARCH
SOCIOLOGICAL ABSTRACTS

Film
Bibliographies, Guides, and Indexes
Armour, Robert A. *Film: A Reference Guide*. Westport, CT: Greenwood, 1980.
Film Literature Index. New York: Film and Television Documentation Center, 1973–date. Quarterly with annual indexes.
Halliwell, Leslie. *Halliwell's Film Guide*. 4th ed. New York: Scribners, 1983.
International Index of Film Periodicals. New York: Bowker, 1975–date.
Oxford Companion to Film. Ed. Liz-Anne Bawden. New York: Oxford UP, 1976.
Performing Arts Research: A Guide to Information Sources. Detroit: Gale, 1976.
Ross, Harris. *Film as Literature, Literature as Film: An Introduction to and Bibliography of Film's Relationship to Literature*. Westport, CT: Greenwood, 1987.
Whalon, Marion K. *Performing Arts Research: A Guide to Information Sources*. Detroit: Gale, 1976.

Encyclopedias, Dictionaries, and Handbooks
Film Encyclopedia. Ed. Phil Hardy. New York: Morrow, 1983–84.

Abstracts and Digests
New York Times Film Reviews. New York: Times Books, 1970–date.

Geography

Bibliographies, Guides, and Indexes
Geographers: Bio-Bibliographical Studies. Ed. T. W. Freeman et al. London: Mansell, 1977–date. Annually.

Geography and Local Administration: A Bibliography. Ed. Keith Hoggart. Monticello, IL: Vancy, 1980.

Geologic Reference Sources: A Subject and Regional Bibliography. Ed. Dedrick C. Ward, Marjorie Wheeler, and Robert A. Bier. 2nd ed. Metuchen, NJ: Scarecrow, 1980.

Guide to Information Sources in the Geographical Sciences. London, England: Croom Helm, 1983.

International List of Geographical Serials. 3rd ed. Chicago: U of Chicago, 1980.

Literature of Geography: A Guide to Its Organization and Use. 2nd ed. Hamden, CT: Shoe String, 1978.

Social Sciences Index. New York: Wilson, 1974–date.

Encyclopedias, Dictionaries, and Handbooks
Encyclopedia of Geographic Information Sources. Ed. J. Mossman. 4th ed. Detroit: Gale, 1986.

Geography and Cartography: A Reference Handbook. Ed. Clara B. Lock. 3rd ed. Hamden, CT: Shoe String, 1976.

Longman's Dictionary of Geography. Ed. L. D. Stamp. London, England: Longman, 1970.

Abstracts and Digests
Geo Abstracts, A–G. Norwich, England: Geo Abstracts, 1972–date. Bimonthly.

Databases
GEOBASE
SOCIAL SCISEARCH

Geology

Bibliographies, Guides, and Indexes
Bibliography and Index of Geology. Boulder, CO: American Geological Institute, 1933–date. Monthly with annual indexes.

Bibliography of North American Geology. 49 vols. Washington, DC: Geological Survey, 1923–71.

General Science Index. New York: Wilson, 1978–date.

Geological Reference Sources: A Subject and Regional Bibliography. Ed. Dedrick C. Ward, Marjorie W. Wheeler, and Robert A. Bier. Metuchen, NJ: Scarecrow, 1981.

Guide to Information Sources in Mining, Minerals, and Geosciences. Ed. S. R. Kaplan. New York: McGraw, 1978.
Publications of the Geological Survey. Washington, DC: GPO, 1979.

Encyclopedias, Dictionaries, and Handbooks
Challinor's Dictionary of Geology. 6th ed. New York: Oxford, 1986.
Encyclopedia of Field and General Geology. Ed. C. W. Finkle. New York: Van Nostrand Reinhold, 1982.
Glossary of Geology. Ed. R. L. Bates and J. A. Jackson. 3rd ed. Falls Church, VA: AGI, 1987.
McGraw-Hill Encyclopedia of the Geological Sciences. New York: McGraw, 1980.

Databases
COMPENDEX
GEOARCHIVE
GEOBASE
GEOREF

Health and Physical Education

Bibliographies, Guides, and Indexes
Annotated Bibliography of Health Economics. Ed. A. J. Culyer et al. New York: St. Martin's, 1977.
Author's Guide to Journals in the Health Field. New York: Haworth, 1980.
Bibliography of Research Involving Female Subjects. Washington, DC: AAHPER, 1975.
Consumer Health Information Source Book. 2nd ed. New York: Bowker, 1984.
Current Index to Journals in Education. Phoenix, AZ: Oryx, 1969–date.
Education Index. New York: Wilson, 1929–date.
Food and Nutrition Information Guide. Englewood, CO: Libraries Unlimited, 1988.
Foundations of Physical Education and Sport. Ed. C. A. Bucher. St. Louis, MO: Mosby, 1986.
Health Maintenance Through Food and Nutrition: A Guide to Information Sources. Ed. Helen D. Ulrich. Detroit: Gale, 1981.
Health Statistics: A Guide to Information Sources. Detroit: Gale, 1980.
Physical Education Index. Cape Giradeau, MO: Oak, 1978–date.
Physical Fitness and Sports Medicine. Washington, DC: GPO, 1978–date.
Sports and Physical Education: A Guide to the Reference Sources. Ed. Bonnie Gratcher et al. Westport, CT: Greenwood, 1983.

Encyclopedias, Dictionaries, and Handbooks
Columbia Encyclopedia of Nutrition. New York: Putnam, 1988.
Encyclopedia of Nutrition Science. Ed. [sic] Rollinson. New York: Wiley, 1988.
Encyclopedia of Physical Education, Fitness and Sport. Ed. Thomas K. Cureton, Jr. 3 vols. Salt Lake City, UT: Brighton, 1980.
Encyclopedia of Sports. 6th ed. rev. New York: Barnes, 1978.
International Dictionary of Sports and Games. Ed. C. J. Cuddon. New York: Schocken, 1979.

Abstracts and Digests

Nutrition Abstracts and Reviews. New York: Wiley, 1931–date.

Databases

ERIC
MEDLINE
MEDOC
SOCIAL SCISEARCH
SPORT AND RECREATION INDEX

History

Bibliographies, Guides, and Indexes

Arts and Humanities Citation Index. Philadelphia: Institute for Scientific Information, 1976–date. Annually.

Combined Retrospective Index to Journals in History, 1838–1974. 11 vols. Arlington: Carrollton, 1977–78.

Guide to Historical Method. Ed. Robert J. Shafer. 3rd ed. Belmont, CA: Wadsworth, 1980.

Harzfeid, Lois. *Periodical Indexes in the Social Sciences and Humanities: A Subject Guide.* Metuchen, NJ: Scarecrow, 1978.

Historical Bibliography. Ed. D. Williamson. Hamden, CT: Shoe String, 1967.

Kaplan, Louis. *A Bibliography of American Autobiographies.* Madison: U of Wisconsin P, 1961.

Prucha, Francis Paul. *Handbook for Research in History.* Lincoln: U of Nebraska P, 1987.

Social Sciences Citation Index. Philadelphia: Institute for Scientific Information, 1979–date. Annual supplements.

Wars of the United States. New York: Garland, 1984–date.

Encyclopedias, Dictionaries, and Handbooks

Dictionary of American History. 8 vols. New York: Scribners, 1976.

Encyclopedia of American History. Ed. Richard B. Morris and Jeffrey B. Morris. 6th ed. New York: Harper, 1982.

Encyclopedia of World History. 5th ed. Boston: Houghton, 1972.

Abstracts and Digests

Recently Published Articles. Washington, DC: American Historical Association, 1976–date.

Writings on American History. Washington, DC: American Historical Association, 1903–date.

Databases

AMERICA: HISTORY AND LIFE
HISTORICAL ABSTRACTS
SOCIAL SCIENCES CITATION INDEX

Journalism and Mass Communications

Bibliographies, Guides, and Indexes

An Annotated Journalism Bibliography: 1958–1968. Minneapolis: U of Minnesota P, 1970.

Annotated Media Bibliography. Ed. Brenda Congdon. Washington, DC: ACC, 1985.

Black Media Directory. Ed. Martin Pollack. Fort Lauderdale, FL: Alliance, 1989.

Black Media in America: A Resource Guide. Ed. G. H. Hill. Boston: Hall, 1984.

Blum, Eleanor. *Basic Books in Mass Media.* 2nd ed. Urbana: U of Illinois P, 1980.

Broadcast Television: A Research Guide. Ed. F. C. Schreibman. Los Angeles: AFI Education Services, 1983.

Business Periodicals Index. New York: Wilson, 1958–date.

Humanities Index. New York: Wilson, 1974–date.

Journalism Bibliographies: Master Index. Detroit: Gale, 1979. Supplements.

Media Research: An Introduction. Ed. R. D. Wimmer and J. R. Dominick. Belmont, CA: Wadsworth, 1982.

Radio and Television: A Selected Annotated Bibliography. Metuchen, NJ: Scarecrow, 1978. Supplements to 1982.

Encyclopedias, Dictionaries, and Handbooks

Barron, Jerome A., and C. Thomas Dienes. *Handbook of Free Speech and Free Press.* Boston: Little, Brown, 1979.

Paneth, Daniel. *Encyclopedia of American Journalism.* New York: Facts on File, 1983.

Taft, William H. *Encyclopedia of Twentieth Century Journalists.* New York: Garland, 1986.

Abstracts and Digests

Communications Abstracts. San Mateo, CA: Sage, 1978–date.

Databases

AP NEWS
MAGAZINE INDEX
NATIONAL NEWSPAPER INDEX
NEWSEARCH
REUTERS
SOCSCI SEARCH
UPI NEWS

Language

Bibliographies, Guides, and Indexes

American Literature and Language: A Guide to Information Sources. Detroit: Gale, 1982.

Annual Bibliography of English Language and Literature. Cambridge, England: Cambridge UP, 1921–date. Annual.

Cambridge Encyclopedia of Language. Ed. David Crystal. New York: Cambridge UP, 1987.

A Concise Bibliography for Students of English. 5th ed. Stanford, CA: Stanford UP, 1972.

McCrum, Robert, William Cran, and Robert MacNeil. *The Story of English.* New York: Viking, 1986.

The World's Major Languages. Ed. Bernard Comrie. New York: Oxford UP, 1987.

Encyclopedias, Dictionaries, and Handbooks

Barnhart, Robert K. *The Barnhart Dictionary of Etymology.* New York: Wilson, 1987.

Mathews, Mitford M. *Americanisms: A Dictionary of Selected Americanisms on Historical Principles.* Chicago: Chicago UP, 1966.

Oxford English Dictionary. Ed. James A. H. Murray et al. 13 vols. New York: Oxford UP, 1933. Supplements.

Skeat, Walter W. *An Etymological Dictionary of the English Language.* New ed. rev. Oxford, England: Clarendon, 1910.

Webster's Dictionary of English Usage, 1989 ed.

Abstracts and Digests

Language and Language Behavior Abstracts. Chicago: Sociological Abstracts, 1967–date.

Databases

LANGUAGE AND LANGUAGE BEHAVIOR ABSTRACTS
MODERN LANGUAGE ASSOCIATION BIBLIOGRAPHY

Literature

Bibliographies

Bibliographic Guide to Black Studies: 1987. The Schomburg Center for Research in Black Culture. Boston, MA: Hall, 1988.

Bibliographical Guide to the Study of Literature of the USA. Ed. Clarence L. Gohdes. 5th ed. Durham, NC: Duke UP, 1984.

Bibliography of American Literature. New Haven: Yale UP, 1955–date.

Bibliography of Criticism of Contemporary Chicano Literature. Comp. Ernestina N. Eger. Berkeley, CA: Chicano Studies Library Publications, U of California, 1982.

Black American Fiction: A Bibliography. Ed. Carol Fairbanks and Eugene E. Engeldinger. Metuchen, NJ: Scarecrow, 1978.

Black Americans in Autobiography: An Annotated Bibliography of Autobiographies and Autobiographical Books Written Since the Civil War. Durham, NC: Duke UP, 1984.

Contemporary Novels: A Checklist of Critical Literature on the British and American Novel Since 1945. Ed. I. Adelman and R. Dworkin. Metuchen, NJ: Scarecrow, 1972.

A Decade of Chicano Literature (1970–1979): Critical Essays and Bibliography. Ed. Luis Leal et al. Santa Barbara, CA: Editorial La Causa, 1982.

Garland Shakespeare Bibliographies. 18 vols. New York: Garland, 1980–date.

MLA International Bibliography of Books and Articles on the Modern Languages and Literatures. New York: MLA, 1921–date.

New Cambridge Bibliography of English Literature. Ed. George Watson. 5 vols. Cambridge, England: Cambridge UP, 1974.

Poetry Explication: A Checklist of Interpretations Since 1925 of British and American Poems Past and Present. Boston: Hall, 1980.

Guides

American and British Poetry: A Guide to the Criticism. Athens, OH: Swallow, 1984.

American Fiction 1900–1950: A Guide to Information Sources. Ed. James Woodress. Detroit: Gale, 1974.

Cambridge Guide to Literature in English. Ed. Ian Ousby. New York: Cambridge UP, 1988.

Contemporary Literary Criticism. Detroit: Gale, 1973–date.

English Romantic Poets: A Review of Research and Criticism. 4th ed. New York: MLA, 1985.

Literary Research Guide. Ed. Margaret Patterson. 2nd ed. New York: MLA, 1983.

McGraw-Hill Guide to English Literature. Ed. K. Lawrence, B. Seifter, and I. Ratner. New York: McGraw, 1985.

Research Guide for Undergraduate Students: English and American Literature. Ed. Nancy L. Baker. 3rd ed. New York: MLA, 1985.

Histories

Literary History of the United States. Ed. Robert E. Spiller et al. 4th ed. 2 vols. New York: Macmillan, 1974.

Oxford History of English Literature. Oxford, England: Clarendon, 1945–date.

Indexes

Book Review Index. Detroit: Gale, 1965–date.

Cumulated Dramatic Index. 2 vols. Westwood, MA: Faxon, 1965.

Essay and General Literature Index. New York: Wilson, 1934–date.

Granger's Index to Poetry. Ed. William J. Smith and William F. Bernhardt. 7th ed. New York: Columbia UP. 1982.

Humanities Index. New York: Wilson, 1974–date.

Index to Black American Writers in Collective Biographies. Dorothy W. Campbell. Littleton, CO: Libraries Unlimited, 1983.

Index to Book Reviews in the Humanities. Detroit: Thompson, 1960–date.

Index to Full-Length Plays: 1895–1964. 3 vols. Westwood, MA: Faxon, 1956–1965.

Literary Criticism Index. Ed. A. R. Weiner and S. Means. Metuchen, NJ: Scarecrow, 1984.

Play Index. 6 vols. New York: Wilson, 1953–date.

Short Story Index: Collections Indexed 1900–1978. New York: Wilson, 1979.

Encyclopedias

Benet's Reader's Encyclopedia. 3rd ed. New York: Harper, 1987.

Encyclopedia of World Literature in the Twentieth Century. Ed. Leonard S. Klein. 2nd ed. 5 vols. New York: Ungar, 1983.

Dictionaries

Dictionary of Classical Mythology. Ed. Pierre Grimal. Cambridge, MA: Basil Blackwell, 1985.

Oxford Companion to American Literature. Ed. James D. Hart. New York: Oxford UP, 1983.

Handbooks

Cambridge Handbook of American Literature. Ed. Jack Salzman. New York: Cambridge UP, 1986.

Abstracts and Digests

Abstracts of English Studies. Urbana IL: NCTE, 1958–date.
Book Review Digest. New York: Wilson, 1905–date.

Databases

BOOK REVIEW INDEX
MLA BIBLIOGRAPHY

Mathematics

Bibliographies, Guides, and Indexes

Annotated Bibliography of Expository Writing in the Mathematical Sciences. Ed. M. P. Gaffney and L. A. Steen. Washington, DC: Mathematics Association, 1976.
Bibliography of Mathematical Works Printed in America through 1850. Ed. I. Bernard Cohen. Repr. of 1940 ed. Salem, NH: Ayer, 1980.
Index of Mathematical Papers. Vols. 9 & 10. Providence, RI: American Mathematical Society, 1979.
Using Mathematical Literature: A Practical Guide. Ed. B. K. Schaefer. New York: Marcel Dekker, 1979.

Encyclopedias, Dictionaries, and Handbooks

CRC Handbook of Mathematical Sciences. Ed. William Beyer. 5th ed. West Palm, FL: CRC. 1978.
Encyclopedic Dictionary of Mathematics. Ed. Kiyoshi Ito. 2nd ed. 4 vols. Cambridge, MA: MIT P, 1987.
Facts on File Dictionary of Mathematics. Ed. Carol Gibson. Rev. ed. New York: Facts on File, 1988.
Gellert, W., et al., eds. *The VNR Concise Encyclopedia of Mathematics.* Florence, KY: Reinhold, 1977.
Prentice Hall Encyclopedia of Mathematics. Ed. Barry Henderson West et al. Englewood Cliffs, NJ: Prentice Hall, 1982.

Abstracts and Digests

General Science Index. New York: Wilson, 1978–date.
Mathematical Reviews. Providence, RI: American Mathematical Society, 1940–date. Monthly.

Databases

MATHSCI

Medical Sciences

Bibliographies, Guides, and Indexes

Cumulative Index to Nursing and Allied Health Literature. Glendale, CA: Glendale Adventist Medical Center, 1977–date. [Formerly *Cumulative Index to Nursing Literature*, 1956–1976.]

Guide to Library Resources for Nursing. Ed. K. P. Strauch and D. J. Brundage. New York: Appleton, 1980.

Health Statistics: A Guide to Information Sources. Detroit: Gale, 1980.

Hospital Literature Index. Chicago: American Hospital, 1945–date.

Index Medicus. Washington, DC: National Library of Medicine, 1960–date.

Information Sources in the Medical Sciences. Ed. L. T. Morton and S. Godbolt. 3rd ed. London, England: Butterworths, 1984.

Introduction to Reference Sources in Health Sciences. Ed. F. Roper and J. Boorkman. 2nd ed. Chicago: Medical Library, 1984.

Library Research Guide to Nursing. E. Katina Strauch et al. Ann Arbor, MI: Pierian, 1989.

Medical Reference Works, 1679–1966: A Selected Bibliography. Ed. John B. Blake and Charles Roos. Chicago: Medical Library, 1967. Supplements 1970–date.

Morton, Leslie, and Robert J. Moore. *A Bibliography of Medical and Biomedical Biography.* Gower, England: Gower, 1989.

Nursing Studies Index. Ed. Virgina Henderson. 4 vols. Philadelphia: Lippincott, 1957–72.

Polit, Denise, and Bernadette Hungler. *Nursing Research: Principles and Methods.* 3rd ed. Philadelphia: Lippincott, 1987.

Encyclopedias, Dictionaries, and Handbooks

Black's Medical Dictionary. Ed. W. A. R. Thompson. London, England: Black, 1984.

Dorland's Illustrated Medical Dictionary. 26th ed. Philadelphia: Saunders, 1985.

Encyclopedia of Medical History. Ed. Roderick McGrew. New York: McGraw, 1985.

Databases

BIOSIS PREVIEWS
EMBASE
MEDLINE
NURSING AND ALLIED HEALTH
SCISEARCH

Music

Bibliographies, Guides, and Indexes

Bibliographic Guide to Music. Boston: Hall, 1976–date.

Cohn, Arthur. *Recorded Classical Music: A Critical Guide to Compositions and Performances.* New York: Macmillan, 1981.

General Bibliography for Music Research. Ed. K. E. Mixter. 2nd ed. Detroit: Information Coordinators, 1975.

Horn, David. *The Literature of American Music in Books and Folk Music Collections: A Fully Annotated Bibliography.* Metuchen, NJ: Scarecrow, 1977.
Music Article Guide. Philadelphia: Information Services, 1966–date.
Music Index. Warren, MI: Information Coordinators, 1949–date.
Music Reference and Research Materials: An Annotated Bibliography. Ed. Vincent Duckles. 3rd ed. New York: Free Press/Macmillan, 1974.
Popular Music: An Annotated Index to American Popular Songs. 10 vols. New York: Adrian, 1964–85.
RILM (Repertoire Internationale de Litterature Musicale). New York: City U of New York, 1967–date.

Encyclopedias, Dictionaries, and Handbooks
Baker's Biographical Dictionary of Musicians. 7th ed. New York: Schirmer, 1984.
International Cyclopedia of Music and Musicians. Ed. Oscar Thompson. New York: Dodd, 1985.
International Encyclopedia of Hard Rock and Heavy Metal. Ed. Tony Jasper. New York: Facts on File, 1985.
New College Encyclopedia of Music. New York: Norton, 1981.
New Grove Dictionary of Music and Musicians. Ed. H. Wylie Hitchcock and Stanley Sadie. 4 vols. New York: Grove, 1986.
New Oxford Companion to Music. Ed. Denis Arnold. 11th ed. 2 vols. Oxford, England: Oxford UP, 1982.

Databases
RILM ABSTRACTS (Repertoire Internationale de Litterature Musicale)

Philosophy and Religion

Bibliographies, Guides, and Indexes
Bynagle, Hans E. *Philosophy: A Guide to the Reference Literature.* Littleton, CO: Libraries Unlimited, 1986.
The Philosopher's Guide: To Sources, Research Tools, Professional Life, and Related Fields. Ed. R. T. DeGeorge. Lawrence KS: Regents, 1980.
The Philosopher's Index: An International Index to Philosophical Periodicals and Books. Bowling Green, OH: Bowling Green University, 1967–date.
A Reader's Guide to the Great Religions. Ed. Charles J. Adams. 2nd ed. New York: Free Press, 1977.
Religion Index One: Periodicals. Chicago: American Theologian, 1978–date.
Religious Periodicals Directory. Ed. Graham Cornish. Santa Barbara, CA: ABC-Clio. 1986.
Research Guide to Philosophy. Ed. Terence Tice and Thomas Slavens. (Sources of Information in the Humanities, No. 3.) Chicago: ALA, 1983.
Social and Historical Sciences, Philosophy and Religion. Vol. 2 of *Guide to Reference Material.* Ed. A. J. Walford. 4th ed. London, England: Library Association, 1982.

Encyclopedias, Dictionaries, and Handbooks

Dictionary of American Religious Biography. Westport, CT: Greenwood, 1977.
A Dictionary of Philosophy. Ed. P. A. Angeles. New York: Harper, 1981.
Dictionary of Philosophy. Ed. A. R. Lacey. New York: Paul/Methuen, 1987.
Dictionary of the History of Ideas. Ed. P. Winer. 5 vols. New York: Scribners, 1974.
Handbook of World Philosophy: Contemporary Developments Since 1945. Ed. John R. Burr. Westport, CT: Greenwood, 1980.
Harper's Bible Dictionary. Ed. Paul Achteimer. New York: Harper, 1985.
Melton, J. Gordon. *Encyclopedia of American Religions.* 2nd. ed. Detroit: Gale, 1986.
Parrinder, Geoffrey. *A Dictionary of Non-Christian Religions.* Philadelphia: Westminster, 1971.
Who's Who in Religion. Chicago: Marquis, 1985.

Abstracts and Digests

World Philosophy: Essay Reviews of 225 Major Works. Ed. Frank Magill. 5 vols. Englewood Cliffs: Salem, 1982.

Databases

PHILOSOPHER'S INDEX

Physics

Bibliographies, Guides, and Indexes

Applied Science and Technology Index. New York: Wilson, 1958–date.
Current Papers in Physics. London, England: IEE, 1966–date.
Sources of History of Quantum Physics. Ed. T. S. Kuhn et al. Philadelphia: APS, 1967.
Use of Physics Literature. Ed. H. Coblans. Woburn, MA: Butterworth, 1975.

Encyclopedias, Dictionaries, and Handbooks

Encyclopedia of Physics. Ed. Robert Besancon. New York: Van Nostrand Reinhold, 1985.
Encyclopedia of Physics. Ed. Rita G. Lerner and George L. Trigg. Reading, MA: Addison-Wesley, 1981.
McGraw-Hill Encyclopedia of Science and Technology. 20 vols. 6th ed. New York: McGraw, 1987.

Abstracts and Digests

Owen, Dolores B. *Abstracts and Indexes in the Sciences and Technology.* 2nd ed. Metuchen, NJ: Scarecrow, 1985.
Physics Abstracts. Surrey, England: IEE, 1898–date.
Science Abstracts. London, England: IEE, 1898–date.

Databases

SCISEARCH
SPIN

Political Science

Bibliographies, Guides, and Indexes

ABC: Pol Sci. Santa Barbara, CA: ABC-Clio, 1969–date.

Combined Retrospective Index to Journals in Political Science, 1886–1974. 8 vols. New York: Carrollton, 1977–78.

Foreign Affairs Bibliography. New York: Council on Foreign Relations, 1933–date. Published every 10 years.

Hall, K. L. *Bibliography of American Constitutional and Legal History, 1896–1979.* 5 vols. Millwood, NY: Kraus, 1984.

Information Sources in Politics and Political Science: A Survey Worldwide. Ed. D. Englefield and G. Drewry. London, England: Butterworth, 1984.

International Bibliography of Political Science. Paris, France: UNESCO, 1953–date. Annually.

Political Science: A Bibliographic Guide to the Literature. Metuchen, NJ: Scarecrow, 1965. Supplements 1966–date.

Public Affairs Information Service. *Bulletin.* New York: PAIS, 1915–date. Semimonthly.

Social Sciences Citation Index. New York: Wilson, 1973–date.

Social Sciences Index. New York: Wilson, 1974–date.

Encyclopedias, Dictionaries, and Handbooks

American Political Dictionary. Ed. Jack C. Plano and Milton Greenberg. 7th ed. New York: Holt, 1985.

Blackwell Encyclopedia of Political Institutions. Ed. Vernon Bogdanor. Cambridge, MA: Blackwell, 1987.

Encyclopedia of the Third World. Ed. George Thomas Kurian. 3 vols. New York: Facts on File, 1987.

Handbook of Latin American Studies. Gainesville: U of Florida P, 1936–date.

World Encyclopedia of Peace. Ed. Ervin Lazlo et al. 4 vols. New York: Pergamon, 1986.

Abstracts and Digests

International Political Science Abstracts. Oxford, England: Blackwell, 1951–date.

Political Science Abstracts. New York: Plenum, 1967–date.

Sage Urban Studies Abstracts. San Mateo, CA: Sage, 1973–date.

United States Political Science Documents (USPSD). Pittsburgh: U of Pittsburgh P, 1975.

Databases

ASI
CIS
CONGRESSIONAL RECORD ABSTRACTS
GPO MONTHLY CATALOG
NATIONAL NEWSPAPER INDEX
PAIS
U.S. POLITICAL SCIENCE DOCUMENTS
WASHINGTON PRESSTEXT
WORLD AFFAIRS REPORT

Psychology

Bibliographies, Guides, and Indexes

Bibliographical Guide to Psychology. Boston: Hall, 1982.
Bibliography of Aggressive Behavior: A Reader's Guide to the Research Literature. Ed. J. Michael Crabtree and Kenneth E. Moyer. New York: Liss, 1977.
The Harvard List of Books in Psychology. Cambridge, MA: Harvard UP, 1971.
McInnis, Raymond G. *Research Guide for Psychology*. Westport, CT: Greenwood, 1982.
Marken, Richard. *Introduction to Psychological Research*. Monterey, CA: Brooks, 1981.
Mental Health Book Review Index. New York: Research Center for Mental Health, 1956–72.
Psychoanalysis, Psychology, and Literature: A Bibliography. Ed. Norman Kiell. 2nd ed. 2 vols. Metuchen, NJ: Scarecrow, 1982.
Psychological Index. 42 vols. Princeton: Psychological Review, 1895–1936. Succeeded by *Psychological Abstracts* (see below).
Reed, Jeffery J., and Pam M. Baxter. *Library Use: A Handbook for Psychology*. Washington, DC: APA, 1983.
Social Sciences Citation Index. Philadelphia, PA: Institute for Scientific Information, 1969–date. Annually.
Science Citation Index. Philadelphia: Institute for Scientific Information, 1961–date. Annually.

Encyclopedias, Dictionaries, and Handbooks

Encyclopedia of Psychology. 2nd ed. New York: Continuum, 1979.
Encyclopedia of Psychology. Ed. Raymond J. Corsini. 4 vols. New York: Wiley, 1984.
Encyclopedic Dictionary of Psychology. Ed. Rom Harre and Roger Lamb. Cambridge, MA: MIT, 1983.
Oxford Companion to the Mind. Ed. Richard L. Gregory. Oxford, England: Oxford UP, 1987.

Abstracts and Digests

Annual Review of Psychology. Palo Alto, CA: Annual Review, 1950–date.
Child Development Abstracts and Bibliography. Chicago: U of Chicago P, 1927–date.
Psychological Abstracts. Washington, DC: APA, 1927–date.
Sage Family Studies Abstracts. San Mateo, CA: Sage, 1979–date.

Databases

CHILD ABUSE AND NEGLECT
ERIC
MENTAL HEALTH ABSTRACTS
PSYCHOLOGICAL ABSTRACTS
SOCIAL SCISEARCH
SOCIOLOGICAL ABSTRACTS

Sociology
and Social Work

Bibliographies, Guides, and Indexes

Combined Retrospective Index to Journals in Sociology, 1895–1974. 6 vols. Woodbridge, CT: Research Publications, 1978.

Humanities Index. New York: Wilson, 1974–date.

Library Research Guide to Sociology: Illustrated Search Strategy and Sources. Ed. Patricia Macmillan and James R. Kennedy. Ann Arbor, MI: Pierian, 1981.

Reference Sources in Social Work: An Annotated Bibliography. Ed. James H. Conrad. Metuchen, NJ: Scarecrow, 1982.

Social Science Index. New York: Wilson, 1974–date.

Encyclopedias, Dictionaries, and Handbooks

A Dictionary of Social Science Methods. Comp. P. M. Miller and M. J. Wilson. New York: Wiley, 1983.

Encyclopedia of Social Work. Ed. Anne Minahan. 3 vols. Silver Spring, MD: National Association of Social Workers, n.d.

Student Sociologist's Handbook. Ed. P. B. Bart and L. Frankel. 3rd ed. Glenview, IL: Scott, 1981.

Abstracts and Digests

Social Work Research and Abstracts. New York: NASW, 1964–date.

Sociological Abstracts. New York: Sociological Abstracts, 1953–date.

Databases

CHILD ABUSE AND NEGLECT
FAMILY RESOURCES
NCJRS (National Criminal Justice Reference Service)
SOCIAL SCISEARCH
SOCIOLOGICAL ABSTRACTS

Speech

Bibliographies, Guides, and Indexes

Bibliography of Speech and Allied Areas, 1950–1960. Westport, CT: Greenwood, 1972.

Humanities Index. New York: Wilson, 1974–date.

Index to American Women Speakers, 1828–1978. Metuchen, NJ: Scarecrow, 1980.

Index to Speech, Language, and Hearing: Journal Titles, 1954–78. San Diego, CA: College Hill, n.d.

Radio and Television: A Selected Annotated Bibliography. Metuchen, NJ: Scarecrow, 1978.

Speech Index: An Index to Collections of World Famous Orations and Speeches for Various Occasions, 1935–65. Metuchen, NJ: Scarecrow, 1965–date.

Databases
ERIC
LLBA (Language and Language Behavior Abstracts)
MLA BIBLIOGRAPHIES
SOCIAL SCISEARCH

Women's Studies

Bibliographies, Guides, and Indexes
American Women and Politics: A Selected Bibliography and Research Guide. New York: Garland, 1984.

Ballou, Patricia. *Women: A Bibliography.* 2nd ed. Boston: Hall, 1986.

Bibliographic Guide to Studies on the Status of Women: Development and Population Trends. Paris, France: UNESCO, 1983.

Feminist Library Criticism: A Bibliography of Journal Articles. Ed. Wendy Frost and Michelle Valiquette. New York: Garland, 1988.

Feminist Resources for Schools and Colleges: A Guide. Ed. Anne Chapman. New York: Feminist, 1979.

Fishburn, Katherine. *Women in Popular Culture: A Reference Guide.* Westport, CT: Greenwood, 1982.

Index-Directory of Women's Media. Washington, DC: Women's Institute for Freedom of the Press, 1975–date.

The Progress of Afro-American Women: A Selected Bibliography and Resource Guide. Comp. Janet Sims. Westport, CT: Greenwood, 1980.

Shepard, Bruce D., and Carroll A. Shepard. *Complete Guide to Women's Health.* Tampa, FL: Mariner, 1982.

Social Sciences Index. New York: Wilson, 1974–date.

Women: A Bibliography. Ed. Patricia Ballou. 2nd ed. Boston: Hall, 1986.

Women Helping Women. New York: Women's Action Alliance, 1981.

Women in America: A Guide to Information Sources. Ed. V. R. Terris. Detroit: Gale, 1980.

Women's History Sources: A Guide to Archives and Manuscript Collections in the U.S. 2 vols. New York: Bowker, 1979.

Encyclopedias, Dictionaries, and Handbooks
Encyclopedia of Feminism. Ed. Lisa Tuttle. New York: Facts on File, 1986.

Abstracts and Digests
Women Studies Abstracts. New York: Rush, 1972–date.

Databases
ERIC
SOCIAL SCISEARCH
SOCIOLOGICAL ABSTRACTS

INDEX